Connectionist Models
of Social Reasoning
and Social Behavior

Connectionist Models of Social Reasoning and Social Behavior

Edited by

Stephen J. Read
Lynn C. Miller
University of Southern California

LAWRENCE ERLBAUM ASSOCIATES, PUBLISHERS
1998   Mahwah, New Jersey   London

Lawrence Erlbaum Associates, Inc., Publishers
10 Industrial Avenue
Mahwah, New Jersey 07430

Cover design by Kathryn Houghtaling Lacey

Library of Congress Cataloging-in-Publication Data

Connectionist models of social reasoning and social behavior / edited
   by Stephen J. Read, Lynn C. Miller.
      p.   cm.
   Includes bibliographical references and index.
   ISBN 0-8058-2215-1 (cloth : alk. paper). — ISBN 0-8058-2216-X
(pbk. : alk. paper)
      1. Social psychology. 2. Social perception. 3. Social
interaction. 4. Connectionism. 5. Cognitive psychology. I. Read,
Stephen J. II. Miller, Lynn C.
   HM251.C686   1997
   302—dc21   97-44954
                                                           CIP

Books published by Lawrence Erlbaum Associates are printed on acid-free paper,
and their bindings are chosen for strength and durability.

Printed in the United States of America
10 9 8 7 6 5 4 3 2 1

CONTENTS

PREFACE

Neural network models, also called connectionist or parallel distributed processing models, seem to represent a major paradigm shift in cognitive psychology, cognitive science, and artificial intelligence. Such models move us away from the idea of mind as computer, and instead promise the possibility of brain style models of the mind, admitting the possibility that models of high level cognitive processing can be built from simple neuron-like units. That is, we can build computational models of the mind composed of units functionally similar to the physical units that compose a real brain. This approach has led to some fundamental new insights about the way the mind might work and the way it might interact with the environment.

Surprisingly, given the importance of these models, until recently social psychologists had paid little attention to them. Yet, these models directly address several fundamental characteristics of social perception and social interaction: the simultaneous integration of multiple pieces of information and the quite short time frame within which such integration occurs. Any mundane act of social perception (and any resulting behavior) results from the simultaneous integration of multiple pieces of information, such that the meaning of each piece of information mutually influences and constrains the meaning of each other piece. Thus, social perception can be viewed as the solution of simultaneous mutually interacting constraints. Moreover, this integration typically takes place in a very short time frame, much shorter than would be possible for any kind of reasonable serial integration process. Thus, much of social perception must occur in parallel. Both of these are central characteristics of neural network models (Rumelhart & McClelland, 1986).

Social psychologists' lack of involvement with these models is surprising for another reason. As Read, Vanman, and Miller (1997) have recently shown, there are a number of important parallels between characteristics of these models and the Gestalt principles that formed the theoretical foundation of much of modern social psychology (Asch, 1946; Festinger, 1950, 1957; Heider, 1958; Lewin, 1935, 1947a, 1947b).

However, there has been a recent surge of interest in the application of these kinds of models to social phenomena. This volume brings most of this work together in one place, allowing the reader to appreciate the breadth of these approaches, as well as the theoretical commonality of many of these models. Each of the chapters provides an explicit connectionist model of a central problem in social psychology. Because most of the authors either use a standard architecture, can provide a computer program for their model, or use a publically available system for modeling, interested readers, with a little work, should be able to implement their own variation of a model.

The authors in this volume address a number of central issues in social psychology and show how these kinds of models provide insight into a number of classic issues. Moreover, many of the chapters provide hints that this approach provides the seeds of a theoretical integration the field has long lacked.

Smith and DeCoster, and Kashima, Woolcock, and King outline models of the learning and application of social categories and stereotypes. Kunda and Thagard, Read and Miller, and Van Overwalle and Van Rooy describe models of causal reasoning, social explanation, and person perception. Shoda and Mischel present a model of personality and social behavior. Shultz and Lepper show how a neural network model can capture many of the classic dissonance phenomena, while Ranney and Schank grapple with belief change and the coherence of large scale belief systems. Finally, Nowak and Vallacher, and Eiser, Claessen, and Loose show that these are not just models of individual cognition, but that they can also capture important aspects of social influence and group interaction.

CONNECTIONIST MODELS

In the following we present a very brief overview of connectionist models. We considered (briefly) a more extensive tutorial. However, there are a number of good introductions, some aimed at cognitive psychologists and two recent ones aimed specifically at social psychologists. Thus, it seemed pointless to repeat what had already been said in much more detail elsewhere.

There is probably still no better introduction to neural network models and their psychological implications than the two edited volumes by Rumelhart and McClelland and the PDP research group (1986; McClelland & Rumelhart, 1986). Other good resources for the social psychologist are Anderson's (1995) recent textbook and Bechtel and Abrahamsen's (1991) book, which was written as a companion to the PDP volumes. And recently, Smith (1996) and Read, Vanman, and Miller (1997) have specifically focused on the implications of these kinds of models for the kinds of problems with which social psychologists are concerned. Moreover, Read, Vanman, and Miller (1997) extensively discuss the numerous parallels between key aspects of neural network models and the Gestalt psychological principles that formed the theoretical foundations of much of modern social psychology.

Connectionist modeling (e.g., Hertz, Krogh, & Palmer, 1991; McClelland & Rumelhart, 1986; Rumelhart & McClelland, 1986) treats the processing involved in perceptual and cognitive tasks in terms of the passage of activation, in parallel, among simple, neuron-like units. The most important components of these models are: (a) simple processing units or nodes, which sum the incoming activation, following a specified equation, and then send the resulting activation to the nodes to which they are connected, (b) equations that determine the activation of each node at each point in time, based on the incoming activation from other nodes, previous activation, and the decay rate, (c) weighted connections between the nodes, where the weights affect how activation is spread, and (d) a learning rule that specifies how the weights change in response to experience (Bechtel & Abrahamsen, 1991). Processing in a connectionist model proceeds solely by the spread of activation among nodes, where the pattern of connections affects how activation spreads. There is no higher order executive or control process. Moreover, knowledge in a connectionist model is represented entirely in the pattern of weights among nodes.

Although there are a number of differences among potential neural network models, here we focus on two important differences. One is whether there are feedback relations among the nodes. In feed forward networks, units have unidirectional connections, with no feedback relations. The network is organized in layers, with inputs fed into the input layer and outputs generated at the top layer as a result of a single forward sweep of activation. The simplest such network has two layers, an input and an output layer, although more complicated networks may have intervening or "hidden" layers (so called because they have no direct connections to the environment). Networks with hidden layers, such as the well-known back propagation network, have greater computational power. A prototypical example of a feed forward network is the pattern associator, in which the system learns an arbitrary association between an input represented as a pattern of activation on the input layer and a pattern represented on the output layer. Such networks can learn to categorize objects or assign names to objects.

By contrast, in interactive or feedback networks, at least some connections are bidirectional, resulting in feedback relations, and processing occurs dynamically across a large number of cycles. Nodes in these networks have a minimum and maximum possible activation (typically ranging from 0 to 1, or from -1 to 1). The activation of the nodes is updated many times as the activation of the units moves towards asymptote, and as the system works toward settling into a solution to a particular input. In contrast, in feed forward networks, activation is updated only once.

Because of the feedback relations, interactive or feedback networks are dynamic systems whose behavior evolves over time. As a result they have interesting and useful properties that are not characteristic of feed forward networks. One of the most useful properties of such networks is that they function as parallel constraint satisfaction systems, acting to satisfy multiple simultaneous constraints among elements in a network. Most of the networks in this book are feedback networks and the constraint satisfaction abilities of the networks are central aspects of the models.

A second important difference among models is whether concepts have a distributed or a localist representation. In a localist representation, a concept or perhaps an entire proposition is represented by a single node. In contrast, in a distributed representation a concept is represented by a pattern of activation over a number of nodes. Although some researchers see distributed representations as a defining characteristic of connectionism, we take the view of many researchers that the representation one should use should depend on one's question.

Each of these types of representations has their strengths and weaknesses. We see three major advantages to a distributed representation. First, such a representation does seem more in line with the attempt to model the mind using neuron-like units and does seem to fit our intuition that the representation of a concept should be in terms of the action of large clusters of neurons, rather than an individual neuron. Second, a distributed representation has the property of graceful degradation. That is, loss of a small number of neurons has little if any impact on the representational ability of the model. In contrast, in a localist model loss of a single neuron leads to the loss of the corresponding concept. Third, during learning a distributed representation implicitly calculates the degree of similarity among inputs. That is, if the activation vectors representing different inputs are sufficiently similar, they will tend to receive a common representation in the network. This underlies the ability of such models to learn prototypes from related exemplars. In contrast, a localist model has no such ability.

However, localist models have their own strengths, which are the flip side of some of the weaknesses of distributed models. First, localist models are often much more interpretable, as each concept corresponds to a single node. In contrast, in a distributed representation, because each concept is represented by a pattern of activation over a large number of nodes, it can often be quite difficult to interpret the behavior of such models. Second, localist models are often much more computationally tractable. Consider a simple model with 20 concepts. In a localist model, this will only take 20 units and a 20 × 20 weight matrix. In contrast, assume we had a distributed representation in which each concept was represented by 20 elements. In this model we need 400 units and a 400 × 400 weight matrix. The distributed model has 400 times as many weights. And the problem only gets more serious as the model gets bigger.

One other point is relevant to the issue of whether one should use a localist or a distributed representation. Assume that one is developing a model of high-level cognition, such as a model of analogical reasoning, explanation, or cognitive consistency. In these kinds of models, one is typically interested in relationships among concepts, such as causal or implicational relationships. And frequently the key theoretical mechanism is the parallel satisfaction of mutual constraints among concepts. What is central is the relations among concepts, rather than the representation of concepts. In such cases, it seems likely that the pattern of activation of an ensemble of neurons can be treated as if it were a single node, with little or no loss of theoretical power. In that case a distributed representation would have no advantages and many costs.

Thus, one's choice of representation, we argue, should be a function of one's question. If graceful degradation is important or if one is looking at questions of concept learning or categorization, where sensitivity to similarity is central, then a distributed representation would seem essential. However, in cases where the special strengths of distributed representations are unnecessary, then the relative conceptual and computational simplicity of localist models would seem more desirable.

The various chapters in this book represent some of the conditions under which each kind of representation would seem most appropriate. For instance, several authors—such as Smith and DeCoster, and Kashima, Woolcock, and King—are explicitly interested in models of category learning. Or Read and Miller are interested in the learning of the components of trait concepts. Here distributed representations would seem critical. However, other chapters, such as Shultz and Lepper's chapter on dissonance, Shoda and Mischel's model of personality–behavior relationships or Thagard and Kunda's chapter on the role of coherence, are primarily interested in the implications of processing in recurrent networks, specifically the fact that such networks function as systems for the parallel satisfaction of multiple simultaneous constraints. In these chapters, distributed representations would have provided no additional insights and would have tremendously complicated the models.

OVERVIEW OF THE BOOK

We considered two possible ways to conceptually group the current chapters: in terms of the underlying neural network architecture that is used, or in terms of the specific topic being investigated. Our ultimate choice was the latter, on the assumption that most readers would be primarily interested in the specific topic and how the different investigators approached it. However, in the following descriptions of the chapters we have briefly noted the kind of model that was used. It is an interesting side note that 8 of the 10 chapters use a recurrent or feedback architecture, while only three use a feedforward architecture (Eiser, Claessen, and Loose explore both kinds of architectures). So here follows an overview of each of the 10 chapters.

Thagard and Kunda argue that coherence mechanisms play a central role in three different processes by which people make sense of other people's behavior, how we: (a) integrate a number of concepts, such as traits, to form an impression of another, (b) arrive at an attribution or explanation of someone's behavior, and (c) use analogies to familiar others to make sense of someone's behavior. Not surprisingly to anyone familiar with their work, Thagard and Kunda argue that coherence mechanisms can be treated as constraint satisfaction problems that can be captured by recurrent or feedback connectionist networks.

They then review their work in each of these three areas. First, they describe their recent model of impression formation (Kunda & Thagard, 1996) and how it can capture such phenomena as shifts in meaning of concepts during impression formation and the development of new or emergent concepts from combinations of other concepts. Second, they discuss Thagard's (1989, 1992) model of explanatory coherence and its implications for the understanding of social explanation (see also Miller & Read, 1991; Read & Marcus-Newhall, 1993; Read & Miller, 1993). Third, they describe Holyoak and Thagard's (1989, 1995) work on constraint satisfaction models of analogical reasoning and analog retrieval and they discuss its possible application to a number of phenomena in social perception, such as social comparison, using the self as a model to understand others, and using parents and friends to understand new acquaintances. As part of their discussion they demonstrate how each of these somewhat different phenomena can be treated in terms of the same underlying principle, as a coherence mechanism, operationalized as a constraint satisfaction process. In line with this conclusion, they also discuss the likelihood that these three types of coherence mechanisms are integrated when we actually try to make sense of behavior in social interaction. Finally, following a major focus in social cognition, they examine the extent to which each of these different processes is automatic or controlled.

Read and Miller present an interactive activation and competition (IAC) model of social perception, based on work by McClelland and Rumelhart

(1981; McClelland & Elman, 1986; Rumelhart & McClelland, 1982) on word recognition and speech perception. This model is a feedback or recurrent network, with the nodes organized into multiple layers, where each layer does a different kind of processing and sends the results to higher levels. One interesting aspect of this kind of model is that not only do lower levels, such as feature analysis, send activation to higher levels, but higher levels can also affect lower levels. For instance, a highly activated trait node can send activation back to the feature nodes that compose the original behavior, disambiguating unclear or ambiguous inputs.

Read and Miller propose a four-level network, with each level sending activation to the level above, and in turn receiving activation from the higher level. The nodes in such a model can be treated as hypotheses about the presence or absence of the corresponding concept, with alternative construals or hypotheses having inhibitory links and consistent or supportive hypotheses having excitatory links. The first level in their model is the Feature level, composed of nodes sensitive to the features of human beings, objects, and behavior. Activation from this level then goes to an Identification level, where the individual features are used to identify social actors, objects, and behaviors. Actors, objects, and behaviors identified at this level are then assembled into a coherent representation of the social action at the third level, the Story or Scenario level.

A central aspect of Read and Miller's model is the proposal that social concepts at this level are represented in terms of plot units or frame-based structures, with a case-role structure, where each action centers around a verb or action unit that identifies the various roles, such as actor, patient, and instrument that participate in that action. For instance, they argue that many traits are composed of underlying story structures.

Finally, information from the Story level is used to arrive at the meaning of the interaction at the Conceptual or Meaning level. For example, the instantiated story structure may be used to access various trait characterizations for a social actor.

This model naturally implements various principles of Explanatory Coherence (Thagard, 1989, 1992) that have been shown to play a central role in social reasoning (Ranney & Schank, this volume; Read & Marcus-Newhall, 1993; Read & Miller, 1993), as well as capturing the impact of a limited capacity working memory. Read and Miller also discuss some of the implications of such feedback or attractor models for both learning of social concepts and the combination of old concepts to form novel ones. They note that during learning such models perform a componential analysis of concepts. For example, readers can learn subcomponents of words or social perceivers can learn subcomponents of traits, such as goals, plans, and beliefs. As a result, such a model can capture the acquisition of primitive concepts during learning. Moreover, they discuss how such models can take advantage of such a componential analysis to combine previously learned concepts to form novel concepts. This focus on conceptual combinations is also shared with Thagard and Kunda, and Smith and DeCoster.

Finally, Read and Miller apply their model to two major topics in social perception. First, they discuss how it provides an explicit process model of spontaneous trait inferences, capturing the inferential processing involved in going from the features of the social interaction to the final trait inference. Second, they show how their model can provide an account of Trope's (1986) two-stage model of dispositional inference, and in particular how it can capture the impact of higher level concepts on the identification of social actions.

Kashima, Woolcock, and King use an architecture that is fairly novel in this literature, the tensor product model. However, the central issues they address, the representation of social categories and stereotypes, overlap with those of Smith and DeCoster.

Kashima et al. note that because little work has been done specifying the details of the representation of social groups, they intend their model as a step toward addressing that issue. Further, they note that the little work that has been done has taken two divergent paths: one looking at how impressions of groups are formed, and the other at how individuals are classified into social groupings, that is, how social categories are represented. The aim of their chapter is to present a model that can explain the findings in both of these areas.

They first present a mechanism for how memories are initially encoded and then examine how those memories can be used for judgment and memory retrieval. Their model uses a distributed representation in which a given feature is represented as a pattern of activation over a set of nodes. One unique characteristic of the model is that it provides a mechanism for the representation of attribute–value pairs (or what Kashima et al. call aspects and features), such as skin color: black, or eye color: blue. For example, assume we have an individual, John, with an attribute, skin color, that has a value, black. Representing this notion of an attribute which applies to an object and has a particular value, is difficult to do in standard connectionist models that use distributed representations. For example, a typical connectionist model with a distributed representation would directly associate the individual John with black skin. This is because the standard representation is in terms of a two-dimensional weight matrix that gives the association of two vectors. There is no easy way to represent the idea of an attribute that can take on multiple values. Thus, one could not easily ask the model, "What is John's skin color?"

Let us see how this works. Assume that we have two features, each represented by a vector, **a** and **b**. Multiplying the two vectors together (taking the outer product) gives a matrix, where the elements in the matrix represent the degree of association between each element in **a** and each element in **b**. The tensor formulation is a generalization of this to the association among **n** vectors. Thus, if we had a third vector **c**, we would multiply **a**, **b**, and **c** and end up with a three-dimensional array that represents all the associations among all the elements in each of the three vectors. In this representation, one vector can represent John, a second vector can represent the attribute skin color, and the third vector can represent the value, black. And the resulting three-dimensional array represents the association among John, skin color, and black. Once one has this array, one could then do the equivalent of asking for John's skin color, by taking the two-dimensional matrix representing the association among John and skin color, and then apply it to the three-dimensional array with appropriate mathematical manipulations to retrieve the third vector representing black.

In this model different memory traces are superimposed on each other by simply adding together the tensor products for different memories. Thus, one ends up with one array in which are superimposed a large number of memories.

Kashima et al. then apply their model to several phenomena. First, they demonstrate how characteristics of the group can be used to retrieve a category or group label. As is true of other models, such as Smith and DeCoster's, provision of a partial pattern of cues enables the retrieval of the entire pattern, although the mechanism by which this happens is somewhat different than in Smith and DeCoster's model.

Second, they show how this model can simulate the use of both exemplars and prototypes in classification. As part of this demonstration, they show analytically how the Tensor Product model is consistent with various Context Model theories of classification, first proposed by Medin and Schaffer (1978) and extended by Nosofsky (1984, 1986). These are exemplar-based models which argue that classification of items into a category is based on similarity to exemplars that make up the category. Further, they demonstrate that their model can simulate results of experiments by Smith and Zaraté (1990) supporting a mixture model of classification that seem to show that subjects can use both prototypes and exemplars to classify new items, depending upon the experimental conditions.

Third, they show how this model can simulate judgments or impressions of a group. Essentially, they provide a vector representation of the high and low endpoints of a judgment scale and then calculate the similarity of that vector to the representation of the group. In doing this, they note that judgments of groups seem to fit a weighted averaging model and they show how their model can successfully simulate this. Fourth, they show how the Tensor Product Model can handle Hamilton and Gifford's (1976) work on the distinctiveness based illusory correlation phenomena.

In concluding, they argue that their model has the advantage of capturing both classification and judgment in the same model. And, it is consistent with major models of classification, such as GCM, and major findings in judgment, such as weighted averaging.

Smith and DeCoster apply a recurrent connectionist network, specifically an autoassociative network developed by McClelland and Rumelhart (1986), to key findings in person perception and stereotyping. In an autoassociative model, each unit is linked to every other unit and receives activation from all other units, as well as receiving external input. They use a distributed representation in which a pattern of activation across a set of units represents a concept, rather than having a single node correspond to a single concept. Such a model can do pattern learning, pattern completion of incomplete patterns, and memory reconstruction or schematic processing.

Learning in their model is instantiated by the delta rule (Widrow & Hoff, 1960), which uses the difference between the activation of nodes due to internal inputs from the network and the activation due to external inputs, to adjust the weights. The aim of this procedure is to modify the weights so that the activation of each node from all its internal connections approximates the activation of each node from external or stimulus input. Essentially, the network is learning the pattern of external inputs. One result of this is that the network will learn to reinstantiate the complete pattern from partial input.

Smith and DeCoster show how their model handles four phenomena. First, it can learn characteristics of individual exemplars or cases and then retrieve those characteristics from a partial cue. Second, it can learn a group stereotype or category from multiple exemplars and then, given partial cues, it can retrieve or reconstruct the prototype or stereotype. As Smith and DeCoster note, this demonstrates that a single mechanism and a single representational format can account for these two seemingly different phenomena. This is in contrast to most models in social cognition that assume very different representational forms for exemplars and prototypes. Third, the model can learn multiple knowledge structures in the same network and then create novel or emergent structures by combining the existing structures to form a new structure. This provides a mechanism for the development of novel or emergent concepts. Classic schema models seem to lack a mechanism for combining old concepts to create novel ones (also see Read & Miller, this volume; Thagard & Kunda, this volume). Finally, they show that several aspects of construct accessibility can be captured by such a model, specifically demonstrating that both recency and frequency of activation of a concept increase its impact on future inferences. In addition they show that spaced patterns will have a greater impact than patterns that are massed. They do this by demonstrating that a partial pattern does a better job of reinstantiating a complete pattern when the original pattern has been recently and/or frequently presented, or presented in a spaced fashion.

Smith and DeCoster note that they are able to handle each of these with the same mechanism, although typical work in social cognition proposes a separate model for each. Following work by Rumelhart, Smolensky, et al. (1986) they also observe that such a model can produce what looks like schemas and schematic processing despite the lack of any schematic structures (also see Read & Miller, this volume).

Van Overwalle and Van Rooy investigate how a simple two layer feedforward network using delta rule learning, a pattern associator, can simulate several interesting findings from the literature on causal learning. Their work extends earlier work by others, such as Gluck and Bower (1988a, 1988b) and Shanks (1991, 1993) which has demonstrated that the classic Rescorla–Wagner model of animal learning is formally identical to a two layer (lacking hidden units) feedforward network that uses delta rule learning to learn new associations.

They also compare this kind of model with statistical models, such as Cheng and Novick's (1990) probabilistic contrast model, and show that the connectionist model is sensitive to factors that the probabilistic contrast model is not. The basic difference between statistical models, such as the probabilistic contrast model, and the connectionist model, is that the probabilistic contrast model is sensitive only to relative frequencies of the pairings of different kinds of events, whereas the connectionist model is also sensitive to the absolute frequency of presentation. For instance, according to the probabilistic contrast model the case in which we have one instance of the effect given the cause and no instance of the effect given the absence of the cause, should be equivalent to a case where we have five instances of the effect given the cause and no instances of the effect given the absence of the cause, because in both instances the differences between the probabilities is 1.0. In contrast, the connectionist model is sensitive to the absolute frequency of pairing of the cause and effect. And, they provide evidence that humans have the same sensitivity.

In addition, following other work (e.g., Vallee-Tourangeau, Baker, & Mercier, 1994) they investigate the parallels between effects in the associative learning literature known as blocking and conditioned inhibition and the well known phenomena of discounting and augmenting in the attribution literature. As part of this work they show that in human beings the strength of discounting and augmenting is sensitive to the frequency of instances, which is consistent with the predictions of the associative model, but not with the original version of the probabilistic contrast model.

Finally, they examine the learning of multiple causes and they test the ability of various connectionist models to simulate human responses. They compare the two-layer feedforward network with Pearce's (1994) configural cue model, and with a standard three-layer backpropagation network with hidden units. Pearce's model was explicitly developed to handle configurations of cues, by assigning a single node to the configuration, whereas the back-propagation network should be able, at least in theory, to learn hidden units that represent a configuration of cues. The authors find that Pearce's configural cue model does the best job of simulating results from human subjects.

Shoda and Mischel use an autoassociative, recurrent network to tackle a recent controversy in personality: the apparent paradox between expectations of stable individual differences in patterns of personality and the actually obtained, relatively low, cross-situational consistency in behavior. Their answer to this apparent paradox has been twofold. First, in an extensive body of research they and their colleagues have demonstrated that stable situation–behavior, if–then relationships characterize individuals. That is, while people may not show general cross-situational consistency in behavior, they do show characteristic responses to different situations. For example, two people may be highly aggressive, but in response to different situations. One may be aggressive when dealing with those who try to dominate them and the other when someone is weaker than they are. Thus, we cannot ignore situations in conceptualizing personality, but must deal with the individual's characteristic response to situations.

Second, they have used an autoassociative, recurrent network to investigate whether *stable* patterns of relationships among the "cognitive–affective" units they postulate can give *variable* patterns of behavior in response to differing situations. The different kinds of units they use are: encodings (categories), expectancies and beliefs, affective responses, goals and values, and competencies and self-regulatory plans. In their typical implementation, a set of feature detectors is activated by a situation and activation from these feature detectors then flows to the cognitive affective units. The pattern of activation from the cognitive affective units then activates the behavior node. In their simulations each individual has a stable pattern of relationships among the various cognitive–affective units, although the pattern differs across individuals. Thus, one can view each individual as having a stable "personality."

They demonstrate that each individual model shows a consistent pattern of relationships between the situations and the behavior, although the nature of the pattern differs for different individuals. Thus, each individual has a characteristic set of stable, if–then situation–behavior relationships. But interestingly, the situation–behavior relationships are not completely stable, the impact of the same situation may differ depending upon the recent activation history of the network, or what one may think of as the immediately preceding mental state of the individual. Finally, they provide a real-world example of the application of the model to health protective behavior, specifically breast self-examination.

Shultz and Lepper follow up on some of their earlier work published in *Psychological Review* and use a variant of a Hopfield type network (one type of single layer autoassociative or recurrent network) to successfully simulate the results of a number of different paradigms in the dissonance literature (e.g., Insufficient justification via Initiation, Insufficient justification via Prohibition, Free choice among alternatives). In some cases their simulation better fits the data than does the original dissonance formulation and in one case their simulation leads to a novel prediction which they have experimentally verified. Unfortunately, consistent with the fragility of the work on selective exposure, they were much less successful in capturing the results in this paradigm. As they note, their ability to simulate the results of most of the major paradigms argues that such parallel constraint satisfaction models may provide the basis for theoretical unification within this field.

There are several particularly interesting aspects of their model. First, they are able to use ideas derived from Hopfield's (1982, 1984) notion of the energy of a system to provide a quantitative measure of the overall consonance of the system of beliefs, as well as a measure of the contribution of each belief to the consonance of the system. This was not possible in previous conceptualizations of dissonance. Second, they include the importance of each cognition as a parameter in their model. This allows one to explicitly simulate how dissonance reduction is affected by the degree of importance and amount of support of individual cognitions. Third, they represent each cognition by two negatively linked nodes, where each node can be treated as representing one pole of the cognition. Thus, an attitude toward an activity is represented by the summed activation of both a positive and negative node. Although the negative link will tend to insure that only one of the two nodes is activated, in some cases both could be simultaneously activated, indicating ambivalence.

In addition to simulating the results of the major paradigms, they also examine how their model fares with other recent research. For instance, researchers such as Cooper, Zanna, and Taves (1978) have directly looked at the impact of arousal on attitude change. They have shown that when students write a counterattitudinal essay under high choice, they show the greatest dissonance effect when given a stimulant and the smallest effect when given a tranquilizer. Shultz and Lepper show that their model can simulate the impact of arousal and they include an interesting speculation about the relationship between the role of activation in their model and the impact of stimulants and tranquilizers on cortical arousal. They also successfully address the role of the self-concept in dissonance, including successfully addressing Steele's (1988) work on self-affirmation processes.

As do several authors in this volume, they conclude by making a case for the theoretical unification that can be provided by constraint satisfaction models. Not only can these kinds of models handle the dissonance literature, they can also be applied in a variety of other domains. As they and others have noted, constraint satisfaction models have been employed in a wide variety of domains: belief revision, explanation, comprehension, schema completion, analogical retrieval and mapping, content addressable memory storage and retrieval, attitude change, impression formation, and cognitive balance.

Ranney and Schank try something a little different. Rather than focus on using a particular kind of neural network to address a specific problem, they decide to tackle some broad questions, using their work on the importance of explanatory coherence in thinking. For example, they take the typical distinction that is often made between scientific and social thinking and ask how real this distinction really is. Their answer is: not very. Based on their work in both social reasoning and reasoning about physical systems, they argue that fundamentally, scientific and social thinking rely on the same mechanisms; in particular, principles of explanatory coherence play a central role in both domains.

They also describe some of their work using their program Convince Me. This is a program, partially based on Thagard's model of Explanatory Coherence (1989, 1992), that can be used to uncover people's reasoning about a variety of domains. It can uncover the individual beliefs, the explanatory relations among them, and the coherence or consistency of the set of beliefs. Moreover, by giving subjects feedback on how consistent their beliefs are, it can also be used to encourage people to develop more coherent sets of beliefs. Relevant to the earlier point, in their work with this program, there seems little difference in how people use it to address scientific and social problems.

Finally, they decide to address a really big question: How do we decide what are the most socially significant or important social issues? They use their work with Convince Me and ideas about coherence to explore the role of explanatory coherence in identifying which problems and issues are most socially significant.

Nowak and Vallacher examine how complex social dynamics involving interactions among people in groups can be modeled by neural networks. They argue that such models can provide insights into social dynamics and how such dynamics depend on the connections among people. As part of their discussion, they first introduce another class of models, cellular automata, that have been used to model social dynamics in such social phenomena as social influence and attitude change. They then discuss the limitations of these kinds of models, in particular the rigid nature of social ties, and then note the advantages of neural network models. For example, neural networks can capture negative social relationships, with which cellular automata have trouble. Another attraction is their ability to simulate states of equilibrium; the idea that networks may evolve to certain states but not others.

As an example, they analyze the implications of one type of attractor network, a Hopfield type network where each individual is represented by a node and the connections among nodes represent the relations among them. They also take advantage of the energy function discussed by Hopfield to capture the notion that such systems can have a number of potential equilibria which differ in how good they are, and represent different distributions of beliefs.

They note that one can investigate two kinds of dynamics in these models. First, one can investigate how relations between individuals, such as liking or influence, affect the development of attitudes or similar constructs in a social network. This is equivalent to examining how the links among nodes influence the change of activation of the nodes over time. Second, one can investigate how the opinions of individuals influence the relationships between them, by using what we know about learning in such networks. For example, the Hebbian learning rule states that if two nodes are positively activated at the same time, then the weight between them should increase, whereas if one node is positive and the other negative, then the weight should decrease. This is akin to how similarity in opinion between two individuals can affect their degree of liking.

They also make an interesting set of observations about how the impact of wider societal factors, beyond individual relationships, can be captured in such models. They note that social influence is rarely the only source of opinion change. Typically, in society any individual receives input from a number of other sources, such as media and personal memory. For any particular individual these can be treated as essentially random influences. In neural network terms this can be viewed as noise. They note that as noise in such a network increases, up to a certain point, the number of equilibrium or stable points decreases. This is akin to shaking the system out of the shallower hills and valleys, so that it is more likely to enter the deeper valleys. Thus, the larger the random noise, the greater the likelihood of a small number of ideological positions. This would seem to suggest that at times of great ferment or activity in society, the societal opinion is likely to crystallize into a small number of ideological positions. However, they point out that if the amount of noise becomes too high, then all equilibria disappear; in essence everyone has their own separate, independent opinion.

Eiser, Claessen, and Loose are interested in investigating processes of self-organization in social systems. And like Nowak and Vallacher, they propose using connectionist models to investigate processes occurring in groups of individuals, rather than just looking at intraindividual processes.

Eiser et al. look at two different issues and use two different kinds of architectures. First, they attempt to simulate the development of Cognitive Balance (Heider, 1946) among a group of people (rather than within a single individual). They use a fully recurrent, feedback network in which each individual's feeling about an impersonal object is represented by the activation of a node and the relationship (or amount of liking) between two individuals is represented by the weight between the two corresponding nodes. Thus, similar to Read and Miller (1994) they treat Cognitive Balance as a constraint satisfaction process. Eiser et al. then use this model to study the extent to which the development of balance is due to changes in relationships among individuals versus changes in how individuals feel about impersonal objects. They find that, at least in their particular implementation, changing relationships among individuals is far more important than is changing feelings about objects. As they note, this kind of simulation can be used to extend our analysis of such theories as Balance.

In a second set of simulations, they present a hybrid architecture that combines cellular automata with feedforward, backpropagation networks. In this model, each individual is represented by a cell and the internal state of the cell or individual is represented by the feedforward network. Rules applied to the cells determine how they "talk" to one another. Eiser et al. use this model to study how a group of individuals may come to an agreement about naming an object in their environment; that is, it attempts to model communication among individuals in a social network. As part of their simulation they study various kinds of communication rules that determine who talks to who and how much. Although the model is interesting and innovative, it has one flaw. If it is trying to name two or more different objects, it exhibits what the authors call "Smurfing behavior." That is, all the objects come to receive exactly the same name. So in its current state the model is unable to capture how a group might come to give different names to different objects.

Conclusion

Although social psychologists are just beginning to study the applications of neural network models to social phenomena, it is clear from the chapters in this book that they have great potential for addressing fundamental issues in social psychology. In fact, the present authors have already made significant contributions to our understanding of these issues. We thank the authors for the strength of their contributions.

REFERENCES

Anderson, J. A. (1995). *An introduction to neural networks.* Cambridge, MA: Bradford/MIT Press.
Asch, S. E. (1946). Forming impressions of personality. *Journal of Abnormal and Social Psychology, 41*, 258–290.

Bechtel, W., & Abrahamsen, A. (1991). *Connectionism and the mind: An introduction to parallel processing in networks.* Cambridge, MA: Basil Blackwell.

Cheng, P. W., & Novick, L. R. (1990). A probabilistic contrast model of causal induction. *Journal of Personality and Social Psychology, 58,* 545–567.

Cooper, J., Zanna, M. P., & Taves, P. A. (1978). Arousal as a necessary condition for attitude change following forced compliance. *Journal of Personality and Social Psychology, 36,* 1101–1106.

Festinger, L. (1950). Informal social communication. *Psychological Review, 57,* 271–282.

Festinger, L. (1957). *A theory of cognitive dissonance.* Evanston, IL: Row, Peterson.

Gluck, M. A., & Bower, G. H. (1988a). From conditioning to category learning: An adaptive network model. *Journal of Experimental Psychology: General, 117,* 227–247.

Gluck, M. A., & Bower, G. H. (1988b). Evaluating an adaptive network model of human learning. *Journal of Memory and Language, 27,* 166–195.

Hamilton, D. L., & Gifford, R. K. (1976). Illusory correlation in interpersonal perception: A cognitive basis of stereotypic judgments. *Journal of Experimental Social Psychology, 12,* 392–407.

Heider, F. (1946). Attitudes and cognitive organization. *Journal of Psychology, 21,* 107–112.

Heider, F. (1958). *The psychology of interpersonal relations.* New York: Wiley.

Hertz, J., Krogh, A., & Palmer, R. G. (1991). *Introduction to the theory of neural computation.* Redwood City, CA: Addison Wesley.

Holyoak, K. J., & Thagard, P. (1989). Analogical mapping by constraint satisfaction. *Cognitive Science, 13,* 295–355.

Holyoak, K. J., & Thagard, P. (1995). *Mental leaps: Analogy in creative thought.* Cambridge, MA: MIT Press/Bradford Books.

Hopfield, J. J. (1982). Neural networks and physical systems with emergent collective computational abilities. *Proceedings of the National Academy of Sciences, USA, 79,* 2554–2558.

Hopfield, J. J. (1984). Neurons with graded responses have collective computational properties like those of two-state neurons. *Proceedings of the National Academy of Sciences, USA, 81,* 3088–3092.

Kunda, Z., & Thagard, P. (1996). Forming impressions from stereotypes, traits, and behaviors: A parallel constraint satisfaction theory. *Psychological Review, 103,* 284–308.

Lewin, K. (1935). *A dynamic theory of personality.* New York: McGraw-Hill.

Lewin, K. (1947a). Frontiers in group dynamics: I. *Human Relations, 1,* 2–38.

Lewin, K. (1947b). Frontiers in group dynamics: II. *Human Relations, 1,* 143–153.

McClelland, J. L., & Elman, J. L. (1986). Interactive processes in speech perception: The TRACE model. In J. L. McClelland & D. E. Rumelhart (Eds.), *Parallel distributed processing: Explorations in the microstructure of cognition: Vol. 2. Psychological and biological models* (pp. 58–121). Cambridge, MA: MIT Press/Bradford Books.

McClelland, J. L., & Rumelhart, D. E. (1981). An interactive activation model of context effects in letter perception: Part 1. An account of basic findings. *Psychological Review, 88,* 375–407.

McClelland, J. L., & Rumelhart, D. E. (Eds.). (1986). *Parallel distributed processing: Explorations in the microstructure of cognition: Vol. 2. Psychological and biological models.* Cambridge, MA: MIT Press/Bradford Books.

Medin, D. L., & Schaffer, M. M. (1978). Context theory of classification learning. *Psychological Review, 85,* 207–238.

Miller, L. C., & Read, S. J. (1991). On the coherence of mental models of persons and relationships: A knowledge structure approach. In F. Fincham & G. J. O. Fletcher (Eds.), *Cognition in close relationships* (pp. 69–99). Hillsdale, NJ: Lawrence Erlbaum Associates.

Nosofsky, R. M. (1984). Choice, similarity, and the context theory of classification. *Journal of Experimental Psychology: Learning, Memory, and Cognition, 10,* 104–114.

Nosofsky, R. M. (1986). Attention, similarity, and the identification-categorization relationship. *Journal of Experiment Psychology: General, 115,* 39–57.

Pearce, J. M. (1994). Similarity and discrimination: A selective review and a connectionist model. *Psychological Review, 101*, 587–607.

Read, S. J., & Marcus-Newhall, A. (1993). Explanatory coherence in social explanations: A parallel distributed processing account. *Journal of Personality and Social Psychology, 65,* 429–447.

Read, S. J., & Miller, L. C. (1993). Rapist or "regular guy": Explanatory coherence in the construction of mental models of others. *Personality and Social Psychology Bulletin, 19*, 526–540.

Read, S. J., & Miller, L. C. (1995). Stories are fundamental to meaning and memory: For social creatures, could it be otherwise? In R. S. Wyer, Jr. (Ed.), *Knowledge and memory: The real story, Advances in social cognition, Vol. VIII* (Lead article by R. C. Schank & R. P. Abelson, pp. 139–152). Hillsdale, NJ: Lawrence Erlbaum Associates.

Rumelhart, D. E., Smolensky, P., McClelland, J. L., & Hinton, G. E. (1986). Schemata and sequential thought processes in PDP models. In J. L. McClelland & D. E. Rumelhart (Eds.), *Parallel distributed processing: Explorations in the microstructure of cognition. Vol. 2: Psychological and biological models* (pp. 7–57). Cambridge, MA: MIT Press/Bradford Books.

Rumelhart, D. E., & McClelland, J. L. (1982). An interactive activation model of context effects in letter perception: Part 2. The contextual enhancement effect and some tests and extensions of the model. *Psychological Review, 89,* 60–94.

Read, S. J., & Miller, L. C. (1994). Dissonance and balance in belief systems: The promise of parallel constraint satisfaction processes and connectionist modeling approaches. In R. C. Schank & E. J. Langer (Eds.), *Beliefs, reasoning, and decision making: Psycho-logic in honor of Bob Abelson* (pp. 209–235). Hillsdale, NJ: Lawrence Erlbaum Associates.

Read, S. J., Vanman, E. J., & Miller, L. C. (1997). Connectionism, parallel constraint satisfaction processes, and Gestalt principles: (Re)Introducing cognitive dynamics to social psychology. *Personality and Social Psychology Review, 1*, 26–53.

Rumelhart, D. E., & McClelland, J. L. (1986). *Parallel distributed processing: Explorations in the microstructure of cognition: Vol. 1. Foundations.* Cambridge, MA: MIT Press/Bradford Books.

Shanks, D. R. (1991). Categorization by a connectionist network. *Journal of Experimental Psychology: Learning, Memory and Cognition, 17*, 433–443.

Shanks, D. R. (1993). Human instrumental learning: A critical review of data and theory. *British Journal of Psychology, 84*, 319–354.

Smith, E. R. (1996). What do connectionism and social psychology offer each other? *Journal of Personality and Social Psychology, 70*, 893–912.

Smith, E. R., & Zaraté, M. A. (1990). Exemplar and prototype use in social categorisation. *Social Cognition, 8*, 243–262.

Steele, C. M. (1988). The psychology of self-affirmation: Sustaining the integrity of the self. In L. Berkowitz (Ed.), *Advances in experimental social psychology* (Vol. 21, pp. 261–302). New York: Academic Press.

Thagard, P. (1989). Explanatory coherence. *Behavioral and Brain Sciences, 12*, 435–467.

Thagard, P. (1992). *Conceptual revolutions.* Princeton, NJ: Princeton University Press.

Trope, Y. (1986). Identification and inferential processes in dispositional attribution. *Psychological Review, 93*, 239–257.

Vallée-Tourangeau, F., Baker, A. G., & Mercier, P. (1994). Discounting in causality and covariation judgments. *The Quarterly Journal of Experimental Psychology, 47B*, 151–171.

Widrow, G., & Hoff, M. E. (1960). Adaptive switching circuits. *Institute of Radio Engineers, Western Electronic Show and Convention, Convention Record, Part 4*, 96–104.

PERSON PERCEPTION AND IMPRESSION FORMATION

1

MAKING SENSE OF PEOPLE: COHERENCE MECHANISMS[1]

Paul Thagard
Ziva Kunda
University of Waterloo

THREE WAYS OF MAKING SENSE[1]

When trying to make sense of other people and ourselves, we may rely on
several different kinds of cognitive processes. First, we form impressions of
other people by integrating information contained in concepts that represent
their traits, their behaviors, our stereotypes of the social groups they belong
to, and any other information about them that seems relevant. For example,
your impression of an acquaintance may be a composite of personality traits
(e.g., friendly, independent), behaviors (e.g., told a joke, donated money to
the food bank), and social stereotypes (e.g., woman, doctor, Chinese). Second, we understand other people by means of causal attributions in which
we form and evaluate hypotheses that explain their behavior. To explain
why someone is abrupt on one occasion, you may hypothesize that this
person is impatient or that he or she is under pressure from a work deadline.
You believe the hypothesis that provides the best available explanation of
the person's behavior. A third means of making sense of people is analogy:
You can understand people through their similarity to other people or to
yourself. For example, you may understand the stresses that your friend is
experiencing by remembering an occasion when you yourself experienced

[1]We are grateful for grant support from the Social Sciences and Humanities Research Council
of Canada and the Natural Sciences and Engineering Research Council of Canada. We thank
Steve Read for helpful comments on an earlier draft.

similar stresses. This will allow you to predict your friend's likely feelings and behavior.

All three of these ways of understanding people can be applied to oneself as well as to others. I may gain insight into myself by applying new concepts to myself (e.g., realizing I am impatient), forming new hypotheses about myself (e.g., conjecturing that I may be more upset by a setback than I realized), and by seeing myself as similar to others (e.g., noticing that I am acting just like my father did).

We propose that making sense of people through conceptual integration, explanation, and analogy can all be understood in terms of cognitive mechanisms for maximizing coherence. When integrating information about a person, we attempt to achieve coherence among concepts by reconciling conflicts among the different pieces of information that we have about an individual (Kunda & Thagard, 1996). Knowing that someone who is a lawyer responded meekly to an insult requires us to balance conflicting expectations generated by the stereotype that lawyers are aggressive and the unaggressive behavior (Kunda, Sinclair, & Griffin, 1997). Similarly, in causal attribution, we need to reconcile different explanations for an individual's behavior, choosing, for example, between explanations in terms of personality traits and explanations in terms of situational factors. Such choices require us to maximize explanatory coherence, accepting those explanations that fit best with the rest of our beliefs (Read & Miller, 1993a, 1993b; Thagard, 1989). Finally, making sense of people in terms of other similar people requires us to assess analogical coherence, finding a good fit between the complex of attributes of one person and the complex of attributes of another (Holyoak & Thagard, 1995).

In the next section, we first outline a general characterization of coherence that provides a uniform vocabulary for understanding a wide variety of cognitive processes in terms of parallel constraint satisfaction. We then show in more detail how conceptual integration, causal attribution, and analogical understanding (including empathy) can be understood as different kinds of coherence. We argue that connectionist models of conceptual, explanatory, and analogical coherence provide computationally powerful and psychologically plausible explanations of diverse ways in which people think about other people and themselves.

Coherence as Constraint Satisfaction

To make sense of people, we need to represent different kinds of information about them. These include concepts such as traits and stereotypes that apply to individuals as well as propositions such as *Mary loves John* that describe relations between people. Some representations fit together, but others conflict. For example, describing someone as *loving* fits with describing that person as *kind*, but conflicts with describing that person as *hateful*. The proposition that *Mary loves John* fits with the proposition that *Mary is nice to John*, but conflicts with the proposition that *Mary hates John*. When two representations fit together, there is a positive constraint between them: If you apply one of the representations to someone, then you will tend to apply the other representation as well. If two representations conflict, there is a negative constraint between them: If you apply one of the representations to someone, then you will tend not to apply the other representation. Coming up with a coherent interpretation of people is a matter of applying some representations to them and not applying others. Generally, coherence is a matter of accepting some representations and rejecting others in a way that maximizes compliance with positive and negative constraints.

Thagard and Verbeurgt (1998) provide a general definition of coherence problems. A coherence problem arises when one encounters a set of elements that mutually constrain each other, and wishes to accept some of these elements and reject the remaining ones. For example, one needs to decide which of a set of interrelated traits are characteristic of John (the accepted elements) and which are not (the rejected elements). The constraints among the elements may be positive or negative. A positive constraint among two elements means that the two should go together—they should both be accepted or both be rejected. For example, if John is loving, he should be kind as well, and if he is not loving, he should not be kind either. A negative constraint means that the two elements should not go together—if one is accepted, the other should be rejected. For example, if John is loving, he should not be hateful; if he is hateful, he should not be loving. Each of the constraints carries a weight that reflects its importance.

When partitioning the elements into the accepted set and the rejected set, it is often not possible to satisfy all of the constraints because they may conflict with each other. For example, a person who is manipulative should also be interpersonally skilled. But a person who is interpersonally skilled should also be loving, whereas a person who is manipulative should not. It will be impossible to satisfy all of these constraints simultaneously. The coherence problem is to satisfy as many of the constraints as possible, while giving preference to the more important ones. More technically, the aim is to partition the elements into an accepted and rejected set in a way that maximizes the weight of the satisfied constraints. For a more precise definition, see the appendix.

In later sections, we show how conceptual, explanatory, and analogical coherence can all be understood as special cases of this general characterization of coherence. Each kind of coherence involves different sorts of elements and constraints.

Maximizing coherence is a difficult computational problem: Thagard and Verbeurgt (1998) prove that it belongs to a class of problems generally considered to be computationally intractable, so that no algorithms are available that are both efficient and guaranteed to be correct. Nevertheless, good approximation algorithms are available, in particular connectionist algorithms from which the above characterization of coherence was originally abstracted.

Here is how to translate a coherence problem into a problem that can be solved in a connectionist network:

1. Each element is represented as a unit (node) in a network of units. These units are very roughly analogous to neurons or groups of neurons in the brain.

2. A positive constraint between two elements is represented as an excitatory link between the corresponding units. Each link has a weight representing the strength of the constraint, as determined, for exam ple, by the strength of association between two concepts.

3. A negative constraint between two elements is represented as an inhibitory link between the corresponding units.

4. Each unit is assigned an equal initial activation, say .01. The activation of all the units is then updated in parallel. The updated activation of a unit is calculated on the basis of its current activation, the activation of the units to which it is linked, and the weights of these links. The activation of a given unit is increased with the activation of units to which it has excitatory links, and decreased with the activation of units to which it has inhibitory links. A number of equations are available for specifying how this updating is done (McClelland & Rumelhart, 1989). Typically, activation is constrained to remain between a minimum (e.g., −1) and a maximum (e.g., +1).

5. The network goes through many cycles in which the activation of all units is updated. Updating is repeated until all units have settled, that is, achieved stable activation values that change only minimally from one cycle to another.

6. If a unit's final activation exceeds a specified threshold (e.g., 0), then the element represented by that unit is deemed to be accepted. Otherwise, that element is rejected.

This process results in a partition of elements into accepted and rejected sets by virtue of the network settling in such a way that some units end up with activation levels that are above the critical threshold for acceptance, and others do not. The final levels of activation can also be taken to represent degrees of acceptance and rejection.

Intuitively, this solution is a natural one for coherence problems. Just as we want two coherent elements to be accepted or rejected together, so two units connected by an excitatory link will be activated or deactivated to-

TABLE 1.1
Comparison of Coherence Problems and Connectionist Networks

Coherence	Connectionist Network
Element	Unit
Positive Constraint	Excitatory Link
Negative Constraint	Inhibitory Link
Constraint Satisfaction	Parallel Updating of Activation
Element Accepted	Unit Activated Above Threshold
Element Rejected	Unit Activated Below Threshold

gether. Just as we want the outcome for two incoherent elements to be such that one is accepted and the other is rejected, so two units connected by an inhibitory link will tend to suppress each other's activation, with one activated and the other deactivated. A solution that enforces positive and negative constraints on maximizing coherence is provided by the parallel update algorithm that adjusts the activation of all units at once based on their links and previous activation values. Table 1.1 summarizes the correspondences between coherence problems and connectionist networks.

Impression Formation as Coherence Among Concepts

Sometimes we form impressions of others by integrating their diverse characteristics—their behavior, their traits, the stereotypes of the groups they belong to, and any other kind of information deemed relevant. This process may be viewed as a coherence problem in which the elements are concepts representing the person's characteristics, and the positive and negative constraints are imposed by the positive and negative associations among these concepts and their associates.

Kunda and Thagard (1996) developed a parallel constraint-satisfaction theory of impression formation. This theory assumes that stereotypes, traits, and behaviors can be represented as interconnected nodes in a spreading activation network. The nodes can have positive, excitatory associations, or negative, inhibitory ones. To illustrate the model, consider the well-documented finding that stereotypes can affect the meaning of behavior. For example, when a Black person pushes someone, this is interpreted as violent push. But when a White person performs the identical behavior, this is interpreted as a jovial shove (Sagar & Schofield, 1980).

Figure 1.1 shows part of the network of concepts that would be used to make sense of the observation that a Black person or a White person pushed someone. The boxes depict the nodes representing the concepts. The lines connecting these nodes depict the associations among them. Bold lines indicate excitatory associations, and thin lines indicate inhibitory ones. Each of the concepts depicted also has many additional associates that are not

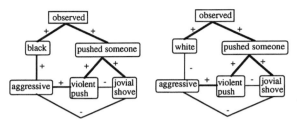

FIG. 1.1. Stereotypes affect the meaning of behavior. The network on the left
activates "violent push" and deactivates "jovial shove." The network on the
right does the opposite. Reprinted from Kunda and Thagard (1996, p. 286).

portrayed in the figure. The observed information, in this case the behavior
(pushed someone) and the stereotyped category (Black or White), is connected to a node termed *observed* to indicate its special status, and to
distinguish it from inferred knowledge—in this case, the traits associated
with the stereotype and the possible interpretations of the behavior. Observed concepts receive strong activation from the *observed* node. Inferred
knowledge becomes activated or deactivated through its positive or negative
associations with the observed information. These associations are based
on perceivers' prior beliefs about the interrelationships among characteristics.

When one observes that a person pushed someone, *pushed someone*
activates both *violent push* and *jovial shove*. If one also observes that the
pusher is Black then, at the same time, *Black* activates *aggressive*, which
further activates *violent push* while deactivating *jovial shove*. If, on the other
hand, one observes that the pusher is White, *White* does not activate *aggressive*. Therefore, both *aggressive* and *violent push* end up with less activation
when the pusher is White than when the pusher is Black. In this manner,
stereotypes color one's understanding of a person's behavior and one's
impression of that person.

As this example illustrates, the identical behavior may be interpreted
differently in different contexts (Kunda & Sherman-Williams, 1993; Sagar &
Schofield, 1980; Wojciszke, 1994). Similar shifts in meaning from one context
to another have been demonstrated for all the major ingredients of impression formation. These include traits (e.g., Asch, 1946; Asch & Zukier, 1984;
Hamilton & Zanna, 1974; Kunda et al., 1997; Zanna & Hamilton, 1977), stereotypes (e.g., Deaux & Lewis, 1984; Kunda, Miller, & Claire, 1990), facial expressions (Trope, 1986), and self-conceptions (e.g., Sanitioso, Kunda, & Fong,
1990). Thus, there is broad support for the notion that the meaning of social
constructs varies from one occasion to another.

Traditional models of representation cannot readily account for such
shifts in meaning. Leading models of social cognition conceptualize representations as schemas, which are typically understood in terms of a filing
cabinet or a storage bin metaphor (e.g., Wyer & Srull, 1986). In such models,

each social construct has a fixed and discrete meaning that may be accessed independently, much like one might pull out a single file from a filing cabinet without affecting any of its neighbors (cf. Kunda et al., 1997; Smith, 1996, in press). In contrast, the parallel constraint-satisfaction model of impression formation assumes that there are no discrete, independent representations of constructs, and the meaning of each construct is not defined in the net but, rather, arises from its pattern of associations with other constructs (cf. Kintsch, 1988). At any time, only a subset of a construct's associates are activated, and these constitute its meaning at that time. Thus, the notion that social constructs vary in meaning from one occasion to another, which conflicts with the assumptions underlying traditional, schema-based models of representation, constitutes a core assumption of the parallel constraint-satisfaction model.

The parallel constraint-satisfaction model of impression formation assumes that a coherent impression of the person is achieved through parallel satisfaction of the constraints imposed by the many concepts applied to the person. This view of impression formation is quite different from the one advocated by earlier serial models of impression formation (Brewer, 1988; Fiske & Neuberg, 1990). These serial models assume that people first try to make sense of other people by applying stereotypes. They may then use individuating information such as traits and behaviors if they are strongly motivated to understand the person or if they cannot successfully categorize the person as belonging to any particular stereotype. Thus, the serial models give special, dominating status to stereotypes. In contrast, the parallel constraint-satisfaction model does not. It treats all kinds of information as equal in status, and assumes that their impact depends entirely on their patterns of association with other pieces of information.

Using this parallel constraint-satisfaction model, Kunda and Thagard (1996) were able to account for most of the phenomena emerging from the literature on how people form impressions of others based on stereotypes and individuating information. Their connectionist program, IMP, successfully simulated the results of experiments that demonstrated these phenomena.

The parallel constraint-satisfaction model can readily account for several phenomena that are not easily accommodated by previous serial models (Brewer, 1988; Fiske & Neuberg, 1990). For example, Kunda, Sinclair, and Griffin (1997) found that the impact of stereotypes on impressions can depend on the perceiver's judgment task. In line with earlier findings (e.g., Locksley, Borgida, Brekke, & Hepburn, 1980), Kunda et al. found that the effects of stereotypes on trait ratings of an individual were undermined by the individual's behavior. Although construction workers are stereotyped as more aggressive than accountants, a construction worker and an accountant were viewed as equally unaggressive after having failed to react to an insult, an unaggressive behavior. But even though the stereotypes no longer affected trait ratings, they continued to influence predictions about the individual's behavior: The construction worker was still viewed as more likely than the accountant to engage in coarse aggressive behaviors such as punching and cursing.

The parallel constraint-satisfaction model predicts such a pattern when the stereotypes are associated with additional traits that are not undermined by the target's behavior and so can continue to influence behavioral predictions. In this case, even though both targets came to be viewed as equally unaggressive, the construction worker continued to be viewed as a member of the working class, and the accountant as a member of the upper middle class. Punching and cursing are positively associated with working-class status but negatively associated with upper middle-class status. Therefore, the working-class construction worker was viewed as more likely than the upper middle-class accountant to punch and curse even though the two were viewed as equally unaggressive.

In this manner, the parallel constraint-satisfaction model can readily account for the differential effects of stereotypes on traits and on behavioral predictions as due to the pattern of associations (constraints) among traits, behaviors, and the different aspects of stereotypes. In contrast, these findings are problematic for the serial models (Brewer, 1988; Fiske & Neuberg, 1990) because these models provide no grounds for distinguishing among different judgment tasks.

The parallel constraint-satisfaction model is also better able than the serial models to account for findings showing that newly encountered combinations of stereotypes (e.g., feminist and bank teller) can jointly influence impressions (Kunda, Miller, & Claire, 1990). Such findings are problematic for the serial models because these assume that only a single stereotype dominates one's impressions at a time. In contrast, the parallel constraint-satisfaction model assumes that stereotypes can be integrated with each other just like any other concepts are integrated, through satisfying the constraints imposed by the knowledge associated with them (cf. Miller & Read, 1991; Read & Miller, 1993a, 1993b).

The fact that the connectionist program, IMP, could successfully simulate the diverse empirical findings on how stereotypes and individuating information influence impressions suggests that the parallel constraint-satisfaction model of impression formation is computationally feasible and psychologically plausible.

It is important to note that this model accounts only for relatively automatic processes of impression formation, that is, processes carried out with little awareness, intention, or effort. It does not model more elaborate, controlled processes that require more effort, intention, and awareness. Thus, this model can account for the relatively automatic processes that take place in the early stages of the attribution process—the identification of behavior, for example, as a friendly act, and the characterization of the person, for example, as a friendly person (Gilbert, 1989; Trope, 1986). But it does not address the more effortful processes that sometimes take place later in the attribution sequence, in which early impressions are corrected by taking situational constraints into account (e.g., the person is on a job interview and so is trying to appear friendly). Similarly, the model explains how racial stereotypes can color initial impressions of members of minority groups, but does not address the processes through which people who are not prejudiced can subsequently attempt to eliminate these automatic influences of stereotypes from their judgments (Devine, 1989). Such higher order reasoning is captured by models of explanatory coherence, which we discuss next.

Note also that this theory of impression formation does not explain how new concepts are formed, only how existing concepts are applied. However, the need for new concepts may be signalled by a lack of coherence, as we discuss later.

In sum, we view the automatic aspects of impression formation as resulting from a process of parallel constraint satisfaction in which one understands people by applying to them a set of concepts in a way that maximizes coherence.

Attribution as Explanatory Coherence

Impression formation is only one way of making sense of people. Another is causal attribution in which we make inferences that explain other people's behavior. Causal attribution is naturally understood in terms of Thagard's (1989, 1992b) theory of explanatory coherence. In this theory, the elements are propositions, including evidence to be explained (observed behavior) and hypotheses about them that would explain the behavior. Suppose, for example, that a normally mild-mannered friend screams at you. Various hypotheses would explain that behavior: Perhaps the friend had a stressful day at work, or stopped taking some needed medication, or learned some secret ugly fact about you. What inference you make to explain your friend's behavior will depend on what best fits with your other beliefs: Maximizing coherence will lead you to accept the most plausible hypothesis that explains your friend's behavior and to reject the alternative hypotheses.

Coherence-based explanatory inferences require specification of the positive and negative constraints among the propositional elements. The main source of positive constraints is explanation: If one proposition explains another, then there is a positive constraint between them. Such constraints can operate at many levels, because we can generate hypotheses that explain other hypotheses as well as hypotheses that explain observed behavior. You may hypothesize that your friend screamed at you because of a stressful day at work, and further hypothesize that the stressful day was

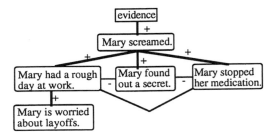

FIG. 1.2. Explanatory coherence network. Positive associations are shown as thick lines and negative associations are shown by thin lines. The evidence that Mary screamed can be explained by three competing hypotheses.

caused by impending layoffs. The result can be a network of propositions of the sort shown in Fig. 1.2. This shows different hypotheses competing to explain the evidence. Positive constraints can be affected by considerations of simplicity: In Thagard's theory, if a number of hypotheses are required to make an explanation, then the positive constraints between hypotheses and evidence are weakened. For example, if you explain Mary's behavior by supposing that she was abducted by aliens who mistreated her, you are making a number of hypotheses whose coherence may suffer as a result of a lack of simplicity as well as incompatibility with other things that you believe.

In explanatory coherence, the sources of negative constraints are contradiction and competition. If two propositions logically contradict each other (Mary is in Florida vs. Mary is in Toronto), then there is a strong negative constraint between them. Moreover, in explanatory situations, people tend to treat hypotheses as negatively constraining each other even if they are not strictly contradictory. It is possible that Mary's behavior should be explained because she had a stressful day *and* she stopped taking her medication *and* she found out something about you, but normally we treat these as independent competing explanations. Explanatory coherence can also be used to assess hypotheses about oneself, as when Mary herself figures out that she screamed because of some previously suppressed hostility.

Thagard (1989, 1992a, 1992b) presented a set of principles for explanatory coherence. Explanatory coherence is a symmetric relation. A hypothesis coheres with what it explains, and the more hypotheses it takes to explain something, the less the degree of coherence. Similar hypotheses that explain similar pieces of evidence cohere. Contradictory and competitive propositions are incoherent with each other. Propositions that describe the results of observations have a degree of acceptability of their own, and the acceptability of a proposition in a system of propositions depends on its coherence with them.

Explanatory coherence has been modeled using a connectionist program called ECHO, which has been applied to many cases of scientific theory evaluation (Nowak & Thagard, 1992a, 1992b; Thagard, 1989, 1991, 1992a, 1992b). It has also been used to model belief revision in the context of science education (Ranney & Thagard, 1988; Schank & Ranney, 1991, 1992). More social applications include adversarial problem solving in which people have to make inferences about the hostile intentions and possible deceptions of their competitors in games, business, and international relations (Thagard, 1992a). ECHO has also been used to model a variety of attributions concerning interpersonal relations. Read and Marcus-Newhall (1993) demonstrated empirically that when people evaluate explanations of social behavior such as "Joanne agrees to marry Bill if they elope immediately," they follow the principles of coherence outlined by Thagard (1989). Further, ECHO successfully simulated these empirical results. It appears then that people make explanatory inferences about others in a manner that maximizes coherence.

Processes of maximizing explanatory coherence are particularly well suited for accounting for jury decision making, where the task is to evaluate the coherence of accounts presented by the prosecution and the defense (cf. Byrne, 1995; Pennington & Hastie, 1992; Read & Miller, 1993a, 1993b). Such processes may also capture the controlled inferences often required for choosing among dispositional and situational attributions for behavior (Gilbert, 1989).

Viewing causal attribution as an attempt to maximize explanatory coherence highlights questions that have received little attention by attribution researchers. Much of the large literature on attribution focused on how people choose between dispositional and situational explanations (Jones, 1990). But there has been little discussion of how people may choose among competing dispositional attributions (is this person friendly or ingratiating?) or among competing situational attributions (is this person driven by pressure at work or by tension at home?) (Kunda, in press). And this tradition has left no room for attributions that incorporate dispositional as well as situational explanations (is this the kind of person who collapses under pressure?) (Mischel & Shoda, 1995; Shoda & Mischel, 1993). Yet, many of our attempts to make sense of others are of precisely this nature. The work on explanatory coherence provides a language and tools for exploring these important kinds of judgment (cf. Miller & Read, 1991; Read & Miller, 1993a, 1993b).

Just as conceptual coherence does not explain concept formation, explanatory coherence does not explain hypothesis formation. The relation of coherence to hypothesis formation is discussed later.

Using One Person to Understand Another via Analogical Coherence

Another valuable cognitive mechanism for making sense of people is analogy, in which we see one person as similar to another with respect to a complex of properties and relations. I may, for example, increase my understanding of Princess Diana by comparing her to Anna Karenina in Tolstoy's novel. This comparison would be much deeper than noticing just that both are women, in that it also involves a set of interlocking relations. Diana is like Anna Karenina in being married to a man, not caring for that man, and being (for a while) passionately involved with another man. The analogy involves noticing not only that Diana corresponds to Anna, but also that Prince Charles corresponds to Anna's husband, and that Diana's lover James Hewitt corresponds to Anna's lover Vronsky.

Such analogical mapping can be viewed as a coherence process that maximizes the satisfaction of multiple constraints (Holyoak & Thagard, 1995). The elements are hypotheses about what corresponds to what, for example that Diana corresponds to Anna and that *loves* in Diana's case corresponds to *loves* in Anna's case. One constraint is perceptual and semantic similarity: Two elements tend to correspond to each other if they look the same or have similar meaning. Other constraints are structural: In order to map *Anna loves Vronsky* to *Diana loves James*, we must consistently map Ann to Diana, loves to loves, and Vronsky to James. Mappings should tend to be one-to-one; without strong reason, we should not map Diana to both Anna and Vronsky. Finally, purpose provides a practical constraint on the mapping, because we should try to come up with mappings that will contribute to the cognitive goals that the analogy is supposed to serve, such as providing an explanation or contributing to a decision.

Finding an appropriate mapping between complex analogs is a computationally difficult problem that can be solved using connectionist models (Holyoak & Thagard, 1989) as well as nonconnectionist methods (Falkenhainer, Forbus, & Gentner, 1989). Here we omit the computational details, but emphasize that analogical understanding, like impression formation and attribution, can be understood as a process of maximizing coherence. To map between two analogous situations involving sets of interrelated people, we must come up with a coherent set of correspondences between the various people and aspects of the situation. Similarly, when our task is to retrieve from memory a person or situation similar to one we want to understand, we must search for one that has a highly coherent set of correspondences.

Making sense of people analogically always involves comparing two individuals, a target to be understood and a source that provides understanding. In the Princess Diana example, the source and target are both other people, but sometimes the source is oneself and the target is another (e.g., empathy), sometimes the target is oneself and the source is another (e.g., some kinds of social comparison), and sometimes both the source and target are oneself, as when a past situation of one's life is used to make sense of a current situation.

Several diverse lines of social psychological research assume, explicitly or implicitly, that people use analogy to make sense of others, that is, they understand individuals by mapping them onto other individuals. Newly encountered individuals are often understood in terms of more familiar others (Smith & Zarate, 1992). For example, people who resembled a significant other (parent, close friend) on some dimensions were falsely recalled as also resembling that person on other dimensions as well (Andersen, Glassmann, Chen, & Cole, 1995). Significant others may be used spontaneously as sources for understanding others because their representations are highly accessible (Andersen et al., 1995). Other individuals may be used as sources of analogical mapping when one is reminded of them. For example, Gilovich (1981) showed that fictitious college football players were understood in terms of famous players when participants were reminded of the famous player, and when that player could be readily mapped onto the fictitious one (as when both played the same position). When mapping was facilitated in this manner, the fictitious players were rated more highly. It appears then that we often understand strangers by mapping them onto people we know well.

We may also understand others by mapping them onto ourselves. When trying to assess others' attitudes and behaviors, we may do so by assuming that they resemble our own. This may be one source of the well-documented false consensus effect, wherein people's estimates of the prevalence of various responses in the population are correlated with their own responses. For example, optimists assume that optimism is more common than do pessimists (Ross, Green, & House, 1977). False consensus effects are exacerbated when the target population is more similar to the self on various demographic dimensions (Marks & Miller, 1987). This may occur because such similarity facilitates mapping the other onto the self.

A particularly important kind of mapping from another to oneself is empathy, in which I establish a correspondence not only between someone else's situation and my own, but also a correspondence between the other's emotional state and an emotional experience of my own. Deep understanding of people's work stress requires not just seeing how their situation corresponds to one that I have been in (unpleasant boss, risk of layoff, etc.) but also appreciating their emotional state (anger, fear). In a purely verbal analogy, I may infer that just as I was angry in my own situation, so the other is likely to be angry in a similar situation. But empathy goes beyond verbal elements by providing a correspondence between some emotional experience of my own and what I can infer analogically to be the emotional experience of the other. By setting up an analogy between another person and myself, I can feel an approximation to what the other feels. Such an analogy should be facilitated if I myself have been in a similar situation. Indeed, Batson et al. (1996) found that women felt greater empathy for someone undergoing a difficult experience if they themselves had had a similar experience (though the same was not true for men). Barnes and

Thagard (in press) have an extended discussion of empathy as analogy. Like other kinds of analogy, empathy can be understood as a coherence mechanism that evaluates a set of correspondences between two people and their situations; empathy differs from other analogies in that the correspondences link representations that are not verbal or visual, but emotional.

Just as the self can serve as a source for understanding others, other people can be used to enrich one's understanding of oneself. An extensive literature on social comparison suggests that people often attempt to evaluate their own abilities and performance by comparing them to those of others. People are particularly likely to seek comparisons with others who are similar to them in various ways (Wood, 1989). Similarly, one's self-views are particularly likely to be affected by exposure to superior others when these superior others are similar to the self. Tesser and his colleagues (Tesser, 1986; Tesser & Campbell, 1983) reasoned that self-evaluations can be threatened when one is outperformed by others. One then engages in thoughts and actions designed to reduce the threat. Such protective action is especially likely to occur when the other person is similar to the self on dimensions such as age, race, gender, or personality. In other circumstances, one can be inspired by the performance of outstanding others, and view oneself more favorably after exposure to them. This too is more likely to occur when the outstanding other resembles the self. For example, future accountants were inspired by reading about an outstanding accountant, but were unaffected by reading about an outstanding teacher. Future teachers, in contrast, were inspired by the outstanding teacher but were unaffected by the accountant (Lockwood & Kunda, 1997). It appears then that we often make sense of ourselves through comparison to others, and we find others most informative about ourselves when we can readily map the other onto the self. Such mapping is facilitated by similarity between the self and the other.

Thus, there is ample evidence that people often make sense of the self and others through analogy to others. And they are more likely to do so when they can construct more coherent analogies among individuals. Similarity between two individuals increases the likelihood that one will be used to make sense of the other. But what determines similarity?

Social psychological research has primarily examined the impact of only one kind of constraint on analogical coherence—surface similarity, that is, relatively superficial similarity that is based only on the number of shared features. This research showed that an individual is more likely to be compared to another when the two are similar in their performance on a given dimension, or when they share one or more attributes. Such surface similarity is indeed an important contributor to the coherence of analogies. But it is not the only one, and it can even be superseded by deeper structural and relational similarity, that is, similarity that is based on the underlying patterns of relations among elements. Structural similarity can lend coherence to analogies among sets of elements even if they are superficially very different from each other (Holyoak & Thagard, 1995). For example, people presented with two pictures, one of a woman receiving a delivery from a food bank employee, and another of a physically similar woman feeding a squirrel will, upon brief reflection, map the woman in the first picture onto the squirrel in the second picture rather than onto the superficially similar woman. The mapping of the first woman onto the squirrel is more coherent because it involves greater correspondence in underlying relations among the objects and characters in each picture, that is, both the woman in the first picture and the squirrel in the second are recipients of food (Markman & Gentner, 1993).

Existing social psychological research cannot speak to the importance of such structural coherence in facilitating analogies among people because it focused on examining similarity on singular dimensions. This focus left no room for detecting the operation of deeper structural similarity. It is possible, therefore, that the conclusion that attribute similarity among individuals will determine whether and how they are used to make sense of one another is overly strong. Intuitively, it seems that we often compare ourselves and others to superficially dissimilar individuals who differ from us in background, nationality, and even gender. Surely, one need not be Indian and male to be inspired by Mahatma Ghandi. Moreover, we can gain important insight into ourselves and others through analogy to the animals in Aesop's fables, and can be inspired by *The Little Engine That Could*. People or things that are highly dissimilar to us in their attributes may nevertheless be similar in their purposes and in the structures of their lives, so that they can be highly informative about ourselves and others. Applying this more complex view of analogical coherence to analogies among individuals may enrich the understanding of the circumstances that lead us to compare one individual to another.

To summarize our discussion so far, coherence theory, which views inference as maximizing satisfaction of positive and negative constraints, provides a general way of understanding how people make sense of each other.[2] Table 1.2 shows how conceptual, explanatory, and analogical coherence can all be viewed as instances of a more broadly defined coherence problem.

---

[2]There are several other kinds of coherence than the three discussed in this paper, but they seem to have less relevance to making sense of other people. In deliberative coherence, actions and goals are evaluated to select plans (Millgram & Thagard, 1996; Thagard & Millgram, 1995). Understanding of other people's decisions may involve appreciation of their assessment of deliberative coherence. In deductive coherence, general principles such as mathematical axioms and ethical rules are evaluated in connection with their deductive implications such as theorems and particular ethical judgments. In visual coherence, interpretations of visual inputs are combined to produce coherent perceptions.

TABLE 1.2
Three Kinds of Coherence

	Conceptual Coherence	Explanatory Coherence	Analogical Coherence
Elements	Concepts	Propositions	Correspondences
Positive Constraints	Positive associations	Explanation	Similarity, purpose, structure
Negative Constraints	Negative associations	Contradiction, competition	One-to-one mappings

Two major problems remain. First, where do the elements and constraints come from? Second, how are the different kinds of constraints related to each other. We address these questions in the next two sections.

The Generation of Elements and Constraints

Although much of cognition can be understood in terms of coherence mechanisms, there is obviously more to cognition than achieving coherence among a set of given elements. Cognition is also generative, producing new concepts, propositions, and analogies. Moreover, for coherence to be assessed, constraints among elements need to have been generated.

Generation of new elements is sometimes driven by *in*coherence. If I am trying to understand someone but fail to form a coherent impression or attribution, I may be spurred to form new elements that can add coherence to the old set of elements. To take an example from Kunda et al. (1990), if I am told that someone is a Harvard-educated carpenter, it may be difficult to reconcile the conflicting expectations associated with the two concepts. Surprise is an emotional reaction signalling that a satisfactory degree of coherence has not been achieved. This reaction triggers hypothesis formation as I ask myself how someone with a Harvard degree could end up working as a carpenter. People show ingenuity in generating explanations, for example, that the Harvard graduate was a counterculture type who preferred a nonprofessional career path. Hence, new hypotheses and possibly also new concepts (the *Ivy League laborer* type) can be added to the set of elements so as to lend greater coherence to the attempt to make sense of this person. In this case, generation of elements is incoherence driven, because it is prompted by a failure to achieve an interpretation that satisfies an adequate number of the positive and negative constraints. In addition to surprise, other emotions such as anxiety may signal incoherence.

Not all element generation is incoherence driven, however. Some representations arise serendipitously, based on things we just happen to encounter. I may form the concept of Albanian as the result of meeting various immigrants from Albania, without having experienced any incoherence in my previous attempts to understand them. In other cases, new representations may arise from curiosity-driven thinking that is motivated not by any incoherence but by the desire to find out more about something that interests me. If I am interested in the Balkans, I will learn more about Serbs and Croats and may form stereotypes about them without having tried and failed to fit them with my other social concepts. Motivation may also lead one to generate new concepts. For example, our desire to protect our stereotypes from change in the face of disconfirmation may lead us assign individuals who threaten our stereotypes into novel subtypes that serve to isolate these individuals from their group (Kunda & Oleson, 1995; Weber & Crocker, 1983). And our desire to view ourselves positively may lead us to construct hypothetical individuals to whom we are superior (Taylor, Wood, & Lichtman, 1983). Thus serendipity, curiosity, and motivation, in addition to incoherence, can spur the generation of new representations.

Where do constraints come from? Some may be innate, capturing basic conceptual relations such as that an object cannot be both red and black all over. Most constraints, however, capture empirically discovered relations between elements. For impression formation, I learn that some concepts (e.g., nurse and benevolent) are positively associated, whereas other concepts (e.g., Nazi and benevolent) are negatively associated. Such associations may be learned through direct observation of nurses or Nazis as well as through cultural transmission. For attribution, the positive constraints come from understanding causal relations. The link between the hypothesis that Mary is in love and the fact to be explained that Mary is very happy depends on the causal judgment gleaned from experience that being in love can cause people to be happy. Negative constraints in explanatory coherence arise from logical contradictions (you cannot be both in love and not in love) and from competing hypotheses (maybe instead she's happy because she got a promotion at work).

Because any full account of human cognition would have to include an account of how new concepts, hypotheses, and other representations are formed, a complete cognitive architecture would have to include generation mechanisms as well as coherence mechanisms (see Thagard, 1996, for a review of different kinds of learning). Our goal in this chapter is not to propose a cognitive architecture, but merely to show how coherence mechanisms contribute to making sense of people.

Automatic and Controlled Processes in Coherence

We presented conceptual integration, explanation, and analogy as three independent ways of making sense of people, each using a different kind of coherence element. In information integration as modeled by IMP, the elements are concepts; in explanation as modeled by ECHO, the elements are propositions; in analogy as modeled by ACME, the elements are correspondences between pairs of concepts, objects, or propositions. However, these three modes of making sense are unlikely to operate in isolation. Our understanding of a given individual will typically reflect a blend of all three mechanisms. For example, after chatting with Jane at a party for a while, your impression of her may be based on the way you integrated her behavior (laughing, talking a lot) with some of the stereotypes applicable to her (single, lawyer, female), on your understanding of how her mood and behavior might be influenced by the fact that she has just received an attractive job offer, and on the fact that she reminds you of your irrepressible friend Meg.

We believe that all three ways of making sense may operate in parallel. However, some aspects of impression formation take place automatically, that is, with little awareness, intention, or effort, whereas others may require more controlled, effortful processes. The process of integrating information modeled by IMP is assumed to take place automatically (Kunda & Thagard, 1996). Traits, behaviors, and stereotypes, as well as some aspects of the situation, influence each other's meaning and jointly influence impressions in a relatively automatic manner. This view is supported by evidence that a person's behavior can provoke automatic trait inference (Gilbert, Pelham, & Krull, 1988; Winter & Uleman, 1984), that the situation can automatically color the meaning of emotional expressions (Trope, 1986, in press), and that stereotypes can automatically influence trait ratings (Devine, 1989) and affective reactions (Fazio, Jackson, Dunton, & Williams, 1995). It appears, then, that a great deal of impression formation arises from automatic integration of available information, without awareness or intention.

Some aspects of causal reasoning may also be relatively automatic. Some behaviors and traits may be automatically viewed as driven by particular causes (e.g., Susan is crying because Tom hit her; John is marrying Ellen because he loves her). Indeed, it has been suggested that underlying goals are often central to the meaning of traits and behaviors (Read, Jones, & Miller, 1990). However, many behaviors are not associated with any obvious causes (e.g., why did David quit his job?), and others are associated with many conflicting ones (Did Melissa lose interest in the lesson because she was too slow to follow it, or because she has long since mastered it?). Moreover, often the context offers alternative causes that compete with a normally strongly associated one (e.g., John is an illegal immigrant; did he marry Ellen because he loves her or because he wants to avoid deportation?). In such cases, when no plausible cause comes to mind, or when one is entertaining several plausible, competing causes and has trouble choosing among them, one is likely to call upon elaborate causal analysis, in a conscious and effortful attempt to determine which is the most likely cause. Thus, controlled causal reasoning can be triggered by the emotional experience of surprise or confusion (Kunda et al., 1990). Note that the availability of multiple competing causes will not necessarily baffle us; often, the context will lead us to favor one cause and suppress the others through relatively automatic constraint satisfaction (see Read & Miller, 1993a, 1993b). But, when we are puzzled or stumped in our attempts to make sense of others, we turn to controlled processes involving elaborate causal analysis.

Recent models of attribution point to such an interplay between automatic and controlled processes (Gilbert, 1989; Trope, 1986). These models suggest that perceivers can automatically view behavior as caused by underlying personality traits (e.g., she acted nervously while talking, so she must be an anxious person; Gilbert et al., 1988; Winter & Uleman, 1984). But when the context offers a competing situational explanation for the behavior (she was discussing an embarrassing topic, that's why she acted nervously), controlled processes are required for this information to be taken into account (Gilbert et al., 1988). Similarly, when the most compelling cause for a behavior is the situation, its causal role is inferred automatically, but controlled processes are required for the actor's personality to be taken into account (Krull, 1993). Thus, a single, strongly associated cause may be inferred automatically. But sorting among multiple competing causes can be more cognitively demanding and so may require more controlled processing.

The third way of making sense of people—analogy—seems likely to involve both automatic and controlled processes. Simple similarity mappings may take place automatically, whereas more complex relational mappings may require elaborate reasoning. There is some evidence that both types of processes may be implicated when making comparisons among individuals. When faced with another person in circumstances similar to their own, people tend to compare themselves automatically to this person; they use information suggesting that the comparison is logically inappropriate only when they have sufficient cognitive resources (Gilbert, Giesler, & Morris, 1995). This suggests that people can map one person onto another automatically, but the mapping can also be influenced, even undone, by more controlled processes. In a similar vein, it has been shown that people spontaneously use surface similarity to map one group of individuals onto another; that is, they base their mappings on the number of shared features among individuals. But, following brief reflection on the similarity between the two groupings, they use deep structural similarities instead; that is, they base their mappings on the underlying relations among sets of individuals (Markman & Gentner, 1993).

Our view of how these automatic and controlled processes interact with each other is similar to that proposed recently by Sloman (1996). Sloman argued that people use relatively automatic, associative processes as well as more controlled, rule-based processes. The two systems may operate simultaneously, with the rule-based system sometimes suppressing the outcomes of the associative one. We would add that the products of one way of making sense may feed into another. Based on the way we integrate information, we may conclude that a person behaved in an unfriendly manner. Our causal analysis may then lead us to conclude that the unfriendly behavior was due to stress, and that the person may well be friendly. This characterizing may then be integrated with our other knowledge of the person. Our resulting impression may lead us to map this person onto another person, and this mapping will trigger further inferences about the person's likely traits and attributes, to be integrated with previous knowledge. As this example illustrates, all three kinds of making sense are dynamically interrelated, and all can contribute to the understanding of a person.

We should note, though, that our attempts to outline how the different ways of making sense of people are interrelated remain speculative. Most empirical and theoretical work to date focuses on understanding each of these processes when examined alone. Thus, there are well-developed models of conceptual integration (Kunda & Thagard, 1996), of causal explanation (Read & Marcus-Newhall, 1993; Thagard, 1989, 1992), and of analogy (Holyoak & Thagard, 1989, 1995), and each is supported by empirical evidence that addresses its particular assumptions. But spelling out the interrelationships among these models remains a major challenge for future theorizing and research.

APPENDIX

Thagard and Verbeurgt (1998) define a *coherence problem* as follows. Let E be a finite set of elements $\{e_i\}$ and C be a set of constraints on E understood as a set $\{(e_i, e_j)\}$ of pairs of elements of E. C divides into $C+$, the positive constraints on E, and $C-$, the negative constraints on E. With each constraint is associated a number w, which is the weight (strength) of the constraint. The problem is to partition E into two sets, A and R, in a way that maximizes compliance with the following two *coherence conditions*:

if (e_i, e_j) is in $C+$, then e_i is in A if and only if e_j is in A. $\qquad$ (1)

if (e_i, e_j) is in $C-$, then e_i is in A if and only if e_j is in R. $\qquad$ (2)

Let W be the weight of the partition, that is, the sum of the weights of the satisfied constraints. The coherence problem is then to partition E into A and R in a way that maximizes W. Because *a coheres with b* is a symmetric relation, the order of the elements in the constraints does not matter. The coherence problem is computationally intractable in that there is no efficient and exact way of solving it, but there are connectionist and other algorithms that provide excellent approximate solutions.

REFERENCES

Andersen, S. M., Glassmann, N. S., Chen, S., & Cole, S. W. (1995). Transference in social perception: The role of chronic accessibility in significant-other representations. *Journal of Personality and Social Psychology, 69*, 41–57.

Asch, S. E. (1946). Forming impressions of personality. *Journal of Abnormal and Social Psychology, 41*, 303–314.

Asch, S. E., & Zukier, H. (1984). Thinking about persons. *Journal of Personality and Social Psychology, 46*, 1230–1240.

Barnes, A., & Thagard, P. (in press). Empathy and analogy. *Dialogue.*

Batson, C. D., Sympson, S. C., Hindman, J. L., Decruz, P., Todd, R. M., Weeks, J. L., Jennings, G., & Burris, C. T. (1996). "I've been there, too": Effect on empathy of prior experience with a need. *Personality and Social Psychology Bulletin, 22*, 474–482.

Brewer, M. B. (1988). A dual process model of impression formation. In T. K. Srull & R. S. Wyer (Eds.), *Advances in social cognition* (pp. 1–36). Hillsdale, NJ: Lawrence Erlbaum Associates.

Byrne, M. D. (1995). The convergence of explanatory coherence and the story model: A case study in juror decision. In J. D. Moore & J. F. Lehman (Eds.), *Proceedings of the Seventeenth Annual Conference of the Cognitive Science Society* (pp. 539–543). Mahwah, NJ: Lawrence Erlbaum Associates.

Deaux, K., & Lewis, L. L. (1984). Structure of gender stereotypes: Interrelationships among components and gender label. *Journal of Personality and Social Psychology, 46*, 991–1004.

Devine, P. G. (1989). Stereotypes and prejudice: Their automatic and controlled components. *Journal of Personality and Social Psychology, 56*, 5–18.

Falkenhainer, B., Forbus, K. D., & Gentner, D. (1989). The structure-mapping engine: Algorithms and examples. *Artificial Intelligence, 41*, 1–63.

Fazio, R. H., Jackson, J. R., Dunton, B. C., & Williams, C. J. (1995). Variability in automatic activation as an unobtrusive measure of racial attitudes: A bona fide pipeline? *Journal of Personality and Social Psychology, 69*, 1013–1027.

Fiske, S. T., & Neuberg, S. L. (1990). A continuum of impression formation, from category-based to individuating processes: Influences of information and motivation on attention and separation. *Advances in Experimental Social Psychology, 23*, 1–74.

Gilbert, D. T. (1989). Thinking lightly about others: Automatic components of the social inference process. In J. A. Bargh & J. S. Uleman (Eds.), *Unintended thought* (pp. 189–211). New York: Guilford.

Gilbert, D. T., Giesler, R. B., & Morris, K. A. (1995). When comparisons arise. *Journal of Personality and Social Psychology, 69*, 227–236.

Gilbert, D. T., Pelham, B. W., & Krull, D. S. (1988). On cognitive busyness: When person perceivers meet persons perceived. *Journal of Personality and Social Psychology, 54*, 733–740.

Gilovich, T. (1981). Seeing the past in the present: The effect of associations to familiar events on judgments and decisions. *Journal of Personality and Social Psychology, 40*, 797–808.

Hamilton, D. L., & Zanna, M. P. (1974). Context effects in impression formation: Changes in connotative meaning. *Journal of Personality and Social Psychology, 29*, 649–654.

Holyoak, K. J., & Thagard, P. (1989). Analogical mapping by constraint satisfaction. *Cognitive Science, 13*, 295–355.

Holyoak, K. J., & Thagard, P. (1995). *Mental leaps: Analogy in creative thought*. Cambridge, MA: MIT Press/Bradford Books.

Jones, E. E. (1990). *Interpersonal perception*. New York: Freeman.

Kintsch, W. (1988). The role of knowledge in discourse comprehension: A construction-integration model. *Psychological Review, 95,* 163–182.

Krull, D. S. (1993). Does the grist change the mill? The effect of the perceiver's inferential goal on the process of social inference. *Personality and Social Psychology Bulletin, 19,* 340–348.

Kunda, Z. (in press). Parallel processing in person perception: Implications for two-stage models of attribution. In J. M. Darley & J. Cooper (Eds.), *Attribution processes, person perception, and social interaction: The legacy of Ned Jones*. Mahwah, NJ: Lawrence Erlbaum Associates.

Kunda, Z., Miller, D., & Claire, T. (1990). Combining social concepts: The role of causal reasoning. *Cognitive Science, 14,* 551–577.

Kunda, Z., & Oleson, K. C. (1995). Maintaining stereotypes in the face of disconfirmation: Constructing grounds for subtyping deviants. *Journal of Personality and Social Psychology, 68,* 565–579.

Kunda, Z., & Sherman-Williams, B. (1993). Stereotypes and the construal of individuating information. *Personality and Social Psychology Bulletin, 19,* 90–99.

Kunda, Z., Sinclair, L., & Griffin, D. (1997). Equal ratings but separate meanings: Stereotypes and the construal of traits. *Journal of Personality and Social Psychology, 72,* 720–734.

Kunda, Z., & Thagard, P. (1996). Forming impressions from stereotypes, traits, and behaviors: A parallel constraint satisfaction theory. *Psychological Review, 103,* 284–308.

Locksley, A., Borgida, E., Brekke, N., & Hepburn, C. (1980). Sex stereotypes and social judgment. *Journal of Personality and Social Psychology, 39,* 821–831.

Lockwood, P., & Kunda, Z. (1997). Superstars and me: Predicting the impact of role models on the self. *Journal of Personality and Social Psychology, 73,* 91–103.

Markman, A. B., & Gentner, D. (1993). Structural alignment during similarity comparisons. *Cognitive psychology, 25,* 431–467.

Marks, G., & Miller, N. (1987). Ten years of research on the false-consensus effect: An empirical and theoretical review. *Psychological Bulletin, 102,* 72–90.

McClelland, J. L., & Rumelhart, D. E. (1989). *Explorations in parallel distributed processing*. Cambridge, MA: MIT Press.

Miller, L., & Read, S. (1991). On the coherence of mental models of persons and relationships. In F. Fincham & G. Fletcher (Eds.), *Cognition in close relationships* (pp. 69–99). Hillsdale, NJ: Lawrence Erlbaum Associates.

Millgram, E., & Thagard, P. (1996). Deliberative coherence. *Synthese, 108,* 63–88.

Mischel, W., & Shoda, Y. (1995). A cognitive-affective system theory of personality: Reconceptualizing situations, dispositions, dynamics, and the invariance in personality structure. *Psychological Review, 102,* 246–268.

Nowak, G., & Thagard, P. (1992a). Copernicus, Ptolemy, and explanatory coherence. In R. Giere (Eds.), *Cognitive models of science* (pp. 274–309). Minneapolis: University of Minnesota Press.

Nowak, G., & Thagard, P. (1992b). Newton, Descartes, and explanatory coherence. In R. Duschl & H. R. (Eds.), *Philosophy of science, cognitive psychology and educational theory and practice* (pp. 69–115). Albany: SUNY.

Pennington, N., & Hastie, R. (1992). Explaining the evidence: Tests of the story model for juror decision making. *Journal of Personality and Social Psychology, 51,* 189–206.

Ranney, M., & Thagard, P. (1988). Explanatory coherence and belief revision in naive physics. In *Proceedings of the Tenth Annual Conference of the Cognitive Science Society* (pp. 426–432). Hillsdale, NJ: Lawrence Erlbaum Associates.

Read, S. J., Jones, D. K., & Miller, L. C. (1990). Traits as goal-based categories: The importance of goals in the coherence of dispositions. *Journal of Personality and Social Psychology, 58,* 1048–1061.

Read, S. J., & Marcus-Newhall, A. (1993). Explanatory coherence in social explanations: A parallel distributed processing account. *Journal of Personality and Social Psychology, 65,* 429–447.

Read, S. J., & Miller, L. C. (1993a). Explanatory coherence in the construction of mental models of others. In *Proceedings of the Fifteenth Annual Conference of the Cognitive Science Society* (pp. 836–841). Hillsdale, NJ: Lawrence Erlbaum Associates.

Read, S. J., & Miller, L. C. (1993b). Rapist or "regular guy": Explanatory coherence in the construction of mental models of others. *Personality and Social Psychology Bulletin, 19,* 526–541.

Ross, L., Greene, D., & House, P. (1977). The "false consensus effect": An egocentric bias in social perception and attribution processes. *Journal of Experimental Social Psychology, 13,* 279–301.

Sagar, H. A., & Schofield, J. W. (1980). Racial and behavioral cues in black and white children's perceptions of ambiguously aggressive acts. *Journal of Personality and Social Psychology, 39,* 590–598.

Sanitioso, R., Kunda, Z., & Fong, G. T. (1990). Motivated recruitment of autobiographical memories. *Journal of Personality and Social Psychology, 59,* 229–241.

Schank, P., & Ranney, M. (1991). Modeling an experimental study of explanatory coherence. In *Proceedings of the Thirteenth Annual Conference of the Cognitive Science Society* (pp. 892–897). Hillsdale, NJ: Lawrence Erlbaum Associates.

Schank, P., & Ranney, M. (1992). Assessing explanatory coherence: A new method for integrating verbal data with models of on-line belief revision. In *Proceedings of the Fourteenth Annual Conference of the Cognitive Science Society* (pp. 599–604). Hillsdale, NJ: Lawrence Erlbaum Associates.

Shoda, Y., & Mischel, W. (1993). Cognitive social approach to dispositional inference: What if the perceiver is a cognitive social theorist? *Personality and Social Psychology Bulletin, 19,* 574–587.

Sloman, S. A. (1996). The empirical case for two systems of reasoning. *Psychological Bulletin, 119,* 3–22.

Smith, E. R. (1996). What do connectionism and social psychology offer each other? *Journal of Personality and Social Psychology, 70,* 893–912.

Smith, E. R. (in press). Mental representations and memory. In D. Gilbert, S. T. Fiske, & G. Lindzey (Eds.), *Handbook of social psychology* (4th ed.). New York: McGraw-Hill.

Smith, E. R., & Miller, F. D. (1983). Mediation among attributional inferences and comprehension processes: Initial findings and a general method. *Journal of Personality and Social Psychology, 44,* 492–505.

Smith, E. R., & Zarate, M. A. (1992). Exemplar-based model of social judgment. *Psychological Review, 99,* 3–21.

Taylor, S. E., Wood, J. V., & Lichtman, R. R. (1983). It could be worse: Selective evaluation as a response to victimization. *Journal of Social Issues, 39,* 19–40.

Tesser, A. (1986). Some effects of self-evaluation maintenance on cognition and action. In R. M. Sorrentino & E. T. Higgins (Eds.), *The handbook of motivation and cognition: Foundations of social behavior* (pp. 435–464). New York: Guilford.

Tesser, A., & Campbell, J. (1983). Self-definition and self-evaluation maintenance. In J. Suls & A. Greenwald (Eds.), *Social psychological perspectives on the self* (pp. 1–31). Hillsdale, NJ: Lawrence Erlbaum Associates.

Thagard, P. (1989). Explanatory coherence. *Behavioral and Brain Sciences, 12,* 435–467.

Thagard, P. (1991). The dinosaur debate: Explanatory coherence and the problem of competing hypotheses. In J. Pollock & R. Cummins (Eds.), *Philosophy and AI: Essays at the interface* (pp. 279–300). Cambridge, MA: MIT Press/Bradford Books.

Thagard, P. (1992a). Adversarial problem solving: Modelling an opponent using explanatory coherence. *Cognitive Science, 16,* 123–149.

Thagard, P. (1992b). *Conceptual revolutions.* Princeton, NJ: Princeton University Press.

Thagard, P. (1996). *Mind: Introduction to cognitive science.* Cambridge, MA: MIT Press.

Thagard, P., & Millgram, E. (1995). Inference to the best plan: A coherence theory of decision. In A. Ram & D. B. Leake (Eds.), *Goal-driven learning* (pp. 439–454). Cambridge, MA: MIT Press.

Thagard, P., & Verbeurgt, K. (1998). *Coherence as constraint satisfaction*. Manuscript submitted for publication.

Trope, Y. (1986). Identification and inferential processes in dispositional attribution. *Psychological Review, 93*, 239–257.

Trope, Y. (in press). Dispositional bias in person perception: A hypothesis-testing perspective. In J. Cooper & J. M. Darley (Eds.), *Attribution processes, person perception, and social interaction: The legacy of Ned Jones*. Mahwah, NJ: Lawrence Erlbaum Associates.

Weber, R., & Crocker, J. (1983). Cognitive processes in the revision of stereotypic beliefs. *Journal of Personality and Social Psychology, 45*, 961–977.

Winter, L., & Uleman, J. S. (1984). When are social judgments made? Evidence for the spontaneousness of trait inferences. *Journal of Personality and Social Psychology, 47*, 237–252.

Wojciszke, B. (1994). Multiple meanings of behavior: Constructing actions in terms of competence or morality. *Journal of Personality and Social Psychology, 67*, 222–232.

Wood, J. V. (1989). Theory and research concerning social comparisons of personal attributes. *Psychological Bulletin, 106*, 231–248.

Wyer, R. S., & Srull, T. K. (1986). Human cognition in its social context. *Psychological Review, 93*, 322–359.

Zanna, M. P., & Hamilton, D. L. (1977). Further evidence for meaning change in impression formation. *Journal of Experimental Social Psychology, 13*, 224–238.

ON THE DYNAMIC CONSTRUCTION OF MEANING: AN INTERACTIVE ACTIVATION AND COMPETITION MODEL OF SOCIAL PERCEPTION

Stephen J. Read
Lynn C. Miller
University of Southern California

In everyday social interaction, people are constantly trying—consciously or not—to make sense of events in social interactions. We readily infer that others are annoyed or frustrated; we infer an individual's competence, caring, good will; we infer that someone wants to help us or impress us, even though these are not explicitly "given." The process by which we make such inferences is incredibly complex. Part of this complexity is reflected in the characteristics of social events themselves: There are often multiple cues involving multiple modalities (e.g., oral, visual), given simultaneously, and changing over time; these cues are typically ambiguous, with meaning highly dependent on the other events, or on the context in which these events and stimuli are embedded. Furthermore, inferences about events, persons, situations, and relationships—and the "evidence" that leads to them—are multiply constrained and interwoven.

Below, we elaborate on this complexity, and the challenges it poses for formulating a theory to address it. We start by examining in greater detail a number of key characteristics of social events that must be taken seriously by any adequate theory of social perception. We then continue by presenting a recurrent or feedback neural network model that addresses these issues.

CENTRAL CHARACTERISTICS OF SOCIAL INTERACTION

Social interaction is characterized by:

1. *Ambiguity.* As many have noted, the meaning of an individual action is typically ambiguous in isolation. Although an action may be clearly a punch, its social meaning may be ambiguous: Is the hit a playful one or an aggressive one?

2. *Meaning is sensitive to context.* Clearly, the meaning of such actions is exquisitely sensitive to context. Whether the punch is seen as playful or aggressive depends on the events in which it is embedded.

3. *Multiple cues simultaneously available.* In social perception, we cannot leisurely consider each piece of information by itself. Instead, a variety of information presses in on us, all at once, such as physical appearance information, behaviors, situational cues, and so on.

4. *Multiple modalities.* Moreover, not only are multiple cues simultaneously present, but they appear in multiple modalities, such as verbal and visual, sometimes tactile, and even olfactory.

5. *Takes place over time, continuous.* And new information is always arriving. In a social interaction of any appreciable length, we continually receive new information that must be integrated with old information and with our current representation. Moreover, this new information may change our previous interpretations, just as our old interpretations affect the meaning of the new information. Thus, the meaning of an interaction is dynamic and evolving (Miller, Bettencourt, DeBro, & Hoffman, 1993; Vallacher & Nowak, 1994).

6. Meaning results from the *solution of multiple, simultaneous constraints.* Our inferences result from the simultaneous integration of a complex web of information. Because we lack the time or capability to deal with each piece individually, a number of different cues must be considered at once, each of which can influence the interpretation of the remaining information.

7. *No two social interactions are precisely alike.* Rarely do we see the same interaction twice. Rather each is distinctive, in ways both subtle and gross. Thus, the representation of each interaction is in some ways unique, requiring the combination of old concepts in novel ways. But how are these concepts combined to form novel representations of unique social interactions?

What kind of model can successfully address all these issues? Clearly, any such model must enable the simultaneous satisfaction of multiple constraints among a variety of sources of information, and must permit information to be integrated in both repeating and novel configurations. One possible model, and the one we pursue here, is a feedback or recurrent neural network model that provides for the parallel satisfaction of multiple constraints.

This model also provides an interesting solution to the question of how well-learned social concepts can be combined to form representations of unique social interactions. One part of the solution is the idea that social concepts are represented in terms of an underlying set of primitive concepts or components, what we refer to as their "deep structure," and that combining concepts when constructing a representation of a social interaction consists of combining these underlying primitives or components.

As part of our discussion of these "deep structures," we make some suggestions about what they may look like, and how these "deep structures" may be combined to create recurring and novel representations. Interestingly, feedback neural network models, as they learn, naturally perform a componential analysis of concepts, so that they should be able to learn the "deep structure," as an integral part of learning. Moreover, we examine how these components can be readily combined by a process of parallel constraint satisfaction taking place in a feedback network. Part of our analysis includes a detailed description of the "deep structures" and processes that humans may use to "get up to" such higher order conceptual representations of sequences of actions, traits, situations, and relationships. Following this analysis we examine the application of our model to two sets of issues in person perception, work on spontaneous trait inferences by Uleman (Uleman, Newman, & Moskowitz, 1996) and others (e.g., Bassili & Smith, 1986; Carlston & Skowronski, 1994), and Trope's (1986; Trope & Liberman, 1993) two stage model of dispositional inference.

Social Perception as an Interactive Activation and Competition Network (IAC)

Our model is an interactive activation and competition (IAC) model, similar to models that McClelland and Rumelhart proposed for word recognition (McClelland & Rumelhart, 1981; Rumelhart & McClelland, 1982) and speech perception (McClelland & Elman, 1986). Such a model is a recurrent or feedback network where nodes have feedback relations among each other. That is, the flow of activation is not one way, but as node "a" sends activation to node "b," node b, in turn, sends activation to node a.

Structure.   The nodes in such a model are organized in layers, with each layer corresponding to a different level of analysis. The nodes can be thought of as representing hypotheses about the presence or absence of specific features or concepts at that level. For example, the lowest level would be an input level, where the input nodes correspond to features of the relevant stimulus and higher levels correspond to meaningful stimuli or concepts. Lower level nodes feed activation up to higher level nodes, and higher level nodes, in turn, can feed activation back down to lower level nodes. Thus, lower level and higher level concepts reciprocally influence each other.

Nature of Links. Links between layers are excitatory when nodes are consistent or support one another and inhibitory when nodes are inconsistent. Moreover, items within the same layer are organized in pools of units where inconsistent items have inhibitory links to one another and items that are consistent with one another have excitatory links.

Example of an IAC Network. A concrete example of this is McClelland and Rumelhart's (1981) model for word recognition. In this model there are three levels: (a) a feature level consisting of various units that are sensitive to different features of letters, such as curves and lines of various orientations; (b) a letter level, where units correspond to specific letters, and letters with the same features have inhibitory links; and (c) a word level where units correspond to specific words, and there are inhibitory links between alternative words that might apply to the same stimulus. (See Fig. 2.1 for a partial representation of such a network.)

In this model, the feature nodes have excitatory connections to the letter nodes in the next level with which they are consistent. Thus, when feature nodes are activated, they activate letter nodes that contain that feature. Moreover, different letters that contain the same features will be organized in competitive pools with inhibitory connections to one another. This insures that the most highly activated letter will inhibit alternative interpretations of the same set of features.

Further, letter units have excitatory connections to the word units with which they are consistent. Thus, if the letter "a" in the third position is activated it will excite all words with a in the third position. In this scheme, the activation of a word is a function of the letters that are activated at the letter level. Words that receive activation from only a subset of their letters will be less strongly activated than words that have all of their letters activated. And alternative words that are consistent with the same set of activated letters will have inhibitory connections with each other. These inhibitory connections serve to sharpen the difference between alternative interpretations.

Feedback or Recurrent Activation. One critical feature of this kind of model is that higher level nodes feed back to lower level nodes. Thus, words that are partially activated by activation from the letter level can send activation back to all the letters that make up that word. Such a feedback

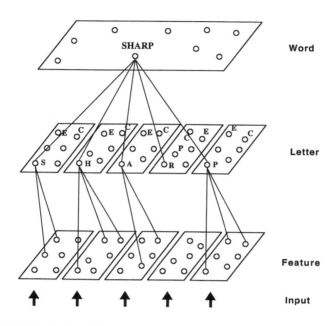

FIG. 2.1. Sketch of the interactive activation model of word perception.

process can "fill in" missing or noisy features or letters from a lower level, or allow one to interpret a stimulus when part of it is ambiguous. For example, assume that the letter in the fourth position of SHA_P is ambiguous as to whether it is a P or an R, but the other letters are clear. Activation from the clear letters would probably be sufficient to fairly strongly activate the word SHARP, because no other word matches this particular pattern of letters as well. This word would then send activation down to its component letters, including the letter R, thus increasing the activation of the letter R. Because R and P in that position would have competitive links, the increased activation of R from the word level would be sufficient to inhibit the P unit, so that the perceiver would interpret the ambiguous letter as an R. One implication of this, important in our subsequent discussion, is that this provides a model for how higher order concepts can affect the interpretation of lower order concepts and can cause the perceiver to fill in missing information.

Parallel Constraint Satisfaction. Another important characteristic of such feedback networks is that they are simultaneously evaluating multiple constraints among a number of sources of information. In such a network, activation passes around symmetrically connected nodes until the activation of all the nodes asymptotes or "relaxes" into a state that satisfies the constraints among the nodes.

As noted, the nodes in these networks represent hypotheses about the presence or absence of various features, where the hypotheses can vary from micro features, such as color or lines, up to concepts or entire propositions, such as traits or a behavior. Links among nodes represent the extent to which the hypotheses are consistent with and support one another, or are inconsistent with and contradict one another. Thus, links can be thought of as representing constraints among the hypotheses. Hypotheses with positive links are mutually supportive, and if one node is activated, it will try to activate the other. In contrast, hypotheses with negative links are contradictory or compete, and therefore, if one node is positively activated, it will try to *deactivate* the other. Weights on the links can vary, indicating the strength of the constraint between the nodes.

The set of constraints among the nodes and their eventual resolution is evaluated by spreading activation among the nodes in parallel. Because the nodes are symmetrically connected and thus have feedback relations, the activation of the nodes evolves over time. As node a is sending activation to node b, it is also receiving activation from node b, as well as from other nodes. Thus, immediately after node a sends activation, its current state is likely to have changed and the amount of activation it can send has also changed. Thus, the activations of the nodes in such a network are continually evolving. However, the activation of the nodes eventually reaches asymptotic values and the network stabilizes and stops changing.

SOCIAL DYNAMICS: A FEEDBACK NEURAL NETWORK

Our interactive activation and competition model of social perception, Social Dynamics, is a feedback neural network. We first describe the process by which activation is spread in such networks. Following this, we describe the structure (4 levels) of this particular model, and the units in the network that enable individuals to "make sense" of everyday social interactions.

This model has some similarities to our previous work (Miller & Read, 1991; Read & Miller, 1993) as well as to Kunda and Thagard's (1996) recent model of impression formation. However, it makes more specific architectural assumptions about the various levels of processing involved in social perception and about the representation of social knowledge.

The activation of each node is a nonlinear function of the sum of the inputs, where the form is sigmoid shaped as in Fig. 2.2. We use the nonlinear activation function used in McClelland and Rumelhart's IAC model of reading

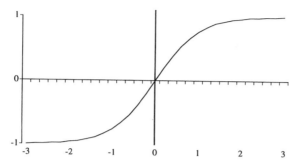

FIG. 2.2. Example of a sigmoid-shaped activation function.

(McClelland & Rumelhart, 1981; Rumelhart & McClelland, 1982) and in other work (e.g., Thagard, 1989):

$$a_j(t + 1) = a_j(t)(1 - d) + \{ net_j(max - a_j(t)) \text{ if } net_j > 0 \text{ and } \\ net_j(a_j(t) - min) \text{ otherwise } \}$$

where $a_j(t + 1)$ is the new activation of the node and $a_j(t)$ is the activation of the node on the previous time step, and d is a decay parameter, net_j is equal to $\Sigma w_{ji}a_i(t)$, where w_{ji} is the weight from node i to j, *min* is the minimum activation value possible (-1.0) and *max* is the maximum activation value (1.0). This activation rule is nonlinear because the possible amount of change in activation of a node is proportional to the difference between its possible maximum or minimum and its current activation. As the current activation approaches the maximum or minimum, this difference decreases and thus the amount of change possible also decreases, resulting in an asymptotic approach to the maximum or minimum. However, because the asymptotic value is a function of both the incoming activation and the decay, the final asymptotic value typically does not reach the max or min activation value. Updating stops when the activation of all nodes reaches asymptote. As can be seen from the equation, the amount of activation sent to a node is a function of the number of nodes connected to it, the strength of the links, whether the link is positive or negative, and the activation of the connected nodes.

Thus, activation is spread in parallel among all the nodes until the activation of each node asymptotes. When activation spreads through such a network, nodes with positive links tend to activate each other and nodes with negative links inhibit each other. Because the activation of a node is a result of all of its positive and negative links to other nodes, the final activation of the node can be thought of as a solution to all the constraints represented by the links. Moreover, because activation is spread in parallel among all the connected nodes, this process results in a global solution to the constraints among the entire set of nodes.

Structure of the Model

Our model has four basic levels (see Fig. 2.3): (1) a *feature or input* level, where nodes corresponding to features of the stimulus are activated; (2) an *identification level*, where the feature information is combined to identify actors, objects, and actions; (3) a *scenario level* where the actors, objects, and action are combined to create a coherent scenario or "ministory" that identifies *who did what to whom and with what consequence*; and (4) the *meaning or conceptual level*, where the meaning of the scenario is identified, often with an overarching conceptual label, such as a trait term.

Input or Feature Layer.   The first layer is the *input* layer or *feature* layer, where perceptual information about the features of social actors, features of objects, features of behaviors, and features of spoken or written language is input. Consistent with other such models, the input information can be

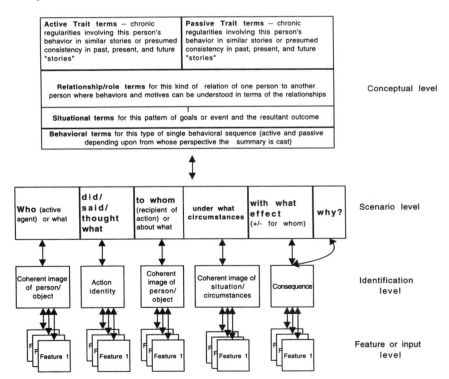

FIG. 2.3. Levels of social dynamics IAC network.

represented as a very long vector of activations, where the value of each element in the vector corresponds to the degree of activation of the corresponding feature node. That is, the value of each element is the value at which the corresponding feature node is activated. Values of each element can range from 0 to 1.

At a lower level of feature analysis, research suggests the plausibility of hard-wired "feature detectors" that capture information about curves, lines, and movement (Sokolov, Izmailov, & Zavgorodnaya, 1985), color, size, orientation, and direction of movement (Treisman & Sato, 1990); elemental sounds and changes in fundamental frequency (Wales & Taylor, 1987), and so forth. These features are assembled into increasingly complex superordinate features such as face (eyes, nose, mouth), black skin, white hair, wrinkled skin, unsteady gait, curved mouth, angular jaw, wide nose, musky smell, beard, syllable, and so forth. Because some of these features may covary with one another (e.g., wide nose, black skin, kinky hair), one feature (black skin) may also simultaneously activate another feature (kinky hair) and deactivate another (blonde hair). We may have an increased adaptive readiness to identify some constellations of features, such as eyes, nose, and mouth, as going together to form a face (Johnson, 1992; Nachson, 1995).

Conceptually, each of these higher order features has a distributed representation, represented by the activation of a number of nodes, but for ease of presentation, such higher order features in the figure are represented by a single node. However, it is important to bear in mind that each of those nodes is "standing in" for a distributed pattern of representations.

Unfortunately, because social psychologists have paid little attention to the perceptual representation of social stimuli it is difficult to develop a principled, distributed representation. This contrasts with the situation in some areas of cognitive psychology, such as models of word recognition, or word pronunciation, where the models depend quite heavily on information about how letters or phonemes are perceptually represented. And research has shown that assumptions about the input representation can play a major role in the adequacy of a model's behavior (Anderson, 1995; Plaut, McClelland, Seidenberg, & Patterson, 1996). Thus, social psychologists need to pay far more attention to the stimulus array and how it is represented perceptually.

Identification Level. At the next level, the *identification level*, clusters of higher level features from the earlier stage (e.g., wrinkled skin, white hair, unsteady gait; black skin, wide nose, black hair; angular jaw, small hip to waist ratio, tall) activate and identify persons, objects, animals, or behaviors (e.g., old; African American; man). This level assembles these characteristics to construct a *coherent image* or representation of a person (e.g., an old Black man; an athletic 20-year-old Black man; an attractive White woman with long blonde hair), an object (e.g., a car), or a behavior (e.g., crossing the street, exchanging money).

There are excitatory links from feature nodes to concepts at the identification layer that the features support. For example, physical features that help define an adult male will have excitatory connections to the concept of an adult male, and features that help identify an adult female will have excitatory connections to the concept of an adult female. Moreover, concepts such as adult male and adult female that are mutually inconsistent identities will have strong inhibitory connections. Such inhibitory connections insure that a specific social actor can only be assigned one of the potential identities. Interestingly, even 9-month-old infants can discriminate male and female faces and appropriately categorize them as one gender or the other (Leinbach & Fagot, 1993). Note that some of these same features that identify adult males and adult females serve to distinguish them from children, animals, or physical objects.

And each of the above animate and inanimate objects or behaviors (and their characteristics) may activate both positive and negative attributes associated with them. One can think of this as activating aspects of a stereotype or schema. Thus, if we identify a man, we might simultaneously activate socially desirable attributes such as instrumental, active, athletic, strong, or assertive, and less desirable attributes, such as aggressive, stereotypically associated with men (Spence & Helmreich, 1978). If we identify a person as old, we may activate concepts such as weak. On the other hand, if we know that a person is a large adult, especially a muscular one, we may activate athletic and strong. Thus, when the physical stimulus activates some features of an actor and allows us to identify them, other associated features are activated at the same time.

Although relatively little processing has occurred at this point, the activated features may activate a strong positive or negative affective response towards the stimulus (Murphy & Zajonc, 1993; Zajonc, 1980), including an immediate "flight or fight" response. Of course, affective responses can activate additional associates (Isen, 1984, 1987) and have an impact on what continues to receive activation.

Excitatory connections also run from the identification level to the feature level. So concepts that are strongly activated at the identification level can affect the perception or interpretation of features. Thus, having identified an individual or a physical object might affect our interpretation of the object's features, particularly if those features are unclear or ambiguous. For example, having misidentified an individual as a woman because of "her" long hair, we may be prone to misperceive some of "her" other features.

Scenario Level. Activation from the nodes corresponding to the identified actors, objects and actions then proceeds to the *scenario level*, where these individual items are assembled into a scenario that assigns participants, objects, and behaviors to their appropriate roles in a "plot unit" (Lehnert & Vine, 1987). For our purposes, a plot unit is defined as a script like representation of *who (or what) did what (how, with what) to whom (or what), and with what effect.*[1] A plot unit essentially contains the basic elements of a story. One or more plot units may be assembled into a larger frame or knowledge structure.

Let us consider an example of a single plot unit: An athletic 20-year-old muscular man, John, pushes an attractive blonde White woman, Mary. Note that at this level of analysis, we have already done a number of things: First, we have identified how many social actors there are (two) and if (as in the present example) they are interacting with each other. Second, we have identified these actors (e.g., a woman; a man). Third, we have identified many things about the physical appearance of these actors and other attributes and concepts that are activated by these features. Fourth, relevant objects might be identified. Fifth, we have identified the nature of the social interaction (e.g., one individual hurts another), and we have assigned the man and woman to the correct roles in this interaction, who is hurting and who is hurt.

As is true for the other levels of analysis, activation from the scenario level can send activation down to the identification level. Thus, construction of a scenario may help in the identification of the various objects and behaviors within it. For example, if we see someone fall, and another's hands engaging in an outward thrust, we may connect the one person's behavior to the fall of the other.

At this point, while plot units are identified, no higher level meaning is attached to these plot units; we do not yet know the meaning of this action. Is the behavior an intentional act of hurting, of aggression, of helping (by moving them out of the way of a predator), an accident, or what? In short, the social meaning has yet to be computed.

Conceptual or Meaning Level. This happens at the next level, the *conceptual* or *meaning* level. This is where inferences are made about such things as the meaning of the behavior (e.g., cooperative, aggressive, etc.), the actors' intentions or goals, characteristics of the actors, such as their traits, or the meaning of the situation. Nodes at the identification level and at the scenario level have excitatory connections to nodes at the conceptual level that they support. For instance, a number of possible explanations

---

[1] One thing we would note as an aside, because to pursue it further would make an already unwieldy situation, totally unmanageable, is that we might have separate modules for identifying agents, objects, and actions, and that the outputs of those modules are then input into a common module where they are integrated into an overall meaning representation. After all, in reading there are very good reasons to assume that there are separate modules for different components of the reading process, semantics, phonetics, graphemics, and so forth.

might become activated by the plot unit "John did this thing to Mary, the effect for Mary was bad"; an accident (John didn't mean to hurt Mary, but he lost his balance, pushed her, and she fell and hurt herself), revenge (John is getting Mary back for hurting him earlier), John is aggressive (he often hurts people in the process of getting what he wants) and so forth.

Additional information about the roles of the characters and their reasons for enacting the behavior might add more or less activation to one of these possibilities. So, too, might adding to the frame with additional plot units: If we also saw that Mary had earlier hit John, the likelihood of activating revenge might increase. Or, as suggested in Fig. 2.4, that concept regarding Mary might be more likely to be activated if she subsequently did something bad to John. Moreover, the observation that John hit Mary might activate the goal of wanting to hurt another, which might increase our perception of John as aggressive. Finally, units within the conceptual layer that are inconsistent, such as the goals of hurting and helping another, will have inhibitory links to each other, so that to the extent that one is activated, it will tend to inhibit the other.

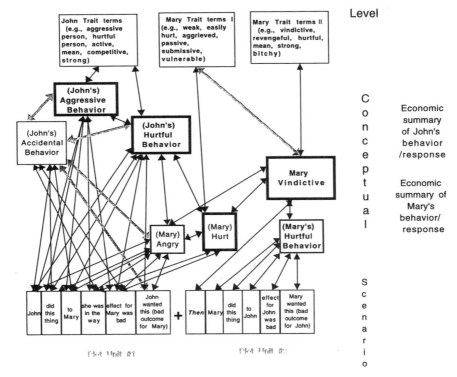

FIG. 2.4. Detailed example of scenario and conceptual levels in the social dynamics IAC network.

A number of different kinds of inferences could be made at the conceptual or meaning level. Here we focus on two. First, social perceivers will frequently make inferences about Why something happened, that is, what are the goals of the actors and their actions. Why inferences, such as John wanted to win and was willing to hurt others to achieve that goal, are central to the meaning of the interaction.

Second, such goal inferences may play an important role in other social inferences, such as trait inferences. In fact, Read, Jones, and Miller (1990) found that perceivers' judgments about whether behaviors are diagnostic or prototypical of traits are mediated by their inferences about actors' goals in enacting these behaviors. Read and Lalwani (1996) provided further evidence that goal inferences mediate the relationship between actions and trait inferences. We suspect that goal inferences are also critical in making other higher order conceptual inferences, such as inferences about relationships (Miller et al., 1993; Miller & Read, 1987, 1991; Read & Miller, 1989) and about situations (Miller, Cody, & McLaughlin, 1994).

Further, goal inferences may also be used in conjunction with additional information (e.g., other behaviors across situations, resources available to the actors, assessments of goal conflicts, other mitigating factors in the situation, etc.) to activate these kinds of inferences. For example, Mary's behavior may involve a pattern in which she systematically tries to "get even" with people who she thinks have kept her from achieving things in the past. She has always hurt others back who have first hurt her (not just John, but Sally, Tim, Molly, and Harry). In short, Mary could be described as vindictive: That is, she intends to harm others who she believes have harmed her in the past, she has the resources to do so, and has done so on more than one occasion. This one trait term not only economically captures a pattern of behavioral response across situations and time, but it also describes Mary's behaviors as limited to particular contexts—she only attacks those who she believes have previously hurt her. Thus, many trait terms are exquisitely sensitive to the situations under which behavior of a particular type is apt to emerge.

Furthermore, the person who uses the trait term is also incorporating other information about the circumstances or characteristics of the actors into the choice of term, besides what this person does (or has been inferred to have done). For example, although men and women may engage in similar behavior, their actions may not be similarly evaluated. Words may be used only for men or women and even the same terms (e.g., aggressive) may have different connotations for men versus women.

Cognitive Capacity: Impact on Social Perception. An additional characteristic of the current model is that higher levels of analysis are increasingly dependent on the cognitive capacity available and on one's focus of attention. Although the feature level is quite automatic, the conceptual level relies heavily on available cognitive capacity. At these higher levels, one can think of processing as taking place in a limited-capacity working memory with two major properties. First, similar to Just and Carpenter (1992), we assume that there is a limited pool of activation available for high level conceptual reasoning, sufficient to activate only a limited set of nodes. To the extent that some nodes are highly activated, less activation is available for other nodes. Second, we assume that focus of attention influences the extent to which nodes can give and receive activation. Concepts that receive greater attention will be able to give and receive more activation. Thus, concepts that are attended to are potentially more influential and more influenceable. For example, assume we have two concepts, say a situational and a dispositional cause of behavior, that receive equal amounts of activation from the input and that have an inhibitory link between them. If we preferentially focus attention on the situational cause, it will be more able to give and receive activation. As a result, it will be more highly activated than the dispositional cause and will be able to more strongly inhibit it.

Principles of Explanatory Coherence

Various principles of explanatory coherence (e.g., Thagard, 1989, 1992) play a central role in the interpretations that develop. These principles, which result from standard assumptions about the structure and behavior of feedback models, require no special or ad hoc assumptions.

What are these principles? First, people prefer broader explanations that account for more of the actions. This preference follows naturally from the fact that nodes with more explanatory relations to other nodes receive more activation and, as a result, are more highly activated. Second, people should prefer explanations that can, in turn, be explained. This follows because explanations that have further explanations, such as a goal being explained in terms of instigating conditions, will receive additional activation from that explanation. Third, people should prefer explanations that retrieve similar events with the same kind of explanation, because the analogous explanations should send additional activation to the target explanation. Fourth, people should prefer simpler explanations that require fewer assumptions. This follows from the limited capacity of working memory. Because there is a limited amount of activation available for items in working memory, the fewer propositions that are maintained as part of an explanation, the greater the activation available for each proposition. Thus, this model naturally implements the principles of Explanatory Coherence discussed by Thagard (1989, 1992) and shown to be important in both social (Ranney & Schank, this volume; Read & Lincer-Hill, 1996; Read & Marcus-Newhall, 1993; Read & Miller, 1993) and nonsocial reasoning (Ranney, Schank, Mosmann, & Montoya, 1993; Schank & Ranney, 1991, 1992; Thagard, 1989, 1992).

Interestingly, the classic attributional principles of discounting and augmenting (Jones & Davis, 1965; Kelley, 1971) also fall naturally out of this kind of model (Read & Marcus-Newhall, 1993; Read & Miller, 1993). Again, no special assumptions are needed. First, let's examine Discounting. A central part of our model is that competing or alternative interpretations have inhibitory connections. As a result, a potential explanation will have lower activation when a competing alternative is activated.

Augmenting is also a result of inhibitory relations, but here, what is important is that there are negative links between the inhibitory cause and the effect, indicating that the cause would typically prevent the effect from occurring, as well as a negative link between the inhibiting and facilitative causes. With this pattern of links, when the event occurs in the face of an inhibiting cause and thus is highly positively activated (e.g., Read & Miller, 1993), then the high positive activation of the event that is sent over the negative link to the inhibitory cause will lead to a high negative activation of the inhibitory cause. Further, the negative activation of the inhibitory cause will be sent over the negative link to the facilitative cause, resulting in positive activation to the facilitative cause. Thus, when an event occurs in the face of an inhibiting cause and thus is highly activated, then the potential cause of the event is more highly activated than when there was no inhibiting event.

LEARNING AND CONCEPTUAL COMBINATIONS IN FEEDBACK NEURAL NETWORKS

We return to issues of higher order inferences involving traits, situations, and relationships in more detail later in this chapter. For now, however, it is important to consider in more detail how such feedback systems operate. In particular, we focus on how such systems can learn the underlying conceptual structures and how they can combine them to create representations of social interactions. Central to understanding both learning and conceptual combination in these kinds of networks is the idea that feedback neural networks can be viewed as "attractor" systems, where the state of the system as it evolves is drawn toward or "attracted to" certain states of the system that represent what the system has learned.

How Do Feedback Systems Learn Complex Associations and Combine Them in Social Perception?

Feedback Systems as Attractor Systems. Hopfield (1982, 1984; also see Amit, 1989; Hertz Krogh, & Palmer, 1991; Rumelhart, Smolensky, McClelland, & Hinton, 1986), relying on extensive work in physics on thermodynamic systems, has shown that feedback systems, with symmetric connections, can be treated as if they have energy, where the "energy" of the system is the sum of the product of the activation of all pairs of nodes times the weight between them, that is, $(w_{ij})(a_i)(a_j)$. Specifically, the "energy" of the system is $E = -\Sigma\Sigma w_{ij}a_i(t)a_j(t)$.

This equation states that the energy of the system decreases when the sign of the product of the activations is consistent with the sign of the weight between them, but increases when the sign of the product of the activations differs from the sign of the weight between them. That is, if the product of the activation of two nodes is consistent with the constraint between them, energy decreases, whereas if the product of the activation of two nodes is inconsistent with the constraint between them, energy increases. Thus, this energy function measures the extent to which the pattern of activations of the nodes is consistent with the relations between them. Hopfield (1982, 1984) demonstrated that neural network systems of this form act so as to minimize the energy function, essentially minimizing the energy of the system.

This energy can be plotted in an n-dimensional space, giving an energy surface that represents the various possible states of the system. This idea is quite powerful in informing intuitions about the behavior of such systems. An energy surface is an n-dimensional representation in which the activation of each of the $n - 1$ nodes defines one of the $n - 1$ dimensions in the representation, and the total energy of the system defines the nth dimension. The shape of the energy surface is defined by the amount of energy (or degree of organization) of the system at each of the possible combinations of activations of all the nodes in the network (see Amit, 1989; Hertz et al., 1991; Rumelhart et al., 1986). Figure 2.5 provides an example of what such an energy surface might look like for a simple network with two nodes and therefore three dimensions.

Thus, solving for the constraints can be viewed as a gradient descent process, moving toward a minimum (or valley) in an energy surface. Over time, the system moves down a gradient or slope until a minimum is reached. A system that has settled or relaxed can be viewed as having reached a valley in the energy surface, representing a minimum state of energy.

Equivalently, minimizing the energy of the system can be thought of as moving from a state where fewer constraints are satisfied to one where more constraints are satisfied (Rumelhart et al., 1986). Essentially, the energy of the system corresponds to its degree of organization. High energy in the system corresponds to less organization and low energy corresponds to greater organization. Thus, such a parallel constraint-satisfaction process can be viewed as attempting to find the maximal degree of organization consistent with the constraints imposed by the relations among the nodes. That is, the system is attempting to maximize the goodness of fit of the network. However, because the system is not guaranteed to find the global minima, it will not necessarily find the state representing the maximum degree of organization.

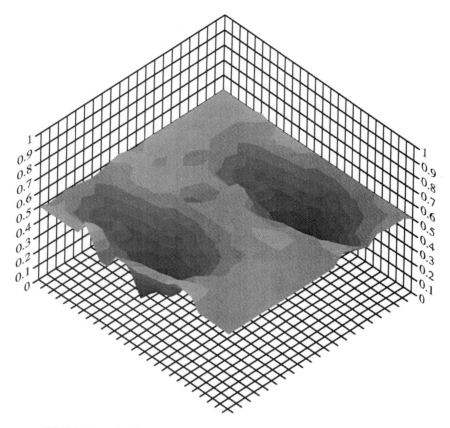

FIG. 2.5. Example of an energy surface for a simple network consisting of two nodes.

The minima in such systems are called "attractors" and can be viewed as having a basin of attraction that corresponds to the valleys or wells in the energy surface. If we probe such a network with a pattern of activations that falls within the basin of attraction of a particular attractor, that is, it falls on the slopes of the basin, the network will evolve toward that attractor. Thus the name attractors, as they are states of the system that act as if they attract nearby states. The systems are called "attractor" systems.

Learning in Attractor Systems

Minima or attractors can represent learned patterns of associations among features. Hopfield (1982, 1984) has shown that learning rules that encode the patterns of associations or correlations among activations of different nodes in the network can be viewed as "digging" valleys or minima in the energy surface and that reaching a minima is equivalent to retrieving the pattern of activation of the nodes that corresponds to the position of the minima in a multidimensional space.

A number of learning rules have been proposed for neural networks. Two of the best known and most straightforward are Hebbian learning and the delta rule. The Hebbian rule is based on a proposal by Hebb (1949) that the strength of the connection between two neurons should increase if they fire at the same time. This rule essentially learns the correlation between the firings of two neurons. The basic version of the rule is (variants have also been proposed): $\Delta w_{ij} = \partial a_i a_j$, where ∂ is the learning parameter, and a_i and a_j are the activations of the two neurons.

The Hebbian rule is an unsupervised rule as there is no explicit teacher or supervisor providing feedback as to whether the learned relationship is correct. Other rules, such as the delta rule (Widrow & Hoff, 1960) and its variant, the backpropagation rule (Rumelhart, Hinton, & Williams, 1986), are supervised rules, because they explicitly try to minimize the difference between a target or teaching output and the output actually obtained. The basic version of the delta rule is: $\Delta w_{ij} = \partial e_i a_j$, where e_i is the error for unit i and is given by $e_i = t_i - a_i$, where t is the teaching input to unit i, or the target activation, and a is its actual activation. The well-known backpropagation rule is a generalization of the delta rule for multilayer networks with hidden units that mediate between input and output units. Note that in the delta rule, the change in the connection strength is an explicit function of the amount of error of prediction in the output unit, that is, the extent to which the output activation deviates from the target or teacher. In contrast, in the Hebbian rule, the change in connection strength is not related to the error of prediction, but only to the actual activation of the output node.

These systems can function as pattern completion devices, filling in missing pieces of a previously learned pattern. If the network has learned a particular pattern and has dug a corresponding attractor, then if the system is given a partial pattern that places the system within the basin of attraction of the attractor, the system will evolve toward the attractor and fill in the rest of the pattern. For example, if given the features "whiskers" and "purrs," the system should evolve toward an attractor with the remaining features and fill in the rest of the pattern for "cat," including the name. This looks very much like using a limited number of cues to activate the schema for a cat (Rumelhart et al., 1986).

A Componential Analysis of Concepts. One further characteristic of attractor systems is that as they learn the patterns of associations among a set of inputs, they can perform a componential analysis of the incoming stimuli. For example, Plaut et al. (1996) had a system learn to pronounce words from written text, going from the written representation of words to their spoken representation. They found that their network spontaneously analyzed the components of the written words and their pronunciation, so that the system developed attractors that corresponded to parts of the correspondence between the written and spoken words. For example, if the system saw a series of words such as *sat, bat, cat, sad, bad, cad, tad, sit, bit, bid,* and so forth, and had to learn the association to their pronunciation, then the system would not only develop attractors for the individual words, but would also learn separate attractors for the correspondence between each of the individual beginning consonants, the vowels, and the ending consonants, and their appropriate pronunciations.

So that the system not only learns attractors for whole words, but also for the pronunciation of the individual consonants and vowels. Plaut et al. (1996) discovered that this capability was important in allowing the system to appropriately pronounce nonwords in the same way that humans would. Thus, given the above set of words, an individual given the nonword "tid," would pronounce it appropriately. Essentially, reading the nonword activates the componential attractors for the components of the nonword, in this case "t," "i," and "d," and when these attractors are activated simultaneously, this leads to the activation of a "spurious attractor" that represents the novel combination and its pronunciation. A spurious attractor is an attractor that does not correspond to any previously learned state of the system, whereas a regular attractor develops in response to a consistently encountered pattern.

Anderson (1995) has shown that with a distributed representation, if the elements within a subgroup (such as the features for the letter "t") co-occur with one another very consistently, whereas the subgroups co-occur with each other somewhat less consistently, the subgroup elements form a tightly associated subgroup of elements that tend to act together as a single unit. For example, if the features that define the letter t always co-occur when the letter t is present, but this set of features occurs with other different features in other different words (e.g., tad, tot, sat, sit), then the elements defining the letter t will have very strong associations within the subgroup defining the letter, while having somewhat weaker associations with the elements defining the features of the other letters in the various words in which it appears. Thus, attractors will develop that correspond to the subgroups of elements.

This work suggests that an attractor network should do a componential analysis of any set of structured concepts as it learns them. Thus, our interactive activation and competition (IAC) model, which is an attractor network, should be able to perform a componential analysis of social concepts such as traits, stereotypes, scripts, and so forth. To the extent that the same lower level concept, such as a goal, behavior, or physical feature, occurs in a number of different concepts, then the lower level concept can be learned as a separate attractor or component.

For example, let us consider learning the relationship between each of a number of different behaviors and the relevant trait concepts. Assume that each of the behavioral exemplars has a distributed representation as a long vector of activations, consisting of a number of subgroups corresponding to each of the different aspects of the behavior, such as the characteristics of the actor, different aspects of the behavior, features of the situation, and the goal(s) of the behavior. As the system is exposed to a large number of different examples, it will perform a componential analysis of the underlying structure of the trait.

Moreover, once this componential structure has been learned, these components can then be combined in new ways, arriving at new or novel conceptual combinations. Shortly, we consider how an attractor model can use knowledge of the structure of social concepts to combine those concepts in novel ways in the interpretation of social action.

In fact, we would argue that mundane social perception involves the combination of a large number of concepts in novel ways. Just as narrative comprehension is a process of conceptual combination in which well-learned concepts are put together in novel ways (Barsalou, 1992), so the process of social perception can be treated similarly. Rarely, if ever, do we see exactly the same interaction twice. Rather, we continually encounter new combinations of old concepts.

Constructing Schemas

As noted, when processing incoming stimuli, these components can then be assembled into complex concepts. Rumelhart et al. (1986) provided an account of how this might happen and some of its implications in their description of how one type of feedback, attractor network, an autoassociative network, can be used to implement the idea of a schema. They first encoded in the network the probability of association among various elements of different rooms in a house. So, for example, there were very strong positive links among items that tend to co-occur in the same room of the house, for example, in the kitchen, between oven and refrigerator, oven and sink, dishwasher and oven, and, in the living room between television and sofa, sofa and fireplace. There were very strong negative links between items that never co-occurred in the same room, such as oven and bathtub, refrigerator and toilet, and there were weak or no links between items that co-occurred infrequently or not at all, for example television and oven. When certain parts of a room, such as stove and sink were activated in the network, they activated the other aspects of the room, such as refrigerator and dishwasher, essentially filling in missing information. Thus, the system seems to have implicitly encoded the schemas for different rooms. This ability to fill in default information is clearly one of the major characteristics of the conception of a schema.

Thus, Rumelhart et al. (1986) proposed that schema are not actually stored, but instead are constructed as needed:

> Schemata emerge at the moment they are needed from the interaction of large numbers of much simpler elements all working in concert with one another. Schemata are not explicit entities, but rather are implicit in our knowledge and are created by the very environment that they are trying to interpret—as it is interpreting them. (p. 20)

Further, ". . . what is stored is a set of connection strengths which, when activated, have implicitly in them the ability to generate states that correspond to instantiated schemata" (p. 21).

One can also have default attribute values for activated objects. For instance, suppose we had a default size for a television set, medium size, that would tend to be turned on when the television node is on. This notion can be captured by having pools of elements, such as small, medium, large, or big screen, where each element in the pool corresponds to one possible slot filler. Each element in the pool has a positive link to the other features of the concept, where the strength of the link is based on prior experience of frequency of association.

If only one element can fill the slot, then there will be very strong negative links among the elements in the pool. For example, if one had a gender slot for a concept, there would be two possible slot fillers, male and female, which would have strong negative links, so that only one gender would be activated. However, if multiple items can fill the slot, then there may be either no links among the elements in the pool, or perhaps weak positive links, so that multiple elements can be turned on at the same time.

Such a network could also learn correlations between a particular room and attributes of the objects in it. For example, we may have learned that if a television is present in the kitchen, it is small, if it is in the living room, it could be medium sized or quite large, whereas a television in the bedroom would almost always be medium sized. This could be captured by having appropriate links between the various possible size attributes of the television and the other objects that appear in the same room.

The notion that schemas are assembled as needed from smaller pieces might help with the observation that various concepts such as traits, situations, and emotions have a great deal of overlapping content. For example, part of the knowledge of both a particular emotion and a trait might be the same kind of situation that would elicit both the emotion and the trait-related behavior. Conversely, part of the knowledge of a particular situation might be how people with various traits would behave in them. In this notion of a schema, the same element could play a role in multiple concepts, because the role of a component in any higher order concept is captured by the pattern of links to the concept.

The idea that schemas are created "on the fly" suggests a possible mechanism for how novel concepts are created. Rumelhart et al. (1986) also showed that their network could "create" novel room representations that had never been explicitly encoded in the network. For example, if one turned on the fireplace, television, and bed nodes, one could get a pattern of activation across all the nodes that described something like a master bedroom suite, even though the network had never been exposed to a master bedroom suite.

One could imagine something similar with novel social combinations. For example, suppose we meet an adult female, who is African American, and a professor of electrical engineering. The resulting pattern of activated nodes might, for many, represent a novel concept to which the network had never been previously exposed.

Below, we turn to a more detailed discussion of persons, situations, and relationship concepts. We begin with a consideration of the importance of story structures in social representation.

MAKING HIGHER ORDER SOCIAL INFERENCES: WHY STORY STRUCTURES ARE CENTRAL UNITS

A key part of our model is the *story* or *scenario* level, where actors, actions, and objects are assembled into a storylike structure. This basic story structure, Who *did what* to whom (or what object) and why, and with what consequences, is central to the representation of social concepts. But why might it be so central? It has been proposed that evolutionary pressures toward increasingly complex social interactions drove cognitive development (Dunbar, 1993). For humans, the most social of all primates, keeping track of who could be relied on, who cheated, and who cooperated was essential; therefore, ways of better understanding, communicating about, and representing other specific humans was basic to human survival (Tooby & Cosmides, 1992). Perhaps that is why gossip, which typically involves the telling of stories about personal and relationship experiences, accounts for 60% of conversational time (Dunbar, 1993). Gossip is, after all, the telling of "who did what to whom and why."

Further, as Read and Miller (1995) suggested, "Stories are central to the human cognitive system because they capture the essence of social interaction, the structure of human action" (p. 139; see also Schank & Abelson, 1995). And "stories are about what happens to goals . . . [and goals] are of tremendous intrinsic interest to human beings" (Read & Miller, 1995, p. 142).

As we argue in considerably more detail in this work (Read & Miller, 1995), there is both developmental and cross-cultural work to suggest that humans may have a readiness to construct basic story structures, or plot units using a set of universals or primes and to build on these depending on the particulars of their given cultural experience. For example, wants (or needs) are among the first concepts children communicate (Gelman, 1990). And, although there are probably few concepts that are universal across cultures, as the linguist Wierzbicka (1992) argued, the *universals across cultures* are apt to include want, as well as all of the words in the following "story": I want this, you do this, this happened, this person did something bad, and something bad happened because of this.

We would argue that there are systematic ways in which humans use these basic concepts and plot units in making inferences about behaviors, persons, situations, relationships, and other complex social inferences (e.g., roles, emotions, states, etc.). We explore some of these possibilities later and how connectionist models allow us to understand how combinations of such relatively simple structures can capture the richness of social inference.

Emotion and Behavior Terms

In everyday parlance, we use terms to describe behaviors and temporary states of persons; these terms are apt to be associated with particular plot units. For example, if Y did a bad thing to X and the effect on X was bad, we are apt to activate a concept such as hurtful to describe the plot sequence. Other behavioral acts might be described in terms of multiple plot units. Thus, the term vindictive act could involve an actor, X, who believes others, Y, did a bad thing to him in the past and the effect was bad (Y hurt X). Now that actor has an opportunity to do a bad thing to those specific others (or associated members), he wants this, and has the resources to do so and has done so (and the effect is bad for Y), creating a double plot unit (Y hurts X; X wants to hurt Y, and does so). Similarly, emotional and motivational states can be framed as plot units with actor goals that are frustrated or achieved. For example, Shaver, Schwartz, Kirson, & O'Connor (1987) provided evidence that many emotion concepts seem to have associated with them a mini story of the events that elicited the emotional response. Anger (Y's response), for example, might be activated by a plot unit like, "Y wanted o; X kept Y from achieving/getting o; the effect on Y was bad" or simply "X did a bad thing, B, to Y; the effect on Y was bad." Note that in these examples, complex concepts used to describe a behavioral act (e.g., vindictive) incorporate a frame with the affective charge of anger. We seem to view the anger as having motivational properties that result in the behavior in the second plot unit in the vindictive frame. Our guess is that the meaning of many constructs used to describe not only persons' behaviors but also traits, situations, and relationships involve plot units linked to emotion terms (see Miller et al., 1994) for a similar argument).

Traits as Economical Scripts

Trait terms are often used as economical labels to capture recurring patterns of goals, plans, resources, and beliefs relevant to behavior for an individual (Miller & Read, 1987). These trait terms, often similar to behavioral terms, capture a chronic pattern of regularity in the lives of persons regarding what they do, to whom (or what), why, and with what effect. Thus, we might say that someone is a vindictive person. When we characterize this person, we are apt to be implying that the person chronically engages in a particular pattern of plot units, that this person is chronically angry with others that they believe have "done bad things to them," and that this person is chronically motivated in such contexts to hurt these others. We now discuss two issues briefly that we have elaborated on in greater detail elsewhere (Miller & Read, 1997). First, what are the possible structures that trait terms may involve, and why are particular trait terms more heavily activated than alternatives.

Structural Combinations: Possible Trait Terms.   Thus, we may say that a person is aggressive, hard driving, irritable or sensitive, depressive, unfocused, extroverted, competent, conservative, open-minded, and so forth. Major determinants of whether these interpretations are apt to be statelike or involve a more chronic trait term include the wealth of linkages between the agent's behavior and similar actions or plot sequences that could be activated (this person hit others on a number of occasions) and the relative absence of competing alternative representations.

Many trait terms appear to involve a basic plot unit that summarizes across analogous patterns of behaviors, either for the target individual or for other individuals, that the perceiver is using to "reason by analogy" to the current actor in making trait inferences. For example, when we observe an action (e.g., John hits Mary with the door and Mary's nose breaks), similar action sequences involving those who do similar things (e.g., Tom who hit Bill and broke Bill's collarbone; Joe who hit Molly) may be activated. These pieces of information might get mapped onto John (e.g., John, like Tom, is generally aggressive). Further, additional plot units may be activated in which the same actor, subject, object, or behavior are involved—especially if they exhibit a similar relationship among the component parts of the representation. Thus, a plot sequence, "John pushed Harry at the dance so hard he hit the wall," and "John ran over the other runner in the race to win" might also be activated, along with associated characteristics of John (e.g., he's generally aggressive). Similarly, we might activate a series of plot sequences about Mary (Mary nearly ran into a car while she was walking) and related associates (Mary seems oblivious to the world around her). Or, we may activate information about similar objects (e.g., doors).

In short, the information that is activated may be precisely the information needed to ascertain whether this action by this actor is typical for this actor, typical for most actors generally, typical for this subject to be the recipient of, or typical for objects of this type. Readers may note that what gets activated at this point is relevant to Kelley's (1971) concepts of consistency, consensus, and distinctiveness.

Often, actors are engaged in multiple sequences of behavior relative to each other and several plot units may be activated and linked together to create a single frame. Imagine that after John hit Mary, Mary hit John. In understanding this sequence of actions, our frame consists of two plot units: (1) John hit Mary (2) Mary hit John. This is a reciprocal action frame with interesting implications for the subsequent assignment of conceptual meaning (e.g., Mary retaliates).

If Mary did not immediately hit John back, but instead bided her time and waited to hurt him when she had the opportunity and resources, we might use a somewhat different term, vindictive. We use this term, vindictive, to indicate that an actor believes that others have hurt him in the past; now this actor has an opportunity to hurt those specific others (or associated members) and has the resources to do so and this actor has acted upon that. If Mary was the type of person who generally engaged in vindictive behavior, we might use the term in a traitlike fashion: That is, this is the type of person who generally hurts those who have previously hurt them when the opportunity arises. Vindictive is part of a reciprocal (acting in kind) complex action frame (e.g., two or more plot units) that involves a class of retaliatory behaviors or propensities, with harming or hurting being the more basic unit. This frame might be abstractly represented as follows: X acted on Y, effect was bad for Y; then Y acted on X, effect was bad for X.

Nodes at the conceptual level (retaliatory) have excitatory connections to nodes and plot units at the identification and scenario level (Mary hit John; John hit Mary). In addition, other concepts would be positively linked to aggressive at the meaning level (e.g., goal of hurting another) which in turn would be linked positively to the identification level (John hits Mary; Mary hit John). Thus, not only would the observation of an aggressive behavior activate the goal of hurting another, but knowing that someone had the goal of hurting someone would increase the activation of the behavior identification as a hit. Finally, units within the conceptual layer that are inconsistent, such as the goals of hurting and helping another, will have inhibitory links to each other, so that to the extent that one is activated, it will tend to inhibit the other.

A second class of reciprocal actions involves reciprocating benefit. Abstractly, such reciprocation would be represented as follows: X acted on Y, effect was good for Y; then Y acted on X, effect was good for X. Cooperation falls into this class of action, with helping being the more basic unit. Note too that which action plot unit precedes the other is important for the assignment of the trait information to the proper actor. In reciprocal action, Y, the initial recipient who later reciprocates, would be more likely to be perceived as retaliatory or cooperative than the initial actor, X.

Similarly, we can also think of concepts that are used to describe nonreciprocal plot units. For example, two plot units could be used to describe the situation where one actor hurts another; that other, however, does not hurt the first actor back (e.g., turns the other cheek). Or, perhaps a first actor helps a second, but that second actor fails to reciprocate a positive outcome; we might refer to that person as having cheated.

Trait terms capture the agent–recipient distinction in narratives; there are active trait terms (to describe the person who does the action) and passive terms (to describe persons who are on the receiving end of the impact of the other's action), an active–passive dimension that is a fundamental one (Osgood, Suci, & Tannenbaum, 1957). It seems probable that other dimensions on which trait terms differ (e.g., potency, evaluation) are also captured in the narrative structure. Evaluation is captured by the consequence of the action (good, bad) and potency seems likely to be captured by whether the actor played an important role in achieving the goal that they desired.

Many trait terms also capture contextual information, recognizing that the behavior in question is sensitive to both the nature of the situation and the identity of others. Consider the general category of aggressive. When we say that someone is a bully, this term suggests a very specific set of circumstances under which aggressive behaviors are apt to be demonstrated (e.g, a bully is someone who threatens another or tries to control another with force or coercion, but that other is someone who is weaker, more dependent, or unable to fight back). Similarly, revengeful is specific to a particular class of others (e.g., those who have done the actor harm).

However, not all traits are so contextually sensitive. When we say that someone is an aggressive person, we are probably making inferences about his or her general propensities regarding a large range of situations and targets (e.g., one form of aggression may involve achieving one's goals regardless of whether others get hurt in the process; another form might be wanting to hurt others generally across situations). Similarly, hurtful, meanspirited, and evil are more general ways of describing how persons might behave with a range of others across situations: A propensity, and the desire, to inflict injury on others.

At the other end of the prosocial spectrum, helpful or altruistic refers to the general propensity to provide a benefit to others, regardless of target or situation, whereas cooperative refers more specifically to someone who helps another to achieve an end with the expectation that this action achieves a common goal (benefits actor) or that the other will reciprocate (or has already done so). Variants of helpful (generous, benevolent, charitable, cooperative, chivalrous, good, etc.) and hurtful (evil, vindictive, aggressive, bad) refer to specific conditions or attributes of giver, recipient, or context.

Now that we have described our assumptions about the representation of social concepts and our IAC model for processing social information, we apply this model to several major issues in social perception. First, we provide an account of how spontaneous trait inferences (Uleman, et al., 1996; Winter & Uleman, 1984) are made; as a process of combining a large number of social concepts to create a coherent representation of a social event. Second, we show how our model can handle experimental results from Trope's (1986) model of dispositional inference.

LINKS BETWEEN SOCIAL DYNAMICS AND OTHER SOCIAL PSYCHOLOGICAL MODELS OF SOCIAL PERCEPTION

Spontaneous Trait Inferences

One of the most consistent bodies of work on trait inference has been the work of Uleman and others on spontaneous trait inferences (e.g., Bassili & Smith, 1986; Carlston & Skowronski, 1994; Uleman et al., 1996). Although this work provides extensive evidence that trait inferences can be made spontaneously, as Uleman et al., (1996) acknowledged, none of this work provides an explicit process model of how trait inferences are made. Here we use our IAC model to provide an explicit model of the process.

When discussing spontaneous trait inferences, researchers typically gloss over the fact that even understanding a single sentence and making a trait inference from it takes a great deal of inferential processing. Consider some of the sentences that Uleman and others frequently used. Each of these seemingly straightforward sentences requires a considerable amount of cognitive processing, such as identification of the concepts, retrieval of their meaning, and extensive inferential processing. The reader will find it instructive to work through each of the sentences and figure out what must be done to arrive at the meaning for each:

The secretary solves the mystery halfway through the book.

The mailman picks his teeth during dinner at the fancy restaurant.

The receptionist steps in front of the old man in line.

The tailor carries the old woman's groceries across the street.

To understand each of these actions, the social perceiver must do the following. (Although the stimuli used here are written sentences, we describe the perceiver's task in such a way as to apply equally well to observed social behavior.) Here we focus on the sentence about the tailor.

Identification of Actors, Objects, and Actions. First, we must identify the important actors and objects involved in the action, as well as the actions in which they are involved. For instance, in the sentence about the tailor carrying the old woman's groceries, we must identify someone as a tailor, someone else as the old woman, the objects as groceries, the action as carrying, and we must identify that the action involved crossing the street. If one is reading the sentence, then one must use the words to identify these concepts, whereas if one is observing the live behavior, then one must use the physical features of the actors and objects to identify them, as well as using the physical features of the actions to identify them.

The identification of the actors, objects, and actions takes place at the feature and identification level of the network. Features of the stimulus turn on the appropriate nodes in the feature level, and the activated feature nodes then send activation to associated nodes in the identification level. For instance, features in the stimulus that identify the old woman, such as physical features that give clues to her gender, and physical features that identify age, such as white hair, slow and stooped gait, wrinkled face, and so forth will turn on corresponding nodes in the feature level. These nodes will then activate concepts at the identification level.

Initially, many different concepts may be partially activated by the same input. For example, for the old woman, gender information will have an excitatory link to young woman, middle-aged woman, old woman, and so forth, white hair and a wrinkled face will have positive links to both old man and old woman. However, ultimately only the old woman concept will be strongly activated, as the old woman concept will be activated by more of the features, and will inhibit alternative identifications through inhibitory links with them. A similar process occurs for each of the other objects, such as tailor, groceries, street, and for the action, carrying.

As we identify the objects and actions, we simultaneously begin to access their conceptual meaning. The meaning includes both other physical features and other conceptual features. Just as the bottom-up activation from the feature level will start to activate concepts at the identification level, activated concepts at the identification level will begin to activate associated features at the feature level. So, once some of the perceptual features of the old woman activate the concept of old woman, the concept of old woman may activate other associated perceptual features that were not activated by the incoming stimulus. For instance, if we did not see her walk, but only saw her hair and face, we might activate features having to do with slow and frail movement. This can be viewed as an example of the kind of filling in that has been identified as a central part of the concept of a schema (Rumelhart et al., 1986).

At the same time, the concepts at the identification level may also activate other associated concepts at the identification level that will add to the conceptual meaning of the concepts. For instance, once the concept old woman is activated, this may activate related concepts, such as stereotypes about where they live, what kind of activities they engage in, or how they talk. Further, the object at the identification level will start to activate related concepts at the meaning level. For instance, the old woman concept may activate traits that are part of the stereotype of old women. All of these additional activated concepts are part of the meaning of the concept and potentially could be part of the interpretation of the action.

At this point, we have a large cloud of concepts activated, but they are not organized into a coherent structure. How might the activated meanings be organized into a coherent structure?

Scenario Level: Creating a Scenario. We propose that the meaning is organized around the central action, in this case, the action of "carrying." But how? Based on work in linguistics and language comprehension on verbs (Barsalou, 1992; Fillmore, 1968; Jackendoff, 1983), we argue that the action or verb provides a particular frame or case with relevant roles or slots, where the various roles correspond to things such as the performer of an action, the recipient, if any, of an action, and the objects involved in the action.

Here, carrying requires an actor role or slot for the individual doing the carrying, in this case the tailor; a role for the thing being carried, which in this case is the old woman's groceries; and a role for the location of the carrying, which is across the street. Further, there is the structure for the meaning of the verb or action "to carry," what this concept means or entails. Each of the roles is specified by a set of features that defines the characteristics of possible role or slot fillers. For example, the carrier should be physically supporting an object and this should be the object being carried. Conversely, the object being carried should be physically supported by the carrier. Moreover, the carrier and the object being carried should be physically moving. Further, the carrier would most likely be animate and human, and the carried a physical object.

Perception of the groceries in the tailor's arms and the observation that he is walking across the street would provide the features necessary to define the tailor as the carrier. That is, the tailor is in physical contact with the groceries, is holding them up, and is physically transporting them across the street. And the perception of the groceries being supported by the tailor's arms would identify the groceries as the thing being carried. Finally, previous observation of the groceries being given to the tailor by the old lady would identify the groceries as belonging to the old lady. Thus, the observation of the interaction would provide the features necessary for assigning the various actors and objects to their appropriate roles.

Once the case-role assignment is done, we now have quite an elaborate representation of the action. Not only do we have a representation of an individual carrying a package for another individual, we also have information about the nature of the actor and the recipient of the action. First, we know that the actor is someone whose occupation is to make and modify clothes for a living. Second, the actor is probably an adult male. Third, we know that the recipient of the action is an elderly female. Fourth, because she is elderly, she may be somewhat frail and weak and would therefore have great difficulty carrying the groceries herself. Fifth, knowing that he has done something for her that would be quite difficult for her to do by herself, we can infer that the man has done her a favor, he has been helpful.

Meaning Level: Why? However, we don't yet know why he did this. As a further part of interpreting this behavior, we must infer why the tailor carried the groceries.

The representation to this point then activates a number of potential related explanations at the meaning level. The initial degree of activation will be a function of the strength of the association between the representation and the potential explanation. Thus, explanations that were highly useful in the past will be more highly activated.

Initially a number of potential explanations, some good and some not, are activated. Once potential explanations have been activated, principles of explanatory coherence (Miller & Read, 1991; Read & Marcus-Newhall, 1993; Thagard, 1989, 1992), such as breadth and simplicity, and other principles, such as discounting and augmenting, come into play in choosing among alternatives.

Thus, the behavior of the tailor carrying the groceries for the old woman could potentially activate several different explanations at the conceptual or meaning level. Potential explanations are that he did it because he wanted to help her, he expected to get paid, or he was trying to get the old woman to like him, and so forth. How strongly each of these or others is initially activated will be a function of the strength of the link to them, where the strength of the link is a function of how useful they have been as explanations in the past for this kind of behavior. For instance, it seems quite likely that in the absence of other information, such as an exchange of money, given that the behavior is a helpful one, the explanation of wanting to help is likely to be more strongly activated than are the other explanations.

Once the alternatives have been activated, then principles of explanatory coherence play a role in selecting among alternatives. As noted earlier, these principles are implemented in terms of patterns of connectivity among the potential explanations and the things to be explained. For example, competing or alternative explanations will have inhibitory links between them, so that the most strongly activated explanation will inhibit the others. This allows stronger explanations to override weaker ones. However, this also implements the principle of discounting, as the presence of an alternative explanation will send activation to the other explanation, and at least partially inhibit it. And, a preference for broad explanations follows from the simple fact that explanations that explain more of the behavior will receive activation from more concepts, and as a result, will be more highly activated.

There are several reasons why we might infer that the goal of the behavior was to be helpful. First, given that the behavior itself was helpful, this should strongly activate the goal of helping. Second, given that the man was a tailor, the grocery carrying was not part of his role responsibilities, and in fact, may have been done instead of his regular job responsibilities. Thus, the fact that he helped in the face of his typical responsibilities, may augment the explanation that he did it because he wanted to help. Because the behavior was out of role, it is more likely that we will infer that the tailor was being helpful (e.g., Jones & Davis, 1965).

In addition to augmenting, the principle of discounting can also play a role. For instance, if we saw the old woman give the tailor $5, we would be far less likely to decide that the behavior was helpful. This would be implemented by an inhibitory link between the alternative explanations of wanting to help and being paid, so that the explanation of being paid would somewhat inhibit the alternative explanation.

Trait Inferences. This representation, which includes the goals of the actor, can then retrieve appropriate trait terms, such as helpful, by sending activation to the relevant traits. As we argued previously (Miller & Read, 1987, 1991; Read & Miller, 1989, 1993), traits are represented as frame-based structures, consisting of one or several plot units, identifying the central actions and the various roles for those actions. Thus, traits can be retrieved and used to characterize a behavior by matching features of the action's representation against the feature representation of various traits.

We propose that aspects of the meaning representation we constructed will send activation to the corresponding components of trait frames. For example, the frame for the trait helpful is something like one individual does something for another individual, the action provides something that the recipient needed or valued, and the actor performed the action with the intent of helping the recipient. As we can see, the components of the meaning representation we constructed for the action, "The tailor carried the old woman's groceries across the street" matches each of these aspects of the trait frame. Thus, each of the matching components should send activation to the trait frame for helpful. As a result, the trait frame for helpful and the trait itself should be highly activated. If this trait frame is highly activated and succeeds in inhibiting alternatives, then this trait should be used to characterize an individual. Thus, this model provides an account of how trait inferences are made from observed behavior.

Trope's Model of Dispositional Inference

This model can also handle the central findings of Trope's model of dispositional inference. A central aspect of the current model is that the passage of activation among levels is symmetrical. Thus, activated concepts in higher levels of the network can send activation to lower level concepts and affect the interpretation of such lower level concepts. For instance, having classified an individual as highly aggressive, we may be more likely to interpret many of their subsequent behaviors as aggressive. This provides an implementation of top-down processing. Interestingly, this aspect of the model maps very nicely onto Trope's recent model of dispositional inference.

According to Trope (1986; Trope & Liberman, 1993), dispositional inference is a two-stage process. The first stage is *behavior identification* where behavior is categorized in disposition-relevant terms (e.g., a friendly behavior), and the second stage is *dispositional inference* where the identified behavior is used to infer whether the target has a disposition that corresponds to the behavior (e.g., a friendly person). A central assumption of Trope's model is that the same information can affect both the identification stage and the dispositional-inference stage. Trope examined most frequently the impact of situational information on these two stages, particularly when the behavior is ambiguous. One of the most interesting implications of Trope's model is that situational information can have opposing effects on the two stages of the model.

For example, Trope showed that if an actor performs an ambiguous behavior, such as an ambiguously aggressive behavior, under strong situational pressure, such as an insult, the situational information may be used at the behavior-identification stage to identify the ambiguous behavior as angry. That is, the situational-constraint information is used to disambiguate the ambiguous behavior, and so we see the behavior as more aggressive than we would have if we did not have the situational information. However, the impact of the situational information is much weaker if the behavior is clear. Such a pattern of results is precisely what one would expect from the IAC model presented here. Activation from higher order concepts should strongly affect the activation of lower order ambiguous concepts, while having weaker effects on nonambiguous concepts.

The situational information should also have an impact on the dispositional-inference stage. However, the direction of the impact will be opposite from its impact on the identification stage. For instance, if an aggressive behavior is performed in response to situational pressures, such as an insult, we should be less likely to see the actor as having a hostile or aggressive disposition than if the behavior was performed without the provocation. This is the classic phenomenon of discounting.

One interesting implication of the opposing effects of situational information on the identification and inference stages is that if situational factors have a greater impact on the identification stage than on the dispositional-inference stage, then people may appear to see the behavior as more dispositionally caused than is "objectively" warranted. For instance, even if the perceiver discounts the angry disposition by the appropriate amount, given the insult, if the insult has a greater impact on the identification of the ambiguous behavior as angry, then the perceiver will see the actor as more dispositionally aggressive than if the perceiver did not know about the insult.

Let us examine in more detail how our model could address this set of findings. We start with the situation shown in Fig. 2.6, where the behavior is unambiguous, the dispositional inference is straightforward, and there is no situational information. (In these examples, our focus was on analyzing Trope's results using the spread of activation among concepts at different levels. Because we were not concerned here with how behaviors are assigned to scenarios, to simplify these analyses, the scenario level was dropped.) Here a set of physical cues, such as fidgeting, nervous laugh, and so forth sends activation to the identification level and the cues jointly and strongly activate the anxious behavior as an identification. The anxious

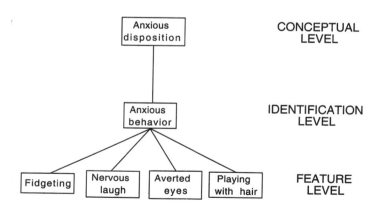

FIG. 2.6. Example of an IAC network for a dispositional inference when the behavior is unambiguous and there is only one potential explanation available. Thin lines indicate excitatory links.

behavior then sends activation to the anxious disposition at the conceptual or meaning level.

But what happens when the perceiver has also been told that the actor who is behaving anxiously was responding to a set of anxiety-provoking questions about things such as their greatest embarrassment and their greatest personal failure. Now two possible explanations for the behavior are activated; anxious disposition and anxiety-provoking questions (see Fig. 2.7). Both of these concepts will receive activation from the anxious behavior node. However, because these are competing explanations, they will also have an inhibitory link between them and will try to suppress or inhibit each other. As a result, the anxious disposition node will be less highly activated than when we did not have the situational information. Thus, we have successfully simulated the classic discounting finding.

Now let's turn to the situation where the behavior is ambiguous and only the anxious disposition is being considered. Suppose it is unclear whether the behavior is anxious or bored. Here, both the anxious-behavior identification and the bored-behavior identification are equally activated by the feature information and there is an inhibitory relation between the two identifications (see Fig. 2.8). The result is that both identifications are equally and only weakly activated by the incoming features. Further, the anxious disposition has an excitatory link to the anxious-behavior node, but an inhibitory link to the bored-behavior node. Because the two behaviors are activated equally, then the opposing excitatory and inhibitory links to the anxious disposition will result in the disposition being only weakly activated and the perceiver will not make a dispositional inference.

But what happens when we add the situational information that the actor is responding to embarrassing questions? As can be seen in Fig. 2.9, the

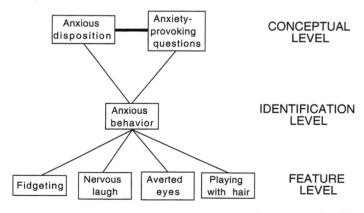

FIG. 2.7. Example of an IAC network for a dispositional inference, when the behavior is unambiguous, but two competing explanations are available. This implements discounting. Thin lines indicate excitatory links and thick lines inhibitory links.

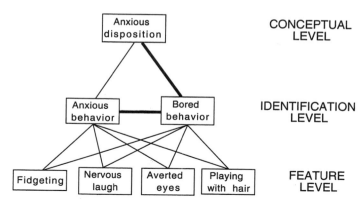

FIG. 2.8. Example of an IAC network for a dispositional inference, when the behavior is ambiguous and only the dispositional explanation is available.

anxiety-provoking questions have an excitatory link to the anxious behavior identifications because they would explain behaving anxiously, but they have inhibitory relations with both the bored-behavior identification, because they would actually inhibit behaving in a bored fashion, and the anxious disposition, because they are an alternative or competing explanation of the behavior. Thus, adding the information about the anxiety-provoking questions will have an impact at both the identification and the conceptual levels. At the identification level, the anxiety-provoking questions will positively activate the anxious behavior and negatively activate the bored behavior. As a result, the anxious behavior will be more highly activated. Further, because the anxious behavior is more highly activated,

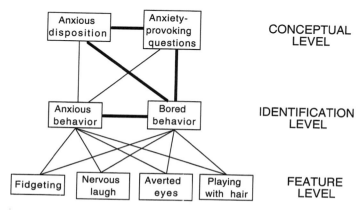

FIG. 2.9. Example of an IAC network for a dispositional inference, when the behavior is ambiguous and both the dispositional and situational explanation are available.

it should also be more successful in inhibiting the bored-behavior interpretation. Thus, the perceiver should see the ambiguous behavior as anxious.

And what happens at the conceptual level? As for the anxious disposition, as a result of the greater activation of the anxious behavior and the reduced activation of the bored behavior, the anxious disposition should be more highly activated. Thus, the situational information can indirectly lead to a greater activation of the dispositional inference. However, at the same time, the anxiety-provoking questions will inhibit the alternative explanation of an anxious disposition.

Thus, consistent with Trope's work, the situational information has opposing effects at the identification and meaning levels. Which of the two effects is strongest will be a function of the strength of the links among the various nodes. For instance, if the situation had strong links to the behavior level, but only weakly competed with the anxious disposition, then the impact of the situation on identification should be much stronger than its discounting effect. As a result, we would find that under high situational pressures, perceivers would make strong dispositional inferences, an apparently counter intuitive result. On the other hand, if the situation had only moderate links to the behavior level and a very strong inhibitory link to the anxious disposition, then we would expect to get the more typical effect of strong discounting.

Thus, our model can handle Trope's central findings. What's more, it provides an explicit process model for this phenomena, something that has been largely lacking in Trope's work. This is particularly interesting because the model was not designed for this purpose. Rather, we used basic principles from neural network models to develop a relatively standard IAC model to handle a variety of phenomena in social perception.

SUMMARY

Although we can handle Trope's results and provide a possible account of spontaneous trait inferences, the model is clearly much broader than these models. It can handle a variety of different kinds of information and is not restricted to just dealing with information in terms of the broad categories of situational and dispositional inference. And it provides an explicit account of how those various kinds of information can interact and be integrated in forming quite complex models of actors and interactions.

Further, this model integrates a number of principles of explanatory goodness that play an important role in how information is integrated. Much of the work on dispositional inference has focused on the principle of discounting and to a lesser extent on the augmenting principle. The current model also contains a number of other principles, such as simplicity and breadth of explanation, that have recently been shown to also play a central role in social inference (e.g., Read & Marcus-Newhall, 1993; Read & Lincer-Hill, 1996). Interestingly, these principles do not require any special or ad hoc assumptions. Rather, they follow directly from the basic architectural assumptions of the model.

In addition, this model begins to provide an explicit process model for how the social perceiver goes from raw stimulus information gathered from social interactions, to higher level inferences, such as traits and goals. As part of this, we have shown how the current model can provide an explicit process model for the making of spontaneous dispositional inferences. As Uleman et al. (1996) noted, such a process model is currently lacking.

A central part of our account is the notion that social interaction is conceptually represented in terms of plot units or frame-based structures, with a case-role structure. Each action centers around a "verb" or action unit that identifies the various roles, such as actor, patient, and instrument, that participate in that action. These plot units play a central role in representing the interaction, as well as in accessing higher level conceptual structures, such as traits, that can be used to characterize or summarize the interaction and the actors in it.

Further, we relied on this notion of plot units or frames to demonstrate how a number of social concepts could be integrated to form a representation for a novel social interaction. In comprehending a social interaction, a number of social concepts will be activated. Parallel-constraint satisfaction processes will operate to keep concepts that satisfactorily characterize the interaction and weed out concepts that do not. Moreover, these same parallel-constraint satisfaction processes can operate to integrate common concepts into novel combinations (see also Kunda & Thagard, 1996).

At the beginning of this chapter we identified a number of characteristics of social perception that an adequate model of social perception should be able to handle. How does the present model fare? We believe quite well.

As we noted at the outset, individual social actions are frequently ambiguous when considered in isolation, but the meaning of such actions is typically quite sensitive to the context. The current model provides a mechanism for how actions that are ambiguous out of context, can be disambiguated by context. Here, the meaning of social actions is the result of the spread of activation, in parallel, through a recurrent or feedback network. The meaning results from the interactions among all the concepts that are concurrently activated. Concepts both at the same level of analysis, as well as concepts at higher and lower levels of analysis can send activation to a social action and affect its interpretation. Thus, the meaning of an action can depend on which higher order concepts are activated and whether they send activation to the target concept, and on whether alternative interpretations of the action are activated and how strongly.

Further, we noted that in any social interaction, myriad cues are available simultaneously and often from different modalities. And new information is always coming in. Again, the parallel spread of activation through a recurrent network allows for the simultaneous integration of multiple sources of information. And because such a network is dynamic and continually changes over time, it can integrate new information as it appears.

Also, the meanings of the different pieces of a social interaction often seem to be mutually interdependent. That is, the meaning of each piece seems to be influenced by the meaning of each other piece. In essence, the meaning of a social interaction seems to result from the solution of multiple, simultaneous constraints.

Finally, we noted that each social interaction is novel and requires us to combine a number of concepts in a unique configuration. Parallel constraint satisfaction processes operating on frame based structures can construct such novel conceptual combinations.

CONCLUSION

Although these models may appear like some newfangled, gee-whiz toy, as we detailed elsewhere (Read, Vanman, & Miller, 1997), their fundamental principles are strikingly similar to many of the Gestalt principles that formed the theoretical foundations for modern social psychology in the work of such giants as Asch, Festinger, Heider, and Lewin. Asch, in his impression formation work, (Asch, 1946) argued that the processing of social stimuli was wholistic. And Heider (1958) relied heavily on Gestalt principles of structure and organization (e.g., good form and equilibrium) in his classic work on attribution theory and causal perception, as he also did in his work on balance theory (Heider, 1946, 1958). Festinger's (1957) theory of cognitive dissonance also relied quite heavily on Gestalt ideas of structural dynamics and Gestalt principles of organization and structure, such as good form and equilibrium. As we noted earlier, the parallel-constraint satisfaction processes that are fundamental to many connectionist models result in wholistic processing, in which principles such as coherence and equilibrium govern the behavior of the system. Moreover, the behavior of such systems is highly dynamic, changing with new inputs.

Further, Lewin's (1947a, 1947b) model of group process and other early work on groups, viewed social interactions in terms of interacting fields of forces, and group properties, such as cohesiveness, as the result of interacting force fields (Festinger, 1950). Similarly, in addressing the dynamics of goal-directed behavior, Lewin (1935) proposed that person–situation interactions could be treated in terms of interacting force fields. Interestingly, a key insight of recent work on connectionist models is that their behavior can be characterized by the same mathematical principles that describe systems of interacting magnetic and electrical fields (Amit, 1989; Hertz et al., 1991; Hopfield, 1982, 1984).

Although connectionist models provide strong conceptual ties to our past, they also hold great promise for our future. As the work in this volume attests, connectionist models provide powerful tools that allow us to take a deeper and more penetrating look at fundamental issues in social reasoning and social behavior.

REFERENCES

Amit, D. J. (1989). *Modeling brain function: The world of attractor neural networks*. Cambridge, England: Cambridge University Press.

Anderson, J. A. (1995). *An introduction to neural networks*. Cambridge, MA: MIT Press/Bradford Books.

Asch, S. E. (1946). Forming impressions of personality. *Journal of Abnormal and Social Psychology, 41*, 258–290.

Asch, S. E. (1952). *Social psychology*. Englewood Cliffs, NJ: Prentice-Hall.

Barsalou, L. W. (1992). *Cognitive psychology: An overview for cognitive scientists*. Hillsdale, NJ: Lawrence Erlbaum Associates.

Bassili, J. N., & Smith, M. C. (1986). On the spontaneity of trait attribution: Converging evidence for the role of cognitive strategy. *Journal of Personality and Social Psychology, 50*, 239–245.

Carlston, D. E., & Skowronski, J. J. (1994). Savings in the relearning of trait information as evidence for spontaneous inference generation. *Journal of Personality and Social Psychology, 66*, 840–856.

Dunbar, R. I. M. (1993). Co-evolution of neocortex size, group size, and language in humans. *Behavioral and Brain Sciences, 16*, 681–735.

Festinger, L. (1950). Informal social communication. *Psychological Review, 57*, 271–282.

Festinger, L. (1957). *A theory of cognitive dissonance*. Evanston, IL: Row, Peterson.

Fillmore, C. J. (1968). The case for case. In E. Bach & R. Harms (Eds.), *Universals in linguistic theory* (pp. 1–88). New York: Holt, Rinehart & Winston.

Gelman, R. (1990). First principles organize attention to and learning about relevant data: Number and the animate–inanimate distinction as examples. *Cognitive Science, 14*, 79–106.

Heider, F. (1946). Attitudes and cognitive organization. *Journal of Psychology, 21*, 107–112.

Heider, F. (1958). *The psychology of interpersonal relations*. New York: Wiley.

Hertz, J., Krogh, A., & Palmer, R. G. (1991). *Introduction to the theory of neural computation*. Redwood City, CA: Addison-Wesley.

Hopfield, J. J. (1982). Neural networks and physical systems with emergent collective computational abilities. *Proceedings of the National Academy of Sciences, USA, 79*, 2554–2558.

Hopfield, J. J. (1984). Neurons with graded responses have collective computational properties like those of two-state neurons. *Proceedings of the National Academy of Sciences, USA, 81*, 3088–3092.

Isen, A. M. (1984). Toward understanding the role of affect in cognition. In R. S. Wyer, Jr., & T. K. Srull (Eds.), *Handbook of social cognition* (Vol. 3, pp. 179–236). Hillsdale, NJ: Lawrence Erlbaum Associates.

Isen, A. M. (1987). Positive affect, cognitive processes, and social behavior. In L. Berkowitz (Ed.), *Advances in experimental social psychology* (Vol. 20, pp. 203–253). San Diego, CA: Academic Press.

Jackendoff, R. (1983). *Semantics and cognition*. Cambridge, MA: MIT Press.

Johnson, M. H. (1992). Imprinting and the development of face recognition: From chick to man. *Current Directions in Psychological Science, 1*, 52–55.

Jones, E. E., & Davis, K. E. (1965). From acts to dispositions: The attribution process in person perception. In L. Berkowitz (Ed.), *Advances in experimental social psychology* (Vol. 2, pp. 219–266). New York: Academic Press.

Just, M. A., & Carpenter, P. A. (1992). A capacity theory of comprehension: Individual differences in working memory. *Psychological Review, 99*, 122–149.

Kelley, H. H. (1971). Attribution in social interaction. In E. E. Jones, D. Kanouse, H. H. Kelley, R. E. Nisbett, S. Valins, & B. Weiner (Eds.), *Attribution: Perceiving the causes of behavior* (pp. 1–26). Morristown, NJ: General Learning Press.

Kunda, Z., & Thagard, P. (1996). Forming impressions from stereotypes, traits, and behaviors: A parallel constraint satisfaction theory. *Psychological Review, 103*, 284–308.

Lehnert, W. G., & Vine, E. W. (1987). The role of affect in narrative structure. Special Issue: Cognitive Science and the understanding of emotion. *Cognition and Emotion, 1*, 299–322.

Leinbach, M. D., & Fagot, B. I. (1993). Categorical habituation to male and female faces: Gender schematic processing in infancy. *Infant Behavior & Development, 16*, 317–332.

Lewin, K. (1935). *A dynamic theory of personality*. New York: McGraw-Hill.

Lewin, K. (1947a). Frontiers in group dynamics: I. *Human Relations, 1*, 2–38.

Lewin, K. (1947b). Frontiers in group dynamics: II. *Human Relations, 1*, 143–153.

McClelland, J. L., & Elman, J. L. (1986). Interactive processes in speech perception: The TRACE model. In J. L. McClelland & D. E. Rumelhart (Eds.), *Parallel distributed processing: Explorations in the microstructure of cognition: Vol. 2. Psychological and biological models* (pp. 58–121). Cambridge, MA: MIT Press/Bradford Books.

McClelland, J. L., & Rumelhart, D. E. (1981). An interactive activation model of context effects in letter perception: Part 1. An account of basic findings. *Psychological Review, 88*, 375–407.

Miller, L. C., Bettencourt, A., DeBro, S., & Hoffman, V. (1993). Negotiating safer sex: Interpersonal dynamics. In J. Pryor & G. Reeder (Eds.), *The social psychology of HIV infection* (pp. 85–123). Hillsdale, NJ: Lawrence Erlbaum Associates.

Miller, L. C., Cody, M. J., & McLaughlin, M. L. (1994). Situations and goals as fundamental constructs in interpersonal communication research. In M. Knapp (Ed.), *Handbook of interpersonal communication* (pp. 162–198). Newberry Park, CA: Sage.

Miller, L. C., & Read, S. J. (1987). Why am I telling you this? Self-disclosure in a goal-based model of personality. In V. Derlega & J. Berg (Eds.), *Self-disclosure: Theory, research, and therapy* (pp. 35–58). New York: Plenum.

Miller, L. C., & Read, S. J. (1991). On the coherence of mental models of persons and relationships: A knowledge structure approach. In G. J. O. Fletcher & F. Fincham (Eds.), *Cognition in close relationships* (pp. 69–99). Hillsdale, NJ: Lawrence Erlbaum Associates.

Miller, L. C., & Read, S. J. (1997). *Primitives, narratives, and trait concepts: How human universals create the tales that traits tell*. Manuscript in preparation, University of Southern California, Los Angeles, CA.

Murphy, S. T., & Zajonc, R. B. (1993). Affect, cognition, and awareness: Affective priming with optimal and suboptimal stimulus exposures. *Journal of Personality and Social Psychology, 64*, 723–739.

Nachson, I. (1995). On the modularity of face recognition: The riddle of domain specificity. *Journal of Clinical & Experimental Neuropsychology, 17*, 256–275.

Osgood, C. E., Suci, G. J., & Tannenbaum, P. H. (1957). *The measurement of meaning*. Urbana, IL: University of Illinois Press.

Plaut, D. C., McClelland, J. L., Seidenberg, M. S., & Patterson, K. (1996). Understanding normal and impaired word reading. *Psychological Review, 103*, 56–115.

Ranney, M., Schank, P., Mosmann, A., & Montoya, G. (1993). Dynamic explanatory coherence with competing beliefs: Locally coherent reasoning and a proposed treatment. In T.-W. Chan

(Ed.), *Proceedings of the International Conference on Computers in Education: Applications of Intelligent Computer Technologies*, 101–106.

Read, S. J., Jones, D. K., & Miller, L. C. (1990). Traits as goal-based categories: The role of goals in the coherence of dispositional categories. *Journal of Personality and Social Psychology, 58*, 1048–1061.

Read, S. J., & Lalwani, N. (1996). *A narrative model of trait inferences: The role of goals*. Unpublished manuscript, University of Southern California.

Read, S. J., & Lincer-Hill, H. M. (1997). *Explanatory Coherence and Principles of Dispositional Inference: The role of parallel constraint satisfaction processes*. Unpublished manuscript, University of Southern California.

Read, S. J., & Marcus-Newhall, A. (1993). Explanatory coherence in social explanations: A parallel distributed processing account. *Journal of Personality and Social Psychology, 65*, 429–447.

Read, S. J., & Miller, L. C. (1989). Inter-personalism: Toward a goal-based model of persons in relationships. In L. Pervin (Ed.), *Goal concepts in personality and social psychology* (pp. 413–473). Hillsdale, NJ: Lawrence Erlbaum.

Read, S. J., & Miller, L. C. (1993). Rapist or "regular guy": Explanatory coherence in the construction of mental models of others. *Personality and Social Psychology Bulletin, 19*, 526–540.

Read, S. J., & Miller, L. C. (1995). Stories are fundamental to meaning and memory: For social creatures, could it be otherwise? In R. S. Wyer, Jr. (Ed.), *Knowledge and memory: The real story: Vol. 8. Advances in social cognition* (pp. 139–152). Hillsdale, NJ: Lawrence Erlbaum Associates.

Read, S. J., Vanman, E. J., & Miller, L. C. (1997). Connectionism, Parallel Constraint Satisfaction Processes, and Gestalt Principles: (Re)Introducing Cognitive Dynamics to Social Psychology. *Personality and Social Psychology Review, 1*, 26–53.

Rumelhart, D. E., Hinton, G. E., & Williams, R. J. (1986). Learning internal representations by error propagation. In D. E. Rumelhart, & J. L. McClelland (Eds.), *Parallel distributed processing: Explorations in the microstructure of cognition: Vol. 1. Foundations* (pp. 319–362). Cambridge, MA: MIT Press/Bradford Books.

Rumelhart, D. E., & McClelland, J. L. (1982). An interactive activation model of context effects in letter perception: Part 2. The contextual enhancement effect and some tests and extensions of the model. *Psychological Review, 89*, 60–94.

Rumelhart, D. E., & McClelland, J. L. (1986). PDP models and general issues in Cognitive Science. In D. E. Rumelhart & J. L. McClelland (Eds.), *Parallel distributed processing: Explorations in the microstructure of cognition: Vol. 1. Foundations* (pp. 110–146). Cambridge, MA: MIT Press/Bradford Books.

Rumelhart, D. E., Smolensky, P., McClelland, J. L., & Hinton, G. E. (1986). Schemata and sequential thought processes in PDP models. In J. L. McClelland & D. E. Rumelhart (Eds.), *Parallel distributed processing: Explorations in the microstructure of cognition: Vol. 2. Psychological and biological models* (pp. 7–57). Cambridge, MA: MIT Press/Bradford Books.

Schank, P. K., & Ranney, M. (1991). An empirical investigation of the psychological fidelity of ECHO: Modeling and experimental study of explanatory coherence. *Proceedings of the Thirteenth Annual Conference of the Cognitive Science Society* (pp. 892–897). Hillsdale, NJ: Lawrence Erlbaum Associates.

Schank, P. K., & Ranney, M. (1992). Assessing explanatory coherence: A new method for integrating verbal data with models of on-line belief revision. *Proceedings of the Fourteenth Annual Conference of the Cognitive Science Society*. Hillsdale, NJ: Lawrence Erlbaum Associates.

Schank, R. C., & Abelson, R. P. (1995). Knowledge and memory: The real story. In R. S. Wyer, Jr. (Ed.), *Knowledge and memory: The real story: Vol. 8. Advances in social cognition* (pp. 1–86). Hillsdale, NJ: Lawrence Erlbaum Associates.

Shaver, P., Schwartz, J., Kirson, D., & O'Connor, C. (1987). Emotion knowledge: Further exploration of a prototype approach. *Journal of Personality and Social Psychology, 52*, 1061–1086.

Sokolov, Y. N., Izmailov, T. A., & Zavgorodnaya, V. L. (1985). Multi-dimensional scaling of configurations of symbols. *Voprosy Psikhologii, 1*, 133–140.

Spence, J. T., & Helmreich, R. L. (1978). *Masculinity and femininity: Their psychological dimensions, correlates and antecedents.* Austin: University of Texas Press.

Thagard, P. (1989). Explanatory coherence. *Behavioral and Brain Sciences, 12*, 435–467.

Thagard, P. (1992). *Conceptual revolutions.* Princeton: Princeton University Press.

Tooby, J., & Cosmides, L. (1992). The psychological foundations of culture. In J. H. Barkow, L. Cosmides, & J. Tooby (Eds.), *The adapted mind: Evolutionary psychology and the generation of culture* (pp. 119–136). New York: Oxford University Press.

Treisman, A., & Sato, S. (1990). Conjunction search revisited. *Journal of Experimental Psychology: Human Perception and Performance, 16*, 459–478.

Trope, Y. (1986). Identification and inferential processes in dispositional attribution. *Psychological Review, 93*, 239–257.

Trope, Y., & Liberman, A. (1993). The use of trait conceptions to identify other people's behavior and to draw inferences about their personalities. *Personality and Social Psychology Bulletin, 19*, 553–562.

Uleman, J. S., Newman, L. S., & Moskowitz, G. B. (1996). People as flexible interpreters: Evidence and issues from spontaneous trait inference. In M. P. Zanna (Ed.), *Advances in experimental social psychology* (Vol. 28, pp. 211–279). San Diego, CA: Academic Press.

Vallacher, R. R., & Nowak, A. J. (1994). *Dynamical systems in social psychology.* San Diego, CA: Academic Press.

Wales, R., & Taylor, S. (1987). Intonation cues to questions and statements: How are they perceived? *Language and Speech, 30*, 199–211.

Widrow, G., & Hoff, M. E. (1960). Adaptive switching circuits. *Institute of Radio Engineers, Western Electronic Show and Convention, Convention Record, Part 4*, 96–104.

Wierzbicka, A. (1992). *Semantics, culture, and cognition: Universal human concepts in culture-specific configurations.* New York: Oxford University Press.

Winter, L., & Uleman, J. S. (1984). When are social judgments made? Evidence for the spontaneousness of trait inferences. *Journal of Personality and Social Psychology, 47*, 237–252.

Zajonc, R. B. (1980). Feeling and thinking: Preferences need no inferences. *American Psychologist, 35*, 151–175.

STEREOTYPING AND SOCIAL CATEGORIZATION

3

THE DYNAMICS OF GROUP IMPRESSION FORMATION: THE TENSOR PRODUCT MODEL OF EXEMPLAR-BASED SOCIAL CATEGORY LEARNING

Yoshihisa Kashima
Jodie Woolcock
Deborah King
La Trobe University

Social psychology has been plagued by metaphysical and methodological individualism. These doctrines assume that there only exist individual human beings and that social psychological phenomena should be examined treating the individual as the unit of analysis (Lukes, 1973). Perhaps reflecting this intellectual tradition, the investigation of *person* impression formation has been central to social psychology ever since Asch (1946). Yet, the human social environment is inhabited not only by individuals, but also by groups (e.g., McGrath, 1984; Tajfel, 1981). At the very least, social groups influence social action to the extent that they are psychologically real. Indicative of this realization is the recent shift of research effort, which includes an examination of how we form impressions about *groups* (Hamilton & Sherman, 1996) and the renewed interest in stereotyping and social identity (see Hilton & von Hippel, 1996, for a recent review).

The sizable literature on these topics in recent times has been mainly concerned about the formation, deployment, and maintenance of mental representations about social groups. However, as Hilton and von Hippel (1996) lamented, "There has been little effort directed at specifying the details of various representational models" (p. 244). A more careful theorizing about cognitive mechanisms is necessary to integrate within a coherent framework diverse inquiries into representations of social groups. More specifically, in dealing with the *formation* of mental representations of groups, there are two divergent lines of research. One deals with the formation of impressions of groups (e.g., Hamilton & Gifford, 1976) in a vein similar to person impression formation; the other is concerned with the classification learning of exemplars into categories (Smith & Zárate, 1990, 1992). In fact, there is no single theoretical framework that can explain these two lines of research (Kashima, in press). The primary aim of this chapter is to show that a parallel distributed processing model called the Tensor Product Model (TPM) can provide a general theory that can explain the findings in these two literatures.

In this chapter, we first introduce the tensor product model, review the major theoretical developments in the two divergent lines of research, and then show how TPM can explain them. In the final section, we discuss how TPM sheds light on Hamilton and Gifford's (1976) classic study on group impression formation, that is, distinctiveness-based illusory correlation.

I. THE TENSOR PRODUCT MODEL OF SOCIAL CATEGORY LEARNING

Many social categories are learned through direct interaction with specific members of the categories and indirect hearsay in the discourse (Linville & Fischer, 1993; Park & Hastie, 1987). As Bruner (1991) emphasized, our informational environment, including social interaction and hearsay, is culturally structured. Most behaviors present themselves as meaningful social actions, which are naturally described by concrete verbs (action verbs in Semin & Fiedler, 1988, 1991; e.g., "helped an old lady crossing the busy street"), whereas people may describe social groups in abstract trait terms or value-laden attributions (adjectives and state verbs in Semin & Fiedler, 1988, 1991; e.g., "helpful"). Direct observations are likely to involve more concrete descriptions, whereas hearsay is bound to include more abstract attributions (Linville & Fischer, 1993). Although the content of the memory traces about a social episode of direct interaction with a group member and an episode of discourse about the group is different, the basis of one's impression about the group is a particular episode directly or indirectly pertaining to the group.[1]

For this reason, we believe a theory of social category learning should be able to model the *episodic* aspect of cognitive processes. Tulving (1983) suggested that specific events in the world are encoded into engrams (or

---

[1]The issue about levels of abstraction regarding the content of an episode is relevant in our later discussion about a mixture model of categorization (section 2.1).

memory traces), which are stored and retrieved for later use. However, just like the exemplar-based theories of social cognition (Linville, Fischer, & Salovey, 1989; Smith & Zárate, 1992), we do not subscribe to his separation between episodic and semantic memory systems (also see Humphreys, Bain, & Pike, 1989).

The exemplar-based theories assume that each memory trace is a meaningful representation (i.e., localist representation). The exemplar-based theories would assume that there are as many memory traces as there are exemplars: For instance, 1,000 exemplars of cats would have to be stored as 1,000 separate memory traces. By contrast, the tensor product model assumes a distributed representational system, in which a meaning is represented by a *pattern* of activation of simple processing units (e.g., Hinton & Anderson, 1981; Rumelhart, McClelland, & the PDP Research Group, 1986). Each processing unit in this case does not have a clearly definable semantic content. Memory traces are all superimposed on each other within the connections among the units. The same processing units participate in the storage of the memories; there is no need to postulate a large number of separate memory traces.

Tensor products have been used to model memory processes (Humphreys et al., 1989; Pike, 1984), analogical reasoning (Halford et al., 1994), and natural language processing (Smolensky, 1990). Special cases of this formulation such as linear associators have been used in a variety of cognitive domains (e.g., Anderson, 1972; Anderson, Silverstein, Ritz, & Jones, 1977; Knapp & Anderson, 1984; Kohonen, 1988) including person impression formation (Kashima & Kerekes, 1994). As we explain later, the tensor product model allows us to describe the formation of associations among multiple features, whereas linear associators (especially heteroassociators) are designed to model the memory link between two features only.

1.1. Encoding, Storage, and Output Processes

The tensor product model assumes that three major processes are involved in the formation of group impressions. In the *encoding process*, social events are encoded and their mental representations are constructed; during the *storage process*, these mental representations are stored; and in the *output process*, memory traces are accessed for some purposes. We illustrate the processes by using a simple example in this section. Figure 3.1 gives an overview.

1.1a. Encoding Process

When a new social event is encountered, the perceiver encodes it into a mental representation. Imagine a man from the United States watching on TV for the first time a scene of an Australian Aboriginal family living in the

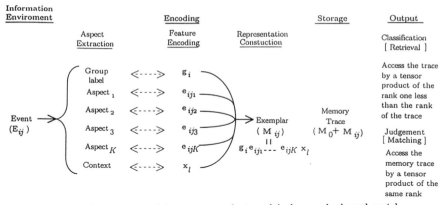

FIG. 3.1.   An overview of the tensor product model of exemplar-based social category learning.

outback of Australia. He may extract *aspects* or *respects* in which Aborigines can be compared to African Americans because of their apparent similarity in skin color. Then, "skin color" is one of the aspects extracted from the new experience. He may think that the Aborigines live in a rural area, extracting the aspect of "area of residence." Context in which the event was encountered (i.e., watching TV) may also be extracted as an aspect.

At the same time, specific *features* with regard to a given aspect are encoded as well. Note that the feature of "living in a rural area" (outback) is encoded with regard to the aspect of area of residence for Australian Aborigines. In our terminology, the relationship between an aspect and a feature is analogous to that between an attribute and a value in another terminology. One can regard an aspect as a psychological dimension on which events vary, and features are specific levels or values on the dimension. By associating the encoded features, a mental representation of the event is constructed. For instance, from the television program, the American man may represent the event as "The Australian Aborigines live in a rural area of Australia according to the TV program." It is this interpreted event that is stored in memory for later use. Turner, Oakes, and their colleagues (Oakes, Haslam, & Turner, 1994; Turner, 1985, 1987) discussed aspect extraction in intergroup setting. Medin, Goldstone, and Gentner (1993) highlighted its importance in the general case of categorization.

The central assumption of the tensor product model is that a social event is encoded into a set of features (with regard to aspects) which are represented in a distributed representational system, and a mental representation of the event that is formed can be mathematically modeled as a tensor product. In the present example, features such as "Australian Aborigines," "rural," and "the TV program" are all extracted; each feature is represented in a distributed manner; and these features are then associated with each other to form a mental representation of the event. Let us use this example to illustrate the model.

To represent this social event, three sets of units, $\{\alpha\}$, $\{\beta\}$, and $\{\gamma\}$, are necessary. We assume for simplicity each set has N units, each of which can be activated, taking a value from negative infinity to positive infinity. Let us assume that the set of units, $\{\alpha\}$, participates in representing a group label, $\{\beta\}$ participates in representing another aspect such as area of residence, and $\{\gamma\}$ participates in representing context. A particular pattern of activation over the units in $\{\alpha\}$ then represents a particular group label such as Aborigines, and so on. A vector notation can be used to designate this pattern of activation, where the level of activation of the ath unit in $\{\alpha\}$ can be indicated by the ath element in the vector $\mathbf{g}_1$. We write this element as $g_1[a]$. Likewise, a particular pattern of activation over $\{\beta\}$ represents "rural area," and another pattern over $\{\gamma\}$ represents TV program. These patterns can be represented by vectors $\mathbf{e}_1$ and $\mathbf{x}_1$. Note that not only the pattern but also the magnitude is also represented. We assume that the magnitude reflects the amount of attention directed to the event. The magnitude of activation is indicated by the length of the vector, which is defined as the square root of the sum of all squared activation values. Figure 3.2 presents a simplified case where each set has only three units. Note that the figure shows only the connections between the bth unit in $\{\beta\}$ and the other units.

When the three patterns are activated simultaneously, the connection among units is strengthened by the product of the activation levels of the units. That is, the connection among the ath unit in $\{\alpha\}$, the bth unit in $\{\beta\}$,

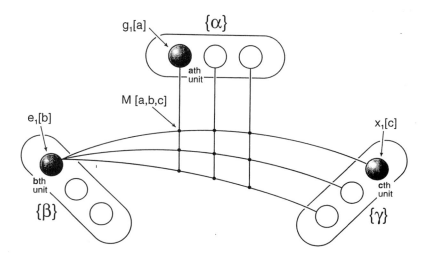

FIG. 3.2. A simple example of the tensor product network.

and the cth unit in $\{\gamma\}$ is strengthened by the product of the activation levels of these units, which are designated as $g_1[a]$, $e_1[b]$, and $x_1[c]$.

Amount by which the connection is strengthened $= M_1[a,b,c]$
$$= g_1[a]e_1[b]x_1[c] \quad (1)$$

Note that there are N^3 connections altogether as all units in different sets are connected, but there are no connections among units within a set. When the three patterns are activated, all these connections are strengthened by the product of the activation levels of the connected units.

In order to describe this learning rule in a simple fashion, we adopt a mathematical form called a tensor, which is a generalization of a matrix. The outer product of two vectors $\mathbf{g}$ and $\mathbf{e}$ can form a matrix $\mathbf{M}$ such that the element $[a,b]$ in $\mathbf{M}$ designated as $M[a,b]$ is the product of $g[a]$ and $e[b]$, which are respectively the ath and bth elements of $\mathbf{g}$ and $\mathbf{e}$. Thus, the rule for constructing $\mathbf{M}$, the matrix product of $\mathbf{g}$ and $\mathbf{e}$, is such that $M[a,b] = g[a]e[b]$. We generalize this rule to construct a tensor. The tensor product of three vectors $\mathbf{g}_1$, $\mathbf{e}_1$, and $\mathbf{x}_1$, which is designated as $\mathbf{M}_1$, can be written as $M_1[a,b,c] = g_1[a]e_1[b]x_1[c]$. Note that this rule gives the amount by which the connection among the three units is strengthened as in Equation 1; $\mathbf{M}_1 = \mathbf{g}_1\mathbf{e}_1\mathbf{x}_1$ where $M_1[a,b,c] = g_1[a]e_1[b]x_1[c]$ gives the amount by which each of the connections is strengthened as a result of activating the three patterns, $\mathbf{g}_1$, $\mathbf{e}_1$, and $\mathbf{x}_1$.

The tensor notation as used here is a straightforward generalization of matrix notation. In fact, an ordinary matrix is a tensor of rank 2, whereas when three vectors are involved, the tensor is said to have rank 3. The rule discussed here can be mathematically generalized to an arbitrary number of vectors and ranks.[2] In fact, the learning rule in Equation 1 is a generalization of the Hebbian learning rule often used in linear associators: For a tensor of rank 2, it reduces to the Hebbian rule. By adopting the general tensor formulation, the tensor product model can describe the formation of associations among more than two features, allowing group representations to have multiple features.

1.1b. Storage Process

Once a mental representation is constructed, it is stored in long-term memory. The central assumption of TPM is that memory traces are all superimposed on each other. The representation in long-term memory is a pattern of connection strengths. Using the same example as before, when the social event of watching on TV Australian Aborigines living in the out-

---

[2]Although somewhat different notations are conventionally used for tensors, we adopt this notation for the sake of exposition.

back of Australia on TV, this event is encoded into $\mathbf{M}_1 = \mathbf{g}_1\mathbf{e}_1\mathbf{x}_1$. Recall that this indicates the amount of connection strengths increased by the simultaneous activation of the three patterns, $\mathbf{g}_1$ (group label), $\mathbf{e}_1$ (rural area), and $\mathbf{x}_1$ (TV program) in $\{\alpha\}$, $\{\beta\}$, and $\{\gamma\}$.

Suppose that the units had been connected with each other, and the connection strengths prior to the processing of the new information about the Aborigines can be described by $\mathbf{M}_0 = \mathbf{g}_0\mathbf{e}_0\mathbf{x}_0$. Then, the storage of the new mental representation is modeled by a simple tensor addition as follows:

$$\mathbf{M} = \mathbf{M}_0 + \mathbf{M}_1$$
$$= \mathbf{g}_0\mathbf{e}_0\mathbf{x}_0 + \mathbf{g}_1\mathbf{e}_1\mathbf{x}_1 \tag{2}$$

where $\mathrm{M}[a,b,c] = \mathrm{M}_0[a,b,c] + \mathrm{M}_1[a,b,c]$. Again, the same rule can be generalized to an arbitrary rank.

1.1c. Output Process

Two types of output processes are particularly relevant to group impression formation. One is a *judgment* process in which the overall impression of a group is reported on a rating scale. The other is a *classification* process where a particular person or a social event is classified into some social categories. The difference between judgment and classification lies in the use of cues to access memory traces. In judgment, a group label is used to retrieve representations of associated social events, and a returned representation is used to make a judgment on a rating scale (see Kashima & Kerekes, 1994). By contrast, in classification, the representation of a social event is used to retrieve a group label.

Although these two types of tasks are used in the investigation of social category learning, it is rarely recognized that they have produced two divergent lines of research in cognitive psychology (Kashima, in press). We discuss this later, and show that TPM can integrate the two sets of literature. However, for now, we describe how TPM models the classification and judgment processes, which can be modeled by reference to Humphreys et al.'s (1989) two ways of accessing stored memory traces, retrieval and matching.

Classification. In the classification process, a given social event is provided (e.g., Australian outback on the TV program), and its mental representation is used to retrieve associated information, typically, a group label (e.g., Australian Aborigines). In the example of Australian Aborigines, then, the retrieval cue is constructed by representing Australian outback, $\mathbf{e}_1$, and the TV program, $\mathbf{x}_1$, in the sets of units, $\{\beta\}$ and $\{\gamma\}$. When this occurs, the activation $\mathrm{e}_1[b]$ in the bth unit in $\{\beta\}$ and the activation $\mathrm{x}_1[c]$ in the cth unit in $\{\gamma\}$ spread to the connection point of these units with the ath unit in $\{\alpha\}$. These activations are multiplicatively combined, and then weighted by the connection strength M[a,b,c] to spread to the ath unit in $\{\alpha\}$. This amount is $M[a,b,c]e_1[b]x_1[c]$. The analogous process occurs for every connection involving the ath unit in $\{\alpha\}$. All activations spreading to the ath unit are summed to generate the activation in that unit, the level of which is the sum of $M[a,b,c]e_1[b]x_1[c]$ for all b and c, $\sum\sum M[a,b,c]e_1[b]x_1[c]$. The analogous process occurs for each unit in $\{\alpha\}$, thus generating a pattern of activation. Let us designate this pattern by $\mathbf{v}$, whose ath element $v[a]$ indicates the activation level of the ath unit. The pattern $\mathbf{v}$ indicates some meaningful, albeit noisy, concept.

This process can be compactly described by a tensor notation. Suppose that the mental representation of "Australian outback on the TV program" is designated by $\mathbf{C} = []e_1x_1$. The $[]$ in this notation is meant to suggest that no activation takes place in $\{\alpha\}$. This retrieval cue generates a pattern of activation designated by a vector, $\mathbf{v}$, as below:

$$\text{Retrieve } (\mathbf{M},\mathbf{C}) = \mathbf{v},$$

where

$$v[a] = \sum_{b=1}\sum_{c=1} M[a,b,c]C[b,c]. \tag{3}$$

Given Equation 3, $\mathbf{v}$ can be rewritten as follows (see Appendix 1 for proof):

$$\mathbf{v} = g_0(e_0.e_1)(x_0.x_1) + g_1(e_1.e_1)(x_1.x_1). \tag{4}$$

Equation 4 assumes that there exist memory associations among the units that resulted from previous cognitive processes, $\mathbf{M}_0$; we assume that this can be written as $g_0e_0x_0$ (see Equation 2). Note that $\mathbf{v} = g_1$ if $(e_0.e_1) = 0$ or $(x_0.x_1) = 0$, and the length of e_1 and x_1 is both unity, where $(\_.\_)$ indicates the dot product. However, $\mathbf{v} \neq g$ under most circumstances. In the present example, Equation 4 suggests that by using the outback and the TV program as joint cues (i.e., "I remember watching on TV something about the outback of Australia . . ."), TPM can retrieve the group label, Australian Aborigines, though the retrieved pattern is likely to be somewhat degraded by some interference from the past memory.

Judgment. The judgment task requires that the object of a judgment be placed on the continuum of a rating scale (e.g., positive vs. negative). We postulate that the endpoints of the scale play a significant role (Kashima & Kerekes, 1994). According to Upshaw's variable perspective model (Ostrom & Upshaw, 1968; Upshaw, 1969), a judgment is a function of the similarity of the object to the higher end of the continuum relative to its similarity to the lower end. Biernat and her colleagues (Biernat & Manis, 1994; Biernat, Manis, & Nelson, 1991) used a similar model in examining the use of double standards in stereotyping (also see Foddy & Smithson, 1989).

Assume that the higher end of the scale is represented by a pattern of activation, **h**, over units, and the lower end, by another pattern, **l**. We suggest that these representations form a part of the retrieval cue for accessing the memory. Suppose that the memory, **M**, as in Equation 2, is accessed to make a likability judgment about the Australian Aborigines on a scale varying from likable to unlikable. First, the group label, g_1, is activated in $\{\alpha\}$, and another vector representation, **r**, which signifies irrelevance of a given aspect, are activated in $\{\gamma\}$. Humphreys et al. (1989) defined **r** as a vector, each of whose elements is $1/\sqrt{N}$. This retrieves a pattern of activation in $\{\beta\}$, which can be designated by vector **w**. The retrieved pattern summarizes the past learning experience pertaining to the group. The pattern, **w**, is then compared to the representations of the higher and the lower ends of the scale, **h** and **l**, to compute the similarities, (**w.h**) and (**w.l**). The similarity between two vectors is defined as the dot product of the two vectors.

If no evaluative information is stored in the memory trace, both (**w.l**) and (**w.h**) will be zero. However, if some evaluative information is present, either (**w.l**) or (**w.h**) or both will be nonzero. In the example of the Australian Aborigines, if the observer has no evaluation about the fact that they live in a rural area, the retrieved pattern, **w**, will not be useful in making an evaluative judgment. Therefore, some additional elaborative processing must be performed or the observer will conclude that he or she has no evaluation about the target group. If the observer does have some evaluative connotation attached to "living in a rural area," then the pattern will be used to make an evaluative judgment. We postulate that an evaluative judgment is the similarity of the object with the higher end of the scale relative to its similarity with the lower end as below:

$$\text{Judgment} = \frac{(\mathbf{w.h})}{(\mathbf{w.h}) + (\mathbf{w.l})}. \tag{5}$$

Again, this process can be mathematically described by tensor operations. We suggest that a memory access cue, $\mathbf{H} = g_1\mathbf{hr}$, is constructed by simultaneously activating the representation of Aborigines, g_1, the representation of the higher end point, **h**, and the representation that indicates no specification, **r**. Similarly, a memory access cue, $\mathbf{L} = g_1\mathbf{lr}$, is constructed by activating the patterns, g_1, **l**, and **r**. According to Humphreys et al., matching involves a comparison of two tensors, which returns a scalar value of similarity. When **M** is matched by **H**, this operation computes a similarity between **M** and **H** as defined in Equation 6 below:

$$\text{Match } (\mathbf{M,H}) = \sum_{a=1}^{N}\sum_{b=1}^{N}\sum_{c=1}^{N} M[a,b,c]H[a,b,c]. \tag{6}$$

Similarly, Match(**M,L**) also returns a similarity between **M** and **L**. It can be shown that Match(**M,H**) = (**w.h**) and Match(**M,L**) = (**w.l**) (see Appendix 2 for proof). Equation 6 can now be expressed by the following quotient:

$$\text{Judgment} = \frac{\text{Match}(\textbf{M,H})}{\text{Match}(\textbf{M,H}) + \text{Match}(\textbf{M,L})}. \tag{7}$$

Equation 7 generalizes Kashima and Kerekes's (1994) formulation.

1.2. General Model

Now we express the tensor product model in a general form involving multiple groups, aspects, and exemplars.

1.2a. Notations

Upper case letters G, E, and X are used to designate a group label, an event, and a context. G_i is the ith group; E_{ij} is the jth event of the ith category; X is the context in which the event took place. We assume that aspects and features are extracted from the events. Lower letters indicate features: e_{ijk} is the feature of E_{ij} in the kth aspect ($i = 1 \ldots I; j = 1 \ldots J_i; k = 1 \ldots K$). So, if the first aspect is "day/night person" as in Smith and Zárate (1990), e_{ij1} may be "day person." Group label or aspect is represented by a set of N cognitive processing units. A particular feature or a specific group label is represented by a column vector with N elements, where the nth element indicates the activation level of the nth unit. A vector is denoted by a bold lower case letter, for example, $\textbf{e}_{ijk}$ is a distributed representation of e_{ijk}. The similarity between two vectors, $s(\textbf{e}_1, \textbf{e}_2)$, can be computed by taking the dot product of these vectors, $(\textbf{e}_1.\textbf{e}_2)$ (i.e., the sum of the products of the corresponding elements of the two vectors). In addition, we define a special vector, $\textbf{r}$, each of whose elements is $1/\sqrt{N}$.

1.2b. Encoding Process

Suppose a group label, G_i, is associated with an event, E_{ij}, that is encoded to have K features, e_{ij1}, e_{ij2}, ... and e_{ijK}. The context in which this event is encountered is X. Then, the configuration of this cognitive episode, [G_i, e_{ij1}, e_{ij2}, ... e_{ijK}, X], is represented by a tensor of rank K+2, $\textbf{M}_{ij} = \textbf{g}_i\textbf{e}_{ij1}\textbf{e}_{ij2} \cdots \textbf{e}_{ijK}\textbf{x}$, where $M_{ij}[m_0, m_1, m_2, \ldots m_{K+1}] = g_i[m_0]e_{ij1}[m_1]e_{ij2}[m_2] \ldots e_{ijK}[m_K]x[m_{K+1}]$.

1.2c. Storage Process

When there are J_i exemplars associated with the group, G_i, all the mental representations are stored in memory, so that the memory pertaining to the group is simply the sum of all the tensors. Further, when I groups are involved, the resultant representation should be as below:

$$M = M_0 + \sum_{i=1}^{I} \sum_{j=1}^{J_i} g_i e_{ij1} e_{ij2} \cdots e_{ijK} x. \tag{8}$$

Again we assume that M_0 is approximated by $\sum g_i e_{i01} e_{i02} \cdots e_{i0K} x$.

1.2d. Output Process

Recall that there are two ways of accessing memory, retrieval and matching. Retrieval is essentially a recall in which a tensor representation of rank K+2, M, is accessed by another tensor of a lower rank.[3] In the present discussion, M is accessed by a tensor of rank K+1, C, which has no feature in the k'th aspect. Retrieval here is modeled as follows:

$$\text{Retrieve } (M,C) = v,$$

where

$$v[m_{k'}] = \sum_{m_0} \cdots \sum_{m_{k-1}} \sum_{m_{k+1}} \cdots \sum_{K+1} M[m_0, \ldots m_{k'-1}, m_{k'}, m_{k'+1}, \ldots m_{K+1}] C[m_0, \ldots m_{k'-1}, m_{k'+1}, \ldots m_{K+1}]. \tag{9}$$

Note that this is a simple generalization of Equation 3. The classification process is a special case of Equation 9 where the missing aspect in C is a group label, so that a group label is retrieved as a result of the retrieval operation.

In matching, memory is accessed by another representation with the same form. For instance, a tensor of rank K+2, M, is accessed by another tensor of rank K+2, H, returning a scalar matching strength. Matching is modeled as follows:

$$\text{Match}(M,H) = \sum_{m_0} \cdots \sum_{m_{K+1}} M[m_0, m_1, \ldots m_{K+1}] H[m_0, m_1, \ldots m_{K+1}]. \tag{10}$$

Suppose that a judgment is required about the i'th group, $G_{i'}$, in terms of the kth aspect. We assume that the higher and lower ends of the judgment scale are represented by H and L, which are tensor products with $g_{i'}$ for the group label, $h_{k'}$ and $l_{k'}$ in the k'th aspect, and r in all the other aspects. Context is x. By generalizing Equation 4, we can model the judgment process:

---

[3]In this discussion, we describe a case in which a tensor memory is accessed by a tensor with one fewer rank. However, retrieval is a general process in which a tensor is accessed by another lower rank tensor. For instance, if a group representation may be accessed by its group label, superimposed memories are retrieved in all aspects that are associated with the label. This model is not limited to the case in which memories about only one aspect are retrieved.

$$\text{Judgment} = \frac{\text{Match}(\mathbf{M},\mathbf{H})}{\text{Match}(\mathbf{M},\mathbf{H}) + \text{Match}(\mathbf{M},\mathbf{L})}. \tag{11}$$

2. GROUP IMPRESSION FORMATION

The main problem in the area of group impression formation is that there is no single theory that adequately explains both the classification and judgment data. On the one hand, there is a well-established class of theories applicable to classification. Among them is Smith and Zárate's (1992) exemplar-based theory. However, it is difficult to see how these theories can be developed to account for the judgment data. Furthermore, PDP theories developed for category learning have difficulty explaining the judgment data. A major advantage of the tensor product model is that it can explain both the classification and judgment data within a single theoretical framework. We will first show that TPM can explain some of the major findings in the classification experiment, and then turn to the judgment literature.

2.1. Classification

A large body of literature has been amassed using the classification task in cognitive psychology. As there are excellent literature reviews (Komatsu, 1992; Smith & Medin, 1981), we are brief about it and move on to its application in group impression formation. In the landmark experiment on prototype acquisition by Posner and Keele (1968), the subjects were given a series of exemplars, to be tested later for their recognition of new and old exemplars. The prototype, which was the pattern from which stimulus exemplars were generated, was classified into the correct category as accurately and as fast as old exemplars, when in fact the subjects had not seen the prototype at all. Their results were widely interpreted as showing an "automatic" acquisition of abstract prototypes from concrete examples.

Nonetheless, exemplar theories such as Medin and Schaffer's (1978) context model were later developed to explain this finding without postulating abstract prototypes. They suggested that because the "prototype" usually had a large number of old exemplars that were similar to it, it tended to be as similar to new exemplars as to the old exemplars. The context model gave rise to a series of theoretical refinements, which we call CM theories. Their core assumption is that classification is based on similarities between new and old exemplars. Assume that there are K dimensions on which exemplars of I categories vary, so that the jth exemplar ($j = 1 \ldots J_i$) of the ith category ($i = 1 \ldots I$), E_{ij}, takes the value, e_{ijk}, on the kth dimension. Suppose a new test exemplar, T, has a value, t_k, on the kth dimension. The similarity (s) between the new exemplar and the old exemplars for the ith category is a multiplicative function of the similarities between the new and the old with respect to all dimensions:

$$s(E_{ij},T) = \prod_{k=1}^{K} s_k(E_{ij},T). \tag{12}$$

Nosofsky (1984, 1986; Nosofsky, Kruschke, & McKinley, 1992) noted that the multiplicative rule can be interpreted in terms of a multidimensional scaling model. More specifically, the similarity between E_{ij} and T, $s(E_{ij},T)$, can be rewritten in terms of the distance between them, $d(E_{ij},T)$, in the following manner: $s(E_{ij},T) = \exp[-\kappa d(E_{ij},T)^p]$, where κ is a free sensitivity parameter and p determines the type of similarity-distance conversion function (an exponential decay function when p = 1; a Gaussian decay function when p = 2). The distance between E_{ij} and T is a Minkowski distance: $d(E_{ij},T)$ $= [\Sigma\alpha_k|t_k-e_{ijk}|^r]^{1/r}$, where α_k is an attention parameter and r determines the type of distance (the city-block metric when r = 1; the Euclidean metric when r = 2). When p = r, the multidimensional scaling model reduces to Medin–Schaffer's multiplicative function (Nosofsky et al., 1992). The probability of categorizing the new exemplar to the ith category, $p(C_i|T)$, is the similarity of T to the exemplars of the ith category divided by the sum of the similarities of T to all exemplars:

$$P(C_i \mid T) = \frac{\displaystyle\sum_{j=1}^{J_i} s(E_{ij},T)}{\displaystyle\sum_{i=1}^{I}\sum_{j=1}^{J_i} s(E_{ij},T)}. \tag{13}$$

More recently, however, Medin, Altom, and Murphy (1984) postulated a mixture model, according to which, people classify an exemplar based on its similarity to other exemplars stored in memory as well as to abstract prototypes of the categories. We use Smith and Zárate's (1990) study to illustrate their theory. Their stimuli and results are listed in Table 3.1. Their stimuli consisted of statements that described nine individuals, who were classified into two groups. Each statement was generated by a frame: [Name] is a (night/day) person. He is (artistic/scientific) and (sociable/unsociable), and thinks it is important to (exercise regularly/eat healthy foods).

Subjects were randomly assigned to two conditions. In the exemplar-only condition, they received nine person descriptions only, whereas in the prototype-first condition, they were told about the prototypes of the two groups first. The prototype of each group had the combination of features of aspects that appeared most frequently for that group.

TABLE 3.1
Stimuli and Results of Smith and Zárate (1990)

					Probability of Classifying as A				
					Smith–Zárate		Simulation Results		
Exemplar	Aspects				Exemplar Only	Prototype First	Exemplar Only	Prototype Only	Prototype + Exemplar
	1	2	3	4					
a1	1	1	1	0	.91	.91	.82	.93	.84
a2	1	0	1	0	.81	.78	.90	.49	.68
a3	1	0	1	1	.91	1.00	.96	.92	.89
a4	1	1	0	1	.88	.94	.91	.93	.87
a5	0	1	1	1	.91	.97	.91	.92	.87
b1	1	1	0	0	.19	.28	.19	.52	.33
b2	0	1	1	0	.28	.16	.15	.48	.32
b3	0	0	0	1	.19	.00	.05	.08	.08
b4	0	0	0	0	.00	.00	.05	.00	.00
n1	1	0	0	1	.62	.72	.64	.53	.52
n2	1	0	0	0	.25	.03	.42	.07	.13
n3	1	1	1	1	.84	1.00	.86	1.00	1.00
n4	0	0	1	0	.28	.03	.38	.07	.13
n5	0	1	0	1	.59	.50	.60	.50	.52
n6	0	0	1	1	.59	.66	.59	.48	.49
n7	0	1	0	0	.19	.00	.20	.09	.08

Note. Four aspects were used, each of which had two contrasting features (indicated by 0 v. 1). a1–a5 were exemplars for Group A; b1–b4 were exemplars for Group B; and n1–n7 were new test exemplars. The prototype for Group A was 1111; that for Group B was 0000.

The experimental procedure consisted of two phases. In the learning phase, exemplars of Groups A and B were presented one at a time and subjects guessed their group membership. Feedback about their classification accuracy was given immediately after each guess. The learning phase continued until subjects could correctly classify all exemplars or until they had seen the exemplars 16 times. In the test phase, the subjects were shown old and some new exemplars, and asked to classify them into Group A or B. Table 3.1 lists the observed probability of classifying each exemplar into Group A.[4]

A mixture model assumes that people would use either the prototypes only or the learned exemplars only in classifying new exemplars. The probability of using the learned exemplars only is a free parameter, e. An observed probability of classifying a given exemplar is a mixture of the prob-

---

[4]Strictly speaking, an "exemplar" in an experiment is cumulated memory traces about a certain individual member of a group, that is, a result of multiple exemplars about the given individual.

ability of classifying it under exemplar model (let this be P_e) and the probability of classifying it under prototype model (let this be P_p), so that the overall probability is $eP_e + (1-e)P_p$. The probabilities of classifying exemplars were predicted by the generalized context model (GCM); however, only the similarities with old exemplars were used for P_e and the similarities with prototypes were used for P_p. The model fit was excellent. The probability of using only exemplars, e, was estimated to be .74 for the exemplar-only condition and .41 for the prototype-first condition. In both conditions, the probability of using exemplars only, e, was significantly different from zero and one, suggesting that people used both prototypes and exemplars in these conditions.

Clearly, a "prototype" in the prototype-first condition is equivalent to an exemplar consisting of modal features. The difference is that the prototype is directly attributed to each group, whereas the exemplars pertain to individual group members. In a way, group prototypes are a kind of hearsay information about a group; it is the experimenter who provided an abstracted summary about the group. We concur with Linville and Fischer (1993): "prototypes" in this sense are a type of exemplar in our terminology. Then, what do we make of the results in the exemplar-only condition? We suggest that subjects spontaneously inferred the modal features of each group. Inferred "prototypes" are nonetheless self-generated exemplars. Based on this and other research, Smith and Zárate (1992) postulated a theory of social judgment that used the generalized context model as the core representational system.[5]

2.2. Modeling Classification

We first analytically show that the tensor product model is consistent with the core assumption of context model-based theories. A simulation experiment is then presented, which simulates Smith and Zárate's (1990) empirical data.

2.2a. Analyzing Classification Process

In the classification experiment, the association between group labels and exemplars are stored in tensor products according to TPM. As before, we assume that each exemplar consists of K aspects, and that E_{ij} is the jth exemplar of the ith group. The cognitive episode of processing the configuration $[G_i, E_{ij}, X]$ is represented as $\mathbf{g}_i\mathbf{e}_{ij1}\mathbf{e}_{ij2} \ldots \mathbf{e}_{ijK}\mathbf{x}$. After all the exemplars are learned, the resultant memory should be described by Equation 8:

---

[5]Recently, Kruschke's ALCOVE (1992) adopted a gradient descent learning algorithm that adjusts the attentional parameters of GCM based on the error feedback from learning trials. We do not discuss ALCOVE further in this chapter as its conceptual core is GCM.

$$\mathbf{M} = \mathbf{M_0} + \sum_{i=1}^{I} \sum_{j=1}^{J_i} g_i e_{ij1} e_{ij2} \cdots e_{ijK} \mathbf{x}. \tag{8}$$

We assume that $\mathbf{M_0}$ is approximated by $\sum g_i e_{i01} e_{i02} \cdots e_{i0K} \mathbf{x}$.

Suppose that memory $\mathbf{M}$ is accessed by a test exemplar, T, which is represented as a rank K+1 tensor, $\mathbf{T} = []t_1 t_2 \cdots t_K \mathbf{x}$. Note that this tensor product does not specify the first aspect as indicated by [] in the first place. The retrieval of a group label by the test exemplar was modeled by Equation 9, which can be rewritten as follows (see Appendix 1 for proof):

$$\text{Retrieve } (\mathbf{M},\mathbf{T}) = \sum_i \sum_j g_i [s_{0i} + \prod_{k=1}^{K} (e_{ijk} \cdot t_k)(\mathbf{x} \cdot \mathbf{x})]. \tag{14}$$

We further assume that the length of $\mathbf{x}$ is unity, and let

$$s(E_{ij},T) = \prod_{k=1}^{K} (e_{ijk} \cdot t_k). \tag{15}$$

If s_{0i} is negligible, the retrieved representation can be interpreted as a weighted sum of the representations of the group labels where the weight for the ith group label is the similarity of T with all of E_{ij}. Note this equation for the similarity of T with E_{ij} is the product of the similarities along the K dimensions, which is consistent with the multiplicative similarity rule of the CM theories (Equation 12).[6] Further, assume that the probability of retrieving a particular group label, G_i, follows Luce's choice rule (1959; Massaro & Friedman, 1990, generalized this and called it Relative Goodness Rule).

$$P(G_i | T) = \frac{\sum_{j=1}^{J_i} s(E_{ij},T)}{\sum_i \sum_j s(E_{ij},T)}. \tag{16}$$

Note that this equation is identical to Equation 13.

2.2b. Simulating Classification Process

We simulated Smith and Zárate's (1990) classification data (Simulation Experiment 1). The simulator was programmed with Mathematica (Wolfram, 1991). Recall that in their experiment two groups of individuals were classi-

---

[6]When $(e_{ijk} \cdot t_k)$ is within [0,1] for all i, j, and k, Equation 15 is equivalent to Equation 12, and can be rewritten by Equation 12 without loss. Therefore, the TPM descriptions can be translated into the distance-based GCM descriptions. When $(e_{ijk} \cdot t_k)$ is outside of [0,1], Equation 15 is not equivalent to Equation 12. However, if the lengths of e_{ijk} and t_k are unity, $(e_{ijk} \cdot t_k)$ falls within the bound of [0,1].

fied in terms of four aspects, each of which had two contrasting features (see Table 3.1). This meant eight different features were involved in the experiment. In the present simulation, it was assumed that each feature was encoded into a random vector with five elements with the length of unity. To generate random vectors, a random number was generated from a uniform distribution (from −1 to +1) for each element in a vector. When all five elements were generated, we normalized the vector by dividing each element by the length of the original vector.

For each simulated subject, the feature vectors were randomly generated. Furthermore, we assumed that the encoding of the same feature would have some random fluctuation each time: We added a random vector with the length of .1 to a feature vector every time a corresponding feature was encoded (amounted to roughly 10% error). After the error was added, each feature vector was again normalized to have the length of unity. Depending on the amount of attention directed to features, we could set parameter values to change the length of the vectors for the features. However, for this simulation, the length of feature vectors was set to unity. Tensor products for learned exemplars were computed based on the error added feature vectors, $e_1 e_2 e_3 e_4$. Forty subjects were simulated in each run.

Recall that there were the prototype-first and exemplar-only conditions in the Smith–Zárate experiment. In the prototype-first condition, the subjects may have learned prototypes only in the beginning, but they should have learned exemplars eventually. By contrast, in the exemplar-only condition, the subjects learned their exemplars in the beginning, but may have inferred the prototypes later. These considerations suggest that the subjects in these conditions might have had both prototype and exemplar representations. Consistent with this reasoning, the final classification performances in the two conditions were very similar to each other in Smith and Zárate's experiment (see Table 3.1). To simulate these conditions, we ran three conditions: one with the prototypes only, one with the exemplars only, and one with prototypes and exemplars. For the prototype + exemplar simulation, the prototypes were assumed to attract more attention than exemplars, so that the former would be slightly longer than each exemplar (.90 and .60, respectively). This assumption seems warranted as the subjects in the prototype-first condition were forced to learn the prototypes before they began the learning of the exemplars. There were nine exemplars and two "prototypes," which were basically exemplars with modal features for the groups in the Smith–Zárate experiment.

Each simulated subject classified a test exemplar by the following rule. The similarities of the test exemplar with the learned exemplars and the prototypes for each of the two groups were computed as specified by Equation 15. The test exemplar was classified into the group that had a greater similarity value. For those simulated subjects that used prototypes only, the similarities of a test exemplar *only* with the prototypes were computed. The proportion of the simulated subjects out of 40 that classified a given test exemplar as group A was recorded as a datum. We conducted this simulation 20 times to compute the mean probability of classifying a test exemplar as group A.

The simulation results resemble the human performance (relevant probabilities are reported in Table 3.1). First, In the beginning, the human subjects in the prototype-first condition performed as in the prototype-only simulation, and the subjects in the exemplar-only condition performed as in the exemplar-only simulation. Smith and Zárate (1990) reported that in the first trial, the probability of their subjects to classify the first exemplar to A was greater than the probability for them to classify the second exemplar to A in the prototype-first condition. However, this trend was reversed in the exemplar-only condition. This observation was borne out in the simulations reported in Fig. 3.3.

Further, as the subjects learn exemplars in the prototype-first condition, and as the subjects infer prototypes in the exemplar-only condition, their classification performances should become like the prototype + exemplar simulation. Figure 3.4 reports the simulation results against the final human performances in the Smith–Zárate experiment. Clearly, the pattern of the final performances is similar to the prototype + exemplar simulation results.

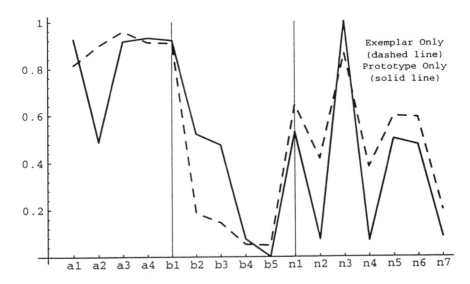

FIG. 3.3. Probability of classifying exemplars to Category A in the prototype-only and exemplar-only simulations: a1–a4 are exemplars of Group A; b1–b5 are exemplars of Group B; and n1–n7 are new test exemplars.

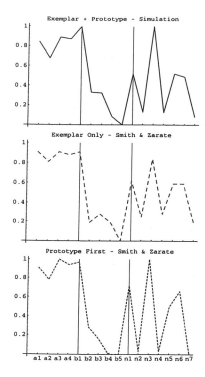

FIG. 3.4. Probability of classifying exemplars to Category A in the prototype + exemplar simulation against the Smith–Zárate results: a1–a4 are exemplars of Group A; b1–b5 are exemplars of Group B; and n1–n7 are new test exemplars.

2.3. Judgment

In the judgment task, people *appear* to average exemplars in forming impressions. In the person impression formation, it is well established that the weighted averaging model (WAM) fits judgment data (see Anderson, 1981; Kashima & Kerekes, 1994, for a review). When people are shown a number of stimuli, their judgment of the overall impression seems as if they are averaging the stimuli:

$$\text{Judgment} = \frac{\sum_{j=0}^{J} w_j s_j}{\sum_{j=0}^{J} w_j},$$

(17)

where w_0 and s_0 are the initial weight and the initial value, and w_j and s_j are the weight and the scale value of the jth stimulus ($j = 1 \ldots$). Although there is no direct test of the weighted averaging model for group impression, most researchers appear to assume that the model holds for it as well (e.g., Ford & Stangor, 1992; Krueger, Rothbart, & Sriram, 1989).

However, the observation that WAM fits the judgment data presents problems to many theories of category learning. A class of theories based on distributed representation systems (DR theories), including Metcalfe-Eich's (Eich, 1982) holographic memory model, Hintzman's (1986) multiple-trace memory model, Knapp and Anderson's (1984) distributed memory model, and McClelland and Rumelhart's (1985) connectionist model, possess three common properties, *linearity*, *time invariance*, and *noninterference* (Busemeyer & Myung, 1988; Myung & Busemeyer, 1992). Linearity means that a prototype estimate is a linear additive function of the exemplars; time invariance suggests that the additive weight for each exemplar is a function of the time lag between its presentation and output; and noninterference implies that variations of exemplars along one dimension do not influence the production of prototypes along another dimension. Algebraically, the following equation embodies these properties (Busemeyer & Myung, 1988, p. 5).

$$\text{Prototype Estimate} = \sum_{j=1}^{J} w_{(J-j)} e_j, \tag{18}$$

where the prototype is estimated after the Jth exemplar, the weight for the jth exemplar, e_j, is a function of the time lag between J and that exemplar, $(J-j)$. However, WAM predicts time variability. In the simplest case, WAM predicts that the weight for an exemplar should be $1/J$, that is, a function of J, but not of $(J-j)$. Clearly, this violates the time invariance property.

Generally, experiments that used judgment tasks found time variability. Myung and Busemeyer's (1992) research on prototype production, which is a generalization of a judgment task (Kashima, in press; Kashima & Kerekes, 1994), found that the simple averaging model fits the data well. They presented a series of lines, which simulated mass spectrum tests of chemical substance. The lengths of a number of vertical lines indicate readings from a test. The pattern of the line lengths is used to diagnose the chemical substance. The participants were shown four test results for one substance, and told to estimate the central tendency. When the weight for each exemplar was estimated from the participants' estimate of the prototype, it was close to $1/J$. As they suggested, this clearly violates the time invariance property (also see Busemeyer & Myung, 1988). Kashima and Kerekes (1994) showed that person impression judgments were time variable. In our preliminary data (Kashima & Clifford, 1995), time variability was also observed in group impression formation.

Time variability in person impression formation was explained by a special case of the tensor product model (Kashima & Kerekes, 1994), which is also capable of explaining recency effects (i.e., tendency for recent information to influence judgments) in person impression formation. When the target person was judged as each new piece of information came in (continuous judgment), there was a strong recency effect. Although a primacy effect is often obtained in person impression formation, it occurs when a judgment is made after all stimuli are presented (final judgment). Kashima and Kerekes suggested that the representation of a target person changed markedly in the continuous judgment condition because the act of making judgments broke the stream of in-coming stimuli. The recency effect occurred because the most recent representation of the person was used to access the memory trace, thus making the most recent information more accessible. Kashima and Kerekes noted that the change in person representation is best understood as a change in context representation in the tensor product model framework (see footnote 5 on p. 423).

Likewise, in forming impressions of a group, the tendency toward a recency effect appears to be stronger when there is some reason to break the stream of stimuli. In particular, seeing a new individual member of a group may provide good enough reason to break the stream. Strange, Schwei, and Geiselman (1978) presented 12 adjectives with high and low levels of likeability to describe a group. In two of the conditions, the order of positive and negative adjectives were counterbalanced to examine the order effect. Crossed with the order, three conditions were included: Each group was said to consist of 12, 6, or 4 individuals, so that an individual member was described by 1, 2, or 3 adjectives. They found a recency effect when each individual was described by 3 adjectives, but a primacy effect was observed when each individual was described by 1 adjective. Under the 4-person group condition, each individual member may have been encoded separately and the representation of the group may have changed as a new member was encountered, just as in person impression formation. There are two potential reasons for this. First, when an individual is described by a greater amount of information, the person is more likely to be individuated (Fiske & Neuberg, 1990). Second, in this experiment, the 4-person group condition had fewer individual members than in the 12-person group condition. The smaller number of individuals would have made it easier to individuate the members.

Manis and Paskewitz's (1987) results are consistent with this interpretation. They showed a series of verbal definitions of common words that varied in their degree of expressed psychopathology. In the person impression condition, they were attributed to one individual, whereas the same definitions were attributed to a group (patients of one hospital) in the group impression condition. In both conditions, the subjects judged the extent of psychopathology of each definition. Manis and Paskerwitz found that the correlations of the overall impression with the judgments of definitions were greater for the more recent items (recency effect); however, the recency effect was more pronounced in the group impression condition than in the person impression condition. Note that in their experiment, the subjects were required to make judgments of definitions continuously. For one thing, this judgment condition tends toward a recency effect (Kashima & Kerekes, 1994; more generally, Hogarth & Einhorn, 1992). Further, in the group impression condition, each definition was attributed to a new patient. This may have further facilitated the tendency to individuate the group members. By contrast, in the person impression condition, the subjects would have expected a greater consistency (Hamilton & Sherman, 1996).

In sum, the group impression formation research using the judgment task has produced at least two major findings. First, people seem to average (or weighted average) exemplars. Second, there is a recency effect when individual members of a group are individuated.

2.4. Modeling Judgment

We analytically discuss how the tensor product model can explain the weighted averaging phenomenon and a recency effect. We then report computer simulations.

2.4a. Analyzing Judgment Process

The tensor product model predicts that, when required to make a judgment about the ith group with regard to a particular aspect (e.g., sociableness, intellectual capacity), the human subject's judgment can be described by WAM. It is easy to show this. Recall that Equation 11 models a judgment about the i'th group with regard to the k'th aspect anchored by the higher and lower endpoints, $h_{k'}$ and $l_{k'}$. Assuming that the representations of group labels are different from each other (i.e., the dot product of any pair of g is zero), Equation 11 reduces to the following equality (see Appendix 2 for proof):

$$\text{Judgment} = \frac{\sum\limits_{j=0}^{J_r}(e_{ijk'}.h_{k'})\prod\limits_{k=1}^{K}(e_{ijk}.r)(x.x)}{\sum\limits_{j=0}^{J_r}(e_{ijk'}.h_{k'})\prod\limits_{k=1}^{K}(e_{ijk}.r)(x.x) + \sum\limits_{j=0}^{J_r}(e_{ijk'}.l_{k'})\prod\limits_{k=1}^{K}(e_{ijk}.r)(x.x)}. \quad (19)$$

Note that the subscript k is from 1 to K except for k'. Equation 19 reduces to

$$\text{Judgment} = \frac{\sum_{j=0}^{J} w_j s_j}{\sum_{j=0}^{J} w_j}, \tag{20}$$

where

$$s_j = \frac{(e_{ijk'} . h_{k'})}{(e_{ijk'} . h_{k'}) + (e_{ijk'} . l_{k'})}, \tag{21}$$

and

$$w_j = [(e_{ijk'} . h_{k'}) + (e_{ijk'} . l_{k'})] \prod (e_{ijk} . r)(x.x). \tag{22}$$

Equation 20 is the weighted averaging model identical to Equation 17.

This does not imply that the *process* of judgment making is described by the weighted averaging model, but rather its *outcome* can be modeled by it (Kashima & Kerekes, 1994). This property is an advantage of TPM over Smith and Zárate's exemplar theory (1992), which assumes that exemplars are averaged. Note that the weighted averaging model posits that there is a prior scale value, s_0, and its weight, w_0. These can be meaningfully interpreted as an effect of the prior memory trace in the tensor product model.

In addition, the context representation, x_q (q = 1 . . . Q), enables us to explain a recency effect. Suppose the context is represented for each new event. It seems reasonable to assume that contexts for new events may be encoded to be very similar to the previous contexts if there is no discernible break in the flow of events; however, a new context may be encoded as different from the preceding context when there is a clear break in the stream of stimuli. An individuated person in a group may provide such a break as previously discussed. Suppose that the most recent stimuli are encoded with a similar context, x_Q, but prior stimuli were encoded with a different context, $x_{Q'}$. If the subjects assume that the stimuli in the most recent context are most diagnostic, and therefore cue the memory by $g_i r$ . . $h_{k'}$ . . rx_Q and $g_i r$ . . $l_{k'}$ . . rx_Q (both **h** and **l** are for the k'th dimension), this cue would emphasize the most recent context, x_Q, relative to other contexts such as $x_{Q'}$, thereby heavily weighting the exemplars associated with the context x_Q. To put it more formally, according to Equation 22, the weight w_j for a given exemplar is a function of the similarity of the context in which the exemplar was encountered (x_q) and the most recent context representations (x_Q), which is ($x_q.x_Q$). This results in a heavy weighting of the exemplars associated with the context that is similar to the most recent context. Provided that the most recent context is most similar to itself, this implies a recency effect.

2.4b. Simulating Judgment Process

We conducted a computer simulation of the tensor product model to show that the judgment is close to averaging and exhibits time variability even if some random variation in representations is involved. The simulator was written with Mathematica. In this simulation, we assumed that one aspect and context were extracted from stimuli in addition to group label. Group label, aspect, and context were each represented by a five-element vector.

The simulation involved four exemplars. A group label was generated by constructing a vector, each of whose elements was a random number between -1 and 1. The vector for a group label was normalized by dividing it by its length, so that its length was unity. For the aspect about which judgments were to be made, we generated two random vectors, $\mathbf{h}$ and $\mathbf{l}$, which respectively represented the high and low end of the aspect, that is, the two extreme ends (e.g., likable vs. unlikable). Again, the method of generating random vectors was the same as for a group label. We computed two feature vectors, $\mathbf{e}_h$ and $\mathbf{e}_l$, for the extracted aspect, such that $(\mathbf{e}_h.\mathbf{h}) = (\mathbf{e}_l.\mathbf{l}) = .80$. We call $\mathbf{e}_h$ and $\mathbf{e}_l$ at the first serial position as H1 and L1, at the second position as H2 and L2, and so on.

Just as in human experiments, we had the simulator learn a series of four exemplars. We constructed 16 different series. The basic logic of this design was spelled out by Anderson (1973), and adopted by Busemeyer and Myung (1988) and Kashima and Kerekes (1994). The design fixes four pairs of given high and low items (H1 and L1, H2 and L2, etc.), and each pair is assigned to a specific serial position so that a given pair appears only at the position. Then, highs and lows are factorially combined, so that 2^4 combinations are created. This gives us the 16 series listed in Table 3.2. In a human experiment, to avoid the confound of pair and position (e.g., H1 and L1 always appearing at position 1), a Latin square design is adopted to make sure four different pairs appear at a given position across four subjects. In this simulation, we used the same vectors for all serial positions, so that this precaution was unnecessary.

The simulation was run in the following manner. For each simulated subject, random vectors of group label ($\mathbf{g}$), context ($\mathbf{x}_q$; q = 1 to 4), high and low ends of an aspect ($\mathbf{h}$ and $\mathbf{l}$) were generated. Features with high values (high feature) and features with low values (low feature) on the aspect ($\mathbf{e}_h$ and $\mathbf{e}_l$) were computed. The vectors were all normalized so that their lengths were unity. The simulated subject received one stimulus at a time, encoded it into a tensor product ($\mathbf{ge}_q\mathbf{x}_q$), stored it, and made a judgment using the most recent context to access the memory ($\mathbf{ghx}_q$ and $\mathbf{glx}_q$). The judgment was recorded as a datum. The procedure continued for all four stimuli in a given series. The same procedure was repeated for the 16 series according to the plan laid out in Table 3.2 (see Appendix 3 for the method of estimating the serial position weights).

TABLE 3.2
Series of Exemplars Used for Judgment Simulation

Series	Position 1	2	3	4	H(1)	H(2)	H(3)	H(4)
1	H1	H2	H3	H4	x	x	x	x
2	H1	H2	H3	L4	x	x	x	
3	H1	H2	L3	H4	x	x		x
4	H1	H2	L3	L4	x	x		
5	H1	L2	H3	H4	x		x	x
6	H1	L2	H3	L4	x		x	
7	H1	L2	L3	H4	x			x
8	H1	L2	L3	L4	x			
9	L1	H2	H3	H4		x	x	x
10	L1	H2	H3	L4		x	x	
11	L1	H2	L3	H4		x		x
12	L1	H2	L3	L4		x		
13	L1	L2	H3	H4			x	x
14	L1	L2	H3	L4			x	
15	L1	L2	L3	H4				x
16	L1	L2	L3	L4				

Note. H(j) where j = 1 to 4 indicates the set of those series that have high features at the jth serial position. The series that have "x" belong to this set; the rest belong to L(j).

We conducted two simulations. The first simulation (Simulation Experiment 2) set x_q to be constant for all serial positions. The second simulation (Simulation Experiment 3) varied x_q randomly. Figure 3.5 reports the mean serial position weight estimates over 20 simulated subjects for Simulation Experiment 2. Clearly, the serial position weights are equal for a given judgment. The best fitting model in this case is a simple average as Myung and Busemeyer (1992) reported. The simple average model implies a time variability. Figure 3.6 reports the mean serial position weight estimates over 20 simulated subjects for Simulation Experiment 3. The figure shows that the serial position curves have an upward swing toward the end. This implies a recency effect as predicted. To put it simply, when context vectors vary, and the most recent context is used to access the memory trace, the most recent exemplar is weighted most heavily, thus resulting in a recency effect. These simulations show that the general discussion about time variability and recency effects hold when randomness is involved.

2.5. Advantages of the Tensor Product Model

The tensor product model can model both classification and judgment results in group impression formation. The model can provide a general framework in which to integrate the literature on group impression forma-

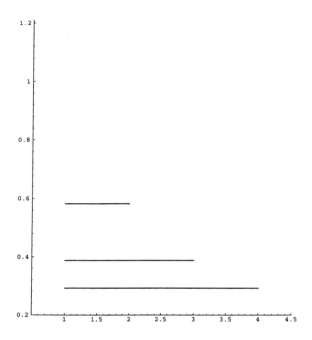

FIG. 3.5. The serial position estimates obtained from Simulation Experiment 2 (context remains constant).

tion in a principled way. TPM is consistent with the core assumption of context model-based theories including the generalized context model for the classification task. For the judgment task, TPM is also consistent with the weighted averaging model, exhibits time variability, and explains a recency effect under some specifiable circumstances.

There are other advantages to the tensor product model. TPM sheds light on conceptual puzzles surrounding the category learning literature. The first puzzle is concerned with psychological similarity. The best accepted (and empirically supported) theory of psychological similarity (Tversky, 1977) postulates an additive model: Psychological similarity between two stimuli is an additive function of the shared and unshared features (see Kashima & Kashima, 1993, for some discussion in the social domain). The same additive similarity model underlies the DR theories. For example, Hintzman (1986) explicitly used Tversky's contrast model. Yet, as we have seen, the DR theories cannot explain the prototype production data because they all imply time invariance. By contrast, though the CM theories explain the classification data admirably, they assume a multiplicative model of similarity: Similarities with respect to different dimensions are multiplicatively combined (see Equation 12). Are there two kinds of psychological similarity?

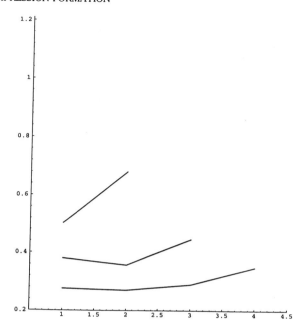

FIG. 3.6. The serial position estimates obtained from Simulation Experiment 3 (context changes over time).

The tensor product model provides one answer to this issue. TPM is based on the additive similarity model, which is consistent with Tversky's contrast model. Yet, by virtue of the tensor product representation, similarities are multiplicatively combined as the CM theories postulate. To see how this is done, recall the retrieval operation. When a tensor, $\mathbf{g}_0\mathbf{e}_0\mathbf{x}_0$ is accessed by $[]\mathbf{e}_1\mathbf{x}_1$, the result is equal to $\mathbf{g}_0(\mathbf{e}_0.\mathbf{e}_1)(\mathbf{x}_0.\mathbf{x}_1)$ (see Equation 4). Note that within each aspect, the retrieval operation computes a dot product, for instance $(\mathbf{g}_0.\mathbf{g}_1)$, and this implies additivity within a given aspect. However, the dot products that are computed within aspects are multiplied to compute the overall similarity, $(\mathbf{e}_0.\mathbf{e}_1)(\mathbf{x}_0.\mathbf{x}_1)$. Thus, TPM implies additive similarity within one aspect, but multiplicative similarity between aspects. This solves the puzzle about additive versus multiplicative similarities.

The second puzzle is that the CM theories of category learning appear to be computationally extremely demanding. They assume that all exemplars are stored in memory, and that similarity of a stimulus to all the stored exemplars is computed. Even the developer of the Generalized Context Model (Nosofsky, Palmeri, & McKinley, 1994) suggested that "[a]lthough the [CM] models have provided impressive accounts of a wide array of categorization phenomena, it is reasonable to question the plausibility of exemplar storage processes and the vast memory resources that they seem to require" (p. 53).

The tensor product model assumes that the process of retrieval is basically a parallel process, and the representations of exemplars are assumed to be superimposed on each other. This reduces the amount of required cognitive resource. The computational resource requirement that Nosofsky et al. (1994) were concerned about is no longer an issue. However, as Halford et al. (1994) suggested, the parallel processing of a tensor product may require a large amount of cognitive resource, and this is likely to constrain the maximum number of aspects that can be processed in parallel.

All in all, the TPM seems to be able to explain many of the findings in the group impression formation literature while shedding new light on some of the conceptual questions in the general area of category learning.

3. DISTINCTIVENESS-BASED ILLUSORY CORRELATION

As a final test of the adequacy of the tensor product model, we will examine TPM's implications for the distinctiveness-based illusory correlation. It is instructive to consider the ways in which TPM handles this paradigmatic case.

3.1. Empirical Findings

Hamilton and Gifford (1976) conducted a pioneering work on group impression formation. In Experiment 1, they showed their subjects a series of 39 behavioral descriptions that differed on their evaluative connotations. Individual members of two groups (A and B) were said to have performed these behaviors. The proportion of positive to negative behaviors was kept constant (9 to 4) for each group; however, the total number of behaviors was varied. Group A was described by 26 behaviors (18 positive and 8 negative), and Group B was described by 13 behaviors (9 positive and 4 negative). The authors argued that the relative infrequency of Group B and negative behaviors makes those items distinctive. According to them, people's tendency to overestimate the co-occurrence of distinctive items leads to a more negative overall impression for Group B than for Group A, that is, a negative stereotyping of a minority group in the absence of any difference in the distribution of positive and negative events associated with the majority and minority groups.

Hamilton and Gifford used both judgment and classification tasks to examine the effect of distinctiveness. They showed that Group B was evaluated more negatively than Group A on judgment scales. In addition, they asked their participants to classify the behavioral descriptions to Group A or Group B. The participants were more likely to classify negative behaviors to Group B more than expected (i.e., 1/3 of total). Both results point to the tendency of a minority group's infrequent behaviors to be weighted more than others. This pattern of findings was replicated in a number of studies (see Hamilton & Sherman, 1994; Mullen & Johnston, 1990, for reviews).

More recently, Fiedler (1991) and Smith (1991) postulated mechanisms other than distinctiveness to explain many of the findings associated with this paradigm. Fiedler (1991) posited that imperfect encoding, retention, and retrieval of information leads to information loss, which results in the over-estimation of infrequent events and underestimation of frequent events. Smith (1991) used Hintzman's (1986) model to simulate the judgment process that relies on the difference between the frequencies of positive and negative behaviors. Group A was judged more positively than Group B because the difference in the frequencies of positive and negative behaviors was larger for Group A than for Group B. Fiedler (1996) showed that both the Fiedler (1991) and Smith (1991) results can be explained within his framework called the Brunswikian Induction Algorithm for Social Cognition (BIAS), which explains the illusory correlation phenomenon in terms of information loss due to fallible observations, and bias reduction due to an aggregation of the observations.

As Hamilton and Sherman (1994) pointed out, although these demonstrations suggest that memory processes may be involved in the illusory correlation phenomenon, their results do not rule out the existence of attentionally driven distinctiveness-based illusory correlation. Stroessner, Hamilton, and Mackie (1992) and Johnson and Mullen (1994) suggested that paired distinctiveness (infrequent event paired with infrequent group) attracts attention at the time of encoding and increases accessibility at the time of retrieval, suggesting the importance of distinctiveness.

3.2. Modeling Distinctiveness-Based Illusory Correlation

The tensor product model offers two explanations for the illusory correlation phenomenon. One is consistent with Hamilton and Gifford's (1976) original explanation of distinctiveness. As we suggested earlier, the amount of attention directed to a stimulus may result in greater activation of the pattern for the stimulus. This means that the magnitude of the activation pattern is greater than others (i.e., the vector is longer). If we assume that the infrequency (or novelty) of an event leads one to pay more attention to it, the paired distinctiveness of a minority member performing a rare behavior can make the magnitude of the activation for infrequent behaviors greater than others. This leads to greater accessibility of the memory trace for a minority's infrequent behaviors.

The tensor product model points to another factor that may contribute to the illusory correlation phenomenon. That is the effect of a prior memory.

TPM postulates that there is a prior memory, M_0, which is assumed to exist before an experiment. When some probe cues are used to access the memory after experimental stimuli are learned, the returned output is not only influenced by the learned stimuli, but also by the prior memory. In typical experimental situations, the effect of the prior memory is constant and can be ignored without many problems. However, in the illusory correlation paradigm, the prior memory may play an important role.

First, let us examine the case of judgment. TPM predicts a weighted averaging of exemplar "scale values" (Equation 20). We can rewrite the equation as follows, assuming that there are N_p positive items and N_n negative items, s_p and s_n indicate the scale values for positive and negative items, and w_p and w_n are the weights for positive and negative items:

$$\text{Judgment} = \frac{w_0 s_0 + N_p w_p s_p + N_n w_n s_n}{w_0 + N_p w_p + N_n w_n}. \tag{23}$$

If $s_0 = (s_n + s_p)/2$ roughly holds and $w_p/w_n > N_n/N_p$, even if the ratio, N_n/N_p, is constant, the judgment increases as the total number of items, $N_p + N_n$, increases.[7] In other words, a more positive rating of a majority group can obtain when the initial value is roughly neutral, and the weight given to positive items relative to that given to negative items is greater than the N_n/N_p ratio. This implies an illusory correlation phenomenon.

Note that much of the explanation hinges on w_0, which represents an effect of the prior memory. If w_0 is zero (i.e., there is no effect of prior memory), the equation implies that there should be no illusory correlation. This is because the judgment should remain constant as long as the ratio, N_n/N_p, remains constant. The interference of the prior memory may be in part responsible for the illusory correlation according to the present formulation.

Now we turn to the case of classification. Equation 14 gives the model prediction when the memory trace of the learned exemplars is accessed by a test exemplar, $T (= t_1 t_2 \ldots t_K)$. The equation is reproduced below:

$$\text{Retrieve } (M,T) = \sum_i \sum_j g_i [s_{0i} + \prod_{k=1}^{K} (e_{ijk} \cdot t_k)]. \tag{14}$$

The model assumes that there is a small effect of the prior memory (represented by s_{0i}). Equation 14 implies that the strength of activation of the group label for the ith group is as follows:

---

[7]This explanation is reminiscent of Anderson's (1981) explanation of a set size effect. When only positive or negative items are involved in person impression formation, likability judgments become more positive or negative as there are more positive or negative items. A weighted averaging model without the w_0 and s_0 predicts no increase; however, with these initial values included, a set size effect can be explained.

$$\text{Strength of Activation of } \mathbf{g_i} = s_{0i} + \sum_{j=1}^{J_i} s(E_{ij}, T). \tag{24}$$

The crucial point to examine is the probability of classifying a negative behavior to a minority group relative to that of classifying it to a majority group. This likelihood ratio is equivalent to the strength of activation of the minority group label relative to that of the majority group label. We can then derive an equation for this likelihood ratio with some simplifying assumptions. If this ratio is greater than the ratio of the number of behaviors for the minority group to that for the majority group, we infer the presence of an illusory correlation.

Suppose that the number of positive and negative behaviors for the minority group is N_p and N_n, and that the comparable figure for the majority group is cN_p and cN_n, where c is a positive integer greater than one. Assuming that the similarity of a negative behavior to both other negative behaviors and positive behaviors to be $s(n,n)$ and $s(p,n)$, we can compute the probability of classifying a negative behavior to the minority group over that of classifying it to the majority group as follows:

$$\frac{p(\text{Minority}\,|\,\text{Negative Behavior})}{p(\text{Minority}\,|\,\text{Negative Behavior})} = \frac{s_{01} + N_n s(n,n) + N_p s(p,n)}{s_{02} + N_n s(n,n) + cN_p s(p,n)}. \tag{25}$$

If $s_{02}/s_{01} < c$, the right hand side of the above equation is greater than $1/c$. In other words, if $s_{01} = s_{02}$ roughly holds, an illusory correlation phenomenon should ensue. However, if s_{01} and s_{02} are both zero (i.e., no effect of the prior memory), there should be no illusory correlation. That is, the interference of the prior memory may be partly responsible for the illusory correlation phenomenon.

The point of this exercise is that the tensor product model suggests two types of mechanisms for the illusory correlation phenomenon. The current empirical literature suggests that the distinctiveness-based attentional process is likely to be involved in the phenomenon. TPM can accommodate this finding, and provides further insights into the operation of memory process as a potential contributor to the illusory correlation phenomenon. TPM basically provides an interference explanation, rather than an information loss explanation, of the distinctiveness-based illusory correlation.

4. CONCLUDING REMARKS

This chapter outlined the tensor product model of exemplar-based social category learning. The model postulates three subprocesses involved in group impression formation: encoding, storage, and output. An analytical distinction was made among aspect extraction, feature encoding, and representation construction in the encoding process. The model assumes distributed representations and some parallel processing capacities, and successfully integrates the existing theories and data from the judgment and classification paradigms. The model provides some further insights into the distinctiveness-based illusory correlation phenomena.

Nevertheless, it is clear that many more additional mechanisms are necessary to account for the full dynamics involved in the formation of group impressions. To this extent, the tensor product model is somewhat different from many other connectionist models; it requires many controlling mechanisms to function as a full fledged theory of human cognition. In addition, one major problem of the tensor product model as it currently stands is its inability to model the aspect extraction and feature encoding process as part inherent to the group impression formation process. The model simply assumes certain features are encoded in the experiment, and cannot describe the process of aspect extraction and feature discovery. These issues are left for future development.

All in all, the virtue of the tensor product model is its potential capacity to integrate a large number of research areas pertaining to judgment and memory. For instance, we contend that the model can be extended to cover not only the formation of group impressions, but also their change (e.g., Weber & Crocker, 1983). Given that TPM can be used to model person impression formation (Kashima & Kerekes, 1994), it may provide a general framework for modeling both person and group impression formation. More generally, the ideas of distributed representation and parallel processing of information offer new concepts with which to theorize about the social psychological process. Rather than replacing the existing theories of social cognition, we see the parallel distributed processing framework as a conceptual tool for generating further theoretical possibilities and empirical questions in the examination of the inherently dynamic social process.

REFERENCES

Anderson, J. (1972). A simple neural network generating an interactive memory. *Mathematical Biosciences, 14,* 197–220.

Anderson, J. A., Silverstein, J. W., Ritz, S. A., & Jones, R. S. (1977). Distinctive features, categorical perception, and probability learning: Some applications of a neural model. *Psychological Review, 84,* 413–451.

Anderson, N. H. (1973). Serial position curves in impression formation. *Journal of Experimental Psychology, 97,* 8–12.

Anderson, N. H. (1981). *Foundations of information integration theory.* New York: Academic Press.

Asch, S. E. (1946). Forming impressions of personality. *Journal of Abnormal and Social Psychology, 41,* 258–290.

Biernat, M., & Manis, M. (1994). Shifting standards and stereotype-based judgments. *Journal of Personality and Social Psychology, 66*, 5–20.

Biernat, M., Manis, M., & Nelson, T. E. (1991). Stereotypes and standards of judgment. *Journal of Personality and Social Psychology, 60*, 485–499.

Bruner, J. (1991). *Acts of meaning.* Cambridge, MA: Harvard University Press.

Busemeyer, J. R., & Myung, I. J. (1988). A new method for investigating prototype learning. *Journal of Experimental Psychology: Learning, Memory, and Cognition, 14*, 3–11.

Eich, J. M. (1982). A composite holographic associative recall model. *Psychological Review, 89*, 1–38.

Fiedler, K. (1991). The tricky nature of skewed frequency tables: An information loss account of distinctiveness-based illusory correlations. *Journal of Personality and Social Psychology, 60*, 24–36.

Fiedler, K. (1996). Explaining and simulating judgment biases as an aggregation phenomenon in probabilistic, multiple-cue environments. *Psychological Review, 103*, 193–214.

Fiske, S. T., & Neuberg, S. L. (1990). A continuum model of impression formation, from category-based to individuating processes: Influences of information and motivation on attention and interpretation. In M. P. Zanna (Ed.), *Advances in experimental social psychology* (Vol. 23, pp. 1–74). San Diego: Academic Press.

Foddy, M., & Smithson, M. (1989). Fuzzy sets and double standards: Modeling the process of ability inference. In J. Berger, M. Zelditch, Jr., & B. Anderson (Eds.), *Sociological theories in progress: New formulations* (pp. 73–99). Newbury Park, CA: Sage.

Ford, T. E., & Stangor, C. (1992). The role of diagnosticity in stereotype formation: Perceiving group means and variances. *Journal of Personality and Social Psychology, 63*, 356–367.

Hamilton, D. L., & Gifford, R. K. (1976). Illusory correlation in interpersonal perception: A cognitive basis of stereotypic judgments. *Journal of Experimental Social Psychology, 12*, 392–407.

Hamilton, D. L., & Sherman, J. W. (1994). Stereotypes. In R. S. Wyer, Jr., & T. K. Srull (Eds.), *Handbook of social cognition* (Vol. 2, pp. 1–68). Hillsdale, NJ: Lawrence Erlbaum Associates.

Hamilton, D. L., & Sherman, S. J. (1996). Perceiving persons and groups. *Psychological Review, 103*, 336–355.

Halford, G. S., Wilson, W. H., Guo, J., Gayler, R. W., Wiles, J., & Stewart, J. E. M. (1994). Connectionist implications for processing capacity limitations in analogies. In K. J. Holyoak, & J. A. Barnden (Eds.), *Advances in connectionist and neural computation theory* (Vol. 2, pp. 363–415). Norwood, NJ: Ablex.

Hilton, J. L., & von Hippel, W. (1996). Stereotypes. *Annual Review of Psychology, 47*, 237–271.

Hinton, G. E., & Anderson, J. A. (Eds.). (1981). *Parallel models of associative memory.* Hillsdale, NJ: Lawrence Erlbaum Associates.

Hintzman, D. L. (1986). "Schema abstraction" in a multiple-trace memory model. *Psychological Review, 93*, 411–428.

Hogarth, R. M., & Einhorn, H. J. (1992). Order effects in belief updating: The belief-adjustment model. *Cognitive Psychology, 24*, 1–55.

Humphreys, M. S., Bain, J. D., & Pike, R. (1989). Different ways to cue a coherent memory system: A theory for episodic, semantic, and procedural tasks. *Psychological Review, 2*, 208–233.

Johnson, C., & Mullen, B. (1994). Evidence for the accessibility of paired distinctiveness in distinctiveness-based illusory correlation in stereotyping. *Personality and Social Psychology Bulletin, 20*, 65–70.

Kashima, E., & Kashima, Y. (1993). Perceptions of general variability of social groups. *Social Cognition, 11*, 1–21.

Kashima, Y. (in press). Tensor product model of exemplar-based category learning. *Proceedings of Australasian Cognitive Science Society.*

Kashima, Y., & Clifford, P. (1995). [Group impression formation experiments]. Unpublished data. School of Psychology, La Trobe University.

Kashima, Y., & Kerekes, A. R. Z. (1994). A distributed memory model of averaging phenomena in person impression formation. *Journal of Experimental Social Psychology, 30*, 407–455.

Knapp, A. G., & Anderson, J. A. (1984). Theory of categorization based on distributed memory storage. *Journal of Experimental Psychology: Learning, Memory, and Cognition, 10*, 616–637.

Kohonen, T. (1988). *Self-organization and associative memory*. New York: Springer Verlag.

Komatsu, L. K. (1992). Recent views of conceptual structure. *Psychological Bulletin, 112*, 500–526.

Krueger, J., Rothbart, M., & Sriram, N. (1989). Category learning and change: Differences insensitivity to information that enhances or reduces intercategory distinctions. *Journal of Personality and Social Psychology, 56*, 866–875.

Kruschke, J. K. (1992). ALCOVE. *Psychological Review, 99*, 22–44.

Linville, P. W., & Fischer, G. W. (1993). Exemplar and abstraction models of perceived group variability and stereotypicality. *Social Cognition, 11*, 92–125.

Linville, P. W., Fischer, G. W., & Salovey, P..(1989). Perceived distributions of the characteristics of in-group and out-group members: Empirical evidence and a computer simulation. *Journal of Personality and Social Psychology, 57*, 165–188.

Luce, R. D. (1959). *Individual choice behavior*. New York: Wiley.

Lukes, S. (1973). *Individualism*. Oxford, England: Basil Blackwell.

Manis, M., & Paskerwitz, J. R. (1987). Assessing psychopathology in individuals and groups: Aggregating behavior samples to form overall impressions. *Personality and Social Psychology Bulletin, 13*, 83–94.

Massaro, D. W., & Friedman, D. (1990). Models of integration given multiple sources of information. *Psychological Review, 97*, 225–252.

McClelland, J. L., & Rumelhart, D. E. (1985). Distributed memory and the representation of general and specific information. *Journal of Experimental Psychology: General, 113*, 159–188.

McGrath, J. E. (1984). *Groups: Interaction and performance*. Englewood Cliffs, NJ: Prentice-Hall.

Medin, D. L., Altom, M. W., & Murphy, T. D. (1984). Given versus induced category representations: Use of prototype and exemplar information in classification. *Journal of Experimental Psychology: Learning, Memory and Cognition, 10*, 333–352.

Medin, D. L., Goldstone, R. L., & Gentner, D. (1993). Respects for similarity. *Psychological Review, 100*, 254–278.

Medin, D. L., & Schaffer, M. M. (1978). Context theory of classification learning. *Psychological Review, 85*, 207–238.

Mullen, B., & Johnson, C. (1990). Distinctiveness-based illusory correlations and stereotyping: A meta-analytic integration. *British Journal of Social Psychology, 29*, 11–28.

Myung, I. J., & Busemeyer, J. R. (1992). Measurement-free tests of a general state-space model of prototype learning. *Journal of Mathematical Psychology, 36*, 32–67.

Nosofsky, R. M. (1984). Choice, similarity, and the context theory of classification. *Journal of Experimental Psychology: Learning, Memory, and Cognition, 10*, 104–114.

Nosofsky, R. M. (1986). Attention, similarity, and the identification-categorisation relationship. *Journal of Experimental Psychology: General, 115*, 39–57.

Nosofsky, R. M., Kruschke, J. K., & McKinley, S. C. (1992). Combining exemplar-based category representations and connectionist learning rules. *Journal of Experimental Psychology: Learning, Memory, and Cognition, 18*, 211–233.

Nosofsky, R. M., Palmeri, T. J., & McKinley, S. C. (1994). Rule-plus-exception model of classification learning. *Psychological Review, 101*, 53–79.

Oakes, P. J., Haslam, S. A., & Turner, J. C. (1994). *Stereotyping and social reality*. Oxford, England: Basil Blackwell.

Ostrom, T. M., & Upshaw, H. S. (1968). Psychological perspective and attitude change. In A. G. Greenwald, T. C. Brock, & T. M. Ostrom (Eds.), *Psychological foundations of attitudes* (pp. 217–242). New York: Academic Press.

Park, B., & Hastie, R. (1987). Perception of variability in category development: instance- versus abstraction-based stereotypes. *Journal of Personality and Social Psychology, 53*, 621–635.

Pike, R. (1984). Comparison of convolution and matrix distributed memory systems for associative recall and recognition. *Psychological Review, 91,* 281–294.

Posner, M. I., & Keele, S. W. (1968). On the genesis of abstract ideas. *Journal of Experimental Psychology, 77,* 353–363.

Rumelhart, D. E., McClelland, J. L., & The PDP Research Group (1986). *Parallel distributed processing: Explorations in the microstructure of cognition* (Vol. 1). Cambridge, MA: Bradford Books.

Semin, G. R., & Fiedler, K. (1988). The cognitive functions of linguistic categories in describing persons: Social cognition and language. *Journal of Personality and Social Psychology, 54,* 558–567.

Semin, G. R., & Fiedler, K. (1991). The linguistic category model, its bases, applications and range. In W. Stroebe & M. Hewstone (Eds.), *European review of social psychology* (Vol. 2, pp. 1–30). London, England: Wiley.

Smith, E. R. (1991). Illusory correlation in a simulated exemplar-based memory. *Journal of Experimental Social Psychology, 27,* 107–123.

Smith, E. E., & Medin, D. L. (1981). *Categories and concepts.* Cambridge, MA: Harvard University Press.

Smith, E. R., & Zárate, M. A. (1990). Exemplar and prototype use in social categorisation. *Social Cognition, 8,* 243–262.

Smith, E. R., & Zárate, M. A. (1992). Exemplar-based model of social judgment. *Psychological Review, 99,* 3–21.

Smolensky, P. (1990). Tensor product variable binding and the representation of symbolic structures in connectionist systems. *Artificial Intelligence, 46,* 159–216.

Strange, K. R., Schwei, M., & Geiselman, R. E. (1978). Effects of the structure of descriptions on group impression formation. *Bulletin of the Psychonomic Society, 12,* 224–226.

Stroessner, S. J., Hamilton, D. L., & Mackie, D. M. (1992). Affect and stereotyping: The effect of induced mood on distinctiveness-based illusory correlations. *Journal of Personality and Social Psychology, 62,* 564–576.

Tajfel, H. (1981). *Human groups and social categories.* Cambridge, England: Cambridge University Press.

Tulving, E. (1983). *Elements of episodic memory.* New York: Oxford University Press.

Turner, J. C. (1985). Social categorization and the self-concept: A social cognitive theory of group behaviour. In E. J. Lawler (Ed.), *Advances in group processes* (Vol. 2). Greenwich, CT: JAI.

Turner, J. C. (1987). *Rediscovering the social group: A self-categorization theory.* Oxford, England: Basil Blackwell.

Tversky, A. (1977). Features of similarity. *Psychological Review, 84,* 327–352.

Upshaw, H. S. (1969). The personal reference scale: An approach to social judgment. In L. Berkowitz (Ed.), *Advances in experimental social psychology* (Vol. 14, pp. 315–371). New York: Academic Press.

Weber, R., & Crocker, J. (1983). Cognitive processes in the revision of stereotypic beliefs. *Journal of Personality and Social Psychology, 45,* 961–977.

Wolfram, S. (1991). *Mathematica: A system for doing mathematics by computer* (2nd ed.). Redwood City, CA: Addison-Wesley.

APPENDIX I

This appendix provides some technical discussion about the retrieval process and the Retrieve function (Equation 3 in text). We first prove a special case (Equation 4), and prove a general case (Equation 14).

AI.I   Special Case (Equation 4)

Suppose that the connection strengths among the three sets of units are $\mathbf{M} = g_0 e_0 x_0 + g_1 e_1 x_1$, and this memory is accessed by the cue, $\mathbf{C} = []e_1 x_1$. The retrieval function, Retrieve($\mathbf{M,C}$) returns a vector, $\mathbf{v}$, whose element is given as below (Equation 3):

$$\text{Retrieve } (\mathbf{M,C}) = \mathbf{v},$$
$$\text{where } v[a] = \sum_{b=1}\sum_{c=1} M[a,b,c]C[b,c]. \tag{3}$$

We prove that Equation 3 implies Equation 4, which is reproduced below.

$$\mathbf{v} = g_0(e_0.e_1)(x_0.x_1) + g_1(e_1.e_1)(x_1.x_1). \tag{4}$$

The tensors, $\mathbf{M}$ and $\mathbf{C}$, are defined as follows:

$$M[a,b,c] = g_0[a]e_0[b]x_0[c] + g_1[a]e_1[b]x_1[c].$$
$$C[b,c] = e_1[b]x_1[c].$$

Substituting the above into Equation 3, we obtain the following:

$$v[a] = \sum_b\sum_c g_0[a]e_0[b]e_1[b]x_0[c]x_1[c] + \sum_b\sum_c g_1[a]e_1[b]e_1[b]x_1[c]x_1[c]$$
$$= g_0[a]\sum_b(e_0[b]e_1[b])\sum_c(x_0[c]x_1[c]) + g_1[a]\sum_b(e_1[b]e_1[b])\sum_c(x_1[c]x_1[c])$$
$$= g_0[a](e_0.e_1)(x_0.x_1) + g_1[a](e_1.e_1)(x_1.x_1).$$

Q.E.D.

AI.2   General Case (Equation 14)

We prove that when

$$\mathbf{M} = \mathbf{M}_0 + \sum_{i=1}^{I}\sum_{j=1}^{J_i} g_i e_{ij1} e_{ij2} \cdots e_{ijK} x$$

$$\mathbf{T} = [\ ]t_1 t_2 \cdots t_K x,$$

assuming that $M_0 = \Sigma g_i e_{i01} e_{i02} \ldots e_{i0K} x$, Retrieve$(M,T) = v$, where

$$v = \sum_{i=1}^{I} \sum_{j=0}^{J_i} g_i (e_{ij1}.t_1) \ldots (e_{ijK}.t_K)(x.x)$$

$$= \sum_{i=1}^{I} \sum_{j=1}^{J_i} g_i [s_{0i} + \prod_{k=1}^{K} (e_{ijk}.t_k)(x.x) \quad (14)$$

Note that $s_{0i} = (e_{i01}.t_1) \ldots (e_{i0K}.t_K)(x.x)$.

Substituting Equation 8 into Equation 9, we obtain the following:

$$v[m_0] = \sum_{m_1} \ldots \sum_{m_{K+1}} M[m_0, \ldots m_{K+1}] T[m_1, \ldots m_{K+1}]$$

$$= \sum_{i=1}^{I} \sum_{j=0}^{J_i} \sum_{m_1} \ldots \sum_{m_{K+1}} (g_i[m_0] e_{ij1}[m_1] \ldots x[m_{K+1}])(t_1[m_1] \ldots x[m_{K+1}])$$

$$= \sum_{i=1}^{I} \sum_{j=0}^{J_i} \sum_{m_1} \ldots \sum_{m_{K+1}} g_i[m_0](e_{ij1}[m_1] t_1[m_1]) \ldots (x[m_{K+1}] x[m_{K+1}])$$

$$= \sum_{i=1}^{I} \sum_{j=0}^{J_i} g_i[m_0](\sum_{m_1} e_{ij1}[m_1] t_1[m_1]) \ldots (\sum_{m_{K+1}} x[m_{K+1}] x[m_{K+1}])$$

$$= \sum_{i=1}^{I} \sum_{j=0}^{J_i} g_i[m_0](e_{ij1}.t_1) \ldots (e_{ijK}.t_K)(x.x).$$

Q.E.D.

APPENDIX 2

This appendix provides technical discussion about the matching process, and the Match function (Equation 6 in text). We prove a special case (Equation 7) and a general case (Equation 11) about the use of the Match function in judgment.

A2.1 Special Case (Equation 7)

Suppose that the connection strengths among the units in the three sets are $M = g_0 e_0 x_0 + g_1 e_1 x_1$, and this memory is accessed by the cue, $C' = g_1[]x_1$ (i.e., group label and context). Let w be the pattern of activation retrieved by this operation, Retrieve(M,C'), where

$$w = (g_0.g_1)e_0(x_0.r) + (g_1.g_1)e_1(x_1.r).$$

We prove that computing the similarity between w and h, $(w.h)$, is the same as matching M and $H = g_1 h x_1$, Match(M,H) as defined in Equation 6.

$$\text{Match}(\mathbf{M}, \mathbf{H}) = \sum_a \sum_b \sum_c M[a,b,c]H[a,b,c]$$

$$= \sum \sum \sum (g_0[a]g_1[a]e_0[b]h[b]x_0[c]r[c] + g_1[a]g_1[a]e_1[b]h[b]x_1[c]r[c])$$

$$= (\sum_a g_0[a]g_1[a])(\sum_b e_0[b]h[b])(\sum_c x_0[c]r[c])$$

$$+ (\sum_a g_1[a]g_1[a])(\sum_b e_1[b]h[b])(\sum_c x_1[c]r[c])$$

$$= (\mathbf{g_0 \cdot g_1})(\mathbf{e_0 \cdot h})(\mathbf{x \cdot r}) + (\mathbf{g_1 \cdot g_1})(\mathbf{e_1 \cdot h})(\mathbf{x \cdot r})$$

$$= (\mathbf{w \cdot h})$$

Q.E.D.

A2.2 General Case (Equation 11)

Suppose the memory **M** and the matching cue **H** are given as follows:

$$\mathbf{M} = \mathbf{M_0} + \sum_i^I \sum_j^{J_i} \mathbf{g_i e_{ij1}} \dots \mathbf{e_{ijK} x}$$

$$\mathbf{H} = \mathbf{g_{i'} r} \dots \mathbf{h_{k'} r} \dots \mathbf{x}$$

where the judgment is made about the i'th group on the k'th aspect. **L** can be defined analogously. Assume that $(\mathbf{g_i \cdot g_{i'}}) = 0$ for all $i \neq i'$.

Match(**M,H**)

$$= \sum_{m_0} \dots \sum_{m_{K+1}} M_0[m_0, \dots m_{K+1}]g_{i'}[m_0]r[m_1] \dots h[m_{k'}] \dots x[m_{K+1}]$$

$$+ \sum_i \sum_j \sum_{m_0} \dots \sum_{m_{K+1}} (g_i[m_0]e_{ij1}[m_1] \dots x[m_{K+1}])(g_{i'}[m_0]r[m_1] \dots h[m_{k'}] \dots x[m_{K+1}])$$

$$= \sum_{m_0} \dots \sum_{m_{K+1}} M_0[m_0, \dots m_{K+1}]g_{i'}[m_0] \dots h[m_{k'}] \dots x[m_{K+1}]$$

$$+ \sum_i \sum_j (\sum_{m_0} g_i[m_0]g_{i'}[m_0])(\sum_{m_1} e_{ij1}[m_1]r[m_1]) \dots$$

$$\dots (\sum_{m_{k'}} e_{ijk'}[m_{k'}]h[m_{k'}]) \dots (\sum_{m_{K+1}} x[m_{K+1}]x[m_{K+1}])$$

$$= \sum_{m_0} \dots \sum_{m_{K+1}} M_0[m_0, \dots m_{K+1}]g_{i'}[m_0] \dots x[m_{K+1}]$$

$$+ \sum_i (\mathbf{g_i \cdot g_{i'}})[\sum_j^{J_i} (\mathbf{e_{ij1} \cdot r}) \dots (\mathbf{e_{ijk'} \cdot h_{k'}}) \dots (\mathbf{x \cdot x})]$$

$$= (\mathbf{g_{i'} \cdot g_{i'}}) \sum_{j=0}^{J_{i'}} (\mathbf{e_{i'jk'} \cdot h}) \prod_{k=1}^{K} (\mathbf{e_{i'jk} \cdot r})(\mathbf{x \cdot x}),$$

where it is assumed that $M_0 = g_{i'}e_{i'01}e_{i'02} \ldots e_{i'0K}x$ and that $k \neq k'$ in the last term. $Match(M,L)$ can be computed analogously.

APPENDIX 3

This appendix describes the method used to estimate the serial position weights for simulating judgment processes.

Assume that the jth serial position weight for the Jth judgment is $SPW(j,J)$, and the Jth judgment is described by the following formula:

$$R_J = \sum_{j=0}^{J} SPW(j,J)s_j$$

Suppose that there are two series with one that has a high feature at the jth position and another that has a low feature at the jth position, but they have the same features at all other positions. The difference between the Jth judgments of those two series is $(s_H - s_L)SPW(j,J)$, where s_H and s_L are scale values for high and low features, respectively. This difference score should be a linear function of $SPW(j,J)$.

We therefore used the following formula to estimate the serial position weights:

$$SPW(j,J) = \sum_{H(j) \ni i} R_{J(i)} - \sum_{L(j) \ni i} R_{J(i)},$$

where $R_{J(i)}$ refers to the Jth judgment of a series i in which i is an element in a set $H(j)$ or a set $L(j)$. The set $H(j)$ includes those series that had high features at the jth serial position, and the set $L(j)$ includes those series that had low features at the jth serial position (see Table 3.2).

4

PERSON PERCEPTION AND STEREOTYPING: SIMULATION USING DISTRIBUTED REPRESENTATIONS IN A RECURRENT CONNECTIONIST NETWORK

Eliot R. Smith
Jamie DeCoster
Purdue University

The chapters in this book illustrate that the influence of connectionism is beginning to spread from cognitive psychology (e.g., McClelland, Rumelhart, et al., 1986; Rumelhart, McClelland, et al., 1986) to social psychology. In the context of this volume, there is no need for us to outline the basic ideas of connectionist models, or to elaborate on their fundamental differences from the symbolic models that have been traditional in both cognitive and social psychology (see Churchland & Sejnowski, 1992; Clark, 1993; or Smith, 1996 for accessible introductory treatments). These fundamental differences have inspired much excitement, with connectionist models viewed as "cataly[zing] a more fruitful conception of the whole project of cognitive science" (Clark, 1993, p. ix), as spurring a scientific revolution as significant as the transition from behaviorism to information-processing psychology (Schneider, 1987), and even as "requir[ing] a major reorientation in the way we think about ourselves" (Ramsey, Stich, & Garon, 1991, p. 200).

Now, it has become evident to many social psychologists that connectionist models of language processing, categorization, schema use, memory, and decision making have direct relevance to their own central concern. This chapter aims to further explore this relevance, concentrating on the area of person perception and social stereotyping. We focus on two goals. First, we present results of computer simulations applying a recurrent connectionist network model to key findings involving person perception and stereotyping. Second, we attempt to put these results in context, comparing our model to other connectionist work in social psychology—particularly the localist parallel constraint satisfaction models that are well-represented in this volume. We conclude by discussing central issues for further research.

SIMULATIONS: METHOD AND RESULTS

Our model and simulation results can be only briefly described in this chapter; a full report is in Smith and DeCoster (in press). The specific connectionist model we are using was developed by McClelland and Rumelhart (1986), and is portrayed in Fig. 4.1. Individual units do not represent an object or concept; instead, this network uses distributed representations in which a pattern of activation across the entire set of units represents a meaningful concept. The workings of the network are described in more detail later. However, as a brief overview, the figure shows that each unit receives input from the environment as well as from other units in the network. Thus, when a pattern of activation representing an input stimulus enters the network, it initiates processing and causes activation to flow along the connections between units. This processing alters the pattern of activation, and after some time, the resulting output pattern becomes available for further processing in other network modules. This is a recurrent network, which means that units send activation to each other and are able to exert reciprocal influences, in contrast to a feedforward network in which activation flows unidirectionally from input to output. In recurrent networks, flows

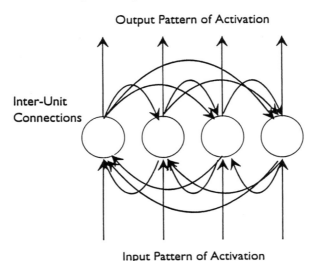

FIG. 4.1. Recurrent connectionist model.

of activation set up by the presentation of an input activation pattern may show various forms of dynamic behavior, including periodic oscillation, chaotic behavior, or—the behavior typical of the McClelland and Rumelhart network—settling to a final state.

We adopt this particular recurrent network because it displays useful behaviors, which can be described as pattern learning, pattern completion, memory reconstruction, or schematic processing. Specifically, as it processes a number of input patterns, the network's connection weights change in a way that encodes information about the patterns. After a pattern has been repeatedly encountered, a set of input cues that resemble the pattern but with some units omitted or some random noise added can elicit the reconstruction of the original pattern on the outputs. This reconstruction is accomplished by the connections between units; if an input pattern has zero or incorrect values of activation for some units, the flows of activation from other units within the network may still give the problematic units approximately correct activation values and thus reinstate the original pattern. This entire process could be described as involving the learning of patterns, and their reconstruction on the basis of partial cues. More broadly, we could say that the network has the ability to form expectations about regularities in its inputs, and to use that knowledge, in addition to the actual input pattern, to make inferences. In many current theories in social cognition, this is termed "schematic processing."

In terms of its place in an overall social-cognitive system, we believe that networks of this type play a role in preconscious conceptual interpretation. The inputs to this module could come either from relatively unprocessed sensory inputs, or from other modules that perform prior processing (see McClelland & Rumelhart, 1986). The outputs of this module, presumably after much additional processing in other modules, help constitute the individual's conscious experience. We do not model the relations of this network's processing to explicit conscious reasoning or inference; see Smolensky (1988) for an extensive account of one possible version of this interface. In recent years, social cognition theorists have heavily emphasized automatic and preconscious processes of the sort that we intend this model to capture (see Banaji & Greenwald, 1994; Bargh, 1994; Higgins, 1996).

Target Phenomena for Simulations

Computer simulations can be conducted in two different ways. For one, the investigator can select a single crucial experiment, usually incorporating many conditions, and try to simulate the empirical data patterns in precise quantitative detail (e.g., McClelland & Rumelhart, 1986). This approach can be valuable if a single experiment exists whose conditions incorporate all the processes of interest to the model, and if the limitations on generality that are inherent to any single study or research paradigm are accepted.

We take the alternative approach: We select robust and well-replicated data patterns from literature, and use the simulation to qualitatively reproduce the data patterns (as in Smith, 1991). This approach has the advantage of generality: If successful, it means that the simulation will capture some major themes in the empirical literature rather than the specific quantitative results of a single experiment. In addition, no one study (to our knowledge) adequately represents all the processes we want to simulate. We target four phenomena, relatively uncontroversial generalizations that are widely represented in textbooks and reviews (Fiske & Taylor, 1991; Wyer & Srull, 1994).

1. People can learn the idiosyncratic characteristics of a specific well-known person; they can apply this knowledge to make inferences about unobserved chararacteristics of a new exemplar (Andersen & Cole, 1990; Lewicki, 1985). (Here and throughout this chapter, these characteristics could be thought of as including personality traits, aspects of physical appearance, behaviors, etc.)

2. People can learn a "group stereotype" or a specific pattern of characteristics from exposure to members of a group; they can apply this knowledge to make inferences about unobserved traits of a new exemplar of the group (Hamilton & Sherman, 1994).

3. People can simultaneously learn multiple knowledge structures; they can apply them in combination to infer new, emergent characteristics of a new exemplar that combines features of several existing categories (Hastie, Schroeder, & Weber, 1990; Kunda, Miller, & Claire, 1990).

4. Recently or frequently encountered patterns will have a bigger impact on future inferences; this is the principle of accessibility (Higgins, 1996). Also, patterns encountered in spaced rather than massed fashion will have a bigger impact on future inferences (Hintzman, 1976); we treat this as an extension of the principle of accessibility.

Details of the Model

We used the autoassociative model discussed in McClelland and Rumelhart (1986) for our simulations in the implementation provided in the Stuttgart Neural Network Simulator[1] (Zell et al., 1994). The network for all our simulations has 40 units interconnected as shown in Fig. 4.1. (The number of units is an arbitrary choice that reflects our available computational resources.) Our fundamental representational assumption is that a person, social group, or other social object is represented by a distributed pattern of activation across these units (Thorpe, 1995; Touretzky, 1995). Conse-

---

[1]This simulator runs on a wide range of UNIX systems and is available at URL ftp://ftp.informatik.uni-stuttgart.de/pub/SNNS.

quently, individual units are not specifically associated with particular concepts and have no meaningful semantic interpretation. However, we do assume that semantically similar concepts are represented by similar patterns of activations across the units (Clark, 1993).

In this model, processing a stimulus occurs in two phases. During the first phase, the pattern applied to the network's external inputs activates the units. Because the units are linked, activation flows within the network so that each unit influences others. The final output pattern will depend not only on the external stimulus but also on the strengths of the interunit connections, which depend on the network's learning history. Although theoretically this process occurs in continuous time, our computer package simulates it as a series of discrete time steps. At first, the activation of units in the network will change significantly during each time step. Assuming the inputs are held constant, however, the unit activations will eventually converge to a particular pattern that represents the network's output. This pattern could be interpreted as an "impression" of the current stimulus. In this way, the autoassociator combines input information with information derived from past experiences. If a stimulus is somehow incongruent with its past training, the output pattern will be modified so that it better matches the prior experiences. The network can use its experience to correct for possible perceptual errors as well as to fill in unobserved details.

The second phase involves learning. The connection weights are modified according to the learning rule, based on the final pattern of activation. This in effect lets the network store information about its final impression based on the input, which may in turn influence the way future inputs are processed. The learning rule is intended to let the network output a complete known pattern when provided with only part of the original pattern as an input. This means that units have to "remember" how their activation levels have generally been associated with the activation of other units in the network so that each unit can reconstruct an appropriate activation level when the network receives incomplete inputs. Each unit in an autoassociator is therefore linked to every other unit in the network (see Fig. 4.1). Activation spreads across these links so that units not receiving input from the stimulus can still become active. Thus each unit receives "internal" inputs from other units in the network as well as its "external" input from outside.

The learning process results in positive connection weights between units that are generally concurrently active, negative weights between units that tend to be active at different times, and near-zero weights between units whose activations are uncorrelated. Loosely, the connection strengths reflect the covariation of the pair of units (though not in the familiar statistical sense; for example, the weights in both directions between a pair of units are generally not equal). Researchers have developed several different learning rules to accomplish this (Hebb, 1949; McClelland & Rumelhart, 1986). Typically, the weight between two units is increased whenever the network observes a pattern where both units are active at the same time and decreased whenever the network observes a pattern where one is active and the other is not.

Mathematically, every unit i in the network receives internal input int_i which is the sum of activation flowing to i from all other units in the network. The input to unit i from unit j is the product of j's activation a_j and the weight w_{ji} of the link from unit j to unit i. Units have no links to themselves; all w_{ii} = 0. The activation of a unit can range from -1 to 1, and the connection weight can be any real value. If the product of unit j's activation and the weight on the connection from j to i is positive it represents an excitatory influence on unit i; if negative, an inhibitory influence. The total internal input for unit i is $int_i = \Sigma_j(a_j * w_{ji})$. The net input N_i for a unit i is the sum of its internal input int_i and the external input ext_i it receives directly from the stimulus pattern: $N_i = int_i + ext_i$. The change in activation for unit i during a processing cycle is determined by the following equations:

$$\Delta a_i = E * N_i * (1 - a_i) - D * a_i \quad \text{if } N_i > 0$$
$$\Delta a_i = E * N_i * (a_i + 1) - D * a_i \quad \text{if } N_i \leq 0$$

Units whose total input is negative tend to decrease their activation whereas those that receive a net positive input tend to increase their activation. The second term in the equations causes the unit activation to naturally decay toward zero. Units with larger activation magnitudes experience greater decay. E and D are global parameters that set the rates of excitation and decay. In our simulations, both of these parameters were fixed at .15. The terms $(1 - a_i)$ and $(a_i + 1)$ act to shunt the excitation, making it more difficult to excite units that have activations close to +1 and more difficult to inhibit units that have activations close to -1. These terms also constrain the activations to the range of -1 to +1. The network is allowed to propagate its activation for 50 processing cycles so that it may develop a stable interpretation of the input. The number 50 is arbitrary, chosen to be much greater than the number of cycles required for the activation pattern to stabilize.

The autoassociator next enters the learning phase, where it modifies its weights to store information about the observed stimulus. We want the network to modify the connection weights so that the summed internal input for each unit predicts the external input as well as possible. The error in this prediction is just the difference between the internal and external inputs for each unit, $\delta_i = ext_i - int_i$.

If this error δ_i is positive, it means that unit i is not receiving enough internal input. If the error is negative, it means that the unit is receiving too much internal input. Thus, the weights are changed by an increment calculated as $\Delta w_{ji} = \eta * \delta_i * a_j$ where η is a global parameter that determines how fast the network learns (fixed at a value of .01 in our simulation runs; see McClelland & Rumelhart, 1988, p. 182), and a_j is the activation of the "sending" unit. This method of altering the weights, called the "delta rule," will cause the weights to take on values so that the internal input approximates the external input for each unit. The internal flows of activation will now allow the network to reinstantiate this pattern even if the input is incomplete. It will also influence the interpretation of future inputs to the extent that they are similar to the observed stimulus pattern, in an automatic generalization process (see Clark, 1993). This indicates that the network has "learned" from this exposure. If the network is exposed to a number of patterns, the sum of these changes will make the connection weights reflect the between-unit covariations that exist in the set of stimuli.

In summary, this recurrent network can show several types of behavior that seem familiar. It can "store" patterns that it processes. It can "abstract" an average or summary of a number of similar patterns because their similarities will produce mutually reinforcing weight changes whereas random differences will produce weight changes that cancel out. The network can then "retrieve" a stored pattern or summary by reinstating it on the outputs given an appropriate set of input cues. It is important to recognize that the network does all these things without any explicit processes of summarizing or averaging input information, constructing representations and storing them as discrete entities, searching among the stored representations, or selecting one to be retrieved and used. These ideas are so familiar as metaphors for memory that it is very difficult for us to think of memory as other than a warehouse filled with separate representations that we search and retrieve. Yet, the functions these metaphorical terms describe can be performed by mechanisms that involve flows of activation among simple interconnected units (Smith, in press). This is one of the most fundamental new insights that differentiates connectionist models from traditional symbolic models.

Simulation Design

We wanted the design of our simulations to capture the conceptual features of the empirical phenomena as well as possible. In a typical person memory experiment, research participants enter with a store of background knowledge (such as group stereotypes), and they may learn additional relevant information in the experiment itself. They are then exposed to a set of social stimuli and report their memory or judgments concerning those stimuli. Therefore, for each simulated topic we built a set of stimulus patterns to represent the subject's pre-experimental knowledge as well as any learning that takes place in the experiment, and had the autoassociative network learn these patterns. We then presented the network with test stimuli representing those used in the experiment to elicit memory reports or social judgments, and recorded the network's output. The specific characteristics of each stimulus set were chosen to conceptually reproduce the experiences of the human participants in the experimental paradigm we were trying to simulate. The specific constraints of each stimulus set are presented later in our discussion of each simulated topic.

In real life, people cannot neatly define those they meet as possessing specific quantities of individual traits or other characteristics. Situational variables as well as our internal states can influence the way we perceive others. Our perceptions, therefore, vary with the presence or absence of these factors. If we wish to generalize from our model to human behavior, we should show that the model reproduces known data patterns not only when stimuli are clear and error-free, but also when variability is included in the stimuli. We therefore added some element of noise, quantitative random variation, to all of our stimulus patterns. The inclusion of random variation means that we cannot run the simulation program a single time and declare that its output represents *the* prediction of the model. To obtain a statistically reliable data pattern, we must average over the results of several independent simulation runs, each with a new set of stimuli that satisfy the constraints for the experiment but that have new random values added. The simulation output with each such stimulus set corresponds conceptually to the responses of an individual research participant in a standard experiment. Correspondingly, we applied standard statistical techniques, such as *t* tests and correlations, to analyze the simulation results.

Simulation 1: Exemplar-Based Inference

Inferences about a newly encountered person can be based on the perceived characteristics of a specific well-known individual. Research by Susan Andersen and her colleagues (e.g., Andersen & Cole, 1990) and by Lewicki (1985) showed that exemplar-based knowledge can affect inferences about newly encountered persons who resemble their significant others in some way. For example, if I have lunch with my uncle who is balding and has a good sense of humor, I might intuitively expect the next balding man I meet to have a good sense of humor as well.

Method. We simulated 10 subjects and exposed each to 1,200 patterns. One thousand were used to represent background knowledge about "people in general" and had all of their characteristics normally distributed with a mean of zero and standard deviation of 0.5, henceforth abbreviated N(0, .5). The remaining 200 patterns were copies of a single exemplar, whose characteristics were randomly drawn from an N(0, .5) distribution. These copies of the exemplar were presented without variation. Though we certainly do not want to claim that the simulation quantitatively reproduces any real-life situation, the presentation of 200 copies of an exemplar was intended to reflect the large number of encounters that people have with their close relationship partners. The presentation order of the 1,200 patterns was determined randomly for each subject.

We tested the network's memory for the exemplar by presenting it with a pattern corresponding to an incomplete version of the exemplar—representing a new individual who resembled the known exemplar. This test pattern had 35 of the original exemplar's values with the other 5 set to zero. We then correlated the values instantiated by the network's output on the 5 omitted units with the corresponding values from the original exemplar.

Results. The mean correlation on the five critical units between the network's output values and the original exemplar pattern was .828. This differs significantly from zero ($t(9) = 26.37$, $p < .0001$).

Discussion. This simulation shows that the network can learn a pattern from multiple presentations. When a new input pattern is similar to the learned one, the network uses its stored knowledge to fill in unobserved parts of the pattern. Conceptually, this process could account for exemplar-based inference in person perception (e.g., Andersen & Cole, 1990).

Simulation 2: Group-Based Stereotyping

A stereotype is defined as a representation of a number of attributes associated with a particular group membership, learned through experience with individual group members or from social learning. The stereotype affects inferences about new group members. Stereotyping research (see Hamilton & Sherman, 1994) typically examines issues of stereotype content and representation, as well as the processes involved in the application of stereotypes in person perception. Our simulation broadens the focus to include the process by which a stereotype is learned, as well stereotype representation and use. In common with other exemplar-based models of stereotype acquisition (e.g., Smith & Zárate, 1992), we assume that stereotypes form when perceivers encounter a number of group members possessing specific characteristics that are perceived to differ from "the average person." These encounters could reflect everyday interactions with real people, biased media portrayals, or social learning from others.

Method. We simulated 10 subjects and exposed each to 1,200 patterns. One thousand were used to represent general background knowledge about people and had all of their characteristics distributed N(0, .5). The remaining

200 were constructed to represent some members of a particular group, with activation patterns that differed systematically from others on 12 units. These 200 patterns had six characteristics distributed N(.5, .5), six characteristics distributed N(−.5, .5), and the remaining 28 characteristics distributed N(0, .5). The presentation order of the 1,200 patterns was determined randomly for each subject. Note that these patterns did not include a single attribute representing "group membership." Instead, we assumed that a distributed pattern of activation represents a number of correlated attributes (such as aspects of physical appearance) that together are cues to group membership, along with other attributes (such as traits) that are perceived to be typical of group members.

After exposure to these patterns, we tested the network's use of the stereotype by presenting it with an incomplete version of the stereotype pattern, containing just 7 of the 12 distinctive units (with the others set to zero), to see if it would infer the group-typical pattern for the 5 missing characteristics.

Results. The activation values across these 5 units were correlated with the group average values (either .5 or −.5 for each characteristic). The value of this correlation, averaged across the 10 simulated subjects, was .647, which is reliably different from 0, $t(9) = 10.54$, $p < .0001$. Thus, the network did complete the pattern, inferring that a new individual who had some features that defined him or her as a member of the stereotyped group has the other aspects of the learned stereotype.

Discussion. This simulation shows that the network learning rule, which extracts information about the input patterns and represents it in the connection weights, can reproduce stereotyping effects. Learned connections among units come to store information about the group-typical patterns, and flows of activation give rise to inferences about new group members. The difference between this simulation and the previous one (exemplar-based inference) is that in this case, the typical pattern was abstracted from many group members that incorporated some variability, whereas for exemplar-based inferences, the pattern was learned from multiple presentations of an unchanged exemplar.

The most important implication of these two simulations considered together is that a common mechanism can account for seemingly disparate phenomena: exemplar-based inference and group-based stereotyping. Existing theories in social cognition generally postulate that these rest on fundamentally different representational formats, such as abstract group-trait associations for stereotypes and more concrete and complex "personalized" representations for specific individuals. Existing theories also face difficult questions such as when to use each type of knowledge representation, which type has priority when they conflict, and so forth (see Kunda & Thagard, 1996; Smith & Zárate, 1992). In contrast, the current model is parsimonious: These simulations show that a common mechanism can reproduce both types of effects. This is because the learning rule can abstract general regularities (e.g., perceived communalities among group members) and ignore random variation, while also preserving specific details about oft-encountered patterns. Other connectionist theorists have similarly emphasized the benefits of a single mechanism that can handle behaviors that seem, on the surface, to involve separate processes using "rules" and "exceptions" (e.g., Seidenberg, 1993).

Simulation 3: Emergent Attributes From Combining Knowledge Structures

Conventional theories of impression formation (e.g., Brewer, 1988; Fiske & Neuberg, 1990; Wyer & Srull, 1989) claim that at least under normal or default processing conditions, perceivers search for a single schema, stereotype, or knowledge structure in memory that fits available information about a target person. The schema is then used to direct the search for further information, to make inferences, and to derive affective and evaluative responses. Recent research demonstrated, however, that people are able to use many sources of knowledge in parallel (Kunda & Thagard, 1996). They can even combine two or more schemata or stereotypes in creative ways, often producing emergent characteristics not present in the input or in any pattern that directly matches the input. For example, a Harvard-educated carpenter might be assumed to be "nonmaterialistic," an attribute that is not highly salient in either the Harvard or carpenter stereotypes (Asch & Zukier, 1984; Hastie et al., 1990; Kunda et al., 1990). Such emergent attributes are difficult to explain from the perspective of a schema theory in which the preferred mode of processing is to fit a single schema to each input. However, they can be accounted for by other types of connectionist models (see Miller & Read, 1991; Read & Marcus-Newhall, 1993). We wished to establish whether our recurrent network could learn multiple knowledge representations and apply them simultaneously to produce such emergent properties.

Method. The design of the stereotypes used in this simulation may be thought of as follows. Three stereotypes, each including three conceptual attributes, are learned by the network:

Stereotype 1: A B C
Stereotype 2: D E F
Stereotype 3: C F G

Given a stimulus pattern A B D E, a model that applied only a single knowledge structure to interpret new input would either activate Stereotype 1 and infer attribute C, or activate Stereotype 2 and infer F. Perhaps a more flexible model might activate both of these stereotypes and infer both C and F. With our model, however, we wanted to test whether the network would be able to draw on *all* of its knowledge—including Stereotype 3, which has no overlap with the stimulus input—to infer attribute G as well. In other words, Stereotype 1 permits an inferential link between A and B in the input and C; Stereotype 2 permits an inference of F from D and E; and Stereotype 3 permits an inference of G from C and F. With all three stereotypes represented in the same set of interunit connections, can the network allow all three to affect the processing of the new input stimulus simultaneously?

To implement this design, we simulated 10 subjects and exposed each to 1,600 patterns in a random order. One thousand were used to form a general background and had all of their characteristics distributed $N(0, .5)$. Two hundred patterns represented each of the three stereotypes. A distributed representation was used, with each of the abstract attributes (represented by a letter in the descriptions above) represented by a specific pattern of positive and negative activation levels across a given set of three units. Thus, the "prototype" pattern for each stereotype had nine units with values of $+.5$ or $-.5$ (corresponding to the three letters), as well as 31 units with zero values. The 200 patterns actually presented to the network were constructed by adding random noise with a standard deviation of .5 to each unit of this prototype. As in the abstract specification described earlier, the characteristics of the first two stereotypes did not overlap, but the pattern for the third stereotype overlapped with each of the first two stereotypes (on those units corresponding to C and F), and also had three unique units with nonzero mean values (i.e., the units corresponding to G).

Results. The network was tested with a stimulus containing the 12 units corresponding to the letters A, B, D, E set to nonzero values (the other 28 were set to zero). We examined the network's output for the unique pattern of activation corresponding to the letter G of the third stereotype. The three units in this pattern were significantly different from zero in the correct directions, $t(9) > 2.4$, $p < .05$ in all three cases. In other words, the network activated the specific pattern corresponding to attribute G.

Discussion. First, this simulation shows that more than one pattern can be simultaneously represented in the network and used to make inferences. In contrast, the two earlier simulations only required the storage of a single pattern. The information in all three stereotypes is maintained in distributed form in the connection weights (van Gelder, 1991), rather than being represented in discrete parcels or chunks that have to be independently retrieved, as assumed in current social psychological theories.

Second, the results show that the network successfully inferred from the input pattern the sub pattern of three characteristics corresponding to the letter G. These characteristics do not appear either in the input stimulus or in Stereotypes 1 and 2. Thus, the network must have activated the first two stored patterns (stereotypes) to infer characteristics C and F for the given input, and also used the third stereotype to infer these three characteristics corresponding to G. The third stereotype had no overlap with the test input stimulus, but was activated as a result of the network's processing. However, this description does not imply that processing is sequential (i.e., first activate Stereotypes 1 and 2 and then Stereotype 3), for all stored knowledge (encoded in the connection weights) actually has effects simultaneously in the network.

In terms of our example, the performance demonstrated by this network could yield the emergent attribute of nonmaterialistic for the Harvard-carpenter stereotype combination. Say Stereotype 1 represents the Harvard stereotype, with attribute C meaning something like "qualified for a high-paying occupation." Stereotype 2 represents carpenter, with attribute F representing "low paid." Stereotype 3 could represent a general knowledge structure stating that if a person is qualified for a high-paying occupation (C) and is low paid (F) it might be because he or she is nonmaterialistic (G). As this simulation shows, activation of the first two stereotypes by other cues besides C and F may, over time, result in the activation of G through the simultaneous use of all three of these knowledge structures.

Simulation 4: Accessibility From Recency, Frequency, and Spacing of Past Exposures

Learned knowledge structures (such as concepts, exemplars, or schemata) generally have larger effects on the interpretation of input information when they have been frequently or recently processed. In social cognition, this property, termed *accessibility* (Higgins, 1996), has been applied to an exceptionally wide range of issues. This simulation is intended to determine whether the connectionist network can not only store and retrieve patterns (as shown by the previous simulations) but also maintain representations of patterns with varying levels of accessibility, qualitatively matching the effects of recent and frequent exposure demonstrated by social-psychological research. In addition, research on memory has obtained a robust finding that when items are studied repeatedly, memory is superior when the presentations of a given item are spaced (separated by presentations of other items) rather than massed (presented sequentially; Hintzman, 1976). This spacing effect is conceptually related to the effects of recency and frequency on accessibility, though it is typically not referenced in the social literature on accessibility.

Method. We simulated a total of 160 subjects per condition for this topic. (The larger number of subjects is due to our desire to find statistically reliable results for all of our conditions, even those not particularly conducive to memory.) Each simulated subject was exposed to a total of 1,000 patterns. The exact makeup of these patterns differed across six conditions. Each set of patterns included multiple copies of a particular exemplar, interspersed among a large number of background patterns. The value of each characteristic in the exemplar was independently drawn from an $N(0, .5)$ distribution. The same exemplar was used in all simulations, and was presented without variation. The general background patterns had all of their characteristics drawn from an $N(0, .5)$ distribution. The number and order of presentation varied across conditions, as described in Table 4.1.

As the table shows, recency was manipulated by presenting the exemplar patterns either centered around position 300 or at the end of the stimulus sequence. Frequency was manipulated by presenting either 50 or 200 copies of the exemplar. The specific values used for both of these manipulations were arbitrarily chosen. We tested each network's memory for the exemplar by presenting it with an incomplete version of the exemplar (containing 35 units) and then correlating the network's output on the remaining 5 units with the original exemplar pattern.

TABLE 4.1
Description of Conditions Used in Simulation 4

Condition	Description	Sequence of Presentations
1	Neither recent nor frequent	275 background patterns 50 copies of exemplar 675 background patterns
2	Recent, not frequent	950 background patterns 50 copies of exemplar
3	Frequent, not recent	200 background patterns 200 copies of exemplar 600 background patterns
4	Recent and frequent	800 background patterns 200 copies of exemplar
5	Not recent, frequent spaced	300 background patterns randomly mixed with 200 copies of the exemplar 500 background patterns
6	Recent, frequent spaced	500 background patterns 300 background patterns randomly mixed with 200 copies of the exemplar

Results and Discussion. The mean r-to-z transformed correlations are graphed in Fig. 4.2. The transformation was used because comparisons among conditions (not simply a mean difference from zero) were important in this simulation. T tests comparing each condition's mean separately against a mean of zero, the expected value if no instances of the specific exemplar had ever been encountered, were significant in all conditions except the first, which was $p < .06$.

All six conditions yielded results in the predicted direction, although as expected, the effect in the not recent, not frequent condition is small (marginally significant with 160 simulated subjects). The more important results involved comparisons among conditions, based on t tests on the r-to-z-transformed correlations. All comparisons discussed here were significant at $p < .05$ unless indicated otherwise. Recency had a clear and strong effect on the magnitude of accessibility, demonstrated by comparing Condition 2 versus 1 (effect of recency with only 50 exposures) and also 4 versus 3 (recency with 200 exposures).

Frequency also had an effect, although a smaller one; compare Condition 3 versus 1 (effect of 200 vs. 50 nonrecent exposures; this comparison was nonsignificant but in the expected direction) and 4 versus 2 (effect of 200 vs. 50 recent exposures). One cannot conclude that the model *generally* predicts that frequency effects will be smaller than recency effects, for the specific effect sizes depend, of course, on such arbitrary details as the use of 200 versus 50 exposures and the placement of nonrecent exposures centered at position 300 in the sequence. In general, the simulation results show that the model qualitatively matches patterns of accessibility found with human subjects: Both recency and frequency increase accessibility. The connectionist network is not only able to store representations of patterns, but also to maintain representations at appropriately varying levels of accessibility depending on the specific history of stimulus exposures.

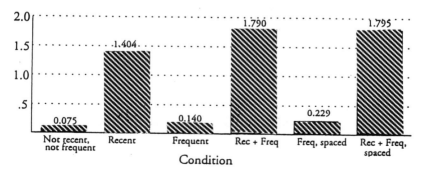

FIG. 4.2. Results of Simulation 4: Accessibility effects. Mean r-to-z transformed correlation (higher value means more accessibility).

Spaced exposures produce more accessibility than massed exposures, in the model as in human experiments. Comparing Condition 5 (not recent, frequent spaced) to 3 (not recent, frequent massed) shows a significant difference in favor of spaced exposures. What is most impressive is that the recent, frequent spaced Condition 6 results in virtually the same accessibility level as the recent, frequent massed Condition 4 (1.795 vs. 1.790), despite the fact that the latter condition involved exposure of the specific exemplar on every one of the 200 most recent trials. In this comparison, spacing of the exposures is pitted against recency because spacing exposures out from a condition in which they are the last 200 necessarily moves some to less recent positions. Still, the spacing effect produces virtually equal accessibility for the target pattern.

Why does the spacing effect occur? Our network, like most connectionist models, uses error-driven learning. Connection weights are modified (that is, learning takes place) in an amount and direction that is a function of the error or difference between the network's current performance and the desired performance. Error-driven learning produces spacing effects because when presentations of a given stimulus are massed, the initial exposures change the weights so that the error is reduced to near zero, and then further presentations have little or no effect on the weights. In contrast, when presentations are spaced, the weight changes induced by exposures to other, unrelated patterns intervene between trials with the specific pattern of interest. Thus, weight changes in the direction of recording a representation of that pattern continue to be made, for the error on that pattern is less likely to approach zero. Paradoxically, then, poorer performance during learning (in the sense that the error in reproducing the target pattern does not reach zero) means better performance at test (greater accessibility of that pattern). This seeming paradox is a general feature of error-driven learners (see Clark, 1993 for discussion).

As these simulations suggest, the effects of spacing versus massing can be considered in a common framework with the effects of recency and frequency of exposure, which are more often dealt with in the social-psychological literature on accessibility (Higgins, 1996). All of these involve the effects of the temporal history of exposures to a specific stimulus on the stimulus pattern's current potential for activation given appropriate cues. Recent, frequent, and well-spaced exposures result in the highest activation potential. It is important to recognize that in this model, accessibility is not explained as some extra property (such as position in a storage bin or charge on a storage battery) added on to discrete representational entities. In fact, this model does not have any discrete representations in the first place. The relative accessibilities of *all* the patterns known to the network, in the sense of their respective potentials for activation, are an emergent property determined by the entire set of connection weights. The weights influence the rapidity and precision with which a pattern appears on the output as activation flows throughout the network given a related set of input cues. Processing a given pattern changes the weights (through the learning rule) in the direction of making that pattern and similar ones a bit easier to activate. Simultaneously, unrelated patterns become a bit harder to activate, because from their perspective, random noise is being added to the weights. In this way, the connectionist framework uses an extremely simple and general mechanism to qualitatively reproduce the known aspects of accessibility effects, as well as including spacing effects within the same framework.

DISCUSSION AND CONCLUSIONS

Summary of Simulation Results

The connectionist model qualitatively reproduces

- effects of a frequently encountered exemplar on inferences,
- effects of a group stereotype learned from varying group exemplars,
- simultaneous use of multiple learned representations (rather than just one) to make inferences, and
- effects of recency, frequency, and spacing on accessibility.

Traditional theories in social cognition can also explain each of these phenomena. But to do so, they employ several distinct types of mechanisms, including a schematic abstraction process that produces generic schemata or group prototypes and uses them to make inferences, an exemplar storage and retrieval process, and a special-purpose mechanism attached to each distinct representation to track its current level of accessibility. This recurrent connectionist network is able to simulate all these phenomena using only a single mechanism. The model thus avoids difficult questions that tend to remain unanswered in traditional models, such as the question of when to stop storing individual exemplars and engage in an abstraction process instead; and whether to use a group stereotype or a well-known exemplar as a basis for inferences. In addition, the model's account of the learning of representations such as stereotypes is more precise and explicit than current accounts in social cognition, which tend to neglect learning altogether.

The model uses the dynamics of activation flows in a recurrent network to reproduce these phenomena. The network's connections allow units to affect each other (as well as to be influenced by the inputs) and the overall pattern of activity gradually settles into a stable state representing the network's interpretation of the input based on its past experiences. This method of computation can be viewed as finding a solution to many constraints in parallel, where the constraints arise jointly from the input and from stored knowledge. As Rumelhart, Smolensky, McClelland, and Hinton (1986) argued, this approach is a powerful one that incorporates most of the functions typically attributed to schematic knowledge structures. However, in this view

> schemata are not "things." There is no representational object which is a schema. Rather, schemata emerge at the moment they are needed from the interaction of large numbers of much simpler elements all working in concert with one another. Schemata are not explicit entities, but rather are implicit in our knowledge and are created by the very environment that they are trying to interpret. (p. 20)

McClelland and Rumelhart (1986) demonstrated that this network is also able to reproduce several findings in the memory literature, such as repetition priming effects, effects of familiarity on response latency, and effects of exemplar exposures on perceptual identification performance. Thus, the model serves the purpose of theoretical integration, offering a single account for a diversity of findings that have typically been attributed to separate mechanisms. In comparison to current social cognition models, such as that of Wyer and Srull (1989), it also offers a considerable advantage in precision and simplicity. Finally, the model also makes several new predictions for which there is preliminary empirical evidence but that are not part of other current models of knowledge representation. These predictions are detailed in Smith and DeCoster (in press). For example, the model suggests that psychological causation will generally be bidirectional (e.g., if one belief or attitude can cause a second, the second probably causes the first as well).

Limitations of the Network

Besides its strengths, this extremely simple connectionist model has some stringent limitations. In particular, as McClelland and Rumelhart (1986) pointed out, the model can learn a set of patterns perfectly only if across the entire set of input patterns, the external input to each unit can be perfectly predicted by a linear combination of the activations of all other units. We believe, however, that perfect reproduction of learned patterns is not an appropriate goal for a network intended as a model of human memory performance. People cannot remember perfectly; they blend separate memories and display interference from related knowledge even when they are trying to retrieve a specific memory exactly. For example, they may remember only the general characteristics of a group rather than the detailed features of each individual exemplar.

In addition, modifications to the model can overcome this constraint on pattern learning. Preprocessing of the inputs by other networks can help: If the input features presented to the network reflect context-sensitive encodings of more basic features, the linearity constraint can be bypassed. Another approach is the incorporation of so-called "hidden units," units without direct connections to the network's inputs or outputs. These can allow the network to develop its own representations of meaningful features. Without hidden units, the network is limited to a fixed set of features (corresponding to the network's inputs) from which to construct distributed representations. But hidden units allow the development of features that are flexible and sensitive to the patterning of the inputs in a particular stimulus set, allowing the network to escape the linearity constraint (McClelland & Rumelhart, 1986).

Another significant limitation is that this model is intended only to account for preconscious "schematic" interpretive processing, modifying and filling out input cues based on previous experience. It does not incorporate any mechanisms for conscious or controlled processing. Thus, we would not expect this network to be able to simulate the recall advantage of expectation-inconsistent over expectation-consistent information demonstrated by Hastie and Kumar (1979) and many other studies. Nor would we expect to be able to simulate the contrast effects that occur under some circumstances when a particular representation is "primed" (made accessible) and then ambiguously related information is presented (Martin, Seta, & Crelia, 1990). This is because both of these effects are thought, on the basis of solid evidence, to depend on effortful conscious processing, which is not incorporated in our current simulation (Kunda & Thagard, 1996, described a similar limitation of their model). This is not to say that connectionist models will never be able to address controlled processing; see Smolensky (1988) for a detailed proposal and Smith (1996) for further discussion of the issue.

Relations to Other Parallel Constraint Satisfaction Models

Local Versus Distributed Representations. Fundamental assumptions about representation constitute one of the greatest differences between connectionist networks of the type described here and the semantic networks or "associative networks" that have typically been used in social cognition to model person perception (e.g., Hamilton, Katz, & Leirer, 1980; Hastie, 1988). The latter models rely on local representations, where each semantically meaningful item stored in memory is represented by its own node. In a distributed representation, however, a stimulus or concept is identified with a pattern of activation across a set of units.

Distributed and local representations each have their own distinct set of advantages and disadvantages. Local representations have the virtues of familiarity and ready understandability. They are conceptually closely related to language and linguistically encoded concepts so that it is easy for theorists to set up configurations of linked nodes to represent a given structure of interrelated knowledge. For these reasons, local representations may be particularly appropriate for modeling conscious, linguistically mediated thought and reasoning processes.

In contrast, distributed representations are somewhat more difficult to grasp conceptually and to work with. Computer simulation rather than a simple pencil-and-paper sketch is generally required to derive implications of a particular representational model. However, in return for these disadvantages, distributed representations offer several important advantages. The most important is that (in most cases) distributed connectionist models *learn* the representations they use, based on exposure to multiple inputs. In contrast, models using local representations typically offer no account of learning and explain only final performance. Another advantage is automatic generalization of learning across similar concepts. Because connectionist learning rules produce similar representations for similar concepts (Clark, 1993), learning something about one concept will influence how the network processes related concepts. As a third advantage, it is much easier to incorporate new concepts into a network that uses distributed representations than one that uses localized representations. In a distributed network, the model represents every possible concept as distinct patterns across the same units. In contrast, in a localist network, each concept must be represented by its own unit. This means that the network itself must grow larger each time it encounters a new concept, and difficult decisions must occasionally be made as to when an input represents an instance of an existing concept versus when a new unit must be created. Finally, distributed representations also offer a "graceful degradation" property; if a certain proportion of units or connections are destroyed, the network will still display approximately correct behavior rather than completely breaking down. More thorough discussion of distributed representations may be found in Hinton, McClelland, and Rumelhart (1986), van Gelder (1991), and Thorpe (1995).

Localist PCS Models. Recently, several theorists advanced localist parallel constraint satisfaction (PCS) models in various domains in social psychology (e.g., Miller & Read, 1991; Read & Marcus-Newhall, 1993; Shultz & Lepper, 1994). Like our simulation, these models simultaneously apply multiple pieces of stored knowledge to generate inferences, rather than selecting a single schema to guide processing. However, they rely on localist representations in which each node represents a belief or proposition and connections between nodes represent their relations of consistency or inconsistency.

In these models, before PCS is applied to a given issue (e.g., to make an inference), a task-specific structure of nodes and links is dynamically constructed. For example, nodes representing specific observed facts ("John criticized Mary") and potential attributions ("John is angry at Mary") and links representing their inferential relationships must be constructed. Many decisions must be made as part of this process: which nodes (propositions) to include as relevant to a given task, what initial activation levels (representing initial belief strengths) to give the nodes, and what sign and weight to give each link. Once all these questions are answered and the proper representations constructed, flows of activation in the network according to the models' rules perform PCS and yield the desired inferences.

These localist PCS models closely resemble semantic networks (Barnden, 1995), which have long been used in cognitive and social psychological theories to represent propositionally encoded information (e.g., Anderson, 1983; Collins & Quillian, 1969; Hamilton et al., 1980). In semantic networks, nodes represent objects or concepts, and labeled links encode specific types of relationships among the nodes. Theorists who invoke semantic networks assume that people can dynamically construct structures of linked nodes— for example, to represent the meaning of a sentence as it is being comprehended. Localist PCS models are based on this same presumed human capability. However, this assumption places the PCS process at a rather high level, involving the same processes that are involved in conscious, reflective, verbally mediated processing. Most of Thagard's (1989) initial applications of his ECHO model, which is the basis for most of the social psychological applications, dealt with just such situations (e.g., reasoning about legal cases or the analysis of evidence relevant to a scientific controversy). It remains an open question whether the localist PCS approach is equally applicable to more automatic, preconscious types of reasoning.

In contrast to localist PCS models, the model described here (as is typical of models using distributed representations) *learns*, from exposure to input stimuli, the representations that it uses to generate inferences. It thus represents a more complete model, covering the construction as well as use of representations. Localist models that deal only with the use of knowledge leave open questions as to how the representations that are assumed to underlie a given inference could be produced in the first place—particularly in the context of preconscious, automatic processing rather than conscious, reflective thought.

Kunda and Thagard's PCS Model. Recently, a new version of a localist PCS model, different from Thagard's ECHO model that inspired most of the earlier PCS models in social psychology, was advanced by Kunda and Thagard (1996). The new model, as applied to person perception and stereotyping, uses nodes that locally represent traits, behaviors, and so forth. Links between nodes represent associations between the concepts. Subject to certain assumptions, when input information activates nodes representing what is observed in a given situation (e.g., a person with a given occupation performing a given behavior), flows of activation across these associative links perform PCS processing and settle on an interpretation of the event.

In contrast to other localist PCS models (e.g., Read & Marcus-Newhall, 1993), the Kunda and Thagard model requires neither the dynamic creation of new nodes with situation-specific meanings, nor the computation of link strengths to represent constraints among nodes within the given situation. Instead, nodes represent long-term, generic constructs that can be applied to individual persons, and links represent associations among them that could be learned from experience (although Kunda and Thagard do not emphasize the learning process). In these respects, the Kunda and Thagard (1996) model resembles our own. Other common points include the idea that social stereotypes can strongly affect person perception but are not *in principle* processed differently from any other type of information (such as behaviors or traits). This assumption, shared by the exemplar model of Smith and Zárate (1992), contrasts with some current accounts that emphasize the uniqueness of stereotypes and their supposed tendency to dominate person impressions. Finally, the Kunda and Thagard model, like our recurrent network and the localist PCS models, can use parallel constraint satisfaction to produce context-specific subtypes and context-dependent meanings of traits. For example, the meaning of "aggressive" in the context of a construction worker versus a lawyer may take on quite different shades.

Still, the Kunda and Thagard (1996) model differs in several ways from our own. Most important is the fact that they use localist representations, whereas we assume that representations of persons and social groups as well as traits, stereotypes, and behaviors are patterns distributed across common sets of units. In addition, Kunda and Thagard do not explicitly account for learning in their model, although as noted above, its basic assumptions are compatible with the learning of the associations between nodes. Further, as we showed earlier, our model can account for effects of accessibility. (Kunda and Thagard, 1996, assume that nodes can vary in accessibility; in our model, it is the accessibility of meaningful patterns of activation, not nodes, that can vary.) Finally, we demonstrated earlier that emergent features can arise from the PCS process when a stimulus pattern has similarities to more than one knowledge structure (e.g., the Harvard-educated carpenter example). In contrast, Kunda and Thagard assume that such emergent features must result from consciously controlled attributional processing triggered by an unexpected combination of features. We agree that such processing could occur in many cases, but believe that PCS processing can also generate seemingly novel features in the way demonstrated by our simulation.

Overall, the similarities between the Kunda and Thagard model and our own are perhaps more impressive than the differences. They are certainly greater than the similarities between either of these models and those models that rely on the construction of a new, problem-specific representation and the computation of appropriate links for each new situation. As argued previously, the latter models share much in common with the traditional conceptions of semantic networks (see Barnden, 1995; Touretzky, 1995).

Place in an Overall Multiple-Module System

The connectionist network simulated here obviously represents only a tiny fraction of the overall system involved in person perception. Functionally, this network processes its inputs based on its past experience to produce outputs that can fill in unobserved details, make "schematic" inferences, and resolve inconsistencies, all by drawing on multiple learned constraints in parallel. This network needs to be supplemented in several ways, as shown in Fig. 4.3.

Input Perceptual Processing Networks. Input networks must turn sensory signals into the meaningful distributed representations that constitute the inputs for the network discussed here. In the first place, such networks may rely on unsupervised learning to detect regularities in stimulus patterns. Supervised learning can then let the network discover which detectable patterns carry social and behavioral significance (see Smith, 1996, for an introduction to these ideas).

These input networks will generally learn only slowly (Singer, 1995). However, several theorists recently suggested that plasticity in their connections accounts for repetition priming, the observation that carrying out a particular process will facilitate a repetition of the same process on the same stimulus for a long time, even weeks or months (e.g., Moscovitch, 1994; Schacter, 1994; Smith, Stewart, & Buttram, 1992). Connectionist learning rules mean that processing the initial stimulus leads to incremental changes in the connection weights. This change is long-lasting, and its effects diminish not with time but with interference from unrelated patterns. Many people have an intuition that the effects of weight changes caused by processing a stimulus on a single occasion could not be demonstrable over days or even weeks, although priming effects clearly can last that long. However, Wiles and Humphreys (1993) argued quantitatively that this intuition is misleading. If even a single encounter with a stimulus can have a long-term effect, it is obvious that when a stimulus is processed frequently over months and

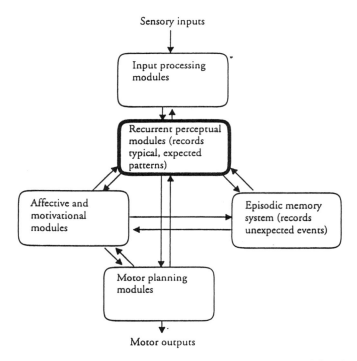

FIG. 4.3. Sketch of multiple-module system. The module shown with heavier lines is the one simulated in this chapter.

years, the resulting systematic shifts in connection weights could influence the individual's processing characteristics for years, even a lifetime (a property termed "chronic accessibility" in the social literature). Thus, as Fig. 4.3 shows, a perceptual processing network located before the network simulated here, which is required in any case to generate the inputs we assume, may be responsible for repetition priming as well as for some accessibility effects.

Two Forms of Learning. Much evidence suggests that people display at least two forms of learning, which differ in speed as well as other characteristics. McClelland, McNaughton, and O'Reilly (1995) used this evidence to argue for a connectionist model with two separate memory systems. One, analogous to the neocortex, changes connection weights only slowly and stores stably structured "schematic" general knowledge. Another, analogous to the hippocampal system, rapidly learns new information and forms episodic traces that are accessible to consciousness. New knowledge is transferred from the latter system into the former in a process analogous to "consolidation," which can take months or years in humans. The authors argued that this dual-memory system can escape from the problems (such as "catastrophic interference" or the destruction of old memories by new learning) to which some single-memory connectionist systems are susceptible.

One important implication of this model for social psychology is a predicted difference in the type of information to which the two systems attend. Schematic learning is chiefly concerned with regularities, so it must record primarily what is typical and expected. In contrast, episodic memories should form on a single exposure to record the details of events that are novel and interesting: In other words, this memory system should attend more to the unexpected and unpredicted. Social psychological studies of person perception show that people attend to and recall mostly expectancy-inconsistent information when forming a new impression, but mostly expectation-consistent information when working with a well-formed and solid expectation (Higgins & Bargh, 1987). It may well be that this observed difference depends on an underlying difference in the properties of two memory systems—one fast learning and responsive to novelty, the other slower learning and attuned to regularities—such as those suggested by McClelland et al. (1995).

Onward to Behavior: Evaluative and Motivational Networks. The network described here is part of a sensory pathway, operating to combine learned constraints with preprocessed input information to generate guesses about the external world. Yet this module is only part of the system that processes incoming information. Bargh (1997) suggested that sensory inputs are processed by evaluative and motivational as well as perceptual systems, giving rise to several types of behavioral effects without the intervention of conscious awareness. Figure 4.3 shows our conception of how this process might work. As sensory information enters the system, encoded as distributed patterns of activation, perceptual modules begin to compute semantic representations of "what's out there" based on the input and prior experience encoded in the connection weights. But the computation is not purely bottom up or stimulus driven. We assume that other modules are connected to the perceptual models with bi-directional or recurrent connections, which are pervasive features of the vertebrate nervous system (Felleman & Van Essen, 1991) as well as of many connectionist models (Movellan & McClelland, 1995).

Among these other networks, as sketched in Fig. 4.3, are evaluative modules that receive their inputs from the semantic representations and attempt to recognize patterns that can be identified as good or bad. Probably these are two separate modules rather than one with a bipolar output signal (see Cacioppo & Berntson, 1994). Affective and motivational modules are similarly connected to the outputs of perceptual interpretive modules, prepared to recognize patterns that represent motivationally significant situations, such as the presence of food, danger, novel stimuli, and so forth. When activated by semantic patterns that they recognize as significant, these modules trigger motor plans and ultimately overt behavior. Motivational modules, such as those that search for food, should have their operation regulated by internal signals representing the individual's state of hunger or satiety (Dorman & Gaudiano, 1995). Motives may be relatively abstract as well as concrete. For example, an affiliation motivation module, when activated, may look for situational features that are conducive to forming or maintaining relationships with others.

The recurrent nature of the between-module connections mean that modules cannot be put into a strict processing sequence. As activation spreads from the perceptual to other evaluative and affective modules, they begin to compute their own representations—and through interactive feedback connections, to influence the pattern of activity into which the "earlier" perceptual module settles. Thus, even as a semantic interpretation of a situation is being constructed, its motivational implications are also being assessed, and feedback from motivational modules may influence the nature of the final perceptual representation into which the network's activity settles. For example, patterns representing motivationally favorable situations may be more stable and form on the basis of less definitive input cues, compared to patterns representing less desirable situations. Self-enhancing and other biases may be due to this sort of mechanism. All this occurs prior to conscious awareness; these modules are part of the system that construct the individual's subjective experience.

Conclusion

Distributed connectionist models offer the potential for theoretical integration in many ways. First, as illustrated by our simulations, a single connectionist model can account for many phenomena that are explained by distinct mechanisms in current models. Second, a given model may account for both findings in social cognition and various aspects of nonsocial memory. As noted earlier, the McClelland and Rumelhart (1986) model does so. Third and more speculatively, a multiple-module system like the one sketched previously may contribute to an integrated account of cognition and motivation. Finally, as many have pointed out, distributed connectionist models offer much promise of building bridges between psychology and neuroscience. (Dare we say "shedding light on the mind-body problem," as Smolensky, 1988, did?) A common language, based on simple units connected by adaptive links and using distributed patterns of activation as representational vehicles, permits theorists like McClelland et al. (1995) to draw on neuroscientific data in support of their model while bringing insights from connectionist modeling to bear on the interpretation of such data. The model that results from this integrative approach successfully fits many kinds of psychological data from studies of memory. This model thus stands as an excellent example of the potential integrative power of distributed connectionist modeling, even in its early stages of development.

We hope that as social psychologists increasingly apply connectionist models, the key areas of concern to our field—person perception, affect, social interaction, motivation-cognition interactions, to name a few—will be incorporated into this emerging synthesis.

ACKNOWLEDGMENTS

Preparation of this chapter was supported by a research grant (R01 MH46840) and a Research Career Development Award (K02 MH01178) from the National Institute of Mental Health.

REFERENCES

Andersen, S. M., & Cole, S. W. (1990). "Do I know you?": The role of significant others in general social perception. *Journal of Personality and Social Psychology, 59,* 384–399.

Anderson, J. R. (1983). *The architecture of cognition.* Cambridge, MA: Harvard University Press.

Asch, S. E., & Zukier, H. (1984). Thinking about persons. *Journal of Personality and Social Psychology, 46,* 1230–1240.

Banaji, M. R., & Greenwald, A. G. (1994). Implicit stereotyping and prejudice. In M. P. Zanna & J. M. Olson (Eds.), *The psychology of prejudice: The Ontario Symposium* (Vol. 7, pp. 55–76). Hillsdale, NJ: Lawrence Erlbaum Associates.

Bargh, J. A. (1994). The four horsemen of automaticity: Awareness, intention, efficiency, and control in social cognition. In R. S. Wyer & T. K. Srull (Eds.), *Handbook of social cognition* (2nd ed., Vol. 1, pp. 1–40). Hillsdale, NJ: Lawrence Erlbaum Associates.

Bargh, J. A. (1997). The automaticity of everyday life. In R. S. Wyer (Ed.), *Advances in social cognition* (Vol. 10, pp. 1–61). Mahwah, NJ: Lawrence Erlbaum Associates.

Barnden, J. A. (1995). Semantic networks. In M. A. Arbib (Ed.), *Handbook of brain theory and neural networks* (pp. 854–857). Cambridge, MA: MIT Press.

Brewer, M. B. (1988). A dual process model of impression formation. In T. Srull & R. Wyer (Eds.), *Advances in social cognition* (Vol. 1, pp. 177–183). Hillsdale, NJ: Lawrence Erlbaum Associates.

Cacioppo, J. T., & Berntson, G. G. (1994). Relationship between attitudes and evaluative space: A critical review, with emphasis on the separability of positive and negative substrates. *Psychological Bulletin, 115,* 401–423.

Churchland, P. S., & Sejnowski, T. J. (1992). *The computational brain.* Cambridge, MA: MIT Press.

Clark, A. (1993). *Associative engines: Connectionism, concepts, and representational change.* Cambridge, MA: MIT Press.

Collins, A. M., & Quillian, M. R. (1969). Retrieval time from semantic memory. *Journal of Verbal Learning and Verbal Behavior, 8,* 240–247.

Dorman, C., & Gaudiano, P. (1995). Motivation. In M. A. Arbib (Ed.), *Handbook of brain theory and neural networks* (pp. 591–594). Cambridge, MA: MIT Press.

Felleman, D. J., & Van Essen, D. C. (1991). Distributed hierarchical processing in the primate cerebral cortex. *Cerebral Cortex, 1,* 1–47.

Fiske, S. T., & Neuberg, S. L. (1990). A continuum of impression formation, from category-based to individuating processes: Influences of information and motivation on attention and interpretation. In M. P. Zanna (Ed.), *Advances in experimental social psychology* (Vol. 23, pp. 1–74). New York: Academic Press.

Fiske, S. T., & Taylor, S. E. (1991). *Social cognition* (2nd ed.). New York: McGraw-Hill.

Hamilton, D. L., Katz, L. B., & Leirer, V. (1980). Organizational processes in impression formation. In R. Hastie, T. M. Ostrom, E. B. Ebbesen, R. S. Wyer, D. L. Hamilton, & D. E. Carlston (Eds.), *Person memory*. Hillsdale, NJ: Lawrence Erlbaum Associates.

Hamilton, D. L., & Sherman, J. W. (1994). Stereotypes. In R. S. Wyer & T. K. Srull (Eds.), *Handbook of social cognition* (2nd ed., Vol. 2, pp. 1–68). Hillsdale, NJ: Lawrence Erlbaum Associates.

Hastie, R. (1988). A computer simulation model of person memory. *Journal of Experimental Social Psychology, 24*, 423–447.

Hastie, R., & Kumar, P. A. (1979). Person memory: Personality traits as organizing principles in memory for behaviors. *Journal of Personality and Social Psychology, 37*, 25–38.

Hastie, R., Schroeder, C., & Weber, R. (1990). Creating complex social conjunction categories from simple categories. *Bulletin of the Psychonomic Society, 28*, 242–247.

Hebb, D. O. (1949). *The organization of behavior*. New York: Wiley.

Higgins, E. T. (1996). Knowledge activation: Accessibility, applicability, and salience. In E. T. Higgins & A. W. Kruglanski (Eds.), *Social psychology: Handbook of basic principles* (pp. 133–168). New York: Guilford.

Higgins, E. T., & Bargh, J. A. (1987). Social cognition and social perception. *Annual Review of Psychology, 38*, 369–426.

Hinton, G. E., McClelland, J. L., & Rumelhart, D. E. (1986). Distributed representations. In D. E. Rumelhart, J. L. McClelland, et al. (Eds.), *Parallel distributed processing* (Vol. 1, pp. 77–109). Cambridge, MA: MIT Press.

Hintzman, D. L. (1976). Repetition and memory. In G. H. Bower (Ed.), *The psychology of learning and memory* (Vol. 11, pp. 47–91). New York: Academic Press.

Kunda, Z., Miller, D. T., & Claire, T. (1990). Combining social concepts: The role of causal reasoning. *Cognitive Science, 14*, 551–577.

Kunda, Z., & Thagard, P. (1996). Integrating stereotypes with individuating information: A parallel constraint satisfaction model of impression formation. *Psychological Review, 103*, 284–308.

Lewicki, P. (1985). Nonconscious biasing effects of single instances of subsequent judgments. *Journal of Personality and Social Psychology, 48*, 563–574.

Martin, L. L., Seta, J. J., & Crelia, R. A. (1990). Assimilation and contrast as a function of people's willingness and ability to expend effort in forming an impression. *Journal of Personality and Social Psychology, 59*, 38–49.

McClelland, J. L., McNaughton, B. L., & O'Reilly, R. C. (1995). Why there are complementary learning systems in the hippocampus and neocortex: Insights from the successes and failures of connectionist models of learning and memory. *Psychological Review, 102*, 419–457.

McClelland, J. L., & Rumelhart, D. E. (1986). A distributed model of human learning and memory. In J. L. McClelland, D. E. Rumelhart, and the PDP Research Group (Eds.), *Parallel distributed processing: Explorations in the microstructure of cognition* (Vol. 2, pp. 170–215). Cambridge, MA: MIT Press.

McClelland, J. L., & Rumelhart, D. E. (1988). *Explorations in parallel distributed processing*. Cambridge, MA: MIT Press.

McClelland, J. L., Rumelhart, D. E., and the PDP Research Group. (Eds.). (1986). *Parallel distributed processing: Explorations in the microstructure of cognition*. (Vol. 2). Cambridge, MA: MIT Press.

Miller, L. C., & Read, S. J. (1991). On the coherence of mental models of persons and relationships: A knowledge structure approach. In G. J. O Fletcher & F. D. Fincham (Eds.), *Cognition in close relationships* (pp. 69–100). Hillsdale, NJ: Lawrence Erlbaum.

Moscovitch, M. (1994). Memory and working with memory: Evaluation of a component process model and comparisons with other models. In D. L. Schacter & E. Tulving (Eds.), *Memory systems 1994* (pp. 269–310). Cambridge, MA: MIT Press.

Movellan, J. R., & McClelland, J. L. (1995). *Stochastic interactive processing, channel separability, and optimal perceptual inference: An examination of Morton's law.* (Technical Report PDP.CNS.95.4). Pittsburgh, PA: Carnegie Mellon University, Department of Psychology.

Ramsey, W., Stich, S. P., & Garon, J. (1991). Connectionism, eliminativism, and the future of folk psychology. In W. Ramsey, S. P. Stich, & D. E. Rumelhart (Eds.), *Philosophy and connectionist theory* (pp. 199–228). Hillsdale, NJ: Lawrence Erlbaum Associates.

Read, S. J., & Marcus-Newhall, A. (1993). Explanatory coherence in social explanations: A parallel distributed processing account. *Journal of Personality and Social Psychology, 65,* 429–447.

Rumelhart, D. E., McClelland, J. L., and the PDP Research Group. (Eds.). (1986). *Parallel distributed processing* (Vol. 1). Cambridge, MA: MIT Press.

Rumelhart, D. E., Smolensky, P., McClelland, J. L., & Hinton, G. E. (1986). Schemata and sequential thought processes in PDP models. In J. L. McClelland & D. E. Rumelhart (Eds.), *Parallel distributed processing: Explorations in the microstructure of cognition* (vol. 2, pp. 7–57). Cambridge, MA: MIT Press.

Schacter, D. L. (1994). Priming and multiple memory systems: Perceptual mechanisms of implicit memory. In D. L. Schacter & E. Tulving (Eds.), *Memory systems 1994* (pp. 233–268). Cambridge, MA: MIT Press.

Schneider, W. (1987). Connectionism: Is it a paradigm shift for psychology? *Behavior Research Methods, Instrumentation, and Computers, 19,* 73–83.

Seidenberg, M. S. (1993). Connectionist models and cognitive theory. *Psychological Science, 4,* 228–235.

Shultz, T. R., & Lepper, M. R. (1994). *Cognitive dissonance reduction as constraint satisfaction.* Unpublished paper, Department of Psychology, McGill University.

Singer, W. (1995). Development and plasticity of cortical processing architectures. *Science, 270,* 758–764.

Smith, E. R. (1991). Illusory correlation in a simulated exemplar-based memory. *Journal of Experimental Social Psychology, 27,* 107–123.

Smith, E. R. (1996). What do connectionism and social psychology offer each other? *Journal of Personality and Social Psychology, 70,* 893–912.

Smith, E. R. (in press). Mental representation and memory. In D. Gilbert, S. Fiske, & G. Lindzey (Eds.), *Handbook of social psychology* (4th ed.). New York: McGraw-Hill.

Smith, E. R., & DeCoster, J. (in press). Knowledge acquisition, accessibility, and use in person perception and stereotyping: Simulation with a recurrent connectionist network. *Journal of Personality and Social Psychology.*

Smith, E. R., Stewart, T. L., & Buttram, R. T. (1992). Inferring a trait from a behavior has long-term, highly specific effects. *Journal of Personality and Social Psychology, 62,* 753–759.

Smith, E. R., & Zárate, M. A. (1992). Exemplar-based model of social judgment. *Psychological Review, 99,* 3–21.

Smolensky, P. (1988). On the proper treatment of connectionism. *Behavioral and Brain Sciences, 11,* 1–74.

Thagard, P. (1989). Explanatory coherence. *Behavioral and Brain Sciences, 12,* 435–502.

Thorpe, S. (1995). Localized and distributed representations. In M. A. Arbib (Ed.), *Handbook of brain theory and neural networks* (pp. 549–552). Cambridge, MA: MIT Press.

Touretzky, D. S. (1995). Connectionist and symbolic representation. In M. A. Arbib (Ed.), *Handbook of brain theory and neural networks* (pp. 243–247). Cambridge, MA: MIT Press.

van Gelder, T. (1991). What is the "D" in "PDP"? A survey of the concept of distribution. In W. Ramsey, S. P. Stich, & D. E. Rumelhart (Eds.), *Philosophy and connectionist theory* (pp. 33–60). Hillsdale, NJ: Lawrence Erlbaum Associates.

Wiles, J., & Humphreys, M. S. (1993). Using artificial neural nets to model implicit and explicit memory test performance. In P. Graf & M. E. J. Masson (Eds.), *Implicit memory: New directions in cognition, development, and neuropsychology* (pp. 141–165). Hillsdale, NJ: Lawrence Erlbaum Associates.

Wyer, R. S., & Srull, T. K. (1989). *Memory and cognition in its social context*. Hillsdale, NJ: Lawrence Erlbaum Associates.

Wyer, R. S., & Srull, T. K. (Eds.). (1994). *Handbook of social cognition* (2nd ed.). Hillsdale, NJ: Lawrence Erlbaum Associates.

Zell, A., Mamier, G., Vogt, M., Mache, N., Hubner, R., Doring, S., Hermann, K.-U., Soyez, T., Schmalzl, M., Sommer, T., Hatzigeogiou, A., Posselt, D., Schreiner, T., Kett, B., & Clemente, G. (1994). *Stuttgart Neural Network Simulator (User Manual, Version 3.2)*. (Technical Report No. 3/94). Stuttgart, Germany: University of Stuttgart, Institute for Parallel and Distributed High Performance Systems.

CAUSAL REASONING

5

A Connectionist Approach to Causal Attribution

Frank Van Overwalle
Dirk Van Rooy
Vrije Universiteit Brussel, Belgium

Attributing a cause to an event is an indispensable mental capacity that enables humans to identify the factors in their environment responsible for their hardship or well-being, to predict similar events in the future, and to increase their control over their occurrences. In fact, not only humans but also animals use the capacity to detect cause–effect relationships in order to prosper and safeguard their everyday adaptation and long-term survival. Given this long evolutionary history from simple invertebrates like the mollusk (Hawkins, 1989) on, it seems reasonable to assume that much, if not all, causal learning is governed by very elementary and simple cognitive processes, operating in animals as well as humans. In this chapter, we argue that the causal learning process involves the development of mental associations or connections between potential causes and the effect, and that this learning process can be profitably analyzed from a connectionist perspective.

The associative approach to causal learning grew from research on animal conditioning (e.g., Rescorla & Wagner, 1972), and has gained increasing support in current cognitive research on human causality and categorization (for reviews, see Allen, 1993; Shanks, 1993, 1995) and in connectionist or adaptive network models of human memory and thinking (e.g., Gluck & Bower, 1988a; McClelland & Rumelhart, 1988). The various theoretical proposals put forward in these diverse areas of research seem to converge to a few fundamental principles. For instance, the popular associative model of animal conditioning proposed by Rescorla and Wagner in 1972 is, in fact, formally equivalent to a specific class of two-layer connectionist models based on the *delta* learning algorithm (i.e., pattern associators; McClelland & Rumelhart, 1988).

In contrast to cognitive psychologists' rising interest in associative or connectionist learning principles, social psychologists have been slow in incorporating these ideas in their theories of human causality judgments. Rather than the descendants of a long evolutionary past, they view humans as naive scientists (Kelley, 1967), logicians (Hewstone & Jaspars, 1987) or statisticians (Cheng & Novick, 1990), who compute causality in analogy to logical and statistical procedures and norms. Although research has repeatedly demonstrated that humans sometimes make biased inferences that deviate from normative probabilities (cf. Kahneman, Slovic, & Tversky, 1982), such findings have been routinely interpreted in terms of unfavorable conditions or lack of cognitive resources to calculate the correct inferences rather than as evidence of an alternative learning process. Even research in social cognition, which adopted notions from earlier network structures (e.g., in person impression; Hamilton, Driscoll, & Worth, 1989) or from recent connectionist network models (e.g., in causal knowledge structures; Read & Marcus-Newhall, 1993), has been mainly concerned with the retrieval of existing memories, rather than with the learning itself of new concepts and causal relationships.

How might we understand the causal learning process? What insights do connectionist approaches offer that go beyond those offered by alternative rule-based (e.g., statistical) models? To address these fundamental questions, we begin this chapter with a review of the normative probabilistic theory of causal attribution as exemplified by the *contrast model* developed by Cheng and Novick (1990) and extended by Van Overwalle (1997; Van Overwalle & Heylighen, 1995), and compare it with a connectionist implementation of Rescorla and Wagner's (1972) model of learning. Next, we present evidence indicating that the connectionist approach provides a better explanation for some phenomena of causal competition like discounting and augmentation (cf. Kelley, 1971). Finally, we present the *configural* model by Pearce (1994), which represents a major advance in connectionist modeling that overcomes several limitations of earlier connectionist models (McClelland & Rumelhart, 1988; Rescorla & Wagner, 1972), and we review some data that suggests that this model is superior in dealing with generalization of causality to factors that are similar to the true cause.

PROBABILISTIC APPROACH

Kelley (1967), one of the founders of attribution theory in social psychology, proposed that perceivers identify the causes of an effect by using a principle of *covariation*, which specifies that an "effect is attributed to that condition which is present when the effect is present and which is absent when the effect is absent" (p. 194). He specified three major comparisons that are important in detecting covariation and causality in the social domain, and later research (e.g., Cheng & Novick, 1990; Hewstone & Jaspars, 1987; Hilton & Slugoski, 1986) demonstrated that each of these comparisons generates an attribution: Low *consensus* (the effect occurs when this person is present but not when others are) produces attributions to the *person*; high *distinctiveness* (the effect occurs when this stimulus is present but not when other stimuli are) generates attributions to the *stimulus*; and low *consistency* (the effect is present on this occasion but not on other occasions) produces attributions to the *occasion*. Although Kelley's (1967) covariation idea is now widely accepted in the attribution literature, there is disagreement about the underlying processes by which covariation and causality are detected. Some attribution researchers took a probabilistic approach to describe this process in more detail.

Probabilistic Contrasts

According to researchers taking a probabilistic perspective, perceivers store in memory the frequencies about cause–effect occurrences, and then perform some quasi-statistical computation on these frequencies in order to produce a causal judgment (for an overview, see Allen, 1993; Cheng & Novick, 1990; Shanks, 1993). In Fig. 5.1, the relevant frequencies (denoted by a–d) are represented in a 2×2 contingency table, where one axis reflects the presence or absence of the potential cause C, and the second axis the presence or absence of the effect.

For reasons that become clear later, the first axis also displays a second factor X, representing the background or context against which the cause C occurs. This context is invariantly present, irrespective of the presence or absence of the target factor C. To distinguish between the two types of factors, the factor C is termed a *contrast* factor (because it is present in one case but not the other), and the factor X is termed a *context* factor (because it reflects the context present in all cases under observation). It should be noted that we define contrast or context factors with respect to a focal set of observations selected by the perceiver or provided by the experimenter;

	Effect	No Effect
C X	*a*	*b*
X	*c*	*d*

FIG. 5.1. A contingency table illustrating a contrast factor (C) and its context factor (X) when the effect is present and absent. The letters a–d reflect frequencies.

they are not necessarily contrastive or contextual under all possible observations of interest.

According to probabilistic theory, causal judgments involve the calculation of the contrast between the probability of the effect given the presence
of the cause minus the same probability given the absence of the cause (see
Allen, 1993; Cheng & Novick, 1990; Shanks, 1993). Stated more simply, causality is attributed to a cause that differs from an invariant background or
context where that cause is absent. This is mathematically expressed by a
probabilistic contrast:[1]

$$\Delta P_c = P(\text{Effect} \mid C) - P(\text{Effect} \mid \sim C)$$

$$= \frac{a}{a+b} - \frac{c}{c+d}, \tag{1}$$

in which P represents the probability in which the effect occurs when the
cause is present (C) or absent ($\sim$C; a tilde denotes the absence of a factor);
and the small letters a–d denote the frequencies in Fig. 5.1. This probabilistic
contrast is closely related to common statistical measures of correlation
between two stimuli such as the χ^2 statistic, and has therefore received a
normative status.

How can the probabilistic contrast equation be applied to Kelley's (1967)
covariation principle? An innovative attempt to tackle this question was
developed by Cheng and Novick (1990) in their probabilistic contrast model.
As their approach is also important in understanding connectionist applications, we discuss one example in more detail. Let us take the target event
"Sarah laughed," and let us focus on Sarah as the potential cause of the
effect laughed. Because the effect (laughed) is always present when the
target person (Sarah) is present, this can be expressed as $P(\text{Laughed} \mid \text{Sarah})$
$= 1$. Now, to estimate Sarah's causal role, we need to contrast this probability
with a relevant causal background where the target person is absent, for
example, with other persons such as Sarah's friends. The low consensus
information that her friends did not laugh at the same event can be expressed as $P(\text{Laughed} \mid \sim \text{Sarah}) = 0$. Then, according to Equation 1, the
contrast between target and comparison persons will be high, or $\Delta P_{\text{Sarah}} =$
1, and Sarah's laughter will consequently be attributed to herself. If, on the
other hand, the high consensus information is given that Sarah's friends
also laughed during the same event or $P(\text{Laughed} \mid \sim \text{Sarah}) = 1$, then ΔP_{Sarah}
$= 0$ and causality will not be attributed to her. The same contrast logic
applies for high distinctiveness and low consistency information. Generally,
a factor will be designated the cause when its outcome is different from that

---

[1]This probabilistic rule is also termed the *delta-P* rule. To avoid any confusion with the *delta*
learning algorithm from connectionist learning models, we do not use this term.

of the comparison cases. Empirical research confirmed that people make attributions to the person, stimulus, or occasion in line with the probabilistic contrast model (Cheng & Novick, 1990).

However, an important shortcoming of probabilistic theory is that it does not specify how attributions are made about the causal background given a focal set of observations. For example, when judging the causal role of Sarah, her behavior was contrasted with that of other persons who constituted a relevant causal background or context; but this causal background itself could not be estimated. Cheng and Novick gave the causal context only a rather shallow interpretation as an enabling condition or an irrelevant factor, and specified that comparisons with an alternative set of observations were necessary to judge their strength. However, as we see, in connectionist approaches, causal contexts can be estimated and do play a crucial role in determining the causal strength of a contrast factor, even within a given set of observations. Given that this is the case, we might simply stop here and note that the probabilistic model is seriously deficient and much more limited than connectionist approaches. However, an alternative approach that seems much more informative is to extend probabilistic theory with additional predictions for causal contexts so that we can still make sensible comparisons between the two approaches.

Probabilistic Contexts

What is a context factor precisely, and how can its causal strength be inferred from a focal set of observations? Fortunately, this issue was already addressed in our earlier work on causal attribution (Van Overwalle, 1997; Van Overwalle & Heylighen, 1995). A context is defined as a relatively constant background condition consisting, for instance, of "situational stimuli arising from the ... environment" (Rescorla & Wagner, 1972, p. 88). Because researchers on the fundamental dimensions of human causality (e.g., Abramson, Seligman, & Teasdale, 1978; Weiner, 1986) already introduced a terminology for factors that correspond very much to our notion of constant background conditions, we borrowed their terms. Hence, the context of a person is denoted as *external* circumstances (that remain constant across different persons); the context of a stimulus is denoted as a *global* cause (that remains constant across different stimuli); and the context of an occasion is denoted as a *stable* cause (that remains permanent over time). As can be seen, each context reflects a constant condition against which a contrast cause may be distinguished. Each pair reflects the two extremes of standard dimensions of causality, including *locus* (personal vs. external), *globality* (stimulus-specific vs. general), and *stability* (occasional vs. stable). Although this terminology still leaves open the question about which specific elements in the context are responsible for the effect, this same problem is in fact also true for contrast causes. For instance, an attribution to the person does not indicate which element inside the person is causality relevant—his or her ability, motivation, and so on (for examples of contrast and context causes, see Weiner, 1986).

To compute the causal strength of a context factor, Van Overwalle (1996, 1997) developed an analogous probabilistic equation that is mathematically expressed by a *probabilistic context*:

$$\Delta P_X = P(\text{Effect} \mid \sim C)$$
$$= \frac{c}{c + d}. \tag{2}$$

The logic behind this equation is straightforward, because it has the same general format as the contrast equation (see Equation 1), but retains only the second term, which represents the causal context X. It specifies that the strength of a causal context can be estimated from the probability of the effect given the relevant comparison cases where the target factor C is absent.

The probabilistic context equation can also easily be applied to Kelley's (1967) covariation variables. In our previous example, the low consensus information that most of Sarah's friends did not laugh can be expressed as $P(\text{Laughed} \mid \sim \text{Sarah}) = 0$, and this low probability indicates that the causal context (e.g., external circumstances) had little causal effect on Sarah's laugh. In contrast, the high consensus information that most of her friends laughed can be expressed as $P(\text{Laughed} \mid \sim \text{Sarah}) = 1$ so that in this case, causality will be strongly attributed to the external context. The same logic applies to low distinctiveness and to high consistency. Thus, in general, a causal context will acquire a substantial amount of causal weight when both the target and comparison cases obtain the same effect.

The probabilistic predictions for both contrast and context causes were combined in what we termed the *joint model* (Van Overwalle, 1997; Van Overwalle & Heylighen, 1995) to reflect the joint operation of the two probabilistic equations. The joint model borrows Equation 1 from Cheng and Novick's (1990) contrast model for the computation of contrast factors, and adds Equation 2 for the computation of context factors. Hence, the two equations are used separately for estimating contrast and context factors. Research on the joint model confirmed that people make attributions to contrast and context causes in line with the predictions of the joint model (Van Overwalle, 1997; Van Overwalle & Heylighen, 1995).

CONNECTIONIST APPROACH

Although the empirical results are supportive of a probabilistic analysis of causal attribution, it seems quite implausible that animals and humans possess the capacity to tally and memorize frequencies in the presence and absence of all potential causes and explicitly compute the relevant contrast and context probabilities. The early associative models and the more recent connectionist approaches addressed these cognitive limitations by assuming that the perceived strength of causes is directly stored in memory under the form of mental connections between the potential cause and the effect. These cause–effect connections are gradually adjusted given information on the co-occurence of the cause and the effect. Various learning mechanisms describing these adjustments were proposed in the animal and human learning literature, but the learning algorithm developed by Rescorla and Wagner in 1972 gained the most popularity. Because this algorithm preceded recent developments in connectionist modeling and still is a major source of inspiration in the field of associative learning (cf. Pearce, 1994), we first discuss the Rescorla–Wagner model and then turn to a connectionist implementation of it.

Rescorla–Wagner Associative Model

A central notion of the Rescorla–Wagner (1992) learning algorithm is that "organisms only learn when events violate their expectations" (p. 75). Thus, changes in associative weights of a causal factor are driven by reducing the difference between the actual effect and the effect expected by the organism. The reduction of this difference or error takes place after each trial in which the factor is present, and the resultant adjustment in weight or Δw of the factor, is expressed in the following learning formula:

$$\Delta w = \alpha \beta_w (\lambda - \Sigma w), \tag{3}$$

where α represents the salience or the probability of attending to the factor, and is normally set to 1 if the factor is present and to 0 if absent; and β_w is a learning rate parameter, ranging between 0 and 1, which reflects the speed of learning. The λ variable denotes the magnitude of the effect, and is typically set to 1 when the effect is present and to 0 when absent; and Σw represents the expected effect based on the summed association weights of all factors present on the trial.

The course of learning in the simple case with one causal factor ($\Sigma w = w_C$) is straightforward. The weight w_C starts at zero, and successive trials cause an increase or decrease until the point is reached when the error or ($\lambda - w_C$) is zero, implying that the effect is perfectly predicted by the cause C, and no further changes are necessary. In that case, we say that learning has reached asymptote. The learning rate parameter β_w determines the proportion or speed by which the discrepancy or error between the expected and the actual effect are taken into account for adjusting associative weights. Thus, causal learning is conceived as a gradual process that is continuously updated rather than a final judgment at the end of a series of observations as assumed by the probabilistic approach.

Connectionist Implementation

An important feature of Rescorla and Wagner's associative model is that their learning algorithm (Equation 3) is identical to the *delta* or Widrow–Hoff updating algorithm that played a major role in some feedforward connectionist models (McClelland & Rumelhart, 1988). Consequently, the Rescorla–Wagner model can be easily implemented by a two-layer feedforward architecture, as illustrated in Fig. 5.2 (see also Gluck & Bower, 1988a; McClelland & Rumelhart, 1988). The first layer comprises input nodes that encode the presence of causal factors, and the second layer comprises the output node representing the predicted effect. The input nodes are connected to the output node via adjustable connections or weights, denoted by dashed lines in Fig. 5.2.

When a factor is present at a trial, the activation of its input node is turned on at value 1; and when a factor is absent, the activation is turned off to 0. There are two features in this input coding that differ somewhat from a typical feedforward network. First, the absence of a factor is coded as an activation of 0 rather than −1 (McClelland & Rumelhart, 1988). This coding scheme reflects the common observation in associative research that animals and humans learn little about objects that are absent. Second,

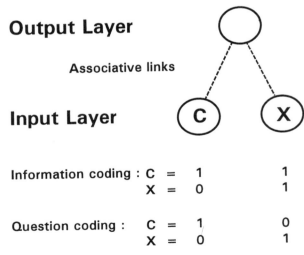

FIG. 5.2. A network representation of the Rescorla–Wagner model given a contrast factor (C) and its context (X), together with some illustrative coding for information presented during learning and questions presented during testing.

there is always a constant context factor X present on every trial, irrespective of the presence of the target cause C (see some illustrative coding in Fig. 5.2). As noted before, this context assumption was also introduced in the probabilistic model by Van Overwalle and Heylighen (1995). Although a very similar idea can be implemented in connectionist models by the use of *bias* terms (see McClelland & Rumelhart, 1988), associative approaches assume that these context factors reflect important and meaningful elements of the environment in which learning takes place (e.g., the animal's cage).

Next, activation from the input nodes spreads automatically to the output node in proportion to their connection weights, and the activations received are summed to determine the activation of the output node. This output activation is thus a linear function of the input activation, and represents the strength of the effect predicted by the network. The actual obtained effect is represented by a teaching value (not shown in the figure), using the same +1 and 0 coding scheme as the input nodes. This teaching value serves as input to the output node; and the error between the output (expected effect) and teaching activations (actual effect) determines the adjustments to the strengths of the connections in the network, as in the Rescorla–Wagner model. The change in the connection weight of factor j (Δw_j) is proportional to this error, and this is formally expressed by the delta learning algorithm (McClelland & Rumelhart, 1988, p. 87):

$$\Delta w_j = \varepsilon(a_t - a_o)a_j, \tag{4}$$

where ε is the learning rate, and the other symbols a_t, a_o, and a_j denote, respectively, the teaching, output, and input activations. Comparing this equation with Equation 3 of Rescorla–Wagner shows that they are completely identical, except for some notational variations. The learning rate β_w in the Rescorla–Wagner equation is represented here by ε, the magnitude of the actual effect λ is replaced by the teaching activation a_t, the expected effect based on the summed association weights Σw is denoted here by the output activation a_o, and the salience α of a factor is reflected in the activation of the corresponding input node a_j of all factors present on the trial.

In research on causal learning, after the subjects have gone through a trial-by-trial acquisition phase, they are presented with questions concerning the causal influence of some factors. An appropriate measure in the network for subjects' causal judgments is simply the activation of the output node, given that the appropriate input nodes are turned on. Thus, to test the predictions of the network, the factors to be tested are turned on at the input layer as before, except that the strength of a contrast factor is now tested separately without its accompanying context (see some illustrative coding in Fig. 5.2). In the present two-layer network, the output activation is identical to the connection weight of each factor tested, because this is the sole factor with its input activation turned on. In the remainder of this chapter, this connectionist implementation of associative learning is referred to as the Rescorla–Wagner network.

Figure 5.3 illustrates two learning histories with six trials for factors C and X, simulated by a connectionist network just described. In the first example where only the contrast factor and its context are followed by the effect (CX → effect; X → no effect; left panel), the weights tend to asymptotic values of $w_C = 1.00$ and $w_X = 0.00$. The contrast factor acquires much positive strength because it is always followed by the effect. Although the context acquires some positive weight when presented together with the contrast factor (when CX → effect), this weight is neutralized every time the context is presented alone (when X → no effect), so that the net result is little causal strength. Conversely, in the second example where only the context is followed by the effect (X → effect, CX → no effect; right panel), the weights tend to asymptotic values of $w_X = 1.00$ and $w_C = -1.00$. The context acquires strong positive strength as it is always followed by the effect. However, the contrast factor attains strong negative causal strength because when it is presented together with the context, the effect is not produced, so that it must compensate for the positive weight of the context.

An important characteristic of the Rescorla–Wagner network is that, given sufficient learning trials, it will arrive at the same causal predictions as the probabilistic contrast and joint models without storing frequencies. This somewhat surprising result was demonstrated mathematically by several authors (Chapman & Robbins, 1990; Van Overwalle, 1996), and suggests that the normative predictions from probabilistic theory are, in fact, also emergent properties of the Rescorla–Wagner learning process. From an

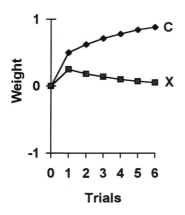

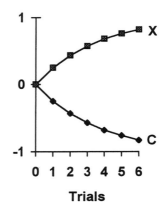

FIG. 5.3. A simulation of causal learning with parameter $\beta_w = .50$. The left panel reflects a learning history of CX → effect and X → no effect trials; whereas the right panel reflects X → effect and CX → no effect trials.

evolutionary perspective, it seems imperative that associative thinking in animals and humans has evolved in such a way that predictive factors are identified with reasonable accuracy (Shanks, 1995).

In sum, the two most important characteristics of a connectionist approach to causal learning that differentiates it from a probabilistic approach are that (a) the connectionist approach does not require that frequency information on all previous trials be tallied and memorized during the learning period, but only the cause–effect connections; and (b) the connectionist approach does not require an explicit and laborious computational process, but immediately integrates incoming information of the last trial by the automatic spreading of activation from input to output and, if inconsistencies arise, immediately adjusts the connections in memory so that causal judgments are readily available. It is evident that the cognitive simplicity and evident generality of connectionist models makes them a very attractive alternative to probabilistic models. However, the validity of the two approaches to causality depends ultimately on their empirical confirmation. It is to such empirical findings that we now turn.

DISCOUNTING AND AUGMENTATION

To distinguish between the probabilistic and connectionist accounts, we explore their predictions in two situations where a perceiver must learn which one among multiple factors caused an event. Despite the central place accorded in attribution theory to the principle of covariation, Kelley (1971) realized that this principle alone was not sufficient to explain how competing causal explanations are selected, and he therefore suggested two auxiliary principles of *discounting* and *augmentation*.

The discounting principle specifies that when the influence of one or more causes is already established, perceivers will disregard other possible causes as less relevant. A common example is when attributions to the person are discounted given evidence on the potent influence of external pressure. The reverse tendency is described in the augmentation principle, which suggests that given two opposing (facilitatory vs. inhibitory) causes, perceivers will value the strength of the cause that produces the effect higher to compensate for the inhibitory influence of the other cause. For instance, success will be more strongly attributed to a person's capacities when the task was hard rather than easy. Numerous investigations showed that these two competitive principles operate in causal judgments of adults (e.g., Hansen & Hall, 1985; Kruglanski, Schwartz, Maides, & Hamel, 1978) and children of 3–4 years of age (e.g., Kassin & Lowe, 1979; Kassin, Lowe, & Gibbons, 1980; Newman & Ruble, 1992).

Discounting and augmentation show a remarkable similarity with effects known in the associative literature as *blocking* and *conditioned inhibition* respectively (cf. Vallée-Tourangeau, Baker, & Mercier, 1994). These terms refer to specific procedures by which competitive effects have been discovered, first in animal conditioning (e.g., Kamin, 1968), and subsequently in causal judgment tasks with humans (e.g., Baker, Mercier, Valée-Tourangeau, Frank, & Pan, 1993; Chapman & Robbins, 1990; Chapman, 1991; Shanks, 1985, 1991). As explained before, a central feature of the Rescorla–Wagner and of other connectionist models is that the adjustments of cause–effect connections are determined by the discrepancy between the actual and expected effect, given not only the target cause but all other simultaneously presented causes, or Σw. Hence, competition for predictive strength between all causes present is an inherent property of associative or connectionist learning.

We conducted an experiment (Van Rooy & Van Overwalle, 1996) in which, in an initial phase, the influence of the context was strengthened in order to explore whether this would lead to the discounting or augmentation of attributions to the target person or to the stimulus later on. The causal strength of the context was enhanced by increasing the number of comparison persons or stimuli—that imply the context—from *one* (small comparison set) to *five* (large comparison set). As discussed before, when several comparison persons or stimuli share the same outcome, strong attributions will be made to the external or global context, respectively (Van Overwalle, 1997; Van Overwalle & Heylighen, 1995). For instance, when many athletes record a very fast time in a sprint race, they are more likely to attribute this outcome to external circumstances such as a favorable back wind rather than to personal talent. The crucial point now is that we expect greater discounting or augmenting effects when five rather than only one comparison person or stimulus is available. For example, attributions to personal athletic talent are more likely to be discounted when the number of other athletes who also record fast times is larger. Conversely, attributions to personal talent are more likely to be augmented the more other athletes record slow rather than fast running times. To what extent can probabilistic or connectionist models reproduce these predictions?

Connectionist Predictions

According to the Rescorla–Wagner network model, an increasing number of comparison cases (or trials) with a similar outcome will cause an increase in the perceived influence of the context. This is illustrated for a person factor and an external context in Fig. 5.4. As can be seen in both the top and bottom panel, the external context acquires a much stronger strength after five trials in the large comparison set ($w_E = .97$), than after one trial in the small comparison set ($w_E = .50$). This course of causal learning was followed in the first phase of our discounting and augmentation conditions.

The two conditions differed in the second phase, after the causal strength of the context was established. In the discounting condition, a novel contrast

Discounting

Large Set

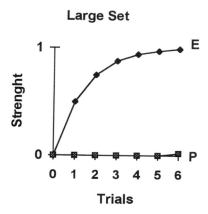

Small Set

Augmentation

Large Set

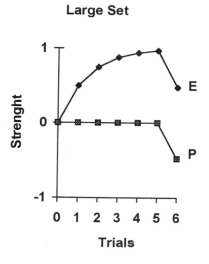

Small Set

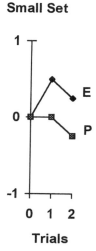

FIG. 5.4. A simulation of discounting and augmentation with parameter $\beta_w =$ .50, illustrated for a person (P) cause and its external (E) context. The conditions involved five (large set) or one (small set) E → effect trials, followed by one PE → effect trial in the discounting condition, or one PE → no effect trial in the augmentation condition.

person or stimulus was introduced sharing the same outcome as the previous comparison cases. According to the Rescorla–Wagner network, in the large comparison set, the role of this contrast factor will be strongly discounted or blocked because the context factor already fully predicts this outcome. This can be seen in the top panel of Fig. 5.4, where more discounting of the contrast person factor was observed in the large comparison set because the context previously acquired strong causal strength, whereas in the small comparison set, the context acquired less strength.

On the other hand, in the augmentation procedure, a novel person or stimulus contrast case is introduced with an outcome opposite to that of the preceding comparison cases. According to the Rescorla–Wagner model, in the large comparison set, this outcome is totally opposite to that predicted by the context factor so that the contrast factor will acquire strong negative strength to compensate for this discrepancy. As can be seen from the bottom panel in Fig. 5.4, the negative strength of the contrast factor was more augmented (i.e., more negative) in the large comparison set where the context acquired a strong causal role than in the small set where the context acquired less strength.

Probabilistic Predictions

These predictions are, however, problematic for probabilistic theory. The reason is that all current probabilistic models of causality (Cheng & Holyoak, 1995; Cheng & Novick, 1990; Van Overwalle, 1997; Waldmann & Holyoak, 1992) based their predictions on a probabilistic calculation of the effect, that is, the relative *proportion* of cause–effect covariation rather than its *raw* frequency. Consequently, all models predict that the probability of the effect given the context is the same whether the number of comparison cases is one or five (i.e., $\Delta P_X = 1/1$ and $5/5$ respectively for both discounting and augmentation), so that the contrast factor is expected to receive the same causal strength in each condition (see Equation 1). Thus, increasing the number of comparison cases should not make any difference to subjects' causal judgments.

Experiments and Results

Subjects were presented with different stories containing information about either five comparison persons or stimuli in the large comparison set, or only one comparison person or stimulus in the small comparison set. This information was followed by one target person or stimulus with the same outcome (discounting) or with an opposite outcome (augmentation). The following description illustrates the discounting of a person factor in the large set (with the small set between brackets): "Five other salesladies [One other saleslady] and also Annie attained high sales figures for perfumes." The next description depicts the augmentation of a person factor: "Five other sportswomen [One other sportswoman] fell during the sprint race, but Sandra did NOT fall during the sprint race." Similar descriptions were given to manipulate the discounting and augmentation of a stimulus factor.

In one condition, the information was presented in a prepackaged summary format (as in the examples above) that captured some aspects of people's verbal interactions with one another, and in another condition the information was presented in a sequential format (i.e., case-after-case) that reflected people's incidental learning during everyday life. After reading each story, subjects rated the causal influence of four factors including the person (i.e., *something about Annie*), the external context (i.e., *something external to Annie*), the stimulus (i.e., *something about perfumes*), and the global context (i.e., *something general about toiletry*), using an 11-point rating scale ranging from 0 (*absolutely no influence*) to 10 (*very strong influence*).

The most relevant attribution ratings are listed in Table 5.1. In line with the connectionist predictions, in the discounting condition, there was significantly more discounting in the large rather than the small comparison sets as shown by the mean attributions to the person and the stimulus; in the augmentation condition, mean attributions were significantly more augmented in the large rather than the small comparison sets. Thus, increasing the number of comparison cases lead to more discounting and more augmentation. This effect was significant in six out of eight comparisons, and most consistent in the summary presentation condition. Overall, these results are consistent with the Rescorla–Wagner network model, but clearly contradict probabilistic models.

TABLE 5.1
Mean Attribution Ratings per Factor and Condition

	Discounting		Augmentation	
	Large Set	*Small Set*	*Large Set*	*Small Set*
	Sequential Presentation			
Person	3.07	< 5.33	8.87	> 7.30
Stimulus	3.13	3.57	7.67	7.23
	Summary Presentation			
Person	4.03	< 7.67	8.63	> 5.93
Stimulus	2.67	< 5.90	7.90	> 6.03

Note. Differences between sets significant at $p < .05$ are indicated by > or <.

Model Simulations

In order to assess the overall performance of the two models, we computed simulations of Van Overwalle's (1997) probabilistic joint model using Equations 1 and 2, and of the Rescorla–Wagner network using Equation 3 (or 4) with weight updates after each trial. The information from the stories was encoded in the models in exactly the same order and number as provided to our subjects. Given that the Rescorla–Wagner network has one free parameter, the learning rate β_w, we sought the best fit for this model by running simulations for the whole range of admissible parameter values (between 0 and 1), and then selected the simulation with the highest correlation between simulated and observed responses (discussed later). Although this procedure may reflect some capitalization on chance, the mere existence of a free parameter might be considered as yet another way in which connectionist models are superior. To our knowledge, there is no published research in which the Rescorla–Wagner learning rate parameter was estimated on social data, so that an appropriate value can only be established post hoc. Note, however, that the reported best-fit parameter values are generally quite robust, and that deviations of .10 in the parameter values decrease the fit only minimally.

The sequential and summary formats were simulated separately with independent learning rates β_w, because we surmised that the format in which information was presented during the experiment might have affected the speed of learning of our subjects. Table 5.2 displays the correlation r between the simulated and observed responses for the contrast and context factors (averaged over all subjects). This measure provides an index of the summary fit of the models (Gluck & Bower, 1988a). As can be seen, although the probabilistic model captured some variance in the data (mean $r = .314$), the Rescorla–Wagner network model fit the data much better (mean $r = .802$). Contrary to our suspicion, the learning rate attained a high value of .80 in both presentation formats. This may suggest that the detection of covariation among social stimuli occurred relatively fast regardless of pre-

TABLE 5.2
Fits of the Models to the Discounting and Augmentation Data

Model	r	Model Parameter
Sequential Presentation		
Probabilistic Joint	.358	
Rescorla–Wagner	.854	$\beta_w = .80$
Summarized Presentation		
Probabilistic Joint	.270	
Rescorla–Wagner	.751	$\beta_w = .80$

Note. r = correlation, β_w = learning rate parameter.

sentation mode, perhaps because the social stories used in our research were quite simple and perhaps familiar to our subjects.

CONFIGURAL ATTRIBUTIONS

So far, we have dealt with single contrast factors and their contexts that make up single dimensions of causality. However, in real life, humans are most often confronted with a more complex situation where multiple dimensions are perceived simultaneously. As Kelley (1967) noted, we not only observe and compare regularly with other people, but also with other situations or stimuli, and with other occasions. When analyzing covariation with multiple dimensions, causality cannot be attributed only to single causes, but also to their interactions or configurations. For example, a car accident is often due to a concurrence of circumstances where various causal factors must be present (e.g., speeding, bad weather, etc.) to produce the effect. Such interactive causes are predicted by the probabilistic model (Cheng & Novick, 1990; Van Overwalle, 1997; Van Overwalle & Heylighen, 1995), but are problematic for the original Rescorla–Wagner model. Several connectionist amendments to the Rescorla–Wagner model were proposed to deal with configurations, but none were particularly elegant or plausible (e.g., Gluck & Bower, 1988b; Van Overwalle, 1996). Recently, however, Pearce (1994) developed a connectionist extension to Rescorla and Wagner's model that deals quite nicely with configurations. We first discuss Pearce's model and then explore some relevant empirical data.

Pearce's Configural Network Model

Pearce was inspired by the common observation in conditioning research that animals respond not only to the training cue but also to other cues that are similar to it, a phenomenon that is termed *generalization*. The more the other cues resemble the training cue, the more the organism expects the same effect and responds in a similar manner (Pearce, 1987, 1994). Similarly, humans may not only attribute causality to the true cause that covaries with the effect, but also to other factors that share similar features with it. However, such similar factors, in and of themselves, do not necessarily covary with the effect. Although generalization may thus be quite suboptimal from a statistical point of view, it does have adaptive value in real life. There may always be some doubt about the critical features in the true cause that produced the effect. Because these critical features may be present in other similar factors, it may be advantageous to generalize causality to these factors. Hence, generalization provides the basis for building generic knowledge that can be applied to many more situations other than the original learning situation.

To address the phenomenon of generalization, Pearce (1994) proposed a connectionist network that assumes that perceivers store in memory representations of *configural exemplars*. Exemplars reflect the whole stimulus configuration as it is encountered in the environment (e.g., a person in a particular situation at a particular time) rather than isolated factors (e.g., a person). Pearce's (1994) connectionist network consists of three layers, in which the exemplars are represented as configural nodes situated at an intermediate layer in between the input and output layers. These configural nodes differ from standard hidden nodes in other well-known connectionist models (McClelland & Rumelhart, 1988). An illustration of the network is given in Fig. 5.5 for four possible combinations of consensus and distinctiveness information. Assuming that the external (E) and global (G) context factors are always present, the PESG configural node reflects the presence of both the target person (P) and the target stimulus (S), PEG reflects the presence of the target person, ESG indicates the presence of the target stimulus, and EG denotes that both the target person and stimulus are absent.

Pearce's (1994) network closely follows the Rescorla–Wagner specifications with respect to the input and target activations; that is, activation is

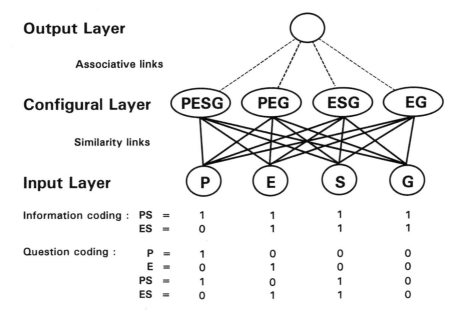

FIG. 5.5. The configural network proposed by Pearce (1994), illustrated for four factors P, E, S, and G.

set to 1 for a factor or effect that is present, otherwise the activation is 0. The input activation then spreads to the configural nodes in proportion to their similarity (discussed later). The more similar a configural node is to the pattern of input nodes, the more it will be activated. Hence, activation from input can spread to various other configurations and thus, indirectly, to other factors due to their mutual similarity rather than to actual covariation with the effect. This produces the effect of generalization.

The similarity between the input and configural nodes is fixed (indicated in the figure by straight lines) and determined by the number of common factors, as formalized below:

$$S_{i,h} = \left(\frac{n_c}{n_i}\right)\left(\frac{n_c}{n_h}\right). \tag{5}$$

In this expression, which is a simplified version of the original formula by Pearce (1987, 1994), n_c is the number of factors common to the input node and the configural node, n_i is the number of factors present in the input node, and n_h is the number of factors present in the configural (hidden) node.

After the configural nodes have been activated, their activation spreads through adjustable connections (indicated by broken lines) to the output node. As noted before, due to generalization, all configural nodes will receive some degree of activation, and all of them cooperate in activating the output node. However, only the configural node that encodes exactly the input information will receive maximum activation (because $S_{i,h} = 1$). Only the connection between this maximally activated configuration and the output is adjusted after each trial, whereas the connections between the other configurations remain unchanged. The adjustment follows the Rescorla–Wagner learning algorithm (Equation 3) except, of course, that the linear summation of the input nodes (Σw) is now replaced by the linear summation of the activation received from the configural nodes. Pearce's (1994) assumption that only the connection of the maximally activated configuration is adjusted stems from the original Rescorla–Wagner model where only the factors present are updated.

Like in the Rescorla–Wagner model, an appropriate measure for subjects' causal judgments is simply the activation of the output node given that the appropriate input nodes are turned on. This procedure works fine when only one contrast–context pair (or causal dimension) is involved. Using a similar logic as Chapman and Robbins (1990), it can be shown mathematically that Pearce's model—like the Rescorla–Wagner model—will converge close to probabilistic norms given sufficient learning trials.

However, when multiple contrast–context pairs are involved, this procedure might not be entirely satisfactory for Pearce's (1994) network, because the activation of one factor generalizes to other factors from other dimensions via the configural nodes, so that the strength of a factor is confounded and cannot be tested in isolation. One possibility to remedy this shortcoming is to assume that when the input nodes are turned on for one contrast–context dimension, the attention or salience for the other dimensions is drastically attenuated. For example, when the perceiver tests the strength of the P or E factor (i.e., locus dimension), then he or she may strongly reduce the attention to factors from other dimensions. This assumption is consistent with the common observation that many dimensions of causality are relatively independent (cf. Weiner, 1986), and thus can be attended to separately. We refer to this selective attention mechanism as the *attention strength for other dimensions* or α_0.

The α_0 mechanism was implemented in Pearce's similarity Equation 5 as follows: If at least one factor of a dimension is present at input, then the default attention (= 1) is used to estimate the number of these factors in Equation 5; conversely, if *no* factor of a dimension is present at input, then their number is estimated by the (much reduced) α_0 attention value. A low α_0 attention value implies that the similarity and strength of a factor (e.g., P) is influenced less by configural nodes containing many different factors (e.g., PESG) and more by configural nodes containing little else but this factor (e.g., PEG). This is true for both contrast and context factors. It is important to note that this selective attention mechanism affects only the testing phase of the model, because, during learning, all the context factors are assumed to be present at input, so that all factors are equally active and contribute equally to the learning of configurations. Given that Pearce (1994) allowed for varying intensity or attention in the terms of his similarity equation, in the network simulations described later, α_0 was freely estimated between 0 and 1. We expect that low values close to 0 will result in a better fit of the model.

Other Networks With Hidden Nodes

Kruschke (1992) recently proposed an exemplar network with a similarity gradient very similar to Pearce's configural network, but this network fell out of favor because its predictions depended too much on learning order (Lewandowsky, 1995). Computer simulations with our data presented in the next section also showed that this network explained less than half of the variance. Therefore, we do not further discuss this model.

Another class of very popular connectionist networks that make use of an intermediate layer are back-propagation networks (McClelland & Rumelhart, 1988). These networks differ, however, from the configural network in several respects. First, the intermediate nodes in the configural network are transparent as they copy exactly the input patterns, whereas back-propagation networks consist of nodes that are hidden in the sense that the network itself searches for an optimal representation without direct intervention from the input. Second, the links between input and configural nodes are fixed and determined by their similarity, whereas the connections between input and hidden nodes in back-propagation networks are adaptive and determined by the discrepancy between the expected and actual effects; this discrepancy is propagated from the output layer to the hidden layer, and then to the input layer. Third, and perhaps more importantly, the two networks were stimulated by a different theoretical concern. Whereas the configural network is based on empirical findings of generalization effects with animals (Pearce, 1987), back-propagation networks were developed mainly from mathematical considerations on how to propagate the error discrepancy efficiently through the network (Rumelhart, Durbin, Golden, & Chauvin, 1995). We surmise that the stronger empirical roots of the configural network make it a more appropriate candidate for modeling causal learning than conventional back-propagation networks. Because the configural network was already tested extensively with animals (see Pearce, 1994), we now turn to some empirical evidence with human subjects to compare the behavior of the configural network with the predictions of other networks.

Experiments and Results

We conducted two experiments (Van Overwalle & Van Rooy, 1996) in which subjects were presented with different scenarios reflecting all possible 2 × 2 combinations of Kelley's three covariation variables. After reading each scenario, the subjects rated the causal influence of single contrast factors (e.g., *something about the person, stimulus,* or *occasion*), single context factors (e.g., *something external, global,* or *stable*) as well as combinations of these factors, using a scale ranging from 0 (*no cause*) to 10 (*most complete cause*). As in the previous experiment, the information was presented under a summary format or a sequential trial-by-trial format. The predictions of the theoretical models under consideration are illustrated in Table 5.3 for consensus and distinctiveness, and can be readily extended to other combinations of covariation variables. To facilitate the discussion, under each information pattern, we listed the configural nodes implied by Pearce's (1994) model that acquire the strongest connection weights.

Because the probabilistic model failed to predict the important phenomenon of discounting and augmentation, we turn immediately to the predictions of Pearce's predecessor, the Rescorla–Wagner network. As suggested before, given sufficient learning trials, this network will converge to probabilistic predictions, provided that the input nodes are coded separately for each contrast–context dimension and their interactions (Van Overwalle, 1996). Hence, the Rescorla–Wagner network predicts that when there is a

TABLE 5.3
Causal Strength Predictions of Rescorla–Wagner's and
Pearce's Network Illustrated for Consensus and Distinctiveness

Consensus	High		Low	
Distinctiveness	Low	High	Low	High
Configural nodes[a]	EG	ESG	PEG	PESG
Causal Prediction				
Positive	EG	ES	PG	PS
	E	E	P	P
	G	S	G	S
Generalized[b]	PG	PS	PS	PG
	ES	EG	EG	ES
Null	PS	PG	ES	EG
	P	P	E	E
	S	G	S	G

Note. P = person, E = external, S = stimulus, G = general.
[a]Configural nodes in Pearce's model that will acquire the strongest weights.
[b]Null strength predicted by Rescorla & Wagner, generalized strength predicted by Pearce.

contrast in the observations, then attributions are made to contrast causes; conversely, when there is no such contrast, attributions are made to the context. Applied to Table 5.3, this implies that attributions will be made to the person (P) given low consensus, and to external (E) causes given high consensus; and similarly, that attributions will be made to the stimulus (S) given high distinctiveness, and to general (G) causes given low distinctiveness. These predictions can be combined to produce attributions to interactions (see top panel). In sum, the Rescorla–Wagner model assumes that these single factors and their interactions will receive significant *positive* causal strength, whereas all other factors (i.e., not tabled in the top panel) are assumed to have approximately *null* causal strength.

Pearce's configural network model makes similar predictions with respect to the causal factors depicted in the top panel of Table 5.3, but for entirely different reasons. As explained earlier, the configural network predicts that most causal strength will be acquired by the configural node that is always followed by the effect (see table header). For instance, high consensus and high distinctiveness indicate that the contrast stimulus (S), together with the external (E) and global (G) contexts, are followed by the effect. This reinforces most strongly the connection weight of the ESG configural node. This weight will then generalize to other causes that form a part of the configuration (e.g., ESG generalizes to E, S, & ES). Therefore, these causes will receive substantial positive causal strength. At his point, Pearce's configural network makes very similar predictions as the Rescorla–Wagner model. In addition, Pearce's network makes the unique prediction that some amount of the causal strength of the maximally connected configural node will also generalize to other interactions that are not part of it, but that share a factor (e.g., ESG generalizes to PS & EG). These interactions are denoted as *generalized* causes because they do not covary at all with the effect, but they do receive some causal strength (see middle panel). The strength of these generalized causes should be stronger than that of the remaining causes that receive null causal strength (see bottom panel).

A summary of the results is given in Table 5.4. As can be seen, the ratings provided by our subjects were most consistent with Pearce's (1994) configural network. There was strong support for the prediction, shared with the Rescorla–Wagner model, that the attribution ratings for positive factors are higher than for generalized and null factors. In support of the unique prediction of the configural network, however, most generalized causes received attribution ratings that were substantially higher than null causes.

Model Simulations

To provide additional confirmation for these results and to test our proposed amendment with respect to the α_o parameter, we computed simulations of Pearce's configural network and compared them with the predictions of the Rescorla–Wagner model. In addition, we computed simulations with the widely used back-propagation network.

We used the same procedure as in the earlier simulations. The information provided to the subjects was encoded in each network, and connection weights were updated after each trial. For the Rescorla–Wagner network, there were separate output nodes for each contrast–context dimension and for their interactions, with a common teaching value and a common β_w learning rate parameter. This architecture guarantees that the network will converge toward probabilistic norms (Van Overwalle, 1996). For Pearce's configural network, the trial information implied four configural nodes (see Table 5.3), with a β_w learning rate and an α_o selective attention parameter. For reasons of comparability, we took the same number of hidden nodes in the back-propagation network, and also the same number of parameters, including a β_w learning rate and an α_m momentum parameter. The momen-

TABLE 5.4
Mean Causal Ratings in Function of Causal Strength Type

	Positive	Generalized	Null
Presentation			
Sequential	5.46	3.87	2.90
Summary	6.84	4.17	2.82

Note. Means differ significantly between all three causal types ($p < .002$).

tum parameter reflects the effect of the past weight update on the current update, and so effectively filters out strong oscillations in the updates (McClelland & Rumelhart, 1988). As noted earlier, because the context factors act as a kind of bias term, we did not include additional bias weights (McClelland & Rumelhart, 1988). As before, for all models, we calculated all admissible parameter values between 0 and 1, and then selected the values that attained the highest correlation between simulated and observed data.

Because the information in the experiments was either presented randomly (in the sequential format) or without any particular order (in the summary format) for each story, we ran 100 simulations with different random trial orders.[2] Table 5.5 presents the summary fit r for each model. The results show that although the Rescorla–Wagner network obtained an adequate fit in the two formats (mean $r = .759$), it was the configural network that reached a slightly better fit overall (mean $r = .793$). The learning rate of both models was highest for the sequential presentation format, suggesting (perhaps contrary to intuition) that the somewhat more complex stimulus material in the present experiments was learned most quickly when presented trial-by-trial. In contrast, the back-propagation simulation failed to reproduce our data to any reasonable degree (mean $r = .171$).

Perhaps the high fit of the configural model was partly due to the introduction of the novel α_o parameter. As expected, the estimates of this parameter were very low, confirming our idea that to test causal strengths independently, the influence of other dimensions needs to be canceled out. Omitting this parameter so that all dimensions were equally activated during testing reduced the r fit measure for the configural network by .086 and .146 in the sequential and summary formats respectively. However, on the basis of the present results alone, it is difficult to assess the generality of our α_o solution for other material.

Why did the back-propagation model perform so poorly? Additional simulations may provide some hints. When 20 instead of 4 hidden nodes were used, the fit did not improve. However, repeating the original trial information of each story improved the fit substantially, but not to the same degree as the other models (mean $r = .277$ with 10 repetitions and mean $r = .430$ with 100 repetitions, all with the same parameter values in Table 5.5). Although perhaps more repetitions or slightly different parameter values might have accommodated the data better, the model seems unable to learn

---

[2]Given that the amount of comparison cases was not specified in the summary format, their number was estimated by running simulations of the probabilistic joint model with different weights for the frequencies of the comparison cases. The highest fit was obtained when the comparison cases received one fifth of the weight of the target cases. The simulations with the connectionist models were then carried out with the number of trials of comparison and target cases adjusted to that same proportion, that is, five target trials for each comparison trial.

TABLE 5.5
Fits of the Models to the Attribution Data

Model	r	Model Parameters
Sequential Presentation		
Rescorla–Wagner	.706	$\beta_w = .62$
Configural	.742	$\beta_w = 1.00;\ \alpha_o = .13$
Back-Propagation	.152	$\beta_w = .81;\ \alpha_m = .52$
Summarized Presentation		
Rescorla–Wagner	.812	$\beta_w = .41$
Configural	.844	$\beta_w = .42;\ \alpha_o = .03$
Back-Propagation	.191	$\beta_w = .88;\ \alpha_m = .99$

Note. r = maximum correlation; Model parameters are: β_w = learning rate; α_o = attention for other dimensions not present at input; α_m = momentum. There were 3 comparison trials in the sequential format; their number in the summary format was simulated as 1/5 (see footnote 2).

the configurations (and their hidden representation) at a reasonable speed. This suggests that Pearce's (1994) exemplar representation of hidden configurations is crucial to the superior and faster performance of his model.

CONCLUSIONS

The data presented in this chapter clearly demonstrate that a connectionist approach has much promise for our understanding of the processes underlying causal reasoning. We have shown how the Rescorla–Wagner network can easily deal with discounting and augmentation effects and how Pearce's configural network predicts generalization of causality, two findings that are problematic for the original covariation principle of Kelley (1967, 1971) as well as for a probabilistic conception of it (Cheng & Novick, 1990). Other cognitive research with humans documented that the Rescorla–Wagner model is superior to the probabilistic approach in explaining competition effects like discounting and augmentation (Baker et al., 1993; Chapman, 1991; Chapman & Robbins, 1990; Gluck, & Bower, 1988a, 1988b; Shanks, 1985, 1993, 1995; Vallée-Tourangeau et al., 1994), and there is also increasing evidence to suggest that animals process covariation information in configural units rather than in elemental features (for a review see Pearce, 1987, 1994). On a theoretical level, the connectionist approach may explain how humans are capable of detecting causal relationships while using little cognitive sources and effort, so that it provides a more plausible account of causal reasoning during the hurry of everyday social life.

The present connectionist approach to attribution leaves a number of unresolved issues. The picture of learning that emerges from connectionist networks is of a rather passive process, in which activations spread automatically and weights are adjusted immediately. However, humans may also take a more active role in which they consider various causal hypotheses that may explain an outcome. Recently, Read (Read & Marcus-Newhall, 1993) proposed a connectionist network to account for this process of hypothesis selection. He suggested that humans' causal knowledge in a particular domain can be represented by a large network structure, with each node representing a domain-relevant causal factor. All these factors compete to acquire some degree of activation, but only the node with the highest activation is chosen as the most plausible hypothesis. However, because the connections in Read's network are *not* adaptive, more work needs to be done to integrate it with the present approach.

Another intriguing question is precisely how connections are adjusted given summarized information. The connectionist approach has no obvious means of explaining this because there are no separate trials during which input activation spreads through the network and weights are adjusted. Our simulations of the summary data were, in fact, carried out by imposing phantom "trials" to the networks. It is possible that the primitive mechanism of associative learning has been adapted during human evolution for the novel task of interpreting verbal summary statements, because nature typically reuses subsystems that are already capable of functioning on their own (Beecher, 1988). One possibility is that humans portray the summary information in the form of dummy entities or mental models (cf. Johnson-Laird, 1983), which are then sequentially analyzed by an associative processor. However, this is mere speculation and we know of no direct evidence that may support this hypothesis.

Leaving these interesting questions aside, we suspect that there is potential for feedforward connectionist models to explain even a broader range of social phenomena in which the detection of covariation plays a role. For instance, the connectionist approach may provide an alternative account for some intriguing findings in group stereotyping, such as illusory correlations (Hamilton & Gifford, 1976). Illusory correlation is the robust effect that perceivers judge minority groups more negatively than majority groups, even when the proportion of their positive and negative behaviors is identical (e.g., twice as much positive to negative behaviors). Because there is less behavioral information about the minority group, and given that learning in a network occurs incrementally, the biased perceptions about the minority group may reflect preasymptotic judgments that are so typical of connectionist models. Indeed, when judgments have not yet reached asymptote in the minority group, any potential difference between the connection weights of positive and negative behaviors is still minimal (so that their contribution seem equal), but that difference grows stronger as the connection weights converge to asymptote in the majority group (so that positive behaviors seem to clearly outweigh negative behaviors).

Given that connectionist models are an idealized reflection of the neural workings of the human brain, we suspect that they will perhaps increase our understanding of other causal phenomena, such as how perceivers infer dispositional attributions about other persons using covariation information (cf. Hilton, Smith, & Kim, 1995), and how people fall prey to other causal illusions, such as the correspondence bias (Gilbert, 1989). We suspect that these and many other phenomena in social reasoning are not so much a tricky result of our social perceptions, societal rules, or of the demanding circumstances of everyday social life, but simply the outcome of a connectionist processing mechanism.

ACKNOWLEDGMENTS

We are very grateful to the editors for their helpful comments on earlier versions of the manuscript. The research reported in this chapter was supported in part by the Belgian National Foundation of Scientific Research (N.F.W.O.) under grant 8.0192.95. Address correspondence to Frank Van Overwalle, Department of Psychology, Vrije Universiteit Brussel, Pleinlaan 2, B–1050 Brussel, Belgium; or by e-mail: Frank.VanOverwalle@vub.ac.be.

REFERENCES

Abramson, L. V., Seligman, M. E. P., & Teasdale, J. D. (1978). Learned helplessness in humans: Critique and reformulation. *Journal of Abnormal Psychology, 87*, 49–74.

Allen, L. G. (1993). Human contingency judgments: Rule based or associative? *Psychological Bulletin, 114*, 435–448.

Baker, A. G., Mercier, P., Vallée-Tourangeau, F., Frank, R., & Pan, M. (1993). Selective associations and causality judgments: Presence of a strong causal factor may reduce judgments of a weaker one. *Journal of Experimental Psychology: Learning, Memory, and Cognition, 19*, 414–432.

Beecher, M. D. (1988). Some comments on the adaptationist approach to learning. In R. C. Bolles & M. D. Beecher (Eds.), *Evolution and learning* (pp. 239–248). Hillsdale, NJ: Lawrence Erlbaum Associates.

Chapman, G. B. (1991). Trial order affects cue interaction in contingency judgment. *Journal of Experimental Psychology: Learning, Memory, and Cognition, 17*, 837–854.

Chapman, G. B., & Robbins, S. J. (1990). Cue interaction in human contingency judgment. *Memory and Cognition, 18*, 537–545.

Cheng, P. W., & Holyoak, K. J. (1995). Adaptive systems as intuitive statisticians: Causality, contingency, and prediction. In H. L. Roiblatt & J. -A. Meyer (Eds.), *Comparative approaches to cognitive science* (pp. 271–302). Cambridge, MA: MIT Press.

Cheng, P. W., & Novick, L. R. (1990). A probabilistic contrast model of causal induction. *Journal of Personality and Social Psychology, 58*, 545–567.

Gilbert, D. T. (1989). Thinking lightly about others: Automatic components of the social inference process. In J. S. Uleman & J. A. Bargh (Eds.), *Unintended thought* (pp. 189–211). New York: Guilford.

Gluck, M. A., & Bower, G. H. (1988a). From conditioning to category learning: An adaptive network model. *Journal of Experimental Psychology: General, 117*, 227–247.

Gluck, M. A., & Bower, G. H. (1988b). Evaluating an adaptive network model of human learning. *Journal of Memory and Language, 27*, 166–195.

Hamilton, D. L., Driscoll, D. M., & Worth, L. T. (1989). Cognitive organization of impressions: Effects of incongruency in complex representations. *Journal of Personality and Social Psychology, 57*, 925–939.

Hamilton, D. L., & Gifford, R. K. (1976). Illusory correlation in interpersonal perception: A cognitive basis of stereotypic judgment. *Journal of Experimental Social Psychology, 12*, 392–407.

Hansen, D. H., & Hall, C. A. (1985). Discounting and augmenting facilitative and inhibitory forces: The winner takes almost all. *Journal of Personality and Social Psychology, 49*, 1482–1493.

Hawkins, R. D. (1989). A biologically realistic neural network model for higher-order features of classical conditioning. In R. G. M. Morris (Ed.), *Parallel distributed processing: Implications for psychology and neurobiology* (pp. 214–247). Oxford, England: Clarendon Press.

Hewstone, M., & Jaspars, J. (1987). Covariation and causal attribution: A logical model of the intuitive analysis of variance. *Journal of Personality and Social Psychology, 53*, 663–673.

Hilton, D. J., & Slugoski, B. R. (1986). Knowledge-based causal attribution: The abnormal conditions focus model. *Psychological Review, 93*, 75–88.

Hilton, D. J., Smith, R. H., & Kim, S. H. (1995). The process of causal explanation and dispositional attribution. *Journal of Personality and Social Psychology, 68*, 377–387.

Johnson-Laird, P. N. (1983). *Mental models: Towards a cognitive science of language, inference, and consciousness.* Cambridge, England: Cambridge University Press.

Kahneman, D., Slovic, P., & Tversky, A. (1982). *Judgments under uncertainty: Heuristics and biases.* Cambridge, England: Cambridge University Press.

Kamin, L. J. (1968). Attention-like processes in classical conditioning. In M. R. Jones (Ed.), *Miami Symposium on the Prediction of Behavior: Aversive Stimulation* (pp. 9–33). Miami, FL: University of Miami Press.

Kassin, S. M., & Lowe, C. A. (1979). On the development of the augmentation principle: A perceptual approach. *Child Development, 50*, 728–734.

Kassin, S. M., Lowe, C. A., & Gibbons, F. X. (1980). Children's use of the discounting principle: A perceptual approach. *Journal of Personality and Social Psychology, 39*, 719–728.

Kelley, H. H. (1967). Attribution in social psychology. *Nebraska Symposium on Motivation, 15*, 192–238.

Kelley, H. H. (1971). Attribution in social interaction. In E. E. Jones, D. E. Kanouse, H. H. Kelley, R. E. Nisbett, S. Valins, & B. Weiner (Eds.), *Attribution: Perceiving the causes of behavior* (pp. 1–26). Morristown, NJ: General Learning Press.

Kruglanski, A. W., Schwartz, S. M., Maides, S., & Hamel, I. Z. (1978). Covariation, discounting, and augmentation: Towards a clarification of attributional principles. *Journal of Personality, 76*, 176–189.

Kruschke, J. K. (1992). ALCOVE: An exemplar-based connectionist model of category learning. *Psychological Review, 99*, 22–44.

Lewandowsky, S. (1995). Base-rate neglect in ALCOVE: A critical reevaluation. *Psychological Review, 102*, 185–191.

McClelland, J. M., & Rumelhart, D. E. (1988). *Explorations in parallel distributed processing: A handbook of models, programs and exercises.* Cambridge, MA: Bradford Book.

Newman, L. S., & Ruble, D. N. (1992). Do young children use the discounting principle? *Journal of Experimental Social Psychology, 28*, 572–593.

Pearce, J. M. (1987). A model for stimulus generalization in Pavlovian Conditioning. *Psychological Review, 94*, 61–73.

Pearce, J. M. (1994). Similarity and discrimination: A selective review and a connectionist model. *Psychological Review, 101*, 587–607.

Read, S. J., & Marcus-Newhall, A. (1993). Explanatory coherence in social explanations: A parallel distributed processing account. *Journal of Personality and Social Psychology, 65*, 429–447.

Rescorla, R. A., & Wagner, A. R. (1972). A theory of Pavlovian conditioning: Variations in the effectiveness of reinforcement and nonreinforcement. In A. H. Black & W. F. Prokasy (Eds.), *Classical conditioning II: Current research and theory* (pp. 64–98). New York: Appleton-Century-Crofts.

Rumelhart, D. E., Durbin, R., Golden, R., & Chauvin, Y. (1995). Back-propagation: The basic theory. In Y. Chauvin & D. E. Rumelhart (Eds.), *Back-propagation: Theory, architecture and applications* (pp. 1–34). Mahwah, NJ: Lawrence Erlbaum Associates.

Shanks, D. R. (1985). Forward and backward blocking in human contingency judgment. *Quarterly Journal of Experimental Psychology, 37B*, 1–21.

Shanks, D. R. (1991). Categorization by a connectionist network. *Journal of Experimental Psychology: Learning, Memory and Cognition, 17*, 433–443.

Shanks, D. R. (1993). Human instrumental learning: A critical review of data and theory. *British Journal of Psychology, 84*, 319–354.

Shanks, D. R. (1995). Is human learning rational? *Quarterly Journal of Experimental Psychology, 48A*, 257–279.

Vallée-Tourangeau, F., Baker, A. G., & Mercier, P. (1994). Discounting in causality and covariation judgments. *Quarterly Journal of Experimental Psychology, 47B*, 151–171.

Van Overwalle, F. (1996). The relationship between the Rescorla–Wagner associative model and the probabilistic joint model of causality. *Psychologica Belgica, 36*, 171–192.

Van Overwalle, F. (1997). A test of the joint model of causal attribution. *European Journal of Social Psychology, 27*, 221–236.

Van Overwalle, F., & Heylighen, F. (1995). Relating covariation information to causal dimensions through principles of contrast and invariance. *European Journal of Social Psychology, 25*, 435–455.

Van Overwalle, F., & Van Rooy, D. (1996). *Generalization beyond covariation: A comparison between probabilistic and connectionist models of causal attribution.* Manuscript submitted for publication.

Van Rooy, D., & Van Overwalle, F. (1996). Een associatieve benadering van discounting en augmentation in causale attributie [An associative approach to discounting and augmentation in causal attribution]. In N. K. De Vries, C. K. W. De Dreu, W. Stroebe, & R. Vonk (Eds.), *Fundamentele sociale psychologie: Deel 10* (pp. 14–28). Tilburg, The Netherlands: Tilburg University Press.

Waldmann, M. R., & Holyoak, K. J. (1992). Predictive and diagnostic learning within causal models: Asymmetries in cue competition. *Journal of Experimental Psychology: General, 121*, 222–236.

Weiner, B. (1986). *An attributional theory of achievement motivation and emotion.* New York: Springer-Verlag.

PERSONALITY AND BEHAVIOR

6

PERSONALITY AS A STABLE COGNITIVE–AFFECTIVE ACTIVATION NETWORK: CHARACTERISTIC PATTERNS OF BEHAVIOR VARIATION EMERGE FROM A STABLE PERSONALITY STRUCTURE

Yuichi Shoda
University of Washington

Walter Mischel
Columbia University

The model of the human mind has undergone a significant evolution in recent years, shifting away from the serial, centralized processing view favored during the 1970s and the early 1980s. Rather than depict the human mind as analogous to a traditional computer program, consisting of a series of logical evaluations and procedures to be executed one step at a time, the new model moves toward a more parallel-distributed processing conception that allows multiple simultaneous processes without a single central control. Yet, the system can produce meaningful, coherent, and adaptive patterns of behavior, reflecting the dynamic interplay among the multiple processes, without necessarily following a specific plan.

Without a central control or a plan, then, what governs the generation of such patterns? The basic premise of the connectionist movement is that the answer lies in the network of relationships among the units that make up the system. And the excitement comes from the many demonstrations and theoretical analyses that show that networks can be built to perform sophisticated information processing, particularly the kinds that are difficult for traditional computers but particularly germane for complex higher level human functions.

Most applications of the connectionist models of information processing so far have concentrated on modeling specific information processing tasks, such as perception and memory. However, if human information processing at the level of such specific performance emerges from dynamic activation of a connectionist network, then the same principle may also underlie "higher level" phenomena commonly considered the domain of social cognition, as evidenced by the work described in this volume. In fact, one of the appeals of the connectionist models is their ability to apply the same principles to provide a unifying account of both molecular- and molar-level phenomena.

The goal of the present chapter is to take such an effort one step further, to the level of the individual's characteristic patterns of social behavior, and their relationships to the external situations and internal conditions in which they unfold. Specifically, we address the question of how the diverse behaviors of an individual in different situations "cohere" or are related in ways that characterize him or her stably. In this attempt, we present an alternative perspective on personality and on the so-called consistency paradox: the apparent contradiction between the persistent empirical findings of behavioral inconsistency across situations, on the one hand, and the belief in personality coherence and stability, on the other (e.g., Mischel & Peake, 1982).

First, we briefly describe this long-standing paradox and then show how the new and still emerging conception of human information processing promises to naturally provide a way to resolve it. We illustrate this model with a computer simulation, and an application of such a conceptualization of personality in a domain of health protective behavior.

BEHAVIORAL EXPRESSIONS OF UNDERLYING INVARIANCES IN THE PERSON: WHAT DEMANDS EXPLANATION?

The core assumption about the nature of personality—built into its very definition—is that individuals are characterized by qualities that are relatively invariant across situations and over a span of time. Guided by that assumption, the pioneer of modern personality, Gordon Allport (1937) urged personality psychologists to "embrace the problem of intra-individual consistency ..." (p. 23). Unclear, however, was the nature of such invariances and their behavioral expressions.

Historically, and quite reasonably, it has been widely assumed that people differ stably in their predisposition to engage in particular types of behaviors (e.g., friendly, conscientious, aggressive). Dispositions and their behavioral expressions were assumed to have a linear, or at least monotonic, relationship, so that the more a person has a trait of friendliness, for example, the more instances of relevant (i.e., friendly) behavior are expected. Thus in this view, personality is conceptualized as a collection of dispositions toward given types of behaviors, which can be represented as follows:

$$\text{Personality} = \begin{array}{l} \text{disposition toward behavior X} \\ \text{disposition toward behavior Y} \\ \text{disposition toward behavior Z} \end{array}$$

Given this assumption, friendlier persons, for example, are expected to display more friendly behaviors than less friendly persons across a wide range of situations. In other words, the assumption was simply that there should be a relatively consistent rank-ordering of individuals in their trait-relevant behaviors. And if one observes that person A is more friendly than person B in one situation, but that B is more friendly than A in another, at least one, or both, of the observations are considered to reflect a temporary fluctuation from the "true" rank ordering of the individuals with respect to their friendliness. Guided by this expectation, personality psychologists pursued cross-situational consistency as evidence of basic coherence in the underlying personality (behavioral) dispositions of individuals. To the surprise of many, however, the results in the search for this type of high cross-situational consistency were unexpectedly discouraging from the start (e.g., Hartshorne & May, 1928; Mischel, 1968; Mischel & Peake, 1982; Newcomb, 1929; Peterson, 1968; Vernon, 1964). After years of study and discussion, although the interpretations continue to differ, the average cross-situational coefficients remain typically low, but nonzero, accounting for only a small percent of the variance (e.g., Mischel, 1993).

Thus, an individual's behaviors in fact significantly fluctuate from the "typical," average level for that person, depending on the specific situations she or he is in. Faced with such findings, and consistent with the assumptions of classic trait theory, the obtained data on situational variability have typically been dismissed as the product of unreliability of measurement or "error." The mainstream solution for dealing with what was thus conceptualized as merely error was to try to eliminate it by aggregating across situations, thereby removing the effects of the situation and focusing on the mean level of behavior as the dispositional index. The net effect was to deliberately exclude the situation from the analysis and conceptualization of the person.

In contrast, we thought it would be reasonable to ask: Do the fluctuations from situation to situation in the individual's social behaviors (e.g., friendlier than most people in situation A but not as friendly as most in situation B) mean that social behaviors are intrinsically unpredictable, and that the best one can do is to predict their average level across situations? Or is there any meaningful pattern and predictability in what appear to be unpredictable variations in behaviors across situations? To address these questions, we undertook an extensive program of empirical research. In this work we explored the proposition that such variability, rather than reflecting only the errors of measurement and unreliability, also might reflect the coherent structure of the underlying personality system, and might also provide clues about its organization and functioning.

Stable Situation–Behavior (if . . . then . . .) Relations Characterize Individuals: Models of Stability Must Incorporate Situations

Results of our empirical investigations over the last 10 years suggest that stable situation-behavior patterns in fact exist, at least in some of the domains we studied, in addition to overall, average individual differences in the tendency to display a type of behavior. For example, at a children's summer camp, as shown in Fig. 6.1, one child was consistently more verbally aggressive than others when warned by an adult. In contrast, another child, although showing a similar overall average level of aggression, was distinctive in that his aggressive behaviors were more visible when approached by a peer than when warned by an adult. For a significant proportion of the children, such stable intraindividual patterns of if . . . then . . . relations were observed (Shoda, Mischel, & Wright, 1993a, 1993b, 1994).

We therefore concluded that the observed situation-to-situation variations in behavior are not all random, but rather, may also reflect stable

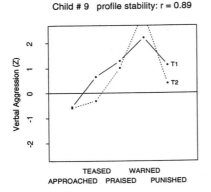
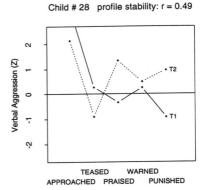

FIG. 6.1. Intraindividual, situation-behavior profiles for verbal aggression in five situations: two illustrative cases. Levels of verbal aggression are shown in z-scores, relative to the normative levels of verbal aggression in each situation (based on data in Shoda, Mischel, & Wright, 1994). Copyright 1994 by the American Psychological Association, adapted with permission.

characteristics of the individual. Generally, and schematically, the data show the following:

Person A: situation 1 → behavior x
situation 2 → behavior y
situation 3 → behavior z

Person B: situation 1 → behavior y
situation 2 → behavior z
situation 3 → behavior x

That is, both individuals A and B sometimes do x, sometimes y, and sometimes z; thus, they are not different in their dispositions toward displaying each type of behavior on the whole. However, they are typically (characteristically) different in the situations in which they display each type of behavior—Person A does x in situation 1, but Person B does it in situation 3; A does y in situation 2, but B does it in situation 1. How might one conceptualize personality to account for this type of individual difference? The traditional conceptualization of the person as a set of dispositions toward a given type of behavior, although parsimonious, cannot readily account for such situation-behavior relations. To do so requires a model of personality that also represents some information about situations and that incorporates the situation explicitly into the model of personality. The present chapter is a step in that direction.

If . . . Then . . . Rules in the Behavior Production System: Predicting Stable Patterns of Variability

At first, one may represent each person as a collection of if . . . then . . . rules, as a classical behaviorist might:

Personality =
```
┌────────────────────┐
│  If S1, then X      │
│  If S2, then Y      │
│      . . .          │
│  If Sn, Then . . .  │
└────────────────────┘
```

However, although this is adequate as a simple description of a person, it is far from being parsimonious in that in order to account for N units of if . . . then . . . relations observed, it requires the same N units of information to be represented in the model. That is, the explanation is as complex as the phenomenon it tries to explain. Thus, in our view, the set of observed if . . . then . . . relations is the data to be accounted for, rather than the account of the data. The latter has to come from the understanding of the intraindividual dynamics that produce the observed if . . . then . . . relationships. It must provide a more parsimonious explanation than conceptualizing personality as a collection of separate if . . . then . . . reflexes, in ways that achieve explanatory coherence (Thagard, 1992).

We need a model of a personality system that generates the observed if . . . then . . . relationships without literally representing each of them separately. As schematically shown below, the model should produce behavior X when in situation S1, but Y when in situation S2, and it must do so while assuming that the personality system itself remains unchanged. How should we conceptualize the processing system that is in the box below?

Situations   Person   Behaviors

    S1→   ┌───────────┐   → X
    S2→   │   │   → Y
            │   ?   │
            │   │
    Sn→   └───────────┘   → . . .

It also has been argued repeatedly that in order to understand social behavior, one must take into account interactions between the person and the situation, and the importance of such interactions in accounting for the observed behavior variance has been demonstrated convincingly (e.g., Magnusson & Endler, 1977). The next challenge is to go beyond acknowledging that Person × Situation interactions exist to understanding just how personality interacts with situations in determining behavior. For that purpose, we believe that the traditional conception of personality as a set of behavioral dispositions is not conducive, because it does not lend itself readily to the analysis of the generative processes that underlie patterns of Person × Situation interaction. For example, from the characterization of a person as "friendly," it is difficult to understand why a person who is typically friendlier than most people with colleagues may also be characteristically less friendly than most people when interacting with students. In contrast, as recent advances in goal-based analyses of personality and its interactions with social situations showed (e.g., Miller & Read, 1989; Read & Miller, 1989), we need a more process-oriented conception of personality to account for meaningful patterns of Person × Situation interactions. In short, we need a model that addresses not only the overall level of different types of behavior that characterize an individual but their predictable pattern of variability across situations (e.g., he always does X when A but Y when B).

Summary of the Model's Requirements

In sum, a model of the personality system that underlies each person's characteristic if . . . then . . . relations must incorporate the role of situations, events, or contexts into the conception of personality. It also must recognize the goal-directed, self-generated nature of human behavior, in which one does not merely react passively to situations, but has a continuous "mental life," including ruminations, imaginations, and construction of future plans. It must deal with cognitive and emotional encoding of situations at multiple levels of awareness and automaticity (e.g., Bargh, 1994a, 1994b; Kihlstrom, 1990). For example, it must be consistent with the findings that people may not be aware of their responses to situations, particularly those that invoke affective responses, and that they may not be able to control such responses (e.g., Bargh, 1994; Zajonc, 1980). In doing so, the concept of the situation must go beyond the simple stimulus in early behaviorism that mechanically pulls responses from an organism's repertoire. Rather, it must encompass the mediating processes, such as the appraisal and construal of the situation, as well as the cognitive and affective processes that follow encoding of the situation.

The processing of the situation must also be fast: When "something" tells a New Yorker to cross a street, or to get off a subway car before the intended destination, the processing is nearly instantaneous; or when someone asks an unexpected question at a party, we may experience a very complex array of emotions within a split second. Like a master chess player (Chase & Simon, 1973; de Groot, 1965), the instant we are exposed to a social situation, we seem to be able to process the very complex set of features present within it. The model also needs to accommodate processing that is not "logical" or "rational." For example, to varying degrees, everyone has the experience of behaving in ways that later are regretted. And despite our best intentions and resolutions, we often find ourselves again doing or saying things that we vowed not to repeat. Sometimes these behaviors seem paradoxical or "ironic," as when we try not to think about something and then find we cannot keep from thinking about it (e.g., Wegner, 1995). Finally, although the goal of the model is to understand social behaviors and personality processes at a molar level, it nonetheless should be compatible with the basic processes that also underlie cognitive, affective, and behavioral responses.

THE COGNITIVE–AFFECTIVE PROCESS SYSTEM (CAPS) MODEL OF THE PERSON

The Units of Analysis

To outline the type of personality system that would satisfy these requirements, our first step was to specify the nature of the units that make up a model of the personality system (Mischel & Shoda, 1995). In a typical study in personality psychology, the unit of analysis employed is an individual, represented by a score on a particular scale. Thus, a variable represents different positions that different people occupy on a dimension. Such a representation tells us how one individual differs (i.e., higher vs. lower) from others in a given dimension, but it does not directly address how each individual's mind works, which requires understanding the intraindividual dynamics that underlie and generate his or her set of stable if . . . then . . . relations. Thus, the unit should allow one to capture the dynamically changing nature of psychological experiences within each person. The units of analysis must refer to the "what," "why," "when," and "how" of the individual's changing experience and behavior, not just to the "how much" of the behavior that is generated.

With that goal in mind, we first considered the types of cognitive and affective mediating units to use as basic ingredients for a dynamic conception of personality. In answering this question, we were guided by the social–cognitive views of personality, broadly defined, in which the units refer to the processes that generate social behaviors, such as goals and motives, expectancies, and values, rather than the phenotypic characteristics of the behaviors themselves (Mischel, 1973; 1990). For example, goals have been shown to provide particularly useful explanatory units by a number of investigators (e.g., Alston, 1975; Gollwitzer & Bargh, 1996; Pervin, 1982; Read & Miller, 1990). Focusing on the distinctive configuration of goals of an individual also allows one to select the features of situations that are relevant and that interact with the qualities of the person (Miller & Read, 1989; Read & Miller, 1989). Furthermore, other aspects of personality, such as plans, resources, competencies, and beliefs and knowledge about the world, are expected to form a coherent pattern organized around the goals (Read, Jones, & Miller, 1990).

Cumulative findings from social, clinical, developmental, and cognitive psychology as well as from cultural anthropology suggested two other major types of mediating units that have long been recognized in the literature (e.g., Mischel, 1973). Namely, one must take into account an individual's characteristic encoding, or perception and identification, of situations, reflecting the selective attention to features of situations, as well as the affective states, which are influenced by and which in turn influence, the cognitive and behavioral responses. Although there are no doubt many more relevant types of units than can be cited here, these cognitive and affective mediating units, as summarized in Table 6.1 (and extensively discussed in Mischel & Shoda, 1995), seem to provide a reasonable, albeit tentative, representation.

The Basic Principles of Dynamic Processing: Activation and Accessibility

Although these units provide a starting point, as Read, Jones, and Miller (1990) put it, a good model of a person "is not a mere feature list but is instead a model of how these components are related to one another" (p. 1060), and it should address how the system "works" dynamically and how the different parts interact. For example, the same person may have contradictory beliefs, values or goals, and different ones may become particu-

TABLE 6.1
Types of Cognitive–Affective Units in the Personality Mediating System

1. Encodings: Categories (constructs) for the self, people, events, and situations (external and internal).
2. Expectancies and Beliefs: About the social world, about outcomes for behavior in particular situations, about one's self-efficacy.
3. Affects: Feelings, emotions, and affective responses (including physiological reactions).
4. Goals and Values: Desirable outcomes and affective states; aversive outcomes and affective states; goals and life projects.
5. Competencies and Self-Regulatory Plans: Potential behaviors and scripts that one *can* do, and plans and strategies for organizing action and for affecting outcomes and one's own behavior and internal states.

Note. From "A Cognitive-Affective System Theory of Personality: Reconceptualizing Situations, Dispositions, Dynamics, and Invariance in Personality Structure," by W. Mischel & Y. Shoda, 1995 *Psychological Review, 102*, p. 253. Copyright 1995 by the American Psychological Association. Reprinted with permission.

larly salient at different times. The question then becomes: What determines which of them leads to behavior at a given time?

A key to answering this question is activation. That is, no matter what beliefs and goals one has, and thus potentially could experience at any time, they must be activated to influence behavior. This view is consistent with most current models of social information processing (e.g., Higgins & Kruglanski, 1996; Higgins & Bargh, 1987). Increasingly, individual differences are conceptualized as differences in the chronic accessibility or activation levels of the particular mental representations available to them (e.g., Gollwitzer & Bargh, 1996; Higgins, 1990; Miller & Read, 1989; Read & Miller, 1989). For example, some encoding of interpersonal situations as personal affronts and violations (e.g., Dodge, 1986) may be more accessible to some individuals, whereas for others, the more accessible representation of situations focus on the potentially threatening, dangerous features (e.g., Miller & Mangan, 1983). Certain affective states, such as depression, may chronically characterize some individuals (e.g., Bargh & Tota, 1988; Nolen-Hoeksema, Parker, & Larson, 1994), whereas distress, irritability, and negative emotions may characterize others (e.g., Eysenck & Eysenck, 1985). Furthermore, stable individual differences in the accessibility of goals and values may affect the type of imaginary scenarios that become activated when faced with ambiguous stimuli (e.g., McClelland, 1985).

Each Person Is Characterized by a Stable and Unique Network of Connections

Chronic activation of cognitive and affective units can thus account for stable individual differences. Activation levels of most units, however, vary over time. In fact, in order to address the dynamic processes, one needs to understand the variations in the psychological experiences of the individuals as they encounter different social situations. Given that the activation levels of most cognitions and affects vary over time and across situations, what, if any, remain constant? Is there a stable pattern in how these experiences come and go, and if so, what regulates it? More specifically, how do the units become activated? What determines the dynamic and adaptive responses of the system to different situations? These questions need to be addressed in order to go from a mere list of cognitive–affective units to a model of a dynamic system. This requires a framework for thinking about how the system functions as a coherent whole within the individual.

In this effort, we drew on a new kind of revolution that has occurred in both cognitive and neuro-science in the last decade, which shifts from the serial, centralized processing that was modeled after the architecture of traditional digital computers to a more parallel, distributed model. Although there are many specific versions within this direction, their theme is that the key to understanding human information processing lies in the organization of the relationships among the units that guide and constrain their activation. It is this pattern of relationships or associations that is the essence of most, if not all, current models of cognition (e.g., Anderson, 1983; Rumelhart & McClelland, 1986) and of the brain (e.g., Churchland & Sejnowski, 1992; Crick & Koch, 1990; Edelman, 1987; Kandel & Hawkins, 1992).

These new models of human information processing were originally developed to deal with phenomena at a lower level of abstraction than with the experiences and behaviors considered in the present chapter. However, it seems reasonable that some basic principles (e.g., activation of one concept by another) also apply to phenomena at a higher level, whereas there may be additional principles that apply only to the more complex higher level constructs (e.g., logical relationships between the two concepts). Curiously, models of the human mind at a higher level of abstraction (e.g., analyses of rational decision making) tended to focus on the latter, at the cost of ignoring the more basic processes. The present model is an attempt to explore the implications of such basic principles of human information processing for identifying and analyzing stable patterns of cognitions, affects, and behaviors that characterize each individual in interaction with social situations.

Encouraged by the successful applications in accounting for such higher level phenomena as analogical reasoning (Spellman & Holyoak, 1992), attitude change (Spellman, Ullman, & Holyoak, 1993), explanatory coherence (Read & Marcus-Newhall, 1993; Thagard, 1989), dissonance reduction (Read & Miller, 1994; Shultz & Lepper, 1996), and impression formation and dispositional inference (Kashima & Kerekes, 1994; Kunda & Thagard, 1996; Read & Miller, 1993), we started with the assumption that the social behaviors reflect the activation of relevant cognitive and affective units connected in a network that characterizes each person. That is, each person is assumed to be characterized by a stable and distinctive network that guides and constrains the activation of the set of cognitions and affects that are potentially accessible. Furthermore, the activation of some of these units are in response to the presence of psychologically salient features of situations. The activation of others leads to the generation of relevant behaviors.

Figure 6.2 illustrates the basic nature of such a CAPS system in a highly simplified, schematic outline. The large circle in the middle represents the personality system. It contains a number of cognitive and affective units, forming a distinctive activation network. A subset of these units become activated when the individual encounters situations that contain a relevant configuration of features. These activated units in turn activate other cognitions and affects, following the network of relations distinctive for the person. Thus, broadly, the pattern of connections is a recurrent, rather than a strictly feedforward, network and the activation levels are assumed to change over time to satisfy, at least locally, the constraints

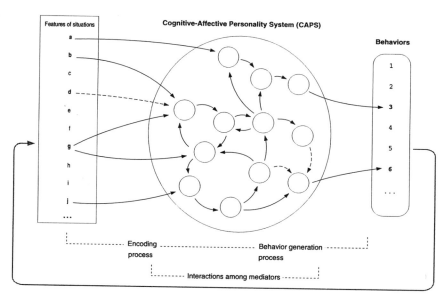

FIG. 6.2. Schematic illustration of the cognitive–affective processing system (CAPS). Situational features activate specific subsets of the mediating units, which in turn activate other mediating units. The network of connections are considered stable and characterize the individual. Arrows indicate activation relationships, such that when one unit is activated, other units that receive arrows from it will receive activation proportional to the weight associated with each arrow. The weight may be positive (solid arrows) or negative (dashed arrows).

represented in the network connection weights (e.g., McClelland & Rumel-hart, 1986).

The figure is a highly simplified view of the rich system of interconnections among the cognitive and affective units that characterize each individual, and that guide and constrain further activation of other units throughout the network. Ultimately, when those units that represent action plans and scripts become sufficiently activated, relevant behaviors are generated. We assume that each individual is characterized by a relatively stable activation network among the units, reflecting the culture and subculture, as well as the individual's learning history. That is, the cognitions and affects that are activated at a given time may change, but how they change, and the relations between one cognition and affect to another, which determines the sequence and pattern of their activation, is assumed to reflect the stable personality structure of the individual.

Obviously, the cognitions and affects that are represented at this abstract, experiential, psychological level are at a much higher level of abstraction than is the cognitive microstructure and, at the extreme other end, the level of the individual neural functions. The network at this point should be considered entirely descriptive, representing the functional relationships among the cognitions and affects. That is, when we say that cognition A "activates" cognition B, what is meant is that for this individual, there is a stable tendency for B to become salient when A is made salient. Furthermore, we make no assumptions as to how the units, or the nodes, that constitute the network are represented at a lower level. For example, each cognitive–affective "node" may itself be represented in a distributed representation, as patterns of activation among the same set of lower level microcognitive units.

It is assumed, however, that the cognitions and affects of each individual follow a predictable and characteristic functional relationship. Whenever an individual encounters a certain kind of person, for example, an absent-minded professor in a school cafeteria, the construal of the encounter, the specific kinds of thoughts and affects that are activated, are not random: Rather, they follow a certain predictable pattern that is characteristic of that individual. Those patterns can be represented by the type of activation network shown in Fig. 6.2, and they characterize the cognitive–affective dynamics that underlie the person's generation of social behavior in that situation.

Behavioral Expressions of Stable Individual Differences in CAPS

In the cognitive–affective processing system model, an individual is characterized by the network of relationships among the thoughts and feelings that guide and constrain their activation, and the features of situations that prime them. Thus, for example, some individuals tend to read malicious intent in others' actions, such as when someone spills milk on them in the cafeteria line (cf. Dodge, 1993), whereas others do not. Some tend to think about their frustrations "when sad" (Wright & Mischel, 1988), whereas for others, the sad state activates a different thought pattern and different behavioral scripts (e.g., Cantor, Mischel, & Schwartz, 1982).

To the extent that the person's internal state is essentially the same, although in reality a person is never really the same, as illustrated later in a computer simulation, the "same" situations should produce the same patterns of activation, reflecting the stable and distinctive network of relations among his or her accessible cognitions and affects. Thus, if one were to record and plot the person's behaviors across different situations and over time, one would find distinctive if ... then ... , situation-behavior profiles generated from this type of personality system.

Predictable Patterns of Variation: The Signatures of Personality

The key point here is that, in the CAPS model, the stable characteristics of the personality system itself are reflected in the way a person's behavior *varies* as a function of specific features of situations. Although the cognitions and affects that are activated change as the individual encounters different situations, the network of connections among the cognitions and affects remains essentially the same. The variation reflects the stable and distinctive organization through which they are interconnected and activate each other. In short, in the CAPS model, the stability of individual differences is reflected in the stability of the network of connections among cognitions and affects, which in turn produces predictable patterns of behavioral variation across situations, or *signatures* of personality.

An Illustrative Computer Simulation

We illustrate the CAPS model in Fig. 6.3, using a simple computer simulation. There, we model the personality system by a recurrent network that performs parallel constraint satisfaction (Rumelhart & McClelland, 1986). Our choice of this class of network architecture, in contrast to a strictly feedforward network, is guided by the assumption that among higher level cognitive–affective units, there is no strict temporal hierarchy. That is, even those units that receive input into the system (e.g., encoding of situations) can be influenced by other units in the system (e.g., beliefs and expectations about the social context). The only distinction we made among the units, from a network architecture standpoint, is that some units receive direct input from

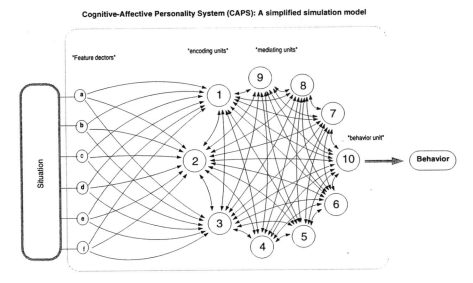

FIG. 6.3. Schematic illustration of the computer model of a CAPS system (see text for details).

the outside world (we call them the encoding units), and some units lead to externally visible behaviors (the behavior units).

A recurrent network generally goes through many cycles of updating (i.e., small adjustments in the levels of activation on each of the unit it contains) before it settles into a pattern of activation that satisfies the constraints imposed by the connection weights. This property allows one to conceptualize the internal state of the system, which continues to change, even if the external situation remains unchanged. Furthermore, the constraint satisfaction is local in that the pattern of activation that the network settles in is not necessarily the best of all possible solutions but is the best among similar patterns of activation. Thus, when this type of network is used to interpret a Necker cube line drawing, the system settles in either one of two equally good interpretations representing a left-facing or right-facing cube, or in a third interpretation, representing an unrealistic solution with two front faces (Rumelhart, Smolensky, McClelland, & Hinton, 1986). The last solution is less than optimal, yet satisfies many constraints, and is better than any of its minor variations.

When the internal cognitive–affective state of an individual is modeled as a parallel constraint satisfaction network, the fact that such a network can settle in one of several final patterns of activation allows for some intrinsic unpredictability in human cognition, affect, and behavior. That is, as noted earlier, people's reactions are of course never exactly the same on two occasions even if the external situations they face are virtually the same. In a parallel constraint satisfaction network, such unpredictability reflects the fact that small differences in the initial activation patterns can result in different final activation patterns, just as the interpretation of a Necker cube may depend on a relatively small initial bias toward one interpretation or another. These properties, as well as the assumptions about the mediating processes, set the present model apart from a strictly stimulus-driven model of the behaviorist view of personality. Finally, given that an individual is usually exposed to a stream of continuously changing external stimuli, the cognitive–affective system may be in a continuous state of flux, never reaching an optimal solution before being exposed to a new set of stimuli. These considerations are incorporated in the design of the illustrative network simulation described in the following paragraphs.

Specifically, the design of the simulation network closely follows the distributed model of memory used by McClelland and Rumelhart (1986). The network consists of 10 cognitive–affective units, 3 of which (encoding units) receive input from social situations, and one of which (behavior unit) determines the strength of a behavioral output, whose activation level we recorded as the simulated person encountered in different situations.[1]

Each of the 10 CAPS units are connected to all other CAPS units with varying activation weights. Given many empirical findings in which associations between two cognitions are asymmetrical (e.g., Tversky, 1977), the connections were allowed to be generally asymmetrical, in that the activation weight going from unit X to Y is generally different from the activation weight going from unit Y to X. We assumed that the input comes from a group of 6 feature detector units (labeled a to f in Fig. 6.3), each of which reflects the presence of a feature in the social situation. The three encoding

---

[1]Actual behavior production may involve the activation levels of multiple, competing, and mutually exclusive behaviors, such as being friendly and being aggressive. Then the process of behavior generation may involve competition among possible behaviors, such that the behavior with the highest level of activation actually becomes displayed. To investigate the effect of that possibility, we created a simulation with a competitive behavior generation process, and found essentially the same results as reported later. We chose to describe the simpler model in the text to make it clear that the property of the model that is the main interest of this chapter is due to the recurrent network itself, rather than depending in part on the competitive behavior production. In fact, it is interesting to note that the competitive behavior production process adds a new characteristic: When we added a competitive behavior production process to our model so that a behavior was displayed only if it was the most strongly activated among the potential behaviors, the result was that in many simulated situations, the behavior of interest was not displayed at all (because other behaviors were more strongly activated). Thus, the effect of the competitive behavior production process was to increase apparent consistency in behavior across situations: It reduced the variation in the activation levels of a given behavioral unit across situations by completely suppressing it when other behaviors were more strongly activated.

units received input from the feature detector units. The term encoding units refers to those cognitive–affective units that receive direct input from the feature detectors.

The first step in the processing of social information is the activation of encoding units when individuals encounter situations. Individual differences in this process are expected to generate differences in the interpretation of the situations, as well as differences in immediate affective responses. Although such differences certainly exist among members of the same culture or subculture, they are expected to be most pronounced between different cultures. That is, to a large extent, members of each culture share the interpretations of features of social situations, such as gestures, facial expressions, and behaviors of other people. Thus, the present model can be generalized to take account of cultural and subcultural differences by introducing differences in the encoding processes (e.g., Shoda, in press). Similarly, members of the same culture may share common pathways in the network of cognitions and affects. For example, independence and autonomy may tend to activate positive affects among members of one culture, whereas they may activate negative affects among members of another.

To simplify the simulation, however, and to illustrate the effect of individual differences in the stable and unique connection patterns among cognitions and affects, we assumed that all 100 individuals shared the same encoding process for the simulation described later. This is analogous to sampling 100 individuals from the same culture or subculture, with culturally shared interpretations of social features.

Specifically, all 100 individuals were characterized by the same set of activation weights that specified the strength of activation the encoding units received from each of the feature detector units (see Table 6.2). Even though they may encode the situations in the same way, these individuals still generally differ in the cognitions and affects that become subsequently activated, reflecting the network of connections among them that are unique to each individual. Thus, in the simulation, each person was characterized by a unique set of weights connecting each of the 10 CAPS units with the others (see Table 6.3, which shows the values chosen for person 80 shown in Fig. 6.4).

In creating each hypothetical person, the weights that characterized their personalities were sampled from a normal distribution with a mean of 0 and a standard deviation of 1. The set of weights for all the connections was further standardized so that the sum of all the weights received by each unit was 0 with a standard deviation of 1. Although Fig. 6.3 uses double-ended arrows to represent interconnections among the 10 CAPS units, as mentioned earlier, the model allowed asymmetrical connection weights. Each double-ended arrow thus represents two arrows, one going in each direction which were set independently with generally different weights.

TABLE 6.2
Connection Weights From Feature Detection Units
to the Encoding Units (i.e., Mediating Units 1–3)

From	To		
Feature Detection Units	Encoding Units		
	1	2	3
1	.69	−1.53	1.24
2	.57	.52	−1.04
3	−1.92	.21	−.14
4	.33	1.33	−.47
5	−.25	.19	1.22
6	.58	−.73	−.82

Note. Mediating units 1 through 3 represent the "encoding units," that is, those cognitions and affects that become activated in relation to feature detection units 1–6. Entries show the activation weights from each of the feature detection units 1 through 6 to each of the three encoding units. Specifically, an entry in row i column j of this table represents the activation contributed to by situation feature i to mediating unit j.

One hundred such persons were created, and they were "exposed" to each of the 15 situations representing all possible combinations of 2 out of 6 features (see Table 6.4). During the simulation, the activation level of each unit was updated simultaneously following a simple, common, nonlinear "squashing" function shown in Equation 1 (e.g., McClelland & Rumelhart, 1986; Shultz & Lepper, 1996), so that the effect of the net input into each unit was proportional to the distance left to the ceiling (when activation < 0) or to the floor (when activation > 0) of the possible range of activation, which was set from −1 to +1.[2]

when $net_i \geq 0$,
$$a_i(t + 1) = d \cdot a_i(t) + net_i \cdot \{ceiling - a_i(t)\}$$
when $net_i < 0$,
$$a_i(t + 1) = d \cdot a_i(t) + net_i \cdot \{a_i(t) - floor\} \qquad (1)$$

where

---

[2]The values of constants c and d that we used in our situation were the same as those used by McClelland & Rumelhart (1986) in their simulation. We also constructed a simulation network that did not use a nonlinear squashing function. In it, the new activation level of each unit was set to its previous activation level times a relatively high decay factor (which we set to 0.5), plus the weighted sum of all the inputs from other units. This simulation was able to produce the same basic results reported here, showing that the results are not dependent on the specific details of the updating function used.

TABLE 6.3

Connection Weights Among the 10 Mediating Units for Person 80

From	*To*									
CAP Mediating Units	*CAP Mediating Units*									
	1	*2*	*3*	*4*	*5*	*6*	*7*	*8*	*9*	*10*
1	—	.43	.94	−.23	.84	.28	−.82	.83	−1.18	−.39
2	.94	—	−.99	−.85	−.30	1.49	−.73	−.87	−.07	−1.61
3	−1.77	−.69	—	−1.39	−.65	−1.50	1.50	−.46	.15	.99
4	.34	−1.11	.89	—	.87	−.98	.63	−1.16	.04	.87
5	−1.18	.36	.44	1.70	—	.69	−1.61	.92	.46	−1.10
6	.50	.58	.25	1.17	.79	—	.04	−.59	.97	−.60
7	.63	.88	−1.76	−.06	.87	−.29	—	.34	−.56	1.59
8	1.26	1.62	−.62	.54	−2.22	1.49	−.10	—	−.89	.12
9	.37	−1.71	1.45	.71	−.46	−.32	.26	1.94	—	−.39
10	−1.04	.17	.09	−.77	−.34	−.76	−.62	.01	2.08	—

Note. Entries are the activation weights connecting the 10 CAP units to each other for the simulated person 80, shown in Fig. 6.4. An entry in row *i* column *j* of this table represents the activation contributed by unit *i* to unit *j*. Unit 10 represents behavioral scripts whose activation produces the behavior that was plotted in Fig. 6.4. Note that situation detection units do not activate this unit directly, but they activate it indirectly through the activation of all the mediating units. Thus, the relationship between the features of situations and the activation of the behavior unit reflects the interactions among the CAP mediating units through the network of interconnections that characterize each individual.

net_i is the net input into unit i from other cognitive–affective units (cau's), such that $net_i = c \cdot \sum_j (w_{ji} \cdot a_j)$, where w_{ji} is the connection weight from unit j to unit i and a_j is the activation level of unit j, and c is a constant (set to 0.15 for the simulations).

$a_i(t)$ is the activation level of unit i at time t;

d is the decay factor (set to 0.85);

ceiling is the upper limit of the range of activation (set to +1);

floor is the lower limit of the range of activation (set to −1).

When its activation exceeded a threshold (which we set at 0), each unit contributed to each of the other units an amount equal to the product of its activation level and the weight of the connection from it to the recipient unit. Thus the contribution increased the recipient unit's activation if the weight was positive, or inhibited it if the weight was negative. When the activation level of a unit was less than the threshold, it had no influence on the activation levels of other units.

The simulation started with the activation values of all CAPS units set to 0. Then each simulated person was exposed to one of the 15 situations, randomly chosen. Depending on the features present in that situation, each

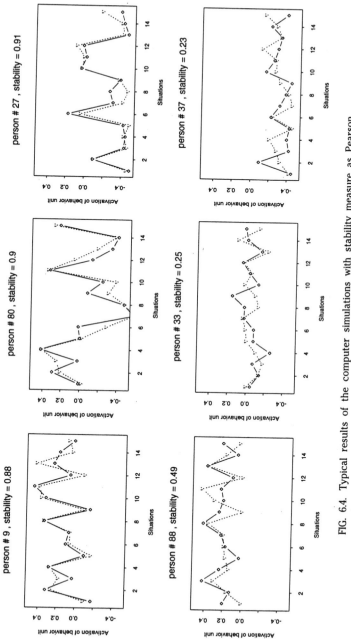

FIG. 6.4. Typical results of the computer simulations with stability measure as Pearson correlation (r).

TABLE 6.4
The Simulated Social World Consisting of 15 Situations

Situations	Features					
	1	2	3	4	5	6
1	1	1	0	0	0	0
2	1	0	1	0	0	0
3	1	0	0	1	0	0
4	1	0	0	0	1	0
5	1	0	0	0	0	1
6	0	1	1	0	0	0
7	0	1	0	1	0	0
8	0	1	0	0	1	0
9	0	1	0	0	0	1
10	0	0	1	1	0	0
11	0	0	1	0	1	0
12	0	0	1	0	0	1
13	0	0	0	1	1	0
14	0	0	0	1	0	1
15	0	0	0	0	1	1

Note. 1 indicates that a feature was present; 0 indicates that a feature was absent.

of the feature detection units was set to either 0 (feature absent) or 1 (feature present). Then the contribution of these feature detection units to the activation of each encoding unit was computed. Because the network went through successive updating, there was a range of possibilities in which the impact of the external features could be added to the encoding units. On the one hand, one could assume that the external features affected only the initial starting state of the network, similar to taking an extremely quick glance and then closing one's eyes while making sense of the stimuli. It seemed that this possibility was extreme, and unlikely to represent what people do in the majority of social interactions. On the other hand, one could assume that the external stimuli continued exerting influence, or that they "clamped" the activation of the encoding units throughout the updating process. These possibilities also seemed extreme, albeit in the opposite direction, because in reality, the encoding of external stimuli can be influenced by other cognitions and affects that are activated in the individual. Thus, the model assumed a continuing but diminishing impact of external situations on the encoding units over time. Specifically, during each cycle of updating, the encoding units received an exponentially decreasing impact of the external stimuli, weighted by the decay factor during each successive updating. Their updating followed the rules described in Equation 1, except that their net input term also included inputs from the feature detectors. That is:

$$net_i = \text{net input into an encoding cognitive–affective unit } i$$
$$= \sum_j (w_{ji} \cdot a_j) + d^n \cdot \sum_k (w_{ki} \cdot f_k). \tag{2}$$

In this equation,

$\sum_j (w_{ji} \cdot a_j)$ is the net input from other cognitive–affects units to unit i, as defined previously.

d is the decay constant also previously described; n represents the number of updating cycles completed; and $\sum_k (w_{ki} \cdot f_k)$ is the net input from external features, where w_{ki} is the weight of the impact of external feature k on cognitive–affective unit i, and f_k indexes the presence (1) or absence (0) of feature k.

The activation levels of all CAPS units were updated simultaneously. As discussed above, to represent the possibility that people are exposed to new stimuli before the activation patterns in reaction to the previous stimulus reaches equilibrium and that they may act before the activation pattern settles, we updated the activation of the CAPS units for only 10 cycles.[3] The final activation level of the "behavior unit" (unit 10 in Fig. 6.3) was recorded as the behavioral output from the person in that situation at that time.

The simulated person was then exposed to another situation. The situation was randomly sampled without replacement from the set of 15 situations, and the same process of computing the activation values of the CAPS units as described earlier was followed. Thus, the simulated person was exposed to each of the 15 situations in random order.

As the person moved from one situation to another, the internal state of the network was not reset before exposure to a new situation. That is, the internal state of the person upon entering a new situation was their final activation value in the immediately preceding situation. Because the order in which the person was exposed to each of the 15 situations was random, the behavior in a particular situation was now, in part, a function of the

---

[3]McClelland and Rumelhart (1986) reported that in a similar network, 50 cycles were "considerably more than enough for it to achieve a stable pattern of activation" (p. 179). To evaluate the effect of the relatively small number of updating cycles we used, we also ran our simulation with 100 cycles of updating, which were in fact more than enough to achieve convergence on stable patterns. The results of such simulations were similar to the ones based on 10 cycles, except that both the intraindividual pattern stability and cross-situational consistency were much higher (.94 and .85, respectively). This suggests that when allowed enough time to settle with exponentially diminishing impact of external stimuli, the system reached more predictable final states with less dependence on the previous situations. Note, however, that the intraindividual profile stability of .94 indicates that the final states still differed predictably from one simulated situation to another following a stable pattern.

history of past exposure to, and experiences in, different situations whose order was randomly chosen. We believe this simulates what occurs in natural social interactions.

After the simulated person was exposed to all 15 situations, we exposed them to the same set of 15 situations for a second time in a new random sequence. This could be considered "Day 2" of exposure, whereas the first exposure to the 15 situations may be considered "Day 1." The internal state of the simulated person entering the first situation on Day 2 was set to be the same as the final state the person was in after being exposed to the last situation on Day 1. We repeated the procedure for each of the 100 hypothetical people, each characterized by a unique and stable pattern of connections among the cognitive–affective units.

The final activation levels of the behavior unit in each situation from Day 1 and Day 2 were plotted separately, and their stability was indexed by computing separately for each person a Pearson product-moment correlation between the 15 observations from Day 1 and the 15 observations from Day 2. Figure 6.4 shows illustrative profiles in which the profile from Day 1 is shown by a solid line, and the profile from Day 2 is shown by a dotted line. The average of the stability coefficients computed separately for each of the 100 simulated persons was .67. The six examples were chosen to represent low (left panels), medium (middle panels), and high (right panels) average levels of behavior unit activation, as well as high (top panels) and moderate (bottom panels) intraindividual profile stability.

Implications of the CAPS Simulations

These results illustrate, as expected, and consistent with our previous work (Mischel & Shoda, 1995), that the simulation of the CAPS model does generate stable patterns of intraindividual variability across situations. Each individual is represented by a unique and stable pattern of connections among the cognitive–affective units that guide and constrain their activation. These connections determine the relationships between the features of situations an individual is exposed to and the activation of each cognitive–affective unit, including the behavior unit. Thus, the unique and stable connection pattern that characterizes each individual is expressed in a stable pattern of relationships between the situations and behavior, resulting in a unique and stable profile of behavioral variability across situations, or a behavioral signature, as shown in Fig. 6.4.

The present simulation extends our previous work (Mischel & Shoda, 1995) by illustrating that the model is capable of producing some degree of unpredictability in the behavior of the same individuals even in the same situation. In the model, such within-situation variability reflects the differences in the internal state of the person as she or he enters a situation.

That is, even in identical external situations, at different times, an individual is never completely the same in his or her cognitive and affective state. The same joking remark may lead to laughter or anger, depending on what the individual is feeling and thinking, which in turn also depends on the situation the person was in before. Thus, the person's internal state forms an ever-evolving stream of experiences, in part reflecting the current situation, in part reflecting the past situation, and in part reflecting the personality of the individual. The present computer simulation of the CAPS model illustrates such real-life processes by starting in one state, and then taking the simulated person through a series of situations, maintaining continuity in the internal states from one situation to another. And in doing so, the model illustrates both the predictable pattern of behavioral variability across situations, or the if ... then ... relations, and what appears from the outside as intrinsic random variation in behavior. No random "noise" was added to the behavior unit or to any other unit in the system, and the only source of randomness in the simulation was in the sequence of situations encountered.

To reiterate, these computer simulations illustrate the central property of the CAPS model: A stable and distinctive activation network of cognitive–affective units, which characterize each individual, determines the relationship between the situations and behaviors. The individual's personality is therefore manifested as a distinctive and stable profile of behavioral variation that is generated as the person moves from one situation to another.

Finally, the six simulated individuals shown in Fig. 6.4 differ not only in the shape of their situation-behavior profiles, but also in the overall height, or elevation, of the profiles. That is, persons 9 and 88 have a higher mean activation level of the behavior unit than persons 27 and 37. If the behavior represented friendliness, then person 9 was friendlier than person 27 in terms of the overall average frequency of friendly behaviors. Such differences were not limited to the examples shown in Fig. 6.4. This is noteworthy because individual differences in the overall levels of behaviors were not directly represented in the model. For each simulated person, all the CAPS units started out with the activation of 0. The only stable individual differences were in the pattern of weights that characterized the connections among them. Furthermore, these weights were normalized such that the total weight received by each unit was 0. Yet the system produced stable individual differences in the elevation of the profiles. Thus the simulation shows that individual differences in the CAPS system can generate differences not just in the shape of the situation-behavior profiles but also in their elevation. Observation of the latter has often been seen as evidence in support of a model with a direct representation in the system of such tendencies, or "traits," that correspond directly to a given type of behavior. The simulation shows that this is not necessarily the case. That is, stable differences in the mean levels of behaviors can be generated even if the behavior-generated system has no direct representation of individual differences in overall behavior tendencies.

The fact that rank ordering of individuals with regard to a behavior can vary considerably across situations has challenged the fundamental assumption and intuitive conviction about personality as a stable characteristic of an individual (e.g., Bem & Allen, 1974; Krahe, 1990; Mischel, 1968; Moskowitz, 1982, 1994; Nisbett & Ross, 1980; Ross & Nisbett, 1991). However, CAPS theory considers the variability of behaviors within individuals across situations not as "error," but as a reflection of a stable personality system as it interacts with the features of situations. When the *if* changes, so will the *then*, but it is the relationship between the two that reflects the underlying stable personality system. The network of cognitions and affects that constitutes the structure of the personality system can remain stable and invariant across situations, while it produces the predictable, characteristic patterns of variation in a given behavior across situations. Thus the theory accounts for the observed variability of behavior as well as the intuitive conviction of the stability of personality. It resolves the consistency paradox by conceptualizing the personality system in ways that allow one to model its interaction with situations, and that make variability of behavior across situations an essential reflection of the stable personality system and indeed its distinctive signature.

PERSONALITY SYSTEM, ITS STATES AND DYNAMICS: TOWARD A CONTEMPORARY DYNAMIC MODEL OF THE PERSON

The present conception of personality also encourages a reexamination and redefinition of some of the core concepts in the study of personality and individual differences. It views the personality system as a CAPS network that activates cognitions and affects, and that generates the individual's behaviors in relation to different situations. Personality states refer to the cognitions and affects activated at a given time. The personality state in part reflects the external situations encountered and the past experiences of an individual. When the current situations change, personality states vary readily and form a continuous stream, reflecting the history of the situations encountered, as well as the distinctive CAPS network that stably characterizes each individual. As an individual moves from one situation to another, if one traces the changes in personality states and plots them as a function of psychologically salient features of situations, a profile with a characteristic elevation and shape should emerge. This profile over time becomes the individual's behavioral signature, reflecting the underlying processing system's stable structure.

Specifying the Contents of the Mediating Units

Rather than being an all-encompassing model of many behavioral domains, the CAPS model we described is deliberately proposed as a meta model, whose purpose is to guide the development of diverse domain-specific models. We next illustrate one example of a domain-specific model that was developed within the CAPS framework. Specifically, the domain chosen was that of health-protective behavior, particularly for dealing with information about risks for breast cancer (Miller, Shoda, & Hurley, 1996).

A basic challenge in applying CAPS to any domain of behavior is to identify a manageably small set of units and connections that play an important role in determining the behavior of interest, from among a very large number of potential mediating units, and an even larger number of possible relationships among them. For this purpose, the first step is to form a cognitive–affective map, which maps the most commonly activated units in the individuals in the population and the significant relationships among them that need to be examined further. Guided by this domain map, research is then directed toward identifying the particular sets of relationships within the map that characterize an individual or a type of individual.

Figure 6.5 illustrates a domain map, showing the types of cognitions and affects for the decision and actual performance of a breast self-examination (BSE) and the network of relations that guide their activation, identified from a literature review (Miller, Shoda, & Hurley, 1996). Although the total configuration is theoretical, the units and the individual pathways are based on those that have been identified in empirical studies that analyzed different aspects of such a configuration.

Constructing such a map is the first step in identifying the cognitive–affective processing that guides the experiences of a woman who is deciding to perform BSE after she has learned that she may have an increased risk (such as a genetic factor) for breast cancer. Examples of internal cognitive and affective events relevant to BSE are illustrated schematically inside the large oval in Fig. 6.5. The formation of BSE-relevant choices, decisions, and intentions are illustrated on the left half of the oval in Fig. 6.5, and their behavioral execution is illustrated on the right half of the oval. A solid arrow connecting one mediating unit to another indicates that the activation of the first unit increases the activation of the second unit. Broken arrows show that the activation of the first reduces or inhibits the activation of the second.

Once such a domain map is built, a real-life instance of the network that characterizes a specific person or a type of people can be conceptualized as a subset of the units and connections in Fig. 6.5. Two possible examples are shown in Figs. 6.6 and 6.7, in which the units and relations that are

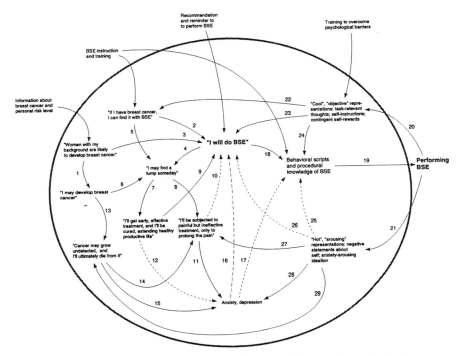

FIG. 6.5. Domain map of cognitive affective units and the network of connections among them that are relevant for performing breast self-examination (BSE). Based on and adapted from Figure 4 of Miller, Shoda, & Hurley, 1996.

important for each example are shown in bold face. These are hypothetical examples, based in part on the empirical investigations of cognitive and affective processes that characterize those who cope well, versus those who do not, with health-risk information, reviewed elsewhere (Miller, Shoda, & Hurley, 1996). The thoughts, affects, and the connections that characterize each example are shown in bold face.

BSE-Relevant Choices, Decisions, and Intentions

We now briefly trace the possible pathways depicted in the domain map. The encoding of the objective risk information affects one's subjective, perceived vulnerability to breast cancer. Thus, one woman may respond to the information that people with a similar background are at high risk for breast cancer with the thought, "I may develop breast cancer," or even with the conviction that she definitely will. In another woman, the objective risk information may not lead to an increased subjective perception of risk. In

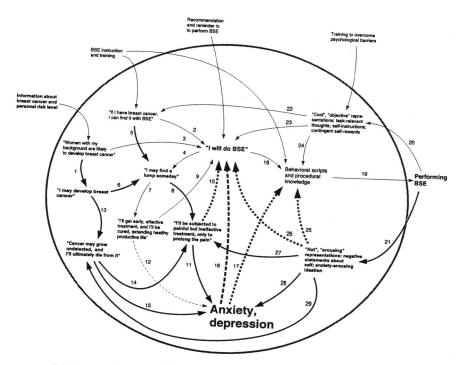

FIG. 6.6. An illustrative CAPS network that undermines intention and performance of BSE. Based on and adapted from Figure 5 of Miller, Shoda, & Hurley,
1996.

Fig. 6.5, this process is illustrated by the solid arrow (Arrow 1) connecting
the health-risk information input to the thought, "I may develop breast
cancer." Individuals may differ in the overall strength with which this thought
is activated. Such individual differences can be shown by arrows of different
thickness. For example, Arrow 1 in Fig. 6.6 is thicker than Arrow 1 in Fig.
6.7, indicating that for a woman whose CAPS network resembles Fig. 6.6, the
objective risk information strongly activates the thought "I may develop
breast cancer." In contrast, for a woman whose CAPS network resembles
Fig. 6.7, the objective risk information does not activate this thought as
strongly.

Information and instructions about how to do a BSE should also increase
self-efficacy expectations for successful performance (e.g., "If I have breast
cancer, I can find it with BSE"). Together, perceived susceptibility and self-
efficacy expectations may jointly activate intentions to perform a BSE (Arrows 2 and 3), which in turn may activate outcome expectations (e.g., "I may
find a lump someday"; Arrow 4). Research has also shown that women differ

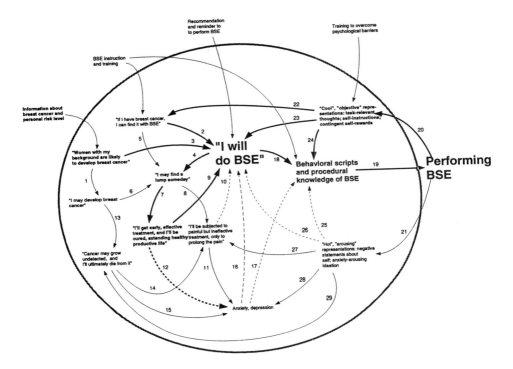

FIG. 6.6.   An illustrative CAPS network that enhances intention and performance of BSE. Based on and adapted from Figure 6 of Miller, Shoda, & Hurley,
1996.

in the types of outcomes that they imagine, following the detection of a
lump. For example, some may imagine a scenario in which early detection
leads to a cure (Arrow 7), whereas for others, more negative outcomes will
be salient (Arrow 8). In Fig. 6.5, Arrows 9 and 10 show the trade-off between
the effects of the different outcome expectancies. The negative outcome
expectancy, "I will be subjected to painful, disfiguring, and potentially ineffective treatment," and the positive outcome expectancy, "I'll get effective,
early treatment," have opposite effects on the intention to do a BSE, "I will
do BSE." Similarly, the negative outcome expectancy increases the arousal
and anxiety that are activated (Arrow 11), whereas the positive expectancy
reduces anxiety (Arrow 12).

As can be seen, the risk information and the intention to do a BSE
regularly are related through many processes with potentially opposing
effects. On the one hand, risk information is expected to strengthen the
intention to perform a BSE, through Arrow 3, as well as through Arrows 1,

6, 7, and 9. On the other hand, risk information also increases the negative affect and anxious arousal that become activated (Arrows 1, 13, and 15, as well as Arrows 1, 6, 8, and 11), which can become overwhelming and thereby activate avoidance (Fig. 6.5, Arrow 16). This would lead a woman to avoid even confronting her situation (e.g., by denial of her breast cancer risk; Rippetoe & Rogers, 1987). The final outcome for each individual will depend on the relative strengths of these two activation pathways. Figure 6.6 shows an example of a type of CAPS network for which exposure to risk information is expected to decrease the intention to do a BSE, while increasing anxiety. Figure 6.7, on the other hand, is a network that characterizes women who are expected to respond to risk information with regular practice of a BSE.

From Intentions to Execution and Adherence

Intentions and plans will be of limited value however, if a woman lacks the mechanisms to activate and maintain a relevant configuration of cognitions and affects for actual adherence to BSE. In fact the number of women who fail to perform a BSE at the recommended frequency despite their intention to do so is significant. Research suggests that how the individual mentally represents the information affects the level of arousal and anxiety (Figs. 6.5–6.7, Arrow 28). Thus, whether she focuses on the "cue" aspects of information (e.g., "Now I need to look for changes in this area," Arrow 20) or on a "hot" aspect (e.g., "if I find a lump, that means hundreds of thousands of cancer cells are already there," Arrow 21) has very different impacts on the continued practice of BSE. In fact, a major problem for maintaining regular screening behaviors like BSE is that the very act of examining primes a cognitive focus on the consequences of these behaviors (Rutledge & Davis, 1988). Such a focus, in turn, may activate the expectation, "I'll be subjected to painful but ineffective treatment" (Arrow 27), and "Cancer may grow undetected, and I may ultimately die from it" (Arrow 29), which in turn increases the anxiety level, further debilitating a woman in her efforts to practice BSE (Arrows 11, 15).

Other self-statements made during the exam also affect adherence to BSE in predictable ways. For example, focusing on the fear of finding a tumor or on the difficulty in discriminating a change in her breast (e.g., "I'm no good at this—I'll never get it right"; Arrow 21) can lead to increased anxiety and decreased intention to continue with BSE. Indeed, in one study, women who reported greater hopelessness and fear used avoidant coping strategies more, and had decreased intentions to perform BSE (Rippetoe & Rogers, 1987). In contrast, task-relevant thoughts (e.g., "Good, now I have to check this area"; Arrow 20) may help sustain the behavior (Dweck & Leggett, 1988; Sarason, Sarason, Keefe, Hayes, & Shearin, 1986; Arrow 24).

CONCLUSION

One of the ultimate and enduring challenges of psychology is to understand and explain why people do what they do, especially those behaviors that seem irrational, puzzling, and inconsistent. Historically, the appeal of Freud's psychodynamic theory was its promise to do exactly that, and it was followed by theorists like Gordon Allport, Henry Murray, and George Kelly, who focused on the dynamics that underlie the observed behavior (e.g., Allport, 1937; Kelly, 1955; Murray, 1938).

Discouraged by the difficulties of finding scientific support for the early dynamic models, the empirical science of personality focused instead on identifying stable differences among individuals on semantic dimensions (e.g., Costa & McCrae, 1992; Goldberg, 1993; Wiggins & Pincus, 1992). In so doing, personality tended to be conceptualized in terms of stable differences in generalized behavior tendencies. This conception captures one meaning of the term "personality" as it is used in everyday discourse, namely as a global summary of individual differences in observed behaviors. But it does not address the other common meaning of the term, as the stable psychological system that generates an individual's characteristic pattern of behavior. Currently, these two meanings of the term, and the two different types of questions they lead to, are pursued in two different subfields of psychology, with distinct construct systems and paradigms (Cervone, 1991; Mischel & Shoda, 1994; Shoda & Mischel, 1996). Ultimately, however, it would be ideal if the same construct system could facilitate our understanding of the behavior-generating system while also providing a way to study individual differences. Toward that goal, we hope that the cognitive–affective processing system (CAPS) model we described here will be a useful step.

ACKNOWLEDGMENTS

Preparation of this article and the research for it by the authors were supported in part by Grants MH39349, MH45994, and MH39263 to Walter Mischel from the National Institute of Mental Health.

We thank the editor of this volume for many valuable and constructive suggestions.

Correspondence concerning this chapter should be addressed to Yuichi Shoda, Department of Psychology, Guthrie Hall, University of Washington, Box 351525, Seattle, WA 98195-1525.

REFERENCES

Allport, G. W. (1937). *Personality: A psychological interpretation*. New York: Holt, Rinehart & Winston.

Alston, W. P. (1975). Traits, consistency and conceptual alternatives for personality theory. *Journal for the Theory of Social Behaviour, 5*, 17–48.

Anderson, J. R. (1983). *The architecture of cognition*. Cambridge, MA: Harvard University Press.

Bargh, J. A. (1994a, June). *First-second: The preconscious in social interaction*. Paper presented at 6th convention of the APS, Washington, DC.

Bargh, J. A. (1994b). The four horsemen of automaticity: Intention, awareness, efficiency, and control as separate issues in social cognition. In R. S. Wyer & T. K. Srull (Eds.), *Handbook of social cognition* (2nd ed., Vol. 1, pp. 1–40). Hillsdale, NJ: Lawrence Erlbaum Associates.

Bargh, J. A., & Tota, M. E. (1988). Context-dependent automatic processing in depression: Accessibility of negative constructs with regard to self but not others. *Journal of Personality and Social Psychology, 54*, 925–939.

Bem, D. J., & Allen, A. (1974). On predicting some of the people some of the time: The search for cross-situational consistencies in behavior. *Psychological Review, 81*, 506–520.

Cantor, N., Mischel, W., & Schwartz, J. (1982). A prototype analysis of psychological situations. *Cognitive Psychology, 14*, 45–77.

Cervone, D. (1991). The two disciplines of personality psychology. *Psychological Science, 2*, 371–377.

Chase, W. G., & Simon, H. A. (1973). The mind's eye in chess. In W. G. Chase (Ed.), *Visual information processing* (pp. 215–281). New York: Academic Press.

Churchland, P. S., & Sejnowski, T. J. (1992). *The computational brain*. Cambridge, MA: MIT Press.

Costa, P. T., Jr., & McCrae, R. T. (1992). Four ways five factors are basic. *Personality and Individual Differences, 13*, 653–665.

Crick, F., & Koch, C. (1990). Towards a neurobiological theory of consciousness. *Seminars in the Neurosciences, 2*, 263–275.

de Groot, A. D. (1965). *Thought and choice in chess*. The Hague, Netherlands: Mouton.

Dodge, K. A. (1986). A social information processing model of social competence in children. *Cognitive perspectives on children's social behavioral development. The Minnesota Symposium on Child Psychology, 18*, 77–125.

Dodge, K. A. (1993). Social-cognitive mechanisms in the development of conduct disorder and depression. *Annual Review of Psychology, 44*, 559–584.

Dweck, C., & Leggett, E. (1988). A social-cognitive approach to personality and motivation. *Psychological Review, 95*, 256–273.

Edelman, G. M. (1987). *Neural Darwinism*. New York: Basic Books.

Eysenck, H. J., & Eysenck, M. W. (1985). *Personality and individual differences*. New York: Plenum.

Goldberg, L. R. (1993). The structure of phenotypic personality traits. *American Psychologist, 48*, 26–34.

Gollwitzer, P. M., & Bargh, J. A. (1996). *The psychology of action: Linking cognition and motivation to behavior*. New York: Guilford.

Hartshorne, H., & May, A. (1928). *Studies in the nature of character: Vol. 1. Studies in deceit*. New York: Macmillan.

Hebb, D. O. (1949). *The organization of behavior*. New York: Wiley.

Higgins, E. T. (1990). Self-state representations: Patterns of interconnected beliefs with specific holistic meanings and importance. *Bulletin of the Psychonomic Society, 28*, 248–253.

Higgins, E. T., & Bargh, J. A. (1987). Social cognition and social perceptions. *Annual Review of Psychology, 38*, 369–425.

Higgins, E. T., & Kruglanski, A. (Eds.). (1996). *Social psychology: Handbook of basic principles*. New York: Guilford.

Hinton, G. E., McClelland, J. L., & Rumelhart, D. E. (1986). Distributed representations. In D. E. Rumelhart & J. L. McClelland (Eds.), *Parallel distributed processing: Explorations in the microstructures of cognition: Vol. I. Foundations* (pp. 77–109). Cambridge, MA: MIT Press/Bradford Books.

Kandel, E. R., & Hawkins, R. D. (1992). The biological basis of learning and individuality. *Scientific American, 267*, 78–86.

Kashima, Y., & Kerekes, A. R. Z. (1994). A distributed memory model of averaging phenomena in person impression formation. *Journal of Experimental Social Psychology, 30,* 407–455.

Kelley, H. (1973). The processes of causal attribution. *American Psychologist, 28,* 107–127.

Kelly, G. A. (1955). *The psychology of personal constructs* (Vols. 1 & 2). New York: Norton.

Kihlstrom, J. F. (1990). The psychological unconscious. In L. A. Pervin (Ed.), *Handbook of personality: Theory and research* (pp. 445–464). New York: Guilford.

Krahe, B. (1990). *Situation cognition and coherence in personality: An individual-centered approach.* Cambridge, England: Cambridge University Press.

Kunda, Z., & Thagard, P. (1996). Forming impressions from stereotypes, traits, and behaviors: A parallel-constraint-satisfaction theory. *Psychological Review, 103,* 284–308.

Magnusson, D., & Endler, N. S. (Eds.). (1977). *Personality at the crossroads: Current issues in interactional psychology.* Hillsdale, NJ: Lawrence Erlbaum Associates.

McClelland, D. C. (1985). How motives, skills, and values determine what people do. *American Psychologist, 40,* 812–825.

McClelland, J. L., & Rumelhart, D. E. (1986). A distributed model of human learning and memory. In J. L. McClelland & D. E. Rumelhart (Eds.), *Parallel distributed processing: Explorations in the microstructures of cognition: Vol. 2. Psychological and biological models* (pp. 170–215). Cambridge, MA: MIT Press/Bradford Books.

Miller, L. C., & Read, S. J. (1989). Inter-personalism: Understanding persons in relationships. In W. Jones & D. Perlman (Eds.), *Perspectives in interpersonal behavior and relationships* (Vol. 2). Greenwich, CT: JAI Press.

Miller, L. C., & Read, S. J. (1991). On the coherence of mental models of persons and relationships: A knowledge structure approach. In G. J. O. Fletcher & F. D. Fincham (Eds.), *Cognition in close relationships* (pp. 69–99). Hillsdale, NJ: Lawrence Erlbaum Associates.

Miller, S. M., & Mangan, C. E. (1983). Interacting effects of information on coping style in adapting to gynecologic stress: Should the doctor tell all? *Journal of Personality and Social Psychology, 45,* 223–236.

Miller, S. M., Shoda, Y., & Hurley, K. (1996). Applying cognitive social theory to health protective behavior: Breast self-examination in cancer screening. *Psychological Bulletin, 119,* 70–94.

Mischel, W. (1968). *Personality and assessment.* New York: Wiley.

Mischel, W. (1973). Toward a cognitive social learning reconceptualization of personality. *Psychological Review, 80,* 252–283.

Mischel, W. (1990). Personality dispositions revisted and revised: A view after three decades. In L. A. Pervin (Ed.), *Handbook of personality: Theory and research* (pp. 111–134). New York: Guilford.

Mischel, W. (1993). *Introduction to personality* (5th ed.). Fort Worth, TX: Harcourt, Brace.

Mischel, W., & Peake, P. K. (1982). Beyond déjà vu in the search for cross-situational consistency. *Psychological Review, 89,* 730–755.

Mischel, W., & Shoda, Y. (1994). Personality psychology has two goals: Must it be two fields? *Psychological Inquiry, 5,* 156–158.

Mischel, W., & Shoda, Y. (1995). A cognitive-affective system theory of personality: Reconceptualizing situations, dispositions, dynamics, and invariance in personality structure. *Psychological Review, 102,* 246–268.

Moskowitz, D. S. (1982). Coherence and cross-situational generality in personality: A new analysis of old problems. *Journal of Personality and Social Psychology, 43,* 754–768.

Moskowitz, D. S. (1994). Cross-situational generality and the interpersonal circumplex. *Journal of Personality and Social Psychology, 66,* 921–933.

Murray, H. A. (1938). *Explorations in personality.* New York: Oxford University Press.

Newcomb, T. M. (1929). *Consistency of certain extrovert-introvert behavior patterns in 51 problem boys.* New York: Columbia University, Teachers College, Bureau of Publications.

Nisbett, R. E., & Ross, L. D. (1980). *Human inference: Strategies and shortcomings of social judgment* (Century Psychology Series). Englewood Cliffs, NJ: Prentice-Hall.

Nolen-Hoeksema, S., Parker, L. E., & Larson, J. (1994). Ruminative coping with depressed mood following loss. *Journal of Personality and Social Psychology, 67*, 92–104.

Pervin, L. A. (1982). *The stasis and flow of behavior: Toward a theory of goals*. Nebraska Symposium on Motivation, 1–53.

Peterson, D. R. (1968). *The clinical study of social behavior*. New York: Appleton.

Read, S. J., Jones, D. K., & Miller, L. C. (1990). Traits as goal-based categories: The importance of goals in the coherence of dispositional categories. *Journal of Personality and Social Psychology, 58*, 1048–1061.

Read, S. J., & Marcus-Newhall, A. (1993). Explanatory coherence in social explanations: A parallel distributed processing account. *Journal of Personality and Social Psychology, 65*, 429–447.

Read, S. J., & Miller, L. C. (1989). Inter-personalism: Toward a goal-based theory of persons in relationships. In L. Pervin (Ed.), *Goal concepts in personality and social psychology* (pp. 413–472). Hillsdale, NJ: Lawrence Erlbaum Associates.

Read, S. J., & Miller, L. C. (1993). Rapist or "regular guy": Explanatory coherence in the construction of mental models of others. *Personality and Social Psychology Bulletin, 19*, 526–540.

Read, S. J., & Miller, L. C. (1994). Dissonance and balance in belief systems: The promise of parallel constraint satisfaction processes and connectionist modeling approaches. In R. C. Schank & E. Langer (Eds.), *Beliefs, reasoning, and decision making: Psycho-logic in honor of Bob Abelson* (pp. 209–235). Hillsdale, NJ: Lawrence Erlbaum Associates.

Rippetoe, P., & Rogers, R. (1987). Effects of components of protection-motivation theory on adaptive and maladaptive coping with a health threat. *Journal of Personality and Social Psychology, 52*, 596–604.

Ross, L., & Nisbett, R. E. (1991). *The person and the situation: Perspectives of social psychology*. New York: McGraw-Hill.

Rumelhart, D. E., & McClelland, J. L. (Eds.). (1986). *Parallel distributed processing: Explorations in the microstructure of cognition: Vol. 1. Foundations*. Cambridge, MA: MIT Press/Bradford Books.

Rumelhart, D. E., Smolensky, P., McClelland, J. L., & Hinton, G. E. (1986). Schemata and sequential thought processes in PDP models. In J. L. McClelland & D. E. Rumelhart (Eds.), *Parallel distributed processing: Explorations in the microstructures of cognition, Vol II. Psychological and biological models* (pp. 7–57). Cambridge, MA: MIT Press/Bradford Books.

Rutledge, D., & Davis, G. (1988). Breast self-examination compliance and the health belief model. *Oncology Nursing Forum, 15*, 175–179.

Sarason, I., Sarason, B., Keefe, D., Hayes, B., & Shearin, E. (1986). Cognitive interference: Situational determinants and traitlike characteristics. *Journal of Personality and Social Psychology, 51*, 215–226.

Shoda, Y. (1997). Cognitive-affective processing system theory and cultural psychology. In K. Kashiwagi, S. Kitayama, & H. Azuma (Eds.), *Cultural psychology*. Toyko: University of Tokyo.

Shoda, Y., & Mischel, W. (1993). Cognitive social approach to dispositional inferences: What if the perceiver is a cognitive-social theorist? *Personality and Social Psychology Bulletin, 19*, 574–585.

Shoda, Y., & Mischel, W. (1996). Toward a unified, intra-individual dynamic conception of personality. *Journal of Research in Personality, 30*, 414–428.

Shoda, Y., Mischel, W., & Wright, J. C. (1989). Intuitive interactionism in person perception: Effects of situation-behavior relations on dispositional judgments. *Journal of Personality and Social Psychology, 56*, 41–53.

Shoda, Y., Mischel, W., & Wright, J. C. (1993a). The role of situational demands and cognitive competencies in behavior organization and personality coherence. *Journal of Personality and Social Psychology, 65*, 1023–1035.

Shoda, Y., Mischel, W., & Wright, J. C. (1993b). Links between personality judgments and contextualized behavior patterns: Situation-behavior profiles of personality prototypes. *Social Cognition, 11*, 399–429.

Shoda, Y., Mischel, W., & Wright, J. C. (1994). Intra-individual stability in the organization and patterning of behavior: Incorporating psychological situations into the idiographic analysis of personality. *Journal of Personality and Social Psychology, 67*, 674–687.

Shultz, T. R., & Lepper, M. R. (1996). Cognitive dissonance reduction as constraint satisfaction. *Psychological Review, 103*, 219–240.

Spellman, B. A., & Holyoak, K. J. (1992). If Saddam is Hitler then Who is George Bush? Analogical mapping between systems of social roles. *Journal of Personality and Social Psychology, 62*, 913–933.

Spellman, B. A., Ullman, J. B., & Holyoak, K. J. (1993). A coherence model of cognitive consistency: Dynamics of attitude change during the Persian Gulf war. *Journal of Social Issues, 49*, 147–165.

Thagard, P. (1989). Explanatory coherence. *Behavioral and Brain Sciences, 12*, 435–467.

Thagard, P. (1992). *Conceptual revolutions*. Princeton: Princeton University Press.

Tversky, A. (1977). Features of similarity. *Psychological Review, 84*, 327–352.

Vernon, P. E. (1964). *Personality assessment: A critical survey*. New York: Wiley.

Wegner, D. M. (1995). Ironic processes of mental control. *Psychological Review, 101*, 34–52.

Wiggins, J. S., & Pincus, A. L. (1992). Personality: Structure and assessment. *Annual Review of Psychology, 43*, 473–504.

Wright, J. C., & Mischel, W. (1988). Conditional hedges and the intuitive psychology of traits. *Journal of Personality and Social Psychology, 55*, 454–469.

Zajonc, R. B. (1980). Feeling and thinking: Preferences need no inferences. *American Psychologist, 35*, 151–175.

ATTITUDES AND
BELIEFS

THE CONSONANCE MODEL OF DISSONANCE REDUCTION

Thomas R. Shultz
McGill University

Mark R. Lepper
Stanford University

THE SEARCH FOR CONSISTENCY

The pursuit of consistency among one's beliefs and attitudes has long been taken as a sign of human rationality (Abelson, 1971), and consistency-seeking has held a prominent place in social-psychological theorizing for over 50 years (e.g., Festinger, 1957; Heider, 1946, 1958; McGuire, 1960; Newcomb, 1953; Osgood & Tannenbaum, 1955). This widespread concern with issues of cognitive consistency culminated in the late 1960s in the publication of an 84-chapter tome, *Theories of Cognitive Consistency*, edited by six of the major social-psychological theorists of the day (Abelson et al., 1968). Theoretical ideas about cognitive consistency, particularly those involving cognitive dissonance (Aronson, 1969; Festinger, 1957; Wicklund & Brehm, 1976) and cognitive balance (Heider, 1946, 1958; Rosenberg & Abelson, 1960), have been thoroughly investigated and largely supported by systematic experimentation. Indeed, the extensive literature on cognitive consistency continues to constitute one major part of the foundation of contemporary social psychology.

However, the study of cognitive consistency seems to have fallen out of favor (Aronson, 1989; Berkowitz & Devine, 1989). With a few prominent exceptions (e.g., Cooper & Fazio, 1984; Steele, 1988; Thibodeau & Aronson, 1992), little empirical work has been done in this area over the past 20 years. Perhaps this decline was due to the fact that so many aspects of the various consistency theories were already so extensively explored; perhaps it was due to an inability to penetrate further the reasoning mechanisms that underlie the search for cognitive consistency.

Recently, we proposed that the striving for cognitive consistency can be understood in terms of constraint satisfaction, a process of simultaneous adjustment of beliefs and attitudes to satisfy as many internal and external constraints as possible (Shultz & Lepper, 1992, 1996, 1997). We illustrated this theoretical reinterpretation with an artificial neural network computer model—the consonance model—that captures many of the findings in the major paradigms of cognitive dissonance theory.

The present chapter summarizes and evaluates this enterprise. The potential payoff for this work would be to offer a novel theoretical interpretation of some of the most basic phenomena in social psychology at an abstract, yet mathematically specified, level that potentially can be unified with many other constraint satisfaction phenomena in psychology. Such a model may also lead to the generation of new predictions for empirical research on important consistency phenomena.

CLASSICAL DISSONANCE THEORY

Classical cognitive dissonance theory postulates that dissonance is a psychological state of tension that people are motivated to reduce (Festinger, 1957). Any two cognitions are said to be dissonant when, considered by themselves, one of them follows from the obverse of the other. The amount of dissonance is defined by the ratio of dissonant to total relevant (i.e., dissonant plus consonant) relations, with each relation being weighted for its importance to the person. Cognitive dissonance can, in principle, be reduced by decreasing the number and/or the importance of the dissonant relations and by increasing the number and/or the importance of consonant relations. The manner in which dissonance will actually get reduced in a particular situation is hypothesized to depend on the resistance to change of the various relevant cognitions, with less resistant cognitions being more likely to change. Resistance, in turn, derives from the extent to which a cognitive change would be likely to produce new dissonance, the degree to which a cognition is firmly anchored in reality, and the difficulty of changing those aspects of reality.

Drawing on these principles, researchers sought to create experimental situations in which dissonance could be produced and, in turn, its reduction channeled into particular predictable changes in attitudes or beliefs. This was often accomplished by the creation of dissonant relationships between people's attitudes or beliefs and their overt actions, producing pressure on them to alter their attitudes or beliefs to justify or fit their presumably irrevocable actions. These studies showed that, under the right circumstances, the result of supposedly rational consistency seeking could be demonstrably irrational behavior. Ironically, as Aronson (1969) put it, dissonance theory portrayed people more as "rationalizing" than as "rational" creatures.

Cognitive dissonance theory proved to be enormously successful. Within five years of the publication of Festinger's original book (1957), the theory had already become the most influential of the consistency models. By now, dissonance theory has generated more than 1,000 published studies covering a great variety of content domains including attitude change, decision rationalization, and responses to belief disconfirmation (Cooper & Fazio, 1984; Thibodeau & Aronson, 1992). The general success of the theory, and its specific ability to encompass both apparently rational and apparently irrational responses, coupled with the possibility that the underlying mechanisms were based on constraint satisfaction, seemed to us to recommend it highly as a candidate for our modeling efforts.

THE CONSONANCE MODEL

Our consonance model is based on the idea that dissonance reduction can be viewed as a constraint satisfaction problem. That is, the motivation to seek cognitive consistency, which is postulated by dissonance and related theories, can be viewed as imposing constraints on the beliefs and attitudes that an individual holds at a given moment (Abelson et al., 1968; Abelson & Rosenberg, 1958; Feldman, 1966). Such consistency problems can be resolved by the satisfaction of a number of soft constraints that can vary in their relative importance. Soft constraints are those that are desirable, but not essential, to satisfy. The fact that constraints can conflict with each other favors softness rather than hardness of constraints and suggests that it is unlikely that inconsistencies can be fully eliminated from most complex belief systems.

Consonance networks correspond to a person's representation of the situation created by the experimental setting for each condition in a particular cognitive dissonance experiment. Units in a network can be variously active, corresponding loosely to the firing rate of neurons. Activations of units represent the direction and strength of the person's attitudes and beliefs. Units can also differ in their resistance to change, reflecting differences in the extent to which particular cognitions may be supported by other cognitions or anchored in reality. Connection weights between cognitions represent psychological implications among a person's beliefs and attitudes. The connections between any two units can be excitatory (+), inhibitory (−), or nonexistent (0). Both unit activations and connection weights can vary across the different conditions of a particular experiment.

Consonance is the degree to which similarly evaluated units are linked by excitatory weights and oppositely valued units are linked by inhibitory weights. Activations change over time cycles in order to satisfy the various constraints and increase consonance. More formally, the consonance contributed by a particular unit i is

$$consonance_i = \sum_j w_{ij} a_i a_j. \tag{1}$$

where w_{ij} is the weight between units i and j, a_i is the activation of the receiving unit i, and a_j is the activation of the sending unit j.

Consonance over the whole network is the sum of the values given by Equation 1 over all receiving units in the network.

$$consonance_n = \sum_i \sum_j w_{ij} a_i a_j. \tag{2}$$

Activation spreads around the network over time cycles in conformity with two update rules:

$$a_i(t+1) = a_i(t) + net_i[ceiling - a_i(t)], \text{ when } net_i \geq 0. \tag{3}$$

$$a_i(t+1) = a_i(t) + net_i[a_i(t) - floor], \text{ when } net_i < 0. \tag{4}$$

where $a_i(t+1)$ is the activation of unit i at time $t+1$, $a_i(t)$ is the activation of unit i at time t, *ceiling* is the maximal level of unit activation, *floor* is the minimal level of unit activation, and net_i is the net input to unit i, defined as

$$net_i = resist_i \sum_j w_{ij} a_j. \tag{5}$$

The parameter $resist_i$ indicates the resistance of receiving unit i to having its activation changed. Smaller values of this parameter indicate greater resistance because smaller values mean less impact of the net input.

At each time cycle, n units are randomly selected and updated according to Equations 3–5. Typically, n is the number of units in the network. The update rules in Equations 3–5 ensure that consonance increases or stays the same across cycles. When consonance reaches asymptote, the updating process is typically stopped.

MAPPING THE CONSONANCE MODEL
TO DISSONANCE PHENOMENA

A generic consonance network is used to instantiate any particular dissonance experiment. To date, our simulations used between two and four cognitions per network, but in principle, there is no limit to the number of cognitions that could be included. Each cognition falls into one of three categories: behaviors, justifications, or evaluations. As noted later, these three categories are differentially resistant to change during dissonance reduction. Our consonance computer program, written in the Common Lisp language, enables us to specify a network including the relevant cognitions, their types and initial activations, and the relations among the cognitions. A concrete example of the start of a network run is given in the next section in which our simulations are presented. At this point, let us turn to a presentation of the set of six theoretical principles that map dissonance theory to the consonance model.

Representation of Cognitions

Principle 1 specifies that a cognition is implemented by the net activation of a pair of negatively connected units, one of which represents the positive pole and the other represents the negative pole. Net activation for the cognition is the difference between activation of the positive unit and activation of the negative unit. Activations range from a floor to a ceiling. In our simulations, the floor parameter is 0 by default. The default ceiling parameter for positive poles is 1 and for negative poles is 0.5. Use of two different default ceilings is based partly on neurological and computational considerations (Anderson, 1995) and partly on the fact that it works well in the domain of cognitive consistency (Shultz & Lepper, 1996). This bipolar representation scheme allows for some degree of ambivalence in cognitions, although the inhibitory connections between the two poles do tend to discourage ambivalence.

Relationships Among Cognitions

Mapping Principle 2 specifies that cognitions are connected to each other based on their causal implications. If quantitative increases in cognition 1 would cause quantitative increases in cognition 2, then cognition 1 is said to be a positive cause of cognition 2. If quantitative increases in cognition 1 would cause quantitative decreases in cognition 2, then cognition 1 is said to be a negative cause of cognition 2. Connection weights range from −1 to 1, with 0 representing a lack of causal relation. The connection scheme for two generic cognitions is illustrated in Fig. 7.1. When two cognitions are positively related, their positive poles are connected with excitatory weights, as are their negative poles; inhibitory weights connect the positive pole of one cognition with the negative pole of the other cognition (Fig. 7.1a). These connections are reversed for cognitions that are negatively related (Fig. 7.1b). Each unit has an inhibitory self-connection specified by the *cap* parameter, and all connection weights are bi-directional. Connection weights

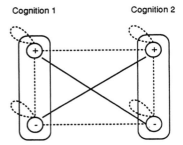

a. Positively related cognitions

Cognition 1   Cognition 2

b. Negatively related cognitions

Cognition 1   Cognition 2

FIG. 7.1. In the consonance model, any two cognitions can be positively (a) or negatively (b) related. Excitatory (positive) weights are portrayed by solid lines, inhibitory (negative) weights by dashed lines. Each cognition is portrayed by a rounded rectangle drawn around the positive and negative poles of the cognition. Each pole is represented as a unit in the network, drawn here as a circle. All connection weights are bi-directional.

have a default value of 0.5, representing a strong or high connection, but we occasionally use a weak or low connection, with a default value of 0.1.

Magnitude of Dissonance

Mapping Principle 3 specifies that total dissonance is the negative of total consonance divided by r, the number of nonzero inter-cognition relations:

$$dissonance = \frac{-consonance_n}{r}. \tag{6}$$

Dividing by r standardizes dissonance across networks by controlling for the number of relevant relations. Self-connections, w_{ii}, are excluded from this computation of dissonance so that dissonance is not an artifact of amount of activation. This definition of dissonance differs from Festinger's (1957) because it is formalized, it measures the amount of dissonance in each inter-cognition relation, it includes within-cognition ambivalence, and it can still vary when all relations are dissonant or all relations are consonant. Our definition of dissonance is analogous to Hopfield's (1982, 1984) notion of energy, and our definition of consonance is analogous to Rumelhart, Smolensky, McClelland, and Hinton's (1986) notion of goodness. Energy (or dissonance) decreases as goodness (or consonance) increases.

Reduction of Dissonance

Principle 4 specifies that networks tend to settle into more stable, less dissonant states as unit activations are updated according to Equations 3, 4, and 5. There are two parameters that affect the dissonance reduction

process, *cap* and *rand%*. A *cap* parameter with a default of −0.5, corresponding to the value of the connection between each unit and itself, w_{ii}, prevents
activations from growing to their ceiling. This sort of activation limitation
seems appropriate for most dissonance experiments, which do not typically
deal with life and death situations. At the start of each run of a network,
connection weights, resistances, caps, and initial activations are all randomized by adding or subtracting a random proportion of their initial amounts.
The *rand%* parameter specifies the proportion range in which additions or
subtractions are randomly selected under a uniform distribution. Typically,
we use small (.1), medium (.5), and large (1.0) levels of *rand%*. This increases
psychological realism in the sense that not everyone can be expected to
share precisely the same parameter values. The randomization of weight
values also violates connection weight symmetry such that $w_{ij} \neq w_{ji}$ and thus
increases the instability of network solutions. Perhaps most importantly,
comparisons of the solutions obtained from networks at various levels of
randomization provide a clear indication of the robustness of the results
across parameter variations.

Changes in Cognitions

Principle 5 specifies that cognition unit activations, but not connection
weights, are allowed to change, and that some cognitions are more resistant
to change than others, as implemented in Equation 5. Beliefs (including
behaviors and justifications) are more resistant to change than are evaluations. Although participants in dissonance experiments are likely to be well
aware of what just happened to them and what they just did, they may not
be so sure of how they feel about aspects of the somewhat novel situation
they are in. The resist parameter has default values of 0.5 for low and 0.01
for high resistance. As specified in Equation 5, the larger the resistance
multiplier, the more readily the unit changes its activation. Additional details
about the consonance model and discussion of its various assumptions are
presented in Shultz and Lepper (1996).

Importance of Dissonance

Recently, we added a sixth mapping principle to account for a variety of
arousal and self-concept phenomena in the dissonance literature (Shultz &
Lepper, 1997). This new Principle 6 concerns the psychological importance
of the dissonant situation. An importance scalar parameter, with default
values of 0.5, 1.0, or 1.5, multiplies all connection weights and unit activations
at the start of each run, before the initial randomizations referred to under
Principle 4. An importance parameter value of 1.0 is used in control conditions; a value of 0.5 is used for conditions that lessen the importance of a

dissonant situation; and a value of 1.5 is used for conditions that enhance the importance of a dissonant situation.

At this point, we move into a review of some of our simulations of cognitive dissonance phenomena.

INSUFFICIENT JUSTIFICATION PARADIGMS

Perhaps the most widely researched and cited experimental paradigm in cognitive dissonance concerns situations that involve psychologically insufficient justification. The "insufficient justification" paradigm deals with situations in which participants are led to engage in some counter-attitudinal action with either rather little or considerably greater justification for that action. Classical dissonance theory predicts that the less the justification for the behavior, the greater the dissonance and, at least when it is difficult to retract one's action, the more people will be motivated to change their attitudes so as to provide additional justification for their actions. Within insufficient justification research, there have been three major sub-paradigms (Lepper, 1983); prohibition, initiation, and forced compliance. Within each of these sub-paradigms, our simulations focused on second-generation experiments that avoided both the plethora of alternative explanations that plagued the original classic experiments and the more narrow and highly qualified interests of most contemporary studies.

Insufficient Justification via Prohibition

The classic study on insufficient justification in a prohibition situation was done by Aronson and Carlsmith (1963) who forbade nursery schoolers from playing with an attractive toy under either mild or severe threat of punishment. In later ratings, children devalued the forbidden toy more in the mild than in the severe threat condition, presumably as a result of greater dissonance under mild threat. In order to rule out a number of alternative explanations of these initial results, Freedman (1965a) included surveillance conditions in this experiment in addition to the original non-surveillance conditions. In the surveillance conditions, the experimenter stayed in the room while the child played with the alternative, less desirable toys. Presumably, the presence of the experimenter lessened dissonance by increasing the potency of the threats. Several weeks later, in another setting, only the children in the mild threat, non-surveillance condition showed significant devaluation of the forbidden toy.

Network specifications for our simulations (Shultz & Lepper, 1996) of the non-surveillance and surveillance conditions of Freedman's experiment are shown in Figs. 7.2a and 7.2b, respectively. There were three cognitions:

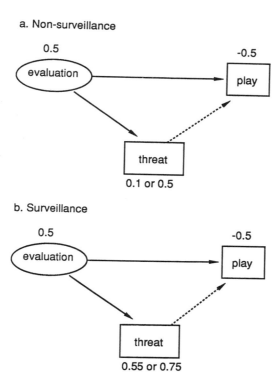

a. Non-surveillance

b. Surveillance

FIG. 7.2. Network specifications for simulation of the Freedman (1965a) experiment. Cognitions with high resistance to change are drawn as rectangles; cognitions with low resistance to change are drawn as ellipses. Positive causal implications are drawn with solid arrows; negative causal implications are drawn with dashed arrows. Each arrow is drawn from cause to effect. Initial activation values are shown next to each cognition. Some details are suppressed in the networks displayed in Figs. 7.2–7.9, in that each cognition is actually implemented with a pair of units and that causal implications among cognitions are implemented with a set of bi-directional connection weights as illustrated in Fig. 7.1.

evaluation of the toy, play with the toy, and threat. Initially, the toy was given a high positive evaluation, play was given a high negative evaluation because it was not done, and threat was either low or high, depending on condition. In the surveillance conditions, the value of these threats was scaled up using a multiplier of 0.5 plugged into Equation 3. The new threat was computed as the old threat plus one half of the difference between 1 and the old threat. Relations among the three cognitions reflected assumed causal relations. The better liked the toy is, the more it would be played with; the better liked the toy, the more threat would be required to prevent play; and the larger the threat, the less the play.

Net evaluation of the toy was computed as the difference between activation of the positive pole and the negative pole of the toy cognition. As shown in Fig. 7.3, after unit activation changes and dissonance reduction reached asymptotic values, the networks showed more devaluation of the forbidden toy under mild than under severe threat, but only in the non-surveillance conditions, thus mirroring the children's data. Figure 7.3 (as well as other figures presenting simulation results in this chapter) shows results for small levels of parameter randomization (*rand%* = .1).

Examples of actual activation updates are shown in Table 7.1 over the first two update cycles from one network run in Freedman's mild threat condition. (For purposes of illustration, the cycles presented in Table 7.1 do not involve any randomization of initial values.) There were six updates per cycle, the number of units in the network. Within each update cycle, the units to be updated were randomly selected. Unit 3, the positive pole of the play cognition, happened to have been selected for the first update. The initial activation for this unit was 0.000, because the toy was not played with. The net input to this unit was −0.050, as specified in Equation 5, before being scaled by the resistance parameter. Net input to a unit is computed as the sum of products of activations on sending units and the connection weights. In this case, there were only three such nonzero products: from unit 1 (activation of 0.5 × weight of 0.5), from unit 4 (activation of 0.5 × weight of −0.5), and from unit 5 (activation of 0.1 × weight of −0.5). Summing these three products yields an unscaled net input of −0.050. Multiplying this net

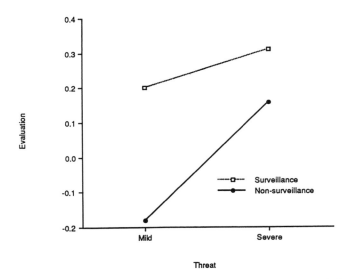

FIG. 7.3. Mean evaluation of the forbidden toy in the simulation of the Freedman (1965a) experiment. Adapted from Shultz and Lepper (1996).

TABLE 7.1
Activation Updates Over the First Two Update Cycles for a Network in
Freedman's Mild Threat, Non-surveillance Condition as Designed in Fig. 7.2a

Unit number (randomly selected)	Unit name	Current unit activation	Net input to unit	Scaled by unit resistance	Distance to floor or ceiling	Updated unit activation
3	play+	0.000	−0.050	0.000	0.000	0.000
6	threat−	0.000	−0.550	−0.006	0.000	0.000
4	play−	0.500	−0.450	−0.005	0.500	0.498
1	evaluation+	0.500	−0.449	−0.224	0.500	0.388
4	play−	0.498	−0.393	−0.004	0.498	0.496
6	threat−	0.000	−0.492	−0.005	0.000	0.000
1	evaluation+	0.388	−0.392	−0.196	0.388	0.312
3	play+	0.000	−0.142	−0.001	0.000	0.000
4	play−	0.496	−0.354	−0.004	0.496	0.494
6	threat−	0.000	−0.453	−0.005	0.000	0.000
5	threat+	0.100	0.353	0.004	0.900	0.103
5	threat+	0.103	0.351	0.004	0.897	0.106

input by the resistance scalar of 0.01 yields −0.0005, which in this Table with only three decimal places rounds to 0.000. The updated activation of this unit was thus still 0.000. The actual running of these networks carried many more decimal places, so this example should be considered as only a rough approximation of what really happens. The interested reader can follow through the next few updates to gain a sense of how the program works. At each update, scaled net input is multiplied by the distance to the floor (in the case of negative net input) or the distance to the ceiling (in the case of positive net input) in the last column of Table 7.1, in conformity with Equations 5 and 6.

Insufficient Justification via Initiation

A second insufficient justification sub-paradigm generated by dissonance theory concerns the consequences of having to suffer an initiation in order to join a group. The initial example of an initiation experiment found that people initiated into a boring group liked the group better after undergoing a severe than after a mild initiation (Aronson & Mills, 1959). The classical dissonance explanation was that the greater dissonance created by a painful initiation could be reduced by increasing one's evaluation of the group for which one had suffered. A follow-up experiment by Gerard and Mathewson (1966) eliminated various alternative explanations for the results of the first experiment, in part by adding non-initiation conditions with the same severe and mild levels of unpleasantness. For this purpose, they used electric shock

at two different levels, administered either as part of an initiation or as part
of an unrelated experiment. Following an overheard boring discussion by a
group they had volunteered to join, participants rated the group. As predicted by dissonance theory, people liked the group better after a severe
than after a mild initiation. However, in the non-initiation condition, participants liked the group better after receiving mild shock than after receiving
severe shock, a finding not predicted by dissonance theory, which speaks
only to the initiation conditions.

Network specifications for simulation of the initiation and non-initiation
conditions of the Gerard and Mathewson experiment (Shultz & Lepper, 1996)
are presented in Figs. 7.4a and 7.4b, respectively. There were three cognitions: evaluation of the group, the behavior of joining the group, and the
level of shock received. Joining received an initially positive evaluation
because participants did volunteer to join. Evaluation of the group received
an initially negative value reflecting the boring discussion that was over-

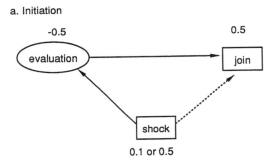

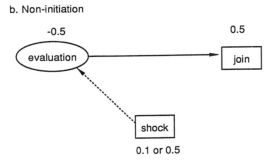

FIG. 7.4. Network specifications for simulation of the Gerard and Mathewson
(1966) experiment.

heard. Shock levels were high or low depending on condition. Relations among the cognitions reflected causal implications: The better you like a group, the more likely you are to join it; the more you pay for something, the more you get; and the more you have to pay, the less likely you are to join.

Network design for the non-initiation conditions was similar except that relations between shock and joining were cut to 0 because, without an initiation, there was no longer a causal relation between them, and relations between shock and evaluation were changed from positive to negative because, with shock no longer paying for joining, the negative experience of being shocked would likely affect how one felt about the whole experimental session.

Net liking for the group was computed as the difference between the positive and negative poles of the evaluation cognition. As shown in Fig. 7.5, when dissonance reduction reached asymptote, attitude results showed the same interaction Gerard and Mathewson found with human subjects: a dissonance reduction effect under initiation conditions, with more liking for the group after severe than after mild initiation; and the reverse, annoyance effect without any initiation. Again, this interaction held up over a wide range of parameter randomization. Thus, the consonance model accounts for the full interaction, whereas classical dissonance theory accounts only for the effects of shock under initiation conditions.

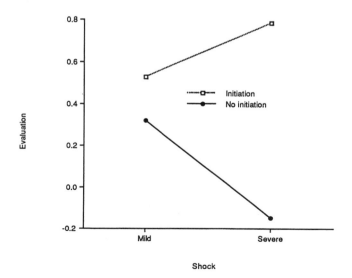

FIG. 7.5. Mean evaluation of the group in the simulation of the Gerard and Mathewson (1966) experiment. Adapted from Shultz and Lepper (1996).

Insufficient Justification via Forced Compliance

The third, and perhaps most famous, insufficient justification sub-paradigm involves what has been called "forced compliance." In the first experiment of this type, Festinger and Carlsmith (1959) found that smaller inducements to voice a belief against one's own attitude led to more change in the direction of the statement than did large inducements. Being paid $1 to lie about how interesting a truly boring task was led to higher subsequent evaluations of the task than did being paid $20 to tell the same lie. Because the receipt of a payment is consonant with telling the lie, it should be more dissonant to lie for a small reward than for a large reward. To rule out a number of alternative explanations, a subsequent study by Linder, Cooper, and Jones (1967) added conditions in which participants were not given a choice about writing a counter-attitudinal essay. They found that the dissonance effect held only when participants had a choice about whether to write the counter-attitudinal essay; without a choice, the opposite effect was found, with higher payment leading to more attitude change in the direction of the view supported in the essay.

Network specifications for this simulation (Shultz & Lepper, 1996) are shown in Fig. 7.6. Again, there were three relevant cognitions: the attitude, writing the essay, and the payment. Initial attitude was high negative, reflecting these liberal college students' negative reactions to banning controversial speakers on campus. Writing the essay was set to high positive because the essay had indeed been written. Payment for writing was either high or low, depending on condition.

Relations among the three cognitions reflected assumed causal implications. In the choice condition, the more one supports the position in the essay, the more likely one would write the essay; the more one is paid, the more one would agree to write the essay; and the more favorable one's attitude, the less one would need to be paid to write an essay at some particular level of support. Relations among cognitions were the same in the no-choice condition, except that the relation between attitude and essay was 0 because, without a choice, there is no causal connection between the two, and the relation between attitude and payment was positive, reflecting a better mood with higher pay.

Attitude toward banning controversial speakers was computed as the difference between activations on the positive and negative poles of the attitude cognition. After dissonance reduction was completed, the networks revealed the same crossover interaction found with Linder et al.'s (1967) college students: a dissonance effect under choice, with more attitude change after low payment than after high payment; and the reverse, mood effect under no choice, with more attitude change after high payment than after low payment (Fig. 7.7). As with the other insufficient justification simu-

a. Choice

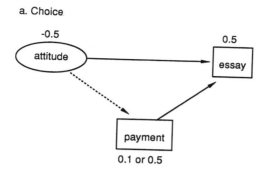

b. No choice

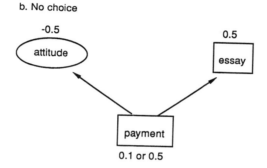

FIG. 7.6. Network specifications for simulation of the Linder et al. (1967) experiment.

lations, the results held up at every level of parameter randomization, but were cleaner at small and medium levels than at high levels. Once again, the consonance model covers the full interaction, whereas classical dissonance theory covers only the dissonance effect under choice.

THE FREE-CHOICE PARADIGM

The second major dissonance paradigm, the free-choice situation, focuses on the effects of people making a choice between alternatives. Making such a decision, it was argued, should create dissonance, due to the fact that the chosen alternative is never perfect and the rejected alternative often has desirable aspects that are necessarily foregone when an irreversible choice is made. Once an irrevocable choice has been made, dissonance can be reduced by viewing the chosen object as more desirable and by viewing the rejected object as less desirable. Such dissonance reduction further sepa-

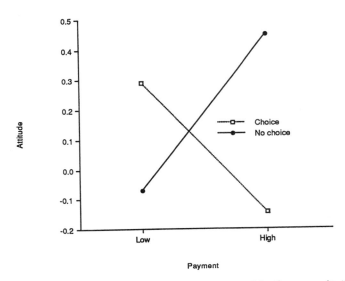

FIG. 7.7. Mean attitude toward the view expressed in the essay in the simulation of the Linder et al. (1967) experiment. Adapted from Shultz and Lepper (1996).

rates the alternative choices in terms of their desirability. Moreover, the magnitude of dissonance should be greater the closer the alternatives are in desirability before the choice is made. The closer the alternatives are in their initial desirability, the more difficult an exclusive choice between them.

In the classic free-choice experiment, Brehm (1956) found that the greater the dissonance created by a choice, the more the increase in separation between the alternatives after the choice was made. There was more separation between alternatives after a difficult choice between two highly preferred alternatives than after an easy choice between a favored and a disliked alternative. Unlike the more counter-intuitive insufficient justification studies, Brehm's free-choice results did not attract many alternative explanations.

However, in planning our simulations, we realized that a third interesting condition could be added, in which participants would be offered a difficult choice, but between two disliked alternatives (Shultz & Lepper, 1996). We referred to this as the difficult/low condition because evaluation of both alternatives starts out relatively low, in contrast to the difficult condition of Brehm (1956) that offered a choice between top-rated alternatives. We referred to that condition as difficult/high. Network specifications for these free-choice simulations are shown in Fig. 7.8. There were three cognitions, two of them evaluations of the alternative objects, and one of them the decision itself. The decision had an initially high value, and the initial values of the alternatives depended on condition. There was a positive relation

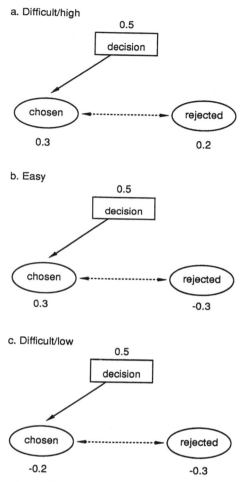

FIG. 7.8. Network specifications for simulation of the Brehm (1956) and Shultz et al. (1996) experiments.

between the decision and the chosen object, reflecting the choice, and a negative relation between the two alternatives reflecting the fact that they were competing for an exclusive choice.

Following Brehm (1956), we computed evaluation differences as final evaluation minus initial evaluation for each alternative. When dissonance reduction in the simulations reached asymptote, evaluation of the chosen object had increased, but more so in the difficult/low condition, and evaluation of the rejected object had decreased, but more so in the difficult/high condition (Fig. 7.9). As parameter randomization increased, the interaction weakened statistically but the pattern of evaluation change remained fairly

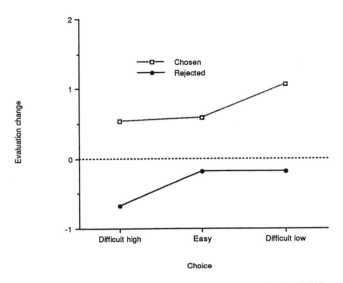

FIG. 7.9. Mean evaluation change in the simulation of the Brehm (1956) and Shultz et al. (1996) experiments. Adapted from Shultz and Lepper (1996).

constant. A new experiment with 13 year olds choosing among posters under these three conditions replicated Brehm's results in the difficult/high and easy choice conditions, and confirmed the predictions of the consonance networks for the difficult/low choice condition (Shultz, Léveillé, & Lepper, 1996).

It is worth noting that the consonance model simulations describe Brehm's (1956) data better than did classical dissonance theory, which only predicts more separation following difficult than following easy choices. Brehm found that most of the action was produced by devaluation of the rejected object in the difficult choice condition, and that was closely simulated by our consonance networks.

AROUSAL AND FORCED COMPLIANCE

More recently, considerable attention has been paid to the study of the arousal properties of cognitive dissonance (e.g., Cooper & Fazio, 1984; Zanna & Cooper, 1974). An important central finding of this work was that dissonance arousal can be externally modulated by administration of a drug, such as an amphetamine, tranquilizer, or placebo. Cooper, Zanna, and Taves (1978), for example, asked university students to write counter-attitudinal essays under either high- or low-choice conditions. These students had taken a pill that they had been led to believe was a placebo. In different conditions, however, the pill actually contained either phenobarbital, amphetamine, or a placebo. The placebo condition produced the usual dissonance effect: more attitude change in the direction of the essay under high choice than under low choice. In the tranquilizer condition, this dissonance effect was eliminated. In contrast, the ingestion of amphetamine enhanced attitude change under both high- and low-choice conditions. This last finding represented the first time that insufficient justification via forced compliance had produced dissonance effects under low-choice conditions.

Network specifications for our simulation (Shultz & Lepper, 1996) of the Cooper et al. (1978) experiment are shown in Fig. 7.10. In a sense, this study was a scaled-down version of Linder et al.'s (1967) forced compliance experiment, without the payment cognition, and with low, rather than no, choice about whether to write the essay. As in the simulation of Linder et al.'s results, the relation between attitude and essay was positive. Rather than cutting this link to 0, as we did to implement the no choice condition of Linder et al., we used a low value for low choice in contrast to a high value for high choice. To instantiate the arousal manipulations, an importance parameter scaled the initial activations and connection weights before they were randomized. This importance scalar was 1.0 for the placebo condition, 0.5 for what we called the downer condition, and 1.5 for what we called the upper condition. This corresponds very roughly to evidence that drugs such as phenobarbital depress neural firing rates and synaptic trans-

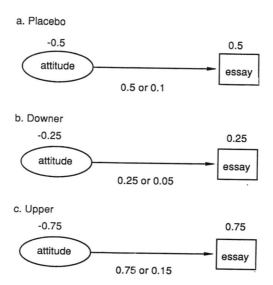

FIG. 7.10. Network specifications for simulation of the three conditions of the Cooper et al. (1978) experiment. Implicational links between attitude and essay are higher for high choice than for low choice.

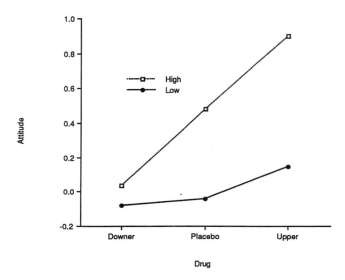

FIG. 7.11. Mean attitude toward the view expressed in the essay in the simulation of the Cooper et al. (1978) experiment. Adapted from Shultz and Lepper (1997).

mission whereas drugs such as amphetamine enhance neural firing rates and synaptic transmission (Quastel, 1975).

Attitude toward the view described in the essay was computed as the difference between activations on the positive and negative poles of the attitude cognition. After the networks had stabilized, the drug by choice interaction effects on attitude mirrored those displayed by Cooper et al.'s university students. There was a dissonance effect in the placebo condition, with more attitude change under high than under low choice; no effect of choice and little attitude change in the downer condition; and enhanced attitude change with the dissonance choice effect in the upper condition (Fig. 7.11). The interaction held for all three levels of parameter randomization.

THE ROLE OF SELF-CONCEPT

There is a contemporary focus on the importance of the self-concept in the arousal of dissonance (Steele, 1988; Thibodeau & Aronson, 1992). The basic idea is that dissonance occurs when behavior is inconsistent with the person's self-concept. Because most people have a positive self-concept, such behaviors as lying or arguing for a position that is contrary to one's own beliefs will arouse dissonance. However, people with a negative self-concept might not experience dissonance from engaging in such behaviors.

Self-Concept in the Forced Compliance Paradigm

Early support for this view can be seen in a study by Epstein (1969), which examined potential differences in the arousal of cognitive dissonance among people scoring high versus low on the trait of Machiavellianism. People scoring low on this trait, it was argued, should experience dissonance in a situation of insufficient justification via forced compliance, but those scoring high on the trait should not. For high Machiavellians, lying or writing a counter-attitudinal essay would not be inconsistent with their self-concept; instead, these sorts of actions would be seen as legitimate tactics of effective social interaction.

Epstein's undergraduate participants all initially supported the fluoridation of water supplies, but those in a dissonance group were induced to give a speech against it. These participants read some anti-fluoridation arguments and were paid $2 to give an anti-fluoridation speech. Participants in a control condition gave no speech, but read the arguments against fluoridation and were paid the $2 anyway.

Consistent with the predictions of classical dissonance theory, Epstein found that attitude change toward an anti-fluoridation position was higher for low Machiavellians who gave a speech than for low Machiavellians who did not give a speech. High scorers on Machiavellianism showed the reverse trend, which Epstein explained by citing evidence that these people are more susceptible to factual arguments than are people scoring low on Machiavellianism.

Network specifications for our simulation (Shultz & Lepper, 1997) of Epstein's experiment are shown in Fig. 7.12. These specifications are identical to those used in our simulations of Linder et al.'s (1967) forced compliance experiment, except that (a) the relation between attitude and speech was low for high Machiavellians (because, for high Machiavellians, there is not such a strong relation between true attitude and public statement), (b) there was an extra cognition for anti-fluoridation arguments (initialized to low) that had a positive relation to attitude (low for low Machiavellians, and high for high Machiavellians), (c) there was no speech cognition in the no-speech condition, and (d) pay was uniformly low.

Attitudes after asymptotes were reached mirrored the crossover interaction found with Epstein's undergraduates. Networks with low Machiavellian parameters revealed a dissonance effect, that is, more attitude change with a speech than without a speech, whereas networks built with high Machiavellian parameters exhibited the reverse effect (Fig. 7.13). The reversal effect for Machiavellians cannot be predicted or explained within classical dissonance theory, but did occur with the various constraints that can be built into consonance networks.

Most recently, even more subtle effects of self-concept on dissonance in a forced compliance situation were found by Steele (1988) in his studies of

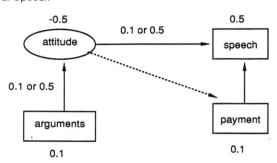

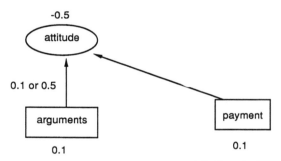

FIG. 7.12. Network specifications for simulation of the Epstein (1969) experiment. For high Machiavellians, the implication between attitude and speech is 0.1 and that between arguments and attitude is 0.5. For low Machiavellians, the implication between attitude and speech is 0.5 and that between arguments and attitude is 0.1.

self-affirmation processes. If dissonance arises when people's actions threaten their self-concepts, then anything that affirms an important aspect of the self-concept, even if it was completely irrelevant to the source of any experimentally induced inconsistency, should minimize the need for people to reduce dissonance via attitude change. Steele's college students were selected for their strong opposition to a tuition hike. These students were then persuaded to write essays in support of a substantial tuition hike, under either high choice or low choice, without any payment for doing so. Some of the students were also previously assessed as having a strong economic-political value orientation. For them, completing a political value scale would presumably affirm a valued part of their self-concept; for others without this value orientation, this task should have little impact. Indeed, Steele found the familiar dissonance effect of more attitude change under high choice than under low choice conditions, but he also found that self-affirmation eliminated attitude change, even under high choice conditions.

Network specifications for our simulations of Steele's experiment (Shultz & Lepper, 1997) are given in Fig. 7.14. As with the experiment of Cooper et al. (1978), this was a scaled-down version of Linder et al.'s (1967) forced compliance experiment. The key cognitions were attitude and essay with a positive relation between them. As with the Cooper et al. experiment, this positive relation was high under high choice and low under low choice. Initial values were high negative for attitude and high positive for essay. Here, the self-affirmation manipulation, designed to minimize the importance of the dissonance produced by the counter-attitudinal behavior, was implemented with an importance scalar of 0.5, as in the downer condition of the Cooper et al. simulation. This dampened all of the unit activations and connection weights prior to the randomization of parameter values.

After these consonance networks stabilized, they showed the same results as Steele's undergraduate participants: more attitude change in the standard high-choice condition than in either the low-choice or the high-choice/self-affirmation conditions (Fig. 7.15).

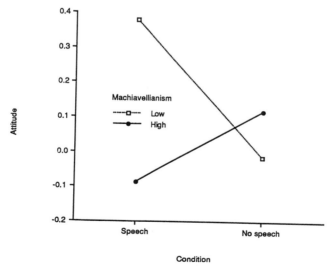

FIG. 7.13. Mean attitude toward the view expressed in the speech in the simulation of the Epstein (1969) experiment. Adapted from Shultz and Lepper (1996).

a. Choice

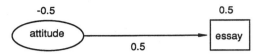

b. Low choice

c. Choice with self-affirmation

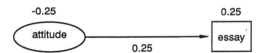

FIG. 7.14. Network specifications for simulation of Steele's (1988) forced compliance experiment. An importance scalar of 0.5 was used in the choice with self-affirmation condition.

Self-Concept in the Free-Choice Paradigm

In a similar vein, Steele (1988) also reported a free-choice experiment that showed self-affirmation effects. In this study, participants rated and ranked 10 record albums and then were given a choice of keeping either their fifth- or sixth-ranked albums. Some of the participants were selected for having a strong scientific value orientation and for having indicated that a lab coat symbolized for them important values and goals; others were selected for whom science was not an important personal value. Within each of these two selected groups, half the participants were asked to wear a lab coat for the rest of the experiment, whereas the others were not. Later, all partici- pants rated the 10 albums once again.

The spreading apart of alternatives after the choice was computed by adding the increase in the value of the chosen item and the decrease in the value of the rejected item. Spread of alternatives was found to be lower in

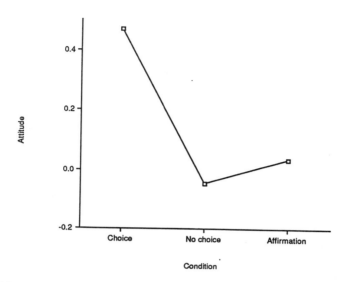

FIG. 7.15. Mean attitude toward the view expressed in the essay in the simulation of Steele's (1988) forced compliance experiment. Adapted from Shultz and Lepper (1996).

the self-affirmation condition, in which scientifically oriented students wore lab coats, than in the other conditions. This result occurred even though the affirmation procedure was irrelevant to the choice that initially produced dissonance.

Network specifications for the standard conditions of this second Steele study are shown in Fig. 7.16 (Shultz & Lepper, 1997). As with the simulations of Brehm's free-choice experiment, there were three principal cognitions: evaluations of each of the two alternatives, and the decision itself. Only a difficult choice was simulated, but otherwise the initial activations and relations were the same as in our simulation of Brehm's experiment (cf. Fig. 7.8). Here, once again, an importance scalar of 0.5 was used to diminish all unit activations and connection weights in the self-affirmation condition.

After stabilization of these consonance networks, spread of evaluation between the two alternative objects was computed as in Steele (1988). Change in the value of one object was the difference between its initial value and its value after stabilization. Spread of evaluation was the sum of the increase in the value of the chosen alternative and the decrease in the value of the rejected alternative. As with Steele's college students, at each level of parameter randomization, there was a smaller spread of the alternatives in the self-affirmation condition than in any of the other three conditions (Fig. 7.17). All of these results on self-concept held at all three levels of parameter randomization.

a. Standard

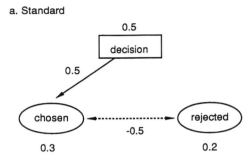

b. Self-affirmation

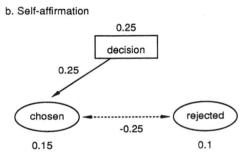

FIG. 7.16. Network specifications for simulation of the standard and self-affirmation conditions of Steele's (1988) free-choice experiment.

THE SELECTIVE EXPOSURE PARADIGM

A third basic paradigm featured in the initial presentation of dissonance theory (Festinger, 1957) involved the phenomenon of selective exposure, referring to biases in the manner in which people seek or avoid additional information that is relevant to a choice they made. In order to reduce cognitive dissonance, people were supposed to prefer information supporting their choices and to avoid information contradicting their choices. Compared to the more successful insufficient justification and free-choice paradigms, however, selective exposure generated much more long-term controversy. This is because of many results that either failed to support the selective exposure predictions or that directly contradicted them by finding a relative preference for dissonant information. Indeed, early reviews of the selective exposure literature concluded that dissonance theory was inapplicable to selective exposure phenomena (Bem, 1967; Freedman & Sears, 1965).

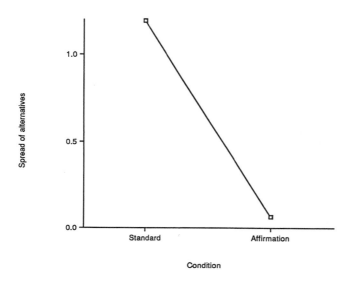

FIG. 7.17. Mean spread of alternatives in the simulation of Steele's (1988) free-choice experiment. Adapted from Shultz and Lepper (1997).

However, subsequent research (reviewed in Frey, 1986) inspired by theoretical reformulations (Festinger, 1964) permitted a somewhat more optimistic appraisal of the ability of dissonance theory to deal with selective exposure effects. These theoretical revisions emphasized, in particular, that there should be a relative preference for dissonant information when this information is perceived to be easily refutable or useful for future decision making (Festinger, 1964).

Replicable Selective Exposure Effects

Nonetheless, because of the controversial nature and relative fragility of selective exposure effects, it is probably wise to consider simulating only results in these areas that have at least one successful reported replication. Two of the phenomena in the selective exposure literature that would seem to meet this requirement concern the effects of variations in the magnitude of dissonance and those of a variety of moderating variables, including the utility, refutability, and credibility of the new consonant or dissonant information.

Selective Exposure and Magnitude of Dissonance. Selective exposure effects are predicted to increase with the magnitude of dissonance, at least in the case of irreversible decisions (Festinger, 1957, 1964). When a decision can be reversed, however, the relation between dissonance and selective exposure is presumably curvilinear, in an inverse U shape. This reflects the idea that, as dissonance approaches a maximum, dissonant information is particularly useful in guiding a decision reversal (Frey, 1986).

One of the first confirmations of the positive relationship between dissonance and selective exposure for irreversible decisions was provided by Mills (1965). Starting with procedures like those used in standard free-choice experiments, Mills asked college women to rank 20 personal care products on desirability and then to make a choice between two of them. In a high dissonance condition, the choice was between two objects that had been ranked very high; in a low dissonance condition, the choice was between one object that had been ranked high and one that had been ranked low. Then, as a measure of selective exposure, participants were asked to rate their interest in reading advertisements for each of the products involved in the choice. As predicted, interest in reading advertisements for the chosen product (i.e., information consonant with the choice) was greater when dissonance was high than when dissonance was low. Contrary to dissonance theory predictions, however, there was no effect of magnitude of dissonance on interest in advertisements for the rejected product (i.e., information dissonant with the choice).

This positive relation between dissonance and preference for consonant information was replicated by Frey (1981). His high school participants ranked 14 books and then were allowed to choose between two of them. Three levels of dissonance were created. High dissonance involved a choice between the second- and third-ranked books, medium dissonance a choice between the second- and seventh-ranked books, and low dissonance a choice between the second- and 13th-ranked books. After the choice was made, participants were allowed to select three commentaries from among six consonant and six dissonant commentaries on their chosen book. The mean number of consonant commentaries chosen was 2.00 in the high dissonance condition, 1.50 for medium dissonance, and 1.41 for low dissonance. The linear trend indicating more preference for consonant information with higher dissonance was statistically significant. As in the Mills (1965) experiment, there was no such effect of magnitude of dissonance on avoidance of dissonant commentaries, contrary to dissonance theory predictions.

Selective Exposure and Utility of Dissonant Information. The direction and strength of selective exposure effects have also been demonstrated to be influenced by a variety of extraneous variables including the utility, refutability, and credibility of the new information (see Frey, 1986, for a review of these studies). In general, dissonant information might actually be preferred to the extent that it is expected to prove useful in future tasks, to be easy to refute, or to originate from a low-credibility source. Some studies of utility have also included a condition in which consonant information is made useful, with the result that the selective exposure effect is enhanced rather than reversed. Potentially, each of these three moderating variables could be simulated in our consonance networks in the same way, by an extra cognition positively connected to the dissonant information cognition (or to the consonant information cognition). Consequently, and because published experiments tend to manipulate only one of these variables at a time, it is probably necessary to only include one of these variables in simulations. Utility of the extra information might be a good choice because its effects are particularly well documented.

One of the first studies of utility in selective exposure was reported by Canon (1964). Male college students selected one of two possible solutions to a business problem. Then they were told that they would take part in either a debate or a presentation of their point of view concerning this decision. To prepare for this session, participants were given the opportunity to read some number of five articles relevant to the case they had decided upon. Two of these articles supported their decision, two contradicted their decision, and one was neutral. Participants were asked to rate their interest in reading each of these articles on a 100-point scale. Preparing for a debate would make the dissonant information more useful, whereas preparing for a presentation of one's own views would render the consonant information more useful. Participants were more interested in consonant information when it was useful and somewhat more interested in dissonant information when it was useful. There was also an orthogonal manipulation of the subject's confidence, with the result that more confidence led to more interest in dissonant information. However, because this effect was not replicated (Freedman, 1965b), it may not be wise to try to capture it in simulations.

Interest in whatever information was more useful was replicated by Freedman (1965b) who also added an equal utility condition in which participants were expecting to merely react to other evaluations of the case. Again, information preference corresponded to the manipulation of information utility. When only one type of information was useful, that type was preferred.

Difficulty of Simulating Selective Exposure Phenomena

Although it might well be worth trying to simulate these selective exposure phenomena, we have not so far had success doing so with our consonance network models. For us, as for many of the early dissonance theorists, selective exposure proved to be a far more elusive target than the other central paradigms presented in Festinger's original book (1957).

Our simulation attempts underscored, though, one feature of selective exposure that was somewhat obscure in the psychological literature. This is the idea that selective exposure deals principally with any residual dissonance that may be present after evaluative change has occurred. That is, only if the relatively more direct process of evaluative change fails to eliminate dissonance would selective exposure operate.

Although this view became clear to us only through attempting to simulate selective exposure effects, it is consistent with both Festinger's (1957) original emphasis on dissonance as a pre-condition of selective exposure and the fundamental distinction between dissonance reduction via evaluative change and dissonance reduction via selective exposure that was drawn in more recent literature. Frey (1986) pointed out that evaluative change does not require any new behavior on the part of the person; an attitude is simply adjusted. In contrast, selective exposure does require additional behavior in terms of further interaction with the environment. Frey's notion that selective exposure is oriented toward the future is consistent with our view that it is primarily useful in dealing with any residual dissonance after dissonance reduction via evaluative change is complete.

Thus, it would appear that at least some of the fragility of selective exposure effects in the psychological literature may have been due to possible inadvertent dissonance reduction via evaluative change. It would seem that substantial dissonance reduction by evaluative change would interfere with selective exposure effects.

DISCUSSION

Using constraint satisfaction neural networks, our consonance model of dissonance reduction successfully captured all of the basics and many of the subtleties of both insufficient justification and free-choice phenomena (Shultz & Lepper, 1996, 1997). These captured effects include the devaluation of a forbidden toy under mild, but not under severe threat, and under non-surveillance, but not under surveillance conditions; greater liking of a group after severe than after mild initiation into the group; more attitude change following small inducements to make counter-attitudinal statements than following larger inducements; and separation of alternatives after a free-choice. Drawing upon later dissonance literature, they also include enhancement of attitude change in forced compliance experiments under stimulating drugs, and elimination of attitude change in forced compliance experiments under calming drugs; elimination of dissonance effects in forced compliance for participants with either Machiavellian personalities or recent self-affirming experiences; and elimination of dissonance effects in free-choice experiments for participants who have just experienced self-affirmation.

In several of these paradigms, our consonance model fit the psychological data better than did classical cognitive dissonance theory. Examples of superior fits to the human data include mood or annoyance effects in insufficient justification via initiation or forced compliance, locus of evaluation change in the free-choice paradigm, and greater attitude change among Machiavellians after not giving a speech than after giving a counter-attitudinal speech. These superior data fits were due to the inclusion of constraints that were not part of classical dissonance theory and to the increased precision inherent to this constraint satisfaction approach.

Consonance constraint satisfaction networks thus seem both more general and more precise in their theoretical coverage than is classical cognitive dissonance theory. In addition, novel predictions generated by the consonance network model for a free-choice between undesirable alternatives were confirmed in a new psychological experiment (Shultz et al., 1996). It is, of course, particularly challenging to generate predictions for new research in an area, such as cognitive dissonance, that has been worked over so thoroughly for so many years. Nevertheless, we hope that this new view of dissonance theory will stimulate further fresh investigations of it and other cognitive consistency phenomena. A particularly fruitful line of predictions might involve more complicated scenarios with more cognitions and relations than found in experiments inspired by dissonance theory. Being a verbally formulated theory, dissonance theory is limited in terms of its ability to deal with complex scenarios.

Perhaps the largest potential payoff for this simulation work, however, is the theoretical unification that can follow successful simulations (Smith, 1996). Constraint satisfaction models have been successfully applied to a wide variety of psychological processes, including belief revision, explanation, comprehension, schema completion, analogical retrieval and mapping, and content-addressable memory storage and retrieval (Holyoak & Thagard, 1989; Kintsch, 1988; Rumelhart et al., 1986; Sloman, 1990; Thagard, 1989). A number of phenomena in social psychology have also been successfully modeled with constraint satisfaction networks, including attitude change, impression formation, and cognitive balance (Kunda & Thagard, 1996; Read & Miller, 1993, 1994; Spellman & Holyoak, 1992; Spellman, Ullman, & Holyoak, 1993). Indeed, in our own present work, we are extending our consonance model to a more complete analysis of the case of cognitive balance theory (Heider, 1946, 1958; Read & Miller, 1994; Rosenberg & Abelson, 1960).

The success of constraint satisfaction models across these varied research areas suggests that cognitive dissonance may not be as unique and exotic as it has often appeared to be. Partly because dissonance researchers chose to focus upon those counter-intuitive dissonance phenomena that could not be easily explained by other models, dissonance theory was historically viewed as distinct from basic and perhaps more mundane psychological processes. Once dissonance and its reduction are viewed as another instance of constraint satisfaction, much of its mystery disappears. Viewing dissonance theory in this new light makes it more understandable within the general scheme of psychological explanation.

Indeed, the use of these sorts of models may help us to remember that dissonance reduction, and the related consonance-seeking processes postulated by other consistency theories, are neither inherently rational nor inherently irrational. Whether the outcome of such a process is one or the other in any given case will depend upon the task and the situation. The same willingness to disregard dissonant feedback that allowed the Wright brothers to succeed in pioneering manned flight also led a number of their predecessors to leap off cliffs while flapping the artificial wings attached to their arms. Perhaps our aspirations to rationality and our propensity for rationalization, these models suggest, are but two sides of the same coin.

ACKNOWLEDGMENTS

This research was supported by a grant to the first author from the Social Sciences and Humanities Research Council of Canada, and by grant MH-44321 to the second author from the U.S. National Institute of Mental Health.

Thomas R. Shultz, Department of Psychology, McGill University, 1205 Penfield Avenue, Montreal, Quebec, Canada H3A 1B1. E-mail: shultz@psych. mcgill.ca. Mark R. Lepper, Department of Psychology, Stanford University, Jordan Hall, Building 420, Stanford, CA 94305-2130. E-mail: lepper@psych.stanford.edu.

REFERENCES

Abelson, R. P. (1971). Are attitudes necessary? In B. T. King & E. McGinnies (Eds.), *Attitudes, conflict, and social change* (pp. 19–32). New York: American Marketing Association.

Abelson, R. P., Aronson, E., McGuire, W. J., Newcomb, T. M., Rosenberg, M. J., & Tannenbaum, P. H. (Eds.). (1968). *Theories of cognitive consistency: A sourcebook.* Chicago: Rand McNally.

Abelson, R. P., & Rosenberg, M. J. (1958). Symbolic psycho-logic: A model of attitudinal cognition. *Behavioral Science, 3,* 1–13.

Anderson, J. A. (1995). *An introduction to neural networks.* Cambridge, MA: MIT Press.

Aronson, E. (1969). The theory of cognitive dissonance: A current perspective. In L. Berkowitz (Ed.), *Advances in experimental social psychology* (Vol. 4, pp. 1–34). Orlando, FL: Academic Press.

Aronson, E. (1989). Analysis, synthesis, and treasuring the old. *Personality and Social Psychology Bulletin, 15,* 508–512.

Aronson, E., & Carlsmith, J. M. (1963). Effect of severity of threat on the devaluation of forbidden behavior. *Journal of Abnormal and Social Psychology, 66,* 584–588.

Aronson, E., & Mills, J. (1959). The effect of severity of initiation on liking for a group. *Journal of Abnormal and Social Psychology, 59,* 177–181.

Bem, D. J. (1967). Self perception: An alternative interpretation of cognitive dissonance phenomena. *Psychological Review, 74,* 183–200.

Berkowitz, L., & Devine, P. G. (1989). Research traditions, analysis, and synthesis in social psychology: The case of dissonance theory. *Personality and Social Psychology, 15,* 493–507.

Brehm, J. W. (1956). Post-decision changes in the desirability of choice alternatives. *Journal of Abnormal and Social Psychology, 52,* 384–389.

Canon, L. K. (1964). Self-confidence and selective exposure to information. In L. Festinger (Ed.), *Conflict, decision, and dissonance* (pp. 83–95). Stanford, CA: Stanford University Press.

Cooper, J., & Fazio, R. H. (1984). A new look at dissonance theory. In L. Berkowitz (Ed.), *Advances in experimental social psychology* (Vol. 17, pp. 229–266). New York: Academic Press.

Cooper, J., Zanna, M. P., & Taves, P. A. (1978). Arousal as a necessary condition for attitude change following forced compliance. *Journal of Personality and Social Psychology, 36*, 1101–1106.

Epstein, G. F. (1969). Machiavelli and the devil's advocate. *Journal of Personality and Social Psychology, 11*, 38–41.

Feldman, S. (Ed.). (1966). *Cognitive consistency.* New York: Academic Press.

Festinger, L. (1957). *A theory of cognitive dissonance.* Evanston, IL: Row, Peterson.

Festinger, L. (1964). *Conflict, decision, and dissonance.* Stanford, CA: Stanford University Press.

Festinger, L., & Carlsmith, J. M. (1959). Cognitive consequences of forced compliance. *Journal of Abnormal and Social Psychology, 58*, 203–210.

Freedman, J. L. (1965a). Long-term behavioral effects of cognitive dissonance. *Journal of Experimental Social Psychology, 1*, 145–155.

Freedman, J. L. (1965b). Confidence, utility, and selective exposure: A partial replication. *Journal of Personality and Social Psychology, 2*, 778–780.

Freedman, J. L., & Sears, D. O. (1965). Selective exposure. In L. Berkowitz (Ed.), *Advances in experimental social psychology* (Vol. 2, pp. 57–97). New York: Academic Press.

Frey, D. (1981). Reversible and irreversible decisions: Preference for consonant information as a function of attractiveness of decision alternatives. *Personality and Social Psychology Bulletin, 7*, 621–626.

Frey, D. (1986). Recent research on selective exposure to information. In L. Berkowitz (Ed.), *Advances in experimental social psychology* (Vol. 19, pp. 41–80). New York: Academic Press.

Gerard, H. B., & Mathewson, G. C. (1966). The effects of severity of initiation on liking for a group: A replication. *Journal of Experimental Social Psychology, 2*, 278–287.

Heider, F. (1946). Attitudes and cognitive organization. *Journal of Personality, 21*, 107–112.

Heider, F. (1958). *The psychology of interpersonal relations.* New York: Wiley.

Holyoak, K. J., & Thagard, P. (1989). Analogical mapping by constraint satisfaction. *Cognitive Science, 13*, 295–355.

Hopfield, J. J. (1982). Neural networks and physical systems with emergent collective computational abilities. *Proceedings of the National Academy of Sciences, USA, 79*, 2554–2558.

Hopfield, J. J. (1984). Neurons with graded responses have collective computational properties like those of two-state neurons. *Proceedings of the National Academy of Sciences, USA, 81*, 3008–3092.

Kintsch, W. (1988). The role of knowledge in discourse comprehension: A construction-integration model. *Psychological Review, 95*, 163–182.

Kunda, Z., & Thagard, P. (1996). Forming impressions from stereotypes, traits, and behaviors: A parallel-constraint-satisfaction theory. *Psychological Review, 103*, 284–308.

Lepper, M. R. (1983). Social-control processes and the internalization of values: An attributional perspective. In E. T. Higgins, D. N. Ruble, & W. W. Hartup (Eds.), *Social cognition and social development* (pp. 294–330). New York: Cambridge University Press.

Linder, D. E., Cooper, J., & Jones, E. E. (1967). Decision freedom as a determinant of the role of incentive magnitude in attitude change. *Journal of Personality and Social Psychology, 6*, 245–254.

McGuire, W. J. (1960). A syllogistic analysis of cognitive relationships. In C. I. Holland & M. J. Rosenberg (Eds.), *Attitude organization and change* (pp. 65–111). New Haven, CT: Yale University Press.

Mills, J. (1965). Effect of certainty about a decision upon postdecision exposure to consonant and dissonant information. *Journal of Personality and Social Psychology, 2*, 749–752.

Newcomb, T. M. (1953). An approach to the study of communicative acts. *Psychological Review, 60*, 393–404.

Osgood, C. E., & Tannenbaum, P. H. (1955). The principle of congruity in the prediction of attitude change. *Psychological Review, 62*, 42–55.

Quastel, J. H. (1975). Effect of drugs on energy metabolism of the brain and on cerebral transport. In L. L. Iversen, S. D. Iversen, & S. H. Snyder (Eds.), *Handbook of psychopharmacology: Vol. 5. Synaptic modulators* (pp. 1–46). New York: Plenum.

Read, S. J., & Miller, L. C. (1993). Rapist or "regular guy"?: Explanatory coherence in the construction of mental models of others. *Personality and Social Psychology Bulletin, 19*, 526–541.

Read, S. J., & Miller, L. C. (1994). Dissonance and balance in belief systems: The promise of parallel constraint satisfaction processes and connectionist modeling approaches. In R. C. Schank & E. Langer (Eds.), *Beliefs, reasoning, and decision making: Psycho-logic in honor of Bob Abelson* (pp. 209–235). Hillsdale, NJ: Lawrence Erlbaum Associates.

Rosenberg, M. J., & Abelson, R. P. (1960). An analysis of cognitive balancing. In M. J. Rosenberg, C. I. Hovland, W. J. McGuire, R. P. Abelson, & J. W. Brehm (Eds.), *Attitude organization and change* (pp. 112–163). New Haven, CT: Yale University Press.

Rumelhart, D. E., Smolensky, P., McClelland, J. L., & Hinton, G. (1986). Schemata and sequential thought processes in PDP models. In D. E. Rumelhart & J. L. McClelland (Eds.), *Parallel distributed processing: Explorations in the microstructure of cognition* (Vol. 2, pp. 7–57). Cambridge, MA: MIT Press.

Shultz, T. R., & Lepper, M. R. (1992). A constraint satisfaction model of cognitive dissonance phenomena. *Proceedings of the Fourteenth Annual Conference of the Cognitive Science Society* (pp. 462–467). Hillsdale, NJ: Lawrence Erlbaum Associates.

Shultz, T. R., & Lepper, M. R. (1996). Cognitive dissonance reduction as constraint satisfaction. *Psychological Review, 103*, 219–240.

Shultz, T. R., & Lepper, M. R. (1997). *Consonance network simulations of arousal and self-concept phenomena in cognitive dissonance: The importance of psychological importance.* Manuscript submitted for publication.

Shultz, T. R., Léveillé, E., & Lepper, M. R. (1996). *Free choice and cognitive dissonance revisited.* Manuscript submitted for publication.

Sloman, S. (1990). *Persistence in memory and judgment: Part-set inhibition and primacy.* Unpublished doctoral dissertation, Stanford University.

Smith, E. R. (1996). What do connectionism and social psychology offer each other? *Journal of Personality and Social Psychology, 70*, 893–912.

Spellman, B. A., & Holyoak, K. J. (1992). If Saddam is Hitler, then who is George Bush? Analogical mapping between systems of social roles. *Journal of Personality and Social Psychology, 62*, 913–933.

Spellman, B. A., Ullman, J. B., & Holyoak, K. J. (1993). A coherence model of cognitive consistency: Dynamics of attitude change during the Persian Gulf war. *Journal of Social Issues, 49*, 147–165.

Steele, C. M. (1988). The psychology of self-affirmation: Sustaining the integrity of the self. In L. Berkowitz (Ed.), *Advances in experimental social psychology* (Vol. 21, pp. 261–302). New York: Academic Press.

Thagard, P. (1989). Explanatory coherence. *Behavioral and Brain Sciences, 12*, 435–502.

Thibodeau, R., & Aronson, E. (1992). Taking a closer look: Reasserting the role of the self-concept in dissonance theory. *Personality and Social Psychology Bulletin, 18*, 591–602.

Wicklund, R. A., & Brehm, J. (1976). *Perspectives on cognitive dissonance.* Hillsdale, NJ: Lawrence Erlbaum Associates.

Zanna, M. P., & Cooper, J. (1974). Dissonance and the pill: An attribution approach to studying the arousal properties of dissonance. *Journal of Personality and Social Psychology, 29*, 703–709.

8

TOWARD AN INTEGRATION OF THE SOCIAL AND THE SCIENTIFIC: OBSERVING, MODELING, AND PROMOTING THE EXPLANATORY COHERENCE OF REASONING

Michael Ranney
University of California, Berkeley

Patricia Schank
SRI International

It may seem odd for two cognitive scientists, each with little specific expertise in social psychology, to present a chapter that focuses on social cognition. Indeed, our past work may seem much more in the realm of scientific reasoning than in that of social reasoning. But one question that we have been asking, both of ourselves and of our colleagues, is, "What is the difference between 'scientific reasoning' and plain old 'reasoning'?" Generally, people hem and haw when confronted with this question, then speak of the latter as if it were social reasoning—and quite often, they mention socially based ruminations that involve suboptimal decisions, faulty heuristics, and inappropriately biased values, goals, and the like (see Gigerenzer, 1991; Tversky & Kahneman, 1974, and many others). Useful follow-up questions to such respondents include, "Well, is the difference between these two sorts of reasoning qualitative or quantitative?" Put another way (as many—including Einstein, 1950—seem to have occasionally wondered), "Is scientific reasoning just (a) more likely to employ formal tools (like deduction or mathematics) and/or (b) more likely to involve the vigilant search for disconfirmation—something that 'just plain folks' (Lave, 1988, p. 4) do, but less frequently?"

Put rather bluntly, we have not been able to reject the hypothesis that the word "scientific" in "scientific reasoning" is superfluous. In an era of specialization, we realize that it is a bit out of fashion to undifferentiate reasoning (although one can argue that interdisciplinary cognitive science itself similarly bucks the trend); still, we are more struck by how much of the everyday is found in scientific reasoning (and vice versa) than by how unique scientific reasoning is. Thus, we believe that the principles of reasoning that have been seen primarily as characterizing scientific reasoning can equally well be viewed as central to social reasoning.[1] Bifurcating the set of reasoning processes into the social and the scientific is a bit like bifurcating a deity and still considering the encompassing religion to be monotheistic. In essence, adding either the modifier "social" or "scientific" seems unnecessary, unless one speaks about the *domain* being reasoned about (discussed later).

Consider the following experience. While at a social gathering, a friend's father remarked that sugar-laden foods dramatically boost children's activity. It was obvious, he claimed, because he had watched a birthday party full of kids "go crazy" after eating the cake. Another guest (perhaps a "better reasoner" on this topic) pointed out a glitch with the father's logic: Several factors other than sugar intake could account for the craziness (e.g., the party atmosphere, the greater disarray in the party room, relaxed supervision, etc.). The critic was essentially reasoning more completely and/or "more scientifically," bringing up issues of control or baseline conditions, alternative hypotheses, critical tests, and covariation detection (see Nisbett & Ross, 1980). (Note, though, that we do not suggest that the father was thus reasoning "more socially" because he failed to initially consider the critic's issues, as this might imply that the critic was *not* reasoning socially.)

Scientists often reason the same way the father did—with biases, untested assumptions, and observations that have no control situations to limit confounding (e.g., they use "fallback heuristics;" cf. Fletcher, 1993, p. 257). However, we believe that scientists appear scientific to the degree to which they spend a higher proportion of time engaging in sciencelike activities, such as criticizing hypotheses (both their own and others'), developing and calibrating precise measuring instruments and methods, engaging in formal (e.g., mathematical, computational, logical, and quasi-logical) analyses of a domain, soliciting extraneous reviews of their work, and the like. We further suggest that the more one has useful, auxiliary, physical, or social artifacts (e.g., calculators, computers, word processors, reasoning engines, logical systems, jargon), the more one can (at least appear to) "act scientifically" (see Fletcher, pp. 260, 265).

---

[1]We thank Stephen Read for help in phrasing this premise. As he and Marcus-Newhall (1993) pointed out, "if these principles are as central in everyday social inference as they are in scientific inference, then it is critical that we gain a better understanding of their role in social inference" (p. 430; also see Fletcher, 1993).

Naturally, no one engages in these behaviors 100% of the time, and there are several reasons for this gap between competence and performance. First, many scholars have noted (in one way or another) that we are limited processors of information, and such temporal, memorial, and computational demands strongly limit the rigor of our thoughts (e.g., Hoadley, Ranney, & Schank, 1994; Ranney, in press; Simon, 1955). To be globally coherent or rational means that one would ruminate so much as to never get out of bed in the mornings due to the exhaustive depth of processing required and the slow speed of our cognitive processors. (And even if one could rouse oneself, she would probably not be much fun.) Again, to the degree that our tools can reduce such processing limitations (for instance, an auditory alert before one's car runs out of fuel), our best-laid plans will indeed seem fairly scientifically (e.g., rigorously) laid out. Put more colloquially, scientists seem like eggheads mostly because of the "cool toys" they can use to study phenomena—in which toys can be both physical objects and special-purpose cognitive representations (Norman, 1988, 1993). Fletcher (1993) provided a similar perspective on processing limitations, grounded more in the literature of social and personality psychology, as to why, at different times, "people are both rational and rationalizers" (p. 255–260; cf. Ranney, 1996, on consistency and rationality).

As is often useful, it is worth reminding ourselves that scientists live in social worlds, just as social people live in scientific worlds (e.g., with at least some of the methods and products of science), regardless of whether either group likes it. Indeed, it is difficult to generate a reasoning scenario that does not involve, to some degree, both the social and the scientific in some way—that is, a purely social or purely scientific situation.[2] This is elaborated upon later when we discuss the relationships between, for instance, values (or goals), and hypotheses. For a quick example, though, note that the value (or at least what seems to be a value), "Don't act like an idiot" can be expressed as the hypothesis "Bad things happen when you act like an idiot" and vice versa.[3] Similarly, the hypothesis "The future will be better if we keep other organisms alive" might be seen as the value (e.g., the commandment) "Do not kill." The language of values often makes us think of social aspects, whereas the language of hypotheses often makes us think of scientific aspects. We suggest that these may be the same basic representations, but with differing perspectives, or "cover stories," if you will.

---

[2]After all, even human languages, which often mediate reasoning processes, result from social consensus (Putnam, 1981), yet they have formal properties as well. In a similar vein, it would seem incorrect to argue that social reasoning does not involve the consideration of constructs that are generally seen as scientific, namely hypotheses or evidence.

[3]Such hypotheses may vary in concreteness or level of analysis. For instance, "People look down on you when you act like an idiot" might replace or supplement the more abstract "Bad things . . ." hypothesis.

As relative outsiders to social psychology, we feel fairly unconstrained to point out different meanings of "social," and that some of these meanings differ from what is usually considered normative in the literature of social/personality psychology (e.g., as involving personality traits, group interactions, judgment, and decision making; cf. Fiske & Taylor, 1984). In this chapter, we highlight three readings of "social." As pointed out earlier, in one reading, some people (at least casually) contrast the social with the scientific, suggesting that social reasoning is a reasoning "style" that has, in principle (i.e., not just practice), less empiricism, less objectivity, less rigor, less accountability,[4] or more emotion. We tend to reject this interpretation, as it seems to merely—that is, nonproductively—substitute "social reasoning" for "poor reasoning" and/or borrow from the following two readings.[5] (Fletcher, e.g., 1993, nicely addresses similar issues, and he occasionally links the "rational" with the "scientific" in his discussions.)

A second reading of "social" regards the *domain* of reasoning; in this form, social reasoning means reasoning about (small-scale) interpersonal situations (e.g., Miller & Read, 1991; Read & Miller, 1993). (This will be our default, but certainly not exclusive, meaning for "social.") Such reasoning might be about whether a certain girl will date a certain boy or how to act regarding an HIV-infected child (e.g., Ritter, 1991; see later discussion). A third meaning of "social" involves us as social creatures within a larger, communal, society—a society that can provide us with both great benefits and terrible hardships. The second and third meanings are occasionally seen as the material for commonsense or "folk" psychology. Fletcher contrasts such folk theories with ("scientific") psychological theories, in that they "have a wider range of uses and aims" and "consist of a more amorphous, flexible and sprawling set of concepts and models . . ." (1993, p. 265).

In this chapter, each of these three meanings of "social" is intermittently addressed, particularly with respect to our research regarding explanatory coherence, a system that was primarily developed to better study and analyze what we conceived of as "scientific" reasoning (Ranney & Thagard, 1988; Thagard, 1989). We begin with a summary of our past empirical work regarding explanatory coherence, in which we highlight aspects of reasoning

---

[4]For example, some people view social reasoning as "cocktail conversation," in which even fairly outlandish and unsupportable statements may be generated when one is not held to account for them. (Tetlock, 1985, 1992, made similar points with respect to the fundamental attribution error and other phenomena.) This might be seen as a *mode* of reasoning to some people—an informal and off-the-cuff mode—but it is hardly the hallmark of good reasoning (as discussed later; cf. Putnam, 1981). (We thank Todd Shimoda and Bob Branstrom for pointing out this dimension to us.)

[5]This is why we use "socio-scientific" (at times) in this chapter. The reader may find it illuminating to try to generate a counterexample to this claim; that is, we invite the reader to try to find an instance of reasoning that is (a) poor *because* it is social and/or (b) does not conflate the following two notions of "social."

about social situations and societal issues. This is followed by a more in-depth description of our studies involving a particularly controversial societal issue—that of the abortion debate—that we believe includes both social and scientific aspects. We then return to further analyze the purported distinction between social and scientific forms of reasoning, as well as distinctions among various component terms such as values, goals, hypotheses, and candidate actions (e.g., to consider whether the plurals "forms" and "terms" are needed). To reiterate for now, though, we believe that the basic principles and forms of social and scientific reasoning are essentially the same; what may differ between the two are aspects such as the amounts (and/or subtypes) of time, effort, systematicity, and cognitive tools used. Toward this chapter's end, we discuss a set of intended future directions for our research, which takes the shape of trying to answer the (perhaps ultimate social) question, "What should we be studying, such that society will maximally benefit?"

STUDYING AND MODELING EXPLANATORY COHERENCE

Much of our work has focused on assessing and applying the Theory of Explanatory Coherence (TEC) and its associated connectionist model, ECHO, which offer an account of how people evaluate the plausibility of beliefs comprising an explanation or argument (e.g., Ranney & Thagard, 1988; Schank, 1995; Thagard, 1989). TEC is comprised of roughly 10 principles that both establish local pairwise relations among cohering and incohering propositions and that empirically appear to play important roles in evaluations of the quality of an explanation (e.g., Read & Marcus-Newhall, 1993; Schank & Ranney, 1991). For instance, TEC assumes that the plausibility of a belief generally increases with (a) the simplicity with which it is explained (e.g., having fewer necessary explaining cohypotheses), (b) increasing breadth (i.e., offering greater coverage of observations), and (c) decreasing competition with alternative (especially entrenched) beliefs. TEC is quasi-positivistic in that, all other things being equal, evidence tends to have "data priority"—that is, more plausibility—than do hypotheses. In addition, TEC has several holistic characteristics; for instance, (a) coherent beliefs are seen as *symmetrically* supportive, (b) incohering beliefs are seen as *symmetrically* conflicting, (c) coexplaining propositions support both an explanandum *and* each other, and (d) the overall coherence of a configuration of beliefs is "the best that it can be" (cf. the Gestalt Law of Prägnanz), given the pairwise (cohering or incohering) interactions of such beliefs (i.e., an argument reaches a state of minimal discord). TEC generally represents a somewhat uncontroversial view of explanatory coherence,[6] although some philosophers of science might quibble with a principle or two (e.g., the notion of data priority or its prevalence). Others offer somewhat different principles, albeit perhaps for somewhat different cognitive realms (e.g., on the epistemic criteria used for theory evaluation; Fletcher, 1993, pp. 254–255).

What considerably distinguishes TEC from other such systems is its embodiment in a computational, constraint-based, model. In essence, such models are homeostasis-seeking devices, driven to find points of equilibrium or minimal energy—in this case, among beliefs in a system of beliefs that may be quite "messy" (e.g., involving multiple contradictory/competitive elements that are centrally embedded in an argument). In this way, constraint-satisfaction models reify what have been, prior to computational modeling, more "hand-waving" notions such as balance theory, impression formation, Gestaltism, and cognitive consistency or dissonance (see Gabrys, 1989; Kunda & Thagard, 1996; Read & Marcus-Newhall, 1993; Read, Vanman, & Miller, in press; Shultz & Lepper, 1992, 1996; Spellman, Ullman, & Holyoak, 1993; Wertheimer, 1982). These were generally promising models of various high-level (and other) forms of thought that were limited by the lack of formal (e.g., computational) ways in which to assess them.

In contrast, connectionist implementations of such constraint-satisfaction systems are computational and considerably more formal. They can generally be thought of as a comingling of constructs or beliefs (nodes in a network) that are, using an interpersonal metaphor, either "buddies" or "enemies" of each other (but usually not both). The "friendship" of the buddies takes the form of excitatory constraints/links, such that friends generally either do well together or poorly together. On the other hand, the "distaste" of the enemies represents inhibitory constraints/links that tend to drive each other's acceptability (or "activation") down. As activation ("popularity") settles among the various beliefs, this computational currency of evaluation will indicate the relative plausibility of each of the beliefs (e.g., which cliques and subcliques of propositions are most exalted). (Also see Bereiter, 1991, and Thagard, 1996, for other descriptions of such implementations.)

TEC's model, ECHO, is based on the claim that beliefs are related explanatory entities, and evaluating their plausibility is an interactive, principled, coherence-seeking process (Ranney, in press; Thagard, 1989). Belief evaluation in ECHO involves the satisfaction of many constraints, determined by the explanatory relations among propositions and a few processing parameters. ECHO employs a connectionist architecture in which each node represents a proposition (hypothesis or piece of evidence) with an associated

---

[6]TEC is more controversial as an account of scientific inference, in which the main competitor is the Bayesian approach (see Thagard, in press, for a comparison of ECHO with probabilistic models of inference).

activation value, and each connection represents an explanatory relation (explanation, contradiction, or competition[7]) with an associated weighting.[8] ECHO's connection weights and propositional relationships are provided, depending upon the methodology employed, by default, by the experimenter, or by the subject (e.g., Ranney & Schank, 1995). For example, consider the following scenario, which involves two different viewpoints about abortion (from Schank, 1995):

> Smith believes that abortion is wrong because fetuses are alive. Jones disagrees, saying that abortion is fine, because we as a society kill living things (e.g., for food) all the time. (p. 214)

Given the following possible encoding (e.g., by a subject) of this argument,

- hypothesis H1 "Abortion is wrong"
- hypothesis H2 "Abortion is fine"
- hypothesis H3 "It's wrong to kill things that are alive"
- evidence E1 "Fetuses are alive"
- evidence E2 "Society kills living things all the time"
- H1 contradicts H2
- E1 and H3 jointly explain H1
- E2 explains H2

ECHO would accept this input and generate the network shown in Fig. 8.1, in which the solid line between E2 and H2 represents an independent explanation, the solid Y-shape represents a joint explanation, and the dashed line represents a contradiction.

Node activations represent propositional acceptabilities, and are initially assigned to zero (neutral). (Final activations range from −1, complete rejection, to 1, complete acceptance.) Links in ECHO are symmetric, and the link weights (which also range from −1 to 1) are specified by three processing parameters—*excitation*, *inhibition*, and *data excitation*. Excitation determines the weights on links between cohering propositions (with the value divided by the number of explanatory propositions in the case of a joint explanation), inhibition determines the weight on links between incohering propositions, and data excitation specifies the weight on links between data (usually evidence) and the "special evidence unit" (SEU, a unit with activation set at a constant 1.0, to give data a bias toward acceptability). The data priority of a particular piece of evidence may also be specified separately, if desired.

---

[7]"Competition," as used here, is a technical term (Thagard, 1992), and is implemented in a variant of ECHO, called ECHO2. However, its utility is questionable (see Ranney, Schank, Mosmann, & Montoya, 1993), so it is not used or discussed here.

[8]More complete descriptions of ECHO's algorithms are available elsewhere (e.g., Thagard, 1989, 1992).

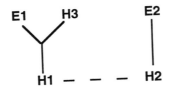

FIG. 8.1. A simplified representation of a small ECHO network.

Continuing with our example above, let us assume that the parameter settings are excitation = .03, inhibition = .06, and data excitation = .055 (our standard default settings). Given these values, the ECHO network shown in Fig. 8.1 would be more completely represented as shown in Fig. 8.2, in which the numbers in italics represent link weights, and the numbers in parentheses represent initial node activations.

After setting up the network, ECHO's constraint-satisfaction engine determines the acceptability of each proposition. Unit activations are updated in cycles until the network settles and the change in all units is asymptotic. At each cycle, the activation of a particular unit u_j is partially determined by a fourth critical parameter—the *decay rate*—and the net input to the unit. Decay specifies the percentage of the activation that a proposition loses at each cycle (when otherwise unchanged). The net input to a unit u_j is the weighted sum of the activation of each neighboring unit u_i, in which a weight is the common link value w_{ij}. Each unit u_j is updated using the following equation (cf. Rumelhart & McClelland, 1986):

$$u_j(t+1) = u_j(t)(1 - decay) + \{\ net_j(max - u_j(t))\text{ if } net_j > 0 \text{ and} \atop net_j(u_j(t) - min) \text{ otherwise}\ \} \tag{1}$$

in which $net_j = \sum_i w_{ij} u_i(t)$

Although ECHO has a few other processing parameters, the four presented here (excitation, inhibition, data excitation, and decay) appear most critical to ECHO's performance (Schank & Ranney, 1991). Returning to our example, the network (in Fig. 8.2) takes 149 cycles to settle, with final activations shown in Fig. 8.3. Note that, for this representation, ECHO essentially predicts that the modeled subject will find that proposition H2 is moderately acceptable (.47 activation) whereas H1 is mildly rejectable (−.29). (For simplicity, link weights are no longer shown because they do not change; the SEU does not change, either, because it is "clamped" at 1.0).

Thus, TEC offers a model (ECHO) that helps us understand how people draw inferences in social environments—one that yields testable and reasonably precise predictions. For example, people might be said to accept hypotheses about others on the basis that these hypotheses are coherent with their current beliefs, and yield coherent explanations of observed behavior

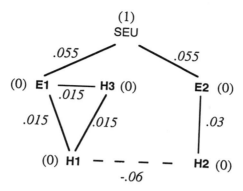

FIG. 8.2. A more explicit initial representation of the ECHO network in Fig. 8.1, with connection weights and initial node activations.

(Thagard, 1989). Pennington and Hastie (1988), as well as Thagard, claim that explanatory coherence plays a crucial role in jurors' decision making, and Read, Miller, and Marcus-Newhall (Miller & Read, 1991; Read & Marcus-Newhall, 1993; Read & Miller, 1993) have used the principles of explanatory coherence to understand and guide models of social interaction and relationships.

Early assessments of ECHO's modeling effectiveness focused on the post hoc modeling of arguments extracted from texts (e.g., scientific treatises and juror reasoning, Thagard, 1992; and social interactions, Miller & Read, 1991) and on subjects' verbal protocols (e.g., regarding their conceptions of physical motion; Ranney & Thagard, 1988). More recently, we have used ECHO to (a priori) predict the strength of subjects' beliefs (see Ranney & Schank, 1995). Initially, we used ECHO to predict subjects' text-based believability ratings (Ritter, 1991; Schank & Ranney, 1991). This methodology involved subjects reading some paragraphs that embodied a particular ECHO network topology; subjects were then asked to rate, on a believability scale,

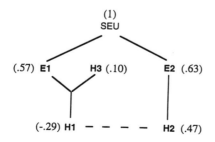

FIG. 8.3. Final activations values (in parentheses) for the network shown in prior figures.

each proposition that was embedded in a text. Texts involving social relationships were particularly salient in Christopher Ritter's work in our laboratory (e.g., Ranney, Schank, & Ritter, 1992). In the following example, between-gender social relations were highlighted:

> A boy wants to ask a girl to see a movie with him. Will Emily say yes or no to Zachary?
> On the one hand, Zachary believes that Emily may dislike him. Emily laughed at him when he fell on the baseball field. Emily did not talk to Zachary when he saw her at the mall. And when Zachary ran for class vice-president, Emily supported Zachary's opponent. The possibility that Emily dislikes Zachary would mean that she will say no to seeing a movie with him.
> On the other hand, Zachary believes that Emily might indeed like him. Emily attends his baseball practices frequently. Sometimes Zachary catches her watching him in class. And he got a valentine from Emily in February. Finally, the assumption that girls are more prone to like boys than to dislike them suggests that she might like Zachary. The possibility that Emily likes Zachary means that she will say yes to seeing a movie with him.
> What do you think? (Ritter, 1991, p. 47)

In initial trials with this scenario, we ended the text with "Should Zachary ask Emily out?" instead of "What do you think?," but biases from subjects' extraneous knowledge indicated that he should ask her out if there were *any* reasonable chance (even significantly less than 50%) that she would agree to it. Thus, the result of comparing ECHO's modeling of this scenario with the believability ratings subjects offered for the text's embedded propositions, and in combination with subjects' verbal protocols, indicated the following: Subjects were clearly bringing extraneous background knowledge and (perhaps past dating) experiences to the situation, reasoning akin to jurors concluding that the "defendant" is "guilty" (cf. Emily saying "no" to a date) only if there were no "reasonable doubt." Schank and Ranney (1991) found similar results, with subjects bringing considerable (and often social) background knowledge to bear, sometimes resulting in divergent interpretations of what we incorrectly assumed would be fairly straightforward linguistic entities such as "think" and "believable."

Such text-based assessments of ECHO were largely successful, modeling even dynamically changing belief evaluations while yielding model-fit correlations, between ECHO's activation predictions and subjects' observed belief evaluations, of up to 0.8 (Schank & Ranney, 1991). This thread of research also allowed for the assessment of TEC's principles (also see Ranney, Schank, Mosmann, & Montoya, 1993; Read & Marcus-Newhall, 1993). Even so, subjects were clearly considering extratextual background knowledge in their deliberations, which was (again) often social in nature. Consider another, larger (full-page), scenario, in which subjects were asked to reason about whether it was safe to send children to a preschool in which another child was tested positive for HIV (Ritter, 1991). Some of these subjects mentioned that preschool children that they knew often engaged in non-casual behaviors (e.g., biting), which dramatically changed their representations of the situation. One said (pp. 22–23):

> I had some strong feelings on this one. Kids bite each other, in preschool. Often. A lot. It's not casual. Both my kids were bit [sic] in their preschool education. Both my kids—they're good kids, well adjusted—bit other kids. Most do, at some point, bite another kid.

Similarly, many subjects dwelled on how the HIV-infected child or his or her parents would feel about what could essentially turn into a discriminating quarantine, adding concerns such as, "I'm very worried about our society isolating HIV-infected people. I'm very concerned about that" (p. 23).

In cases such as these, subjects showed considerably lower correlations between ECHO's activations and their believability ratings. In essence, the set of textual propositions and the text itself was not fully representative of the information that the subjects were considering (due to their extraneous background knowledge), so the fits of the models suffered.

Responses such as these "biting" and "discrimination" ones inspired us to develop a novel method ("bifurcation/bootstrapping"; Schank & Ranney, 1992) to elicit and account for such background knowledge through an on-line interview/protocol session. We concurrently assessed the intercoder reliability of the representations encoders generated as input to ECHO by having multiple encoders "translate" subjects' verbal protocols into (evidential or hypothetical) propositions and (explanatory or inhibitory) relations among the propositions. In this case, we investigated ECHO's ability to model individual subjects' beliefs about physical motion. Our protocol modeling results indicated both reasonably good data fitting and intercoder reliability. Belief revision over time was also well modeled, as were attentional and memorial constraints (e.g., Hoadley et al., 1994; Ranney et al., 1993).

Most recently, our desires to automate the explication of individuals' knowledge bases and belief assessments, and to aid students in articulating and revising their theories, led us to develop our "reasoner's workbench," as described in the next section (Schank, 1995; Schank & Ranney, 1993). This system, Convince Me, is meant to both study and foster aspects of reasoning that are commonly attributed to scientists, for instance: (a) a more articulated and conscious awareness of hypotheses, evidence, and inference, (b) a more systematic way to think about arguments, and (c) more explicit links among beliefs. However, because we claim that these reasoning aspects are hardly unique to scientists, we address them with the aid of some social situations in the following section.

PROMOTING (WHILE OBSERVING) EXPLANATORY COHERENCE

The *Convince Me* System and Some Social Applications

Convince Me is a domain-independent computational "reasoner's work-bench" program that supports argument development and revision, and provides ECHO-based feedback on the coherence of subjects' articulated beliefs. (The system has been employed in diverse realms, e.g., biology, physics, geography, linguistics, etc.; Ranney et al., 1993; Schank, 1995; Schank & Ranney, 1991, 1992; Schank, Ranney, & Hoadley, 1995.) The associated curriculum discusses distinctions between hypotheses and evidence, strate-gies for generating and evaluating arguments and counterarguments, and reasoning biases and how to reduce them. Using Convince Me, individuals can (a) articulate their beliefs regarding a controversy, (b) categorize each notion as being either evidential or hypothetical, (c) connect their beliefs explanatorily and/or inhibitorily, (d) provide ratings to indicate the believ-ability of each statement, and (e) run the ECHO simulation to obtain various forms of feedback. Convince Me also incorporates other important features, such as a tool for diagramming an argument's structure, as well as support for modifying one's arguments, belief ratings, and even the parameters that govern ECHO's "reasoning engine."

Figure 8.4 shows a subject's argument on the aforementioned abortion controversy (one of many in the curriculum) in Convince Me. After entering an argument, specifying believability ratings, and running an ECHO simula-tion, the networked argument's graphed nodes reflect ECHO's activations in a "thermometerlike" fashion (see Fig. 8.4, upper right). The higher the mercury, the more ECHO accepts the statement; the lower the mercury, the more ECHO rejects the statement. (Likert-scaled numerical equivalents are also provided; see the upper left of Fig. 8.4.) In addition, Convince Me can report a "model's fit" correlation between one's believability ratings and ECHO's scaled activation values, indicate how related the two sets of ratings are (e.g., "mildly opposed," "moderately related," "highly related"), and highlight the (three) pairs of values that differ the most (see the middle box in Fig. 8.4).

Convince Me has been used by subjects to reason about various other social situations, such as interpretations of human behavior (e.g., whether yawning indicates a subconscious display of aggression or just a lack of oxygen), and whether the use of marijuana should be legalized. The follow-

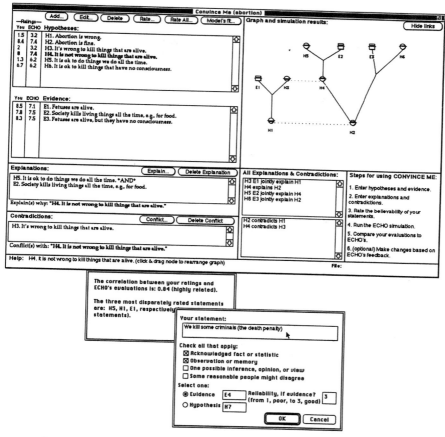

FIG. 8.4. A subject adds a belief related to the abortion controversy ["We kill some criminals (the death penalty)"] and classifies it as reliable evidence (bottom) in response to Convince Me's feedback (middle). Proposition H4, a central node, is highlighted in the main screen area.

ing are two sample texts on these topics, presented to subjects who were using the system (Diehl, 1995; Diehl, Ranney, & Schank, 1995):

(a) Kathryn thinks that marijuana should be legalized because if it were, then it could be regulated, and drug crimes would decrease. Phyllis thinks that marijuana should not be legalized because then it would be used more and lead to further degradation of our society.

(b) Wanda and Dave are walking through Pinetown one night, and both notice that an approaching teenager yawns when passing them.
  Dave thinks that the teenager's yawn was a subconscious aggressive display. He learned in biology that humans are genetically close to apes, and

ape studies suggest that apes engage in "threat yawns." In a group, dominant male apes yawn more—an action that shows off their long canine teeth—while subordinate apes more often cover their yawning mouths with their paws. He says that since Pinetown is a dangerous area, this would explain why the teenager yawned when passing them.

Wanda disagrees with Dave. She notes that people, as well as non-primates such as dogs, yawn when they are alone as well as in groups. She has read that yawning provides more oxygen to the brain and that the more oxygen, the more glucose we can burn for energy. She thinks that since it is late, the teenager is probably tired and yawned to get more oxygen to stay alert. She claims that the hypothesis that yawning is to increase oxygen also explains why it *seems* contagious—people in the same room are all just breathing the same stuffy air, and all need more oxygen.

As we expected from our prior research, subjects generated various alternative hypotheses and extraneous evidence (i.e., that went beyond the given text) regarding these situations. In the marijuana scenario, for example, one subject came up with (and modeled) additional beliefs such as "Marijuana should be legalized for the medical field and not for recreational use," "Patients would benefit from marijuana treatment," and "The economy would benefit from the regulation of marijuana."

Not surprisingly, subjects generated slightly fewer additional beliefs when reasoning about the more elaborated (and perhaps less value-laden) "yawning" scenario. These were usually constrained to why the teenager might be tired (e.g., "The teenager just finished a paper for class"), other reasons for yawning (e.g., boredom, or to alleviate congestion), and potential biases of the viewers ("Wanda is a biologist," "Dave is an anthropologist"). On average, subjects' representations for this argument included four hypotheses, eight pieces of evidence, 18 explanations (four of them joint explanations), and seven contradictions—indicating that the arguments they generated were quite complex. Average belief-activation correlations for subjects using Convince Me to complete this exercise were fairly high at .70, and correlations ranged from .73 to .88 for the other exercises completed using the system (Schank, 1995). These results are in concert with our earlier findings that ECHO can effectively predict subjects' believability ratings for both small- and medium-sized text-based arguments (e.g., Ritter, 1991; Schank & Ranney, 1991), as well as the generally larger subject-generated arguments gathered via our bifurcation/bootstrapping verbal protocol method (Ranney & Schank, 1995; Schank & Ranney, 1992). Completing exercises with the system using scenarios such as this one also appears to improve subjects' abilities to discriminate between the notions of evidence and hypothesis, as discussed more later (and in Ranney, Schank, Hoadley, & Neff, 1996).

Abortion: An Elaborated Example Employing the *Convince Me* Curriculum and System

We recently assessed (e.g., Schank, 1995) Convince Me's effectiveness as a system for fostering reasoning skills by contrasting subjects' performance under two conditions with otherwise identical written tests, instructions, and curricula: instruction involving (a) Convince Me versus (b) no software—a completely on-paper curriculum (the "Written Group"). The abortion example (shown earlier) was one of the four textual stimuli used. Others included competing theories regarding yawning (described earlier), medical diagnosis, and various predictions about pendular release trajectories (from Schank & Ranney, 1992). Results indicate that Convince Me users' beliefs were significantly more in accord with the structures of their arguments (even prior to feedback from the ECHO model), as evidenced by higher belief-activation correlations, compared to the Written Group (e.g., .81 vs. .34 for the abortion text).[9] Further, Convince Me users changed their argument structures twice as often as their ratings, whereas this effect was *reversed* for the Written Group, who changed their ratings twice as often as their arguments. Thus, Convince Me users apparently do not just try to "mimic" ECHO by changing their ratings; on the contrary, compared to students developing arguments on paper, students using the system seem more likely to reflect on and change the fundamental structure of their arguments. Convince Me subjects also tended to employ more explanations and contradictions in their arguments. These results generally explain why Convince Me users' belief-activations correlations were higher—namely, that more explicated and revised arguments should better reflect underlying beliefs.

In addition to assessing the prescriptive utility of Convince Me, we are interested in new descriptive questions that bear upon social psychology, such as, "How do individuals' values affect the coherence of their argument?" For instance, are our abortion findings at all modulated by the side one takes in an argument (e.g., prolife vs. prochoice)? Also, when subjects generate their own propositions, are they proficient at categorizing them as hypothesis or evidence—or are their categorizations questionable? To address such questions, a more detailed analysis of the abortion argument was conducted, because it was the last of four final exercises subjects completed (i.e., they were "warmed up" with the system), and the textual stimulus provided was minimal (two sentences, with about four or fewer propositions; see the earlier text above) so that the majority of the argument came from the subject rather than the text.

---

[9]This was also the case across all four textual stimuli.

Analyses of the abortion data revealed that prolife and prochoice leanings, as evidenced by their central believability ratings, were not correlated with (Convince Me or Written) group membership, nor were belief-activation correlations related to the side taken (e.g., prolife, prochoice, or neutral) in the argument. (Of 20 subjects, 10 were prochoice, 5 prolife, and 5 neutral.) Overall, subjects generated numerically (but nonsignificantly) more propositions for their side of the argument (the ratio of "my side" vs. "other side" propositions was 9:8; see, e.g., Perkins, 1995, on sides), and there were no significant differences between groups on this measure.

The questionability of subjects' categorizations also did not differ significantly between groups. In a blind categorization,[10] one of us questioned (in essence) the categorization of about 16% of the subjects' statements—about 8% of their hypothetical classifications, and about 23% of their evidential ones. However, the disagreements were not distributed evenly across subjects—20% (3 prochoice, 1 prolife) accounted for over half of the questionable categorizations, and 35% (4 prochoice, 2 prolife, 1 neutral) appeared to have no questionable categorizations at all. The most common difficulty occurred when a subject categorized an assertion as a piece of evidence when the researcher viewed it as a hypothesis. For instance, one subject classified the statements "Population is too high" and "Unwanted children only cause more problems" as evidence when both seem clearly arguable (partly because they include vague quantifiers). Another subject listed as evidence "It is a personal not societal issue" and "Everyone has a God-given right to live," which, again, are some of the more controversial (and arguable) assumptions at the center of the debate![11]

In sum, we did not find evidence to suggest that individuals' values (as shown by prolife or prochoice stances) affect the coherence of their argument. On the contrary, our subjects (somewhat surprisingly) did not offer significantly more statements for their own side of the argument, nor did the coherence between believability ratings and argument structures seem related to the side they chose. Some subjects seemed to take liberties in what they called (and failed to call) evidence, but these liberties did not appear to correlate with their (prolife or prochoice) viewpoint. One could credit our curriculum with reducing the biasing influence of such values in the way it fosters the articulation, interrelation, and revision of arguments; either way, the Convince Me software enhances the correlation between subjects' belief evaluations and the structures of their arguments.

---

[10]Additional subject-generated data (e.g., from responses to the check-boxes shown toward the bottom of Fig. 8.4) support the researcher's blind categorizations (see Schank, 1995).

[11]Less common were questionable categorizations of hypotheses that seemed more like evidence, such as "Fetuses are alive" (they *are* made of living tissue—the issue is whether they are alive as people in some independent sense that warrants rights) and "We as a society kill living things" (we clearly kill plants and/or animals for food, we kill some criminals, etc.).

Of course, other considerations should be entertained. For example, analyses of debates on value-laden issues other than abortion (e.g., situations that bring out other values, or have fewer "stock arguments," etc.) may yield different results. The abortion debate is often based on (possibly deeper) politico–religious values and/or the differential valuing of societal versus individual rights, and arguments for both sides are often familiar to subjects. Hence, it may be easier for them to simply reproduce common statements supporting each side of this debate. Similarly, the degrees of dogmatism associated with various values may play a role in the assessments of arguments. It may be that values that are based strongly on doctrine (as could be suggested by extreme ratings), when "unwrapped" into an argument, could lead to less coherence—in the form of beliefs that are either not well explicated, socially difficult to explicate, or are asserted but not well-supported by the offered data. As an example, suppose that part of a subject's support for the prolife stance involves an (even warranted) appeal to authority, such as "my father is prolife." In turn, support for this proposition might include "my father is usually right" and/or "my father was right about my no-good ex." Subjects might feel inhibited to type in such propositions, though, and their arguments would thus be less explicated and less supported. However, note that we did not find much evidence for such dogmatism; only 14% of our subjects' ratings were at the extremes of the scale (i.e., "completely believe" or "completely reject") for the "Abortion is wrong" and "Abortion is okay" statements and all of these extreme ratings came from only 20% of the subjects.[12]

A Modest Proposition

Several recent applications of Convince Me concern our desire to promote both globally coherent reasoning (cf. Ranney, in press) and more environmentally conscious reasoning, a topic that we discuss a bit more toward the end of the chapter. As a societally relevant foreshadowing example, though, consider the proposition, "We should never cause the extinction of another species." Far from an ivory tower controversy, the debate around this hypothesis (or value) can easily reach from our Pacific Northwest, where the survival of the spotted owl is pitted against various economic (e.g., job security) interests, to Washington, DC, where logging industry lobbyists prowl Congress and the administration, to nasty pathogens located in the bowels of the Center for Disease Control in Atlanta.

---

[12]Many other researchers have found that subjects sometimes avoid extreme rating values; this is the well-known "restricted range of variables" problem (e.g., Jensen, 1980). For instance, data collected in conjunction with Florian Kaiser and others indicate that our undergraduate participants from the University of California, Berkeley, behave more homogeneously, ecologically speaking, than a more heterogeneous sample of Swiss auto drivers (cf. Kaiser, Ranney, Hartig, & Bowler, 1997).

One of us has particularly struggled with this controversy, and employed Convince Me to articulate his reasoning. The argument (which is currently too large to usefully portray here in its totality) reflects his confusion: Naturally, all other things being equal, it is better to have more species than fewer species. However, some species are quite deadly to humans. Should they not be destroyed? Certainly, our ancient ancestors would probably not be terribly sad to hear that the last saber-tooth tiger passed on; will we be upset when the last smallpox microbe bites the dust—or when perhaps HIV and the "killer bees" are effectively extinct? The following (paraphrased) dialogue between one of us (M) and his 7-year-old daughter (R) highlights other questions regarding how much human comfort (as in the Pacific Northwest), or even individual lives, mean, in contrast with other species' survival. It was prompted by a James Taylor song ("Mona," 1985), in which the narrator practiced what we might call early euthanasia on his pig because she "got too big to keep and too damn old to eat."

R: Would you shoot me with a 12-gauge if we couldn't both live?
M: No, I'd probably kill myself first to let you have more food; you eat less, and I've already lived about half my life, so it wouldn't be fair for me to live instead of you.
R: Would you kill a pig instead of yourself?
M: Probably, but it depends upon how many pigs remain on Earth. And pigs are awfully smart and useful, compared to many animals.
R: Would you kill me instead of the last pig on Earth if you had to choose?
M: I think I hear your mom coming home! [This statement is highly paraphrased.]

Even intriguing exchanges such as these, which involve the contrast between personal, societal, and global interests, may be analyzed with the assistance of Convince Me. It is our hope that the system will promote both more extensive and more principled reasoning about social issues that we should all be considering. Again, this point is elaborated toward the end of this chapter. For now, we leave this "societal" reading of "social" and return to our criticism of the first reading, in which the social is contrasted with the scientific.

EQUATING THE SOCIAL AND THE SCIENTIFIC: NOT JUST THEORETICAL IMPERIALISM

From the earlier discussion on the proposed unity of reasoning found in both the social and the scientific realms, we might be seen as domain chauvinists. After all, "is not leather the only thing to the cobbler?" A critical reader might suggest that we want to unify the social and the scientific—in terms of hypotheses and evidence and with respect to excitatory and inhibitory relations—because we want our perspective to seem preeminent. As the kids say, "Well, duh!" Of course, we would want that to happen; who wouldn't? Indeed, to a considerable degree, this criticism-and-reply proves our point, as follows: We (as scientists) can of course think of our goal as "Unify apparently disparate phenomena." It follows from our prior, similar, argument regarding values, that having this goal is essentially the equivalent of entertaining the hypothesis, "Unifying disparate phenomena has desirable effects." Naturally, we truly believe that the unification we propose both works and is correct. Still, those who suspect that we are more Machiavellian might suggest that the aforementioned goal stands in for a more directly self-serving goal, such as "Gain more fame" or "Acquire more wealth." But each of these can similarly be converted into hypotheses by a small set of simple transformations (e.g., production rules; Newell & Simon, 1972), such as: "If goal x, then hypothesis 'it is best to x,' " and perhaps vice versa (cf. Putnam, 1981).

Once goals are seen essentially as hypotheses, configurations of other hypotheses and evidence can link with them in explanatory and contradictory/competitive ways, and what initially may have seemed like a value-laden decision is now seen as ("merely") a scientific knowledge base, involving observations and data, predictions and presumed consequences, theories and models (whatever those are)—or even facts.[13] Predictions that have the highest activations may be thought of as reflecting the actions that represent the best decisions currently being considered by the system.

Note the parenthetical "whatever those are" above. This was not meant facetiously. In fact, very few of the terms that we have employed to discuss socio–scientific (or "value–theoretic") reasoning and decision making are even close to being precise ones. We empirically demonstrated, for instance (Ranney et al., 1996; Schank, 1995), that even the distinction between hypothesis and evidence is a fuzzy one. For both novices and experts in scientific reasoning, relatively low interrater reliabilities are obtained when subjects are asked to rate propositions with respect to their hypothesis likeness or evidence likeness. More recent data (Diehl, Castro, & Ranney, 1997) indicate that, although subject-generated exemplars of evidence and hypotheses have certain prototypical linguistic characteristics, what "fact" means—with respect to these other two constructs—is highly variable. For

---

[13]We are, to some degree, implicitly taking the philosophical stance of ethical naturalism here—for instance, that "is" statements can be brought to bear on "ought" statements in one's argument. We also understand that this is part of a rich and ongoing discussion in philosophy and linguistics regarding the purported (and increasingly unfashionable) fact–value dichotomy (e.g., Lakoff, 1987; Millgram, 1995; Putnam, 1981).

instance, is a fact a true piece of evidence, a highly supported hypothesis, or something else? We have obtained a multiplicity of such responses.[14]

Lest we dwell only on the fuzziness of the terms involved in scientific reasoning, we should point out that more socially oriented terms are probably no more clear. Earlier, we proposed that we can pretty much treat hypotheses, goals, values, and candidate actions as a single kind. In other words, there is little agreement about what distinguishes among these terms, and the "noise" swamps the quite variable "signals" of those who believe that they can truly discriminate among such terms (e.g., the variety found in Pervin, 1989; see especially pp. 473–474; also see Gollwitzer & Bargh, 1996). For instance, we propose that a single propositional node in an ECHOlike connectionist network (e.g., "We should reduce the population") might be seen as a goal to some theorists, a hypothesis to others, a value to a third group, and a candidate action to still others. Some theorists might base their categorization on contextual features or even some processing subtleties (e.g., regarding the proposition's embeddedness/connectivity or "priority bias"; cf. Millgram & Thagard, 1996), but there clearly exists a nonuniformity among these views.

As an example of such diverse views, consider ECHO's sibling program, DECO, a similar constraint-satisfying model that is applied to multiaction planning (e.g., Millgram & Thagard, 1996). The theory underlying DECO makes a distinction between goals and candidate actions that seems highly fuzzy (an even fuzzier one than that between hypotheses and evidence, we believe) even though the distinction entails strong computational consequences in that goals gain considerable priority. For instance, in our modeling with ECHO, we have felt rather comfortable representing (albeit somewhat implicitly) goals and actions generally as hypotheses[15] [e.g., "I hypothesize that I should (take the action to) go to the library," or "I hypothesize that I should (have the goal to) meet Florence"; cf. Millgram & Thagard, 1996]. It has also seemed to us that ECHO, as DECO is intended to do, models decision making of sorts (e.g., whether one should decide that a defendant is guilty or innocent, or whether one should decide that some symptoms represent one disease rather than another; Ranney et al., 1993; Schank & Ranney, 1991; Thagard, 1989, 1992). Indeed, given that DECO and

---

[14]Although almost all of our subjects saw fact and evidence as different constructs, they often disagreed about whether one was a type of the other, or if so, which was the superordinate in the categorical hierarchy.

[15]In essence, we do not see the need for a processing priority for goals. Instead, we would view high-priority goals as hypotheses that are very well supported by a complex of reliable evidence and very strong hypotheses. The goal/value, "It is best to stay alive" might be one such hypothesis (e.g., supported by the fear of death evidenced in our culture, the conservatism of avoiding change, the assumption that one will ultimately get to experience death anyway, etc.); even so, it might become rejected (e.g., in order to save the lives of loved ones).

ECHO are so similar (e.g., near isomorphic in their principles, in terms of processing, semantics, etc.), it is not yet clear to us that a separate theory-and-model will, ultimately, be needed. (We have similar concerns regarding IMP, Kunda & Thagard's 1996 model of impression formation.)

Perhaps an even more social term, "values," provides still less termino-logical comfort (e.g., vs. "facts;" Millgram, 1995; Putnam, 1981). What is a "value," anyway? We propose that a value may be seen as a hypothesis that is both so supported by strong propositions (e.g., highly activated evidence and fellow hypotheses) and so distal from all but the weakest competitors, that it seems virtually indubitable, almost like a special evidence unit (Thagard, 1989). Note that, as with goals, we have once again described a fairly socially oriented construct with our "scientific/theoretical fixings." Some will undoubtedly chafe at this, perhaps suggesting that value-laden issues cannot be the subject of scientificlike debate. However, it is our experience, such as with the abortion-debate analysis above (among others), that what appear to be value-laden issues can be captured to a remarkable degree in terms of evidence, hypotheses, explanations, and inhibitory relations. In other words, we remain to be convinced that values, like goals, are not already fundamentally captured by explanatory coherence theory.

In contrast to our view of values as propositional (also see Millgram & Thagard's "intrinsically valuable goals"), some researchers appear to see a value as subpropositional, that is, more like an abstract word (cf. Putnam, 1981) or a phrase rather than as a statement, linguistically. McCarty and Shrum's (1994) work provides an example. Although they acknowledged that the distinction between value orientations and personal values is slippery, they represented value orientations by longish phrases such as "Being a cooperative participant in group activities," and represented (from Kahle, 1983) personal values (and even evidencelike "behaviors") with shorter, one-to-four-word phrases such as "Security" or "Fun and enjoyment." In this paradigm, full propositions (e.g., sentencelike statements) take the form of attitudes, opinions, ideas, goals, and/or beliefs (although distinctions among these also seem slippery to us; cf. Gollwitzer & Bargh, 1996; Pervin, 1989; Scott & Willits, 1994).[16] Because these are often rated on Likert scales of importance, agreement, or behavioral frequency, we believe that subjects might implicitly propositionalize them during these ratings. For instance,

---

[16]For instance, McCarty and Shrum (1994) mixed in such terms when discussing the "value factor" of collectivism, which one might alternatively (we claim) think of as the value orientation "collectives over individuals" or the hypothesis "we are better off promoting the collective rather than individuals." They occasionally suggested that both values and value orientations entail, imply, involve, or perhaps may even *be* goals (see previous discussion) and/or beliefs (e.g., "By definition, values are enduring beliefs and fairly resistant to change"; p. 61). Scott and Willits similarly added to this "word soup" as "ideas," "opinions," and "attitudes" are tossed in. (We thank Florian Kaiser for various discussions about these terms.)

asking subjects to rate, from their perspectives, the importance of "warm relationships with others" is equivalent, in our view, to asking for a rating of the believability of the hypothesis, "Warm relationships with others are very important." Again, in our view, we would expect people to also implicitly consider the alternative, "Warm relationships with others are rather *un*important"—as well as a host of evidence (e.g., some "is" statements) and other hypotheses (e.g., some "ought" statements) that help to support or weaken these propositions.

FUTURE WORK AND FUTURE WORLDS

The Biggest (Social) Problem: Another Instance of Satisfying Constraints

Releases of the Convince Me software are donated to a biology education package (e.g., Schank et al., 1995). But because the system is domain independent, it should be just as applicable to a host of other fields. In thinking of other potential applications, we have tried to focus on the societal good that this reasoner's workbench system might achieve, given our belief that the system is relevant to clarifying how people reason about social problems. More generally, if the system were truly useful, what would be the most important issue that one could address with it? We have actually put this type of question to a number of colleagues and students. The reader is invited to think of your own answer to this question, which we usually word as: What is the biggest problem/challenge facing humankind (or the Earth) during the next 50–100 years?

While you think about the question, you might introspect about your reasoning. Do you leap to a response, perhaps having had thoughts about this before? If so, perhaps you find yourself recalling the response's rationale, generating the argument's structure as you flesh out your memory. However, if you are like most people, you probably have not considered this specific question, and you generate a constraint-based argument from (a) various "big problems" that you have previously noted, (b) new alternative problems that you have just generated, (c) data and hypotheses that support these problems (which are themselves hypotheses) as candidates for "the biggest" problem, and (d) inhibitory relations among various reasons (and, of course, among the problems themselves—because not all can be "the" biggest). In essence, to answer this question, one carries out constraint-based reasoning (which probably involves some social components); this is precisely what Convince Me is designed to facilitate and explicate as it helps people epistemically categorize their propositions and clarify the relations among them. Thus, even the exercise of finding noteworthy problems, an unusually high-level activity, lends itself to analyses involving evidence, hypotheses, and (positive and negative) constraints. Indeed, a constraint-based system like Convince Me might not only help one uncover some of the relationships among various different kinds of problems (described later), it could also be used to explore what the possible trade-offs and synergies would be in addressing different problems.

To date, we have been intrigued by the variety of answers to the "biggest problem" question, although we note that the precise wording (and perhaps the timing and place) of the query may be critical. For instance, polls just prior to our questioning showed that the number one issue for Americans was crime (e.g., over the economy), yet almost none of our subjects answered our question with such responses.[17] Similarly, virtually none of our respondents listed "nuclear war," which would have been most topical less than 10 years ago (and may soon return to prominence). A sample of conference delegates at a recent international symposium in India (comprised of both Indian and other cognitive scientists) yielded proportions that were similar to those found among academic colleagues in the United States: A majority of the respondents chose a category of rather directly resource-related problems, which humankind might (at some point) be able to "fix." Overpopulation appeared to be the modal response (both in the United States and among the international delegates), which the authors would have predicted.[18] But others in this category saw overpopulation as merely a symptom of a more fundamental problem, namely that our resources are poorly distributed, or are either being depleted, have been depleted, or are being used to damage our environment during such depletion.[19] (Thus overpopulation is inhibited for these respondents by alternative, constraint-driven, complexes of data and theory.)

The second category of responses take a more mentality-related approach—in essence, inhibiting responses from the first category. For such respondents (although some subjects offered responses from both categories), they saw the tendency toward intolerance, greed, out-group exclusion, nationalism, not enough love and sharing, and so forth, as the major culprit or culprits. These problems seem less likely to have obvious solutions,

---

[17]Indeed, a poll of 807 registered voters in our state, taken during late January of 1996, showed "immigration" as rivaling "economy/jobs" as the "single most important issue facing California" ("Examiner Poll," 1996). It is unlikely that many other (e.g., nonborder or recession-free) states would have yielded this pattern.

[18]Even industry leaders like Steven Jobs see this as the biggest problem facing humanity (Wolf, 1996).

[19]In concert with such attitudes, Scott and Willits (1994) wrote about part of their 3,500-respondent 1990 Pennsylvania survey: "Only 45% felt that we are approaching the limit of the number of people the earth can support" (p. 245). (Note that various experts report that, although the planet's human population may never double beyond the current number, we will still have too many people for the resources available.)

although some might argue that following the Golden Rule is in some ways easier than getting people to reduce the number of babies they generate.

Depending on the particular demographics of the sample of people queried, the proportions of responses in the two main categories may differ widely.[20] An undergraduate cognitive science class yielded equivalent proportions of about .40 apiece, whereas an arguably more heterogeneous E-mail query (of primarily professionals, many with postgraduate degrees) yielded a majority of the mentality-related responses (e.g., highlighting greed).

One might see these categories of responses as rather mutually exclusive. After all, can there be more than one biggest problem? Still, if a decision maker (perhaps one in government) is having difficulty determining priority among such candidate problems, Convince Me might be able to help generate a kind of triage. For instance, one analyst might believe that overpopulation is a very strong candidate for biggest problem, say, in contrast to either resource management (a competitor from the first category) or "becoming better people" (from the second category). A rationale for this might include the reasoning that neither the best of intentions nor the best of technology and conservation will allow an unlimited number of humans to survive (e.g., given that they would obviously ultimately have only substarvational nutrition/energy resources). On the other hand, an analyst with a resource-management view might point out that, even if only two human beings populated the entire Earth, they still might destroy or eliminate life as we know it—for instance, if each had a million nuclear warheads (targeted around the globe) that were about to fire; in this case, overpopulation pales in comparison to resource management. This same scenario could also allow a third analyst to show that too much malice (e.g., expressed through warfare) can outweigh population and resource usage as problems, especially because one need not eliminate all resources with a multitude of nuclear weapons in order to cause human extinction. Of course, each of the arguments for these three competing "biggest problem" hypotheses could be increasingly more articulated in Convince Me. Determining the biggest problem is obviously a very complex endeavor, and involves difficult trade-offs, such as between the quality and quantity of life, between equity and sustainability in resource usage, and among various other constructs. Such trade-offs are also well suited to constraint-satisfaction analyses, for example, those embodied in Convince Me and its ECHO model.

---

[20]Beyond these two categories, responses are generally too ambiguous, vague, or all inclusive to fit well into either the resource- or mentality-related categories. These include uncertainty, lack of education (e.g., due to a lack of resources, or the undervaluing of education), the vague blaming of groups ("governments," "people," etc.), and even that there is no consensus about what the biggest problem is, which leads to inaction.

Further Avenues of Practical Application

So, are the problems named as biggest by our respondents best considered as social or scientific ones? Again, the distinction seems somewhat irrelevant. Birth control is both a scientific and a social problem, as is resource management, pollution, global warming, and the destruction of rainforests. Similarly, from the mentality-related category, sharing what we have, understanding others, fostering equity—these are also areas in which both the scientific (or science-informed policy) and the social meet.

What, then, must we do? Specifically, what can cognitive scientists and social psychologists interested in constraint-based reasoning do to best increase the social good? Is the writing of archival articles enough? We think not, yet are conflicted as to how to proceed (cf. Kempton, Darley, & Stern, 1992, regarding environmental issues).

One highly attractive, socially responsible, approach would be to widely publicize what the biggest problems are and help address them. However, because few of us actually study these content domains, several drawbacks pop up. For instance, it might make our "day-job research" seem less significant, and it would take a long time to become an expert about these problems. Further, who would listen—and how might one best educate the populace and policymakers? Not only does it take considerable hubris to assume that one can "change things," it takes quite a bit of hubris to even assume that one's analyses and advocacies are correct on such grandiose issues!

For both analysis and policy, we are unfortunately largely reasoning under uncertainty (Tversky & Kahneman, 1974, etc.) in a world that does not provide its own natural control groups. Let us assume, for the sake of argument, that overpopulation is indeed the biggest problem. It may be that doing nothing would actually be best, ultimately, for the human race. Perhaps allowing a population-biologist's nightmare of overshoot-and-catastrophe to occur among humans will actually result in a much better (or even more numerous) subsequent society. On the other hand, slowing population growth now might mean we can successfully "build down" the population to manageable levels before our collective health and welfare diminishes. Constraint-based systems can help with such decision making, although they certainly cannot fully eliminate the uncertainty involved.

As advocates for whichever of these two future-world models one chooses, one must still decide on the tactics to comprise a strategy for addressing the problem. One might try a direct approach, such as that of advertising (e.g., birth control, morality, recycling), or one might try a (seemingly) less direct approach, such as employing governmental rewards and punishments for desired and undesired behaviors. Still, with problems of such complexity and such temporal dynamics, assessments seem more like prognoses and solutions seem more like treatments. Constraint-based systems such as Convince Me can offer tactical help as well, but it remains to be seen whether they can adequately "scale up" to the complexity required by these conundrums (even at some reasonably intermediate level of abstraction).

SUMMARY AND CONCLUSIONS

The theory of explanatory coherence, first employed to model scientific reasoning, has been extended to the realm of social (and societal) reasoning. We suggest that no truly new features are required for this extension, indicating that scientific and social reasoning processes are significantly different primarily in domain, but not in kind. Hypotheses (or theories) and evidence (or facts) are employed in both domains, and even seemingly sociospecific notions such as values, goals, and candidate actions can be plausibly captured with evidence and hypotheses and some excitatory and inhibitory relations expressed among them. Further muddling the scientific/social distinction, scientific reasoning itself often involves social aspects.

We presented model-driven analyses and studies involving socially oriented reasoning (e.g., regarding the abortion debate, HIV quarantines, and marijuana legalization) to illustrate these points. In addition, a software environment, Convince Me, is offered as a reasoner's workbench that helps individuals articulate their thinking about such controversies. The system uses the connectionist model's output as feedback regarding the reasoner's articulation and coherence, suggesting ways in which constraint-satisfaction models may enhance the social good.

As reflected in our subjects' considerable concerns regarding social and scientific (or even technological) "biggest problems," systems that better describe, predict, and foster coherent reasoning will be in increasingly greater demand as the attendant complexities increase. Highlighting such concerns is a poem embedded in a "Calvin and Hobbes" cartoon (Watterson, 1992) in which an alien spacecraft that is plundering our planet's resources provides a metaphor for our considerations regarding the stewardship of the Earth. As the humans complain of the drastically depleted air and water, the alien ship broadcasts: "We're sorry to learn that you soon will be dead, But though you may find this slightly macabre, We prefer your extinction to the loss of our job."

It is likely that our future as a species will hold more (and presumably more important) socioscientific choices than the number of choices we have faced heretofore. Constraint-based models, especially embedded within knowledge-articulation systems such as Convince Me, offer much hope that we can make *better* choices. Therefore, continued research on this class of models seems vital—because the dilemmas represented by our many choices will certainly not be going away.

ACKNOWLEDGMENTS

We thank Christine Diehl, Sergio Castro, Stephen Read, Lynn Miller, Christopher Ritter, Florian Kaiser, Elijah Millgram, Paul Thagard, Todd Shimoda, Steve Adams, Bob Branstrom, Larry Hamel, Michelle Million, George Lakoff, Phil Vahey, Rachel Ranney, the Reasoning Group, and others for their help and comments. Naturally, their assistance does not imply that they endorse each of the ideas expressed herein. We are also grateful to the Spencer Foundation and the Committee on Research of the University of California for funding some of these studies.

REFERENCES

Bereiter, C. (1991). Implications of connectionism for thinking about rules. *Educational Researcher, 20,* 10–16.

Diehl, C. (1995, June). *Pragmatic and conceptual attributes of representational tools influence students' reasoning strategies.* Paper presented at the annual meeting of the American Psychological Society, New York.

Diehl, C., Castro, S., & Ranney, M. (1997, March). *Student models of hypothesis and evidence.* Paper presented at the annual meeting of the American Educational Research Association, Chicago.

Diehl, C., Ranney, M., & Schank, P. (1995, April). *Multiple representations for improving scientific thinking* (Report No. TP-024-671). Paper presented at the annual meeting of the American Educational Research Association, San Francisco. (ERIC Document Reproduction Service No. ED 392 842)

Einstein, A. (1950). *Out of my later years.* New York: Philosophical Library.

Examiner poll. (1996, February 4). *San Francisco Examiner,* p. A-12.

Fiske, S., & Taylor, S. (1984). *Social cognition.* New York: Random House.

Fletcher, G. J. O. (1993). The scientific credibility of commonsense psychology. In K. H. Craik, R. Hogan, & R. N. Wolfe (Eds.), *Fifty years of personality psychology* (pp. 251–268). New York: Plenum.

Gabrys, G. (1989). HEIDER: A simulation of attitude consistency and attitude change. In S. Ohlsson (Ed.), *Aspects of cognitive conflict and cognitive change* (Tech. Rep. No. KUL-89-04). Pittsburgh: University of Pittsburgh, Learning Research and Development Center.

Gigerenzer, G. (1991). From tools to theories: A heuristic of discovery in cognitive psychology. *Psychological Review, 98,* 254–267.

Gollwitzer, P. M., & Bargh, J. A. (Eds.). (1996). *The psychology of action: Linking cognition and motivation to behavior.* New York: Guilford.

Hoadley, C., Ranney, M., & Schank, P. (1994). WanderECHO: A connectionist simulation of limited coherence. In A. Ram & K. Eiselt (Eds.), *Proceedings of the Sixteenth Annual Conference of the Cognitive Science Society* (pp. 421–426). Hillsdale, NJ: Lawrence Erlbaum Associates.

Jensen, A. R. (1980). *Bias in mental testing.* New York: The Free Press.

Kahle, L. R. (Ed.). (1983). *Social values and social change: Adaptation to life in America.* New York: Praeger.

Kaiser, F. G., Ranney, M., Hartig, T., & Bowler, P. A. (1997). *Ecological behavior, environmental attitudes, and feelings of responsibility for the environment.* Manuscript in preparation, University of California, Berkeley.

Kempton, W., Darley, J. M., & Stern, P. C. (1992). Psychological research for the new energy problems: Strategies and opportunities. *American Psychologist, 47,* 1213–1223.

Kunda, Z., & Thagard, P. (1996). Forming impressions from stereotypes, traits, and behaviors: A parallel-constraint-satisfaction theory. *Psychological Review, 103,* 284–308.

Lakoff, G. (1987). *Women, fire, and dangerous things: What categories reveal about the mind.* Chicago: University of Chicago Press.

Lave, J. (1988). *Cognition in practice: Mind, mathematics, and culture in everyday life.* New York: Cambridge University Press.

McCarty, J. A., & Shrum, L. J. (1994). The recycling of solid wastes: Personal values, value orientations, and attitudes about recycling as antecedents of recycling behavior. *Journal of Business Research, 30,* 53–62.

Miller, L. C., & Read, S. J. (1991). On the coherence of mental models of persons and relationships: A knowledge structure approach. In F. Fincham & G. J. O. Fletcher (Eds.), *Cognition in close relationships* (pp. 69–99). Hillsdale, NJ: Lawrence Erlbaum Associates.

Millgram, E. (1995). Inhaltsreiche ethische Begriffe und die Unterscheidung zwischen Tatsachen und Werten [Thick ethical concepts and the fact-value distinction]. In C. Fehige & G. Meggle (Eds.), *Zum moralischen Denken* (pp. 354–388). Frankfurt: Suhrkamp.

Millgram, E., & Thagard, P. (1996). Deliberative coherence. *Synthese, 108,* 63–88.

Newell, A., & Simon, H. A. (1972). *Human problem solving.* Englewood Cliffs, NJ: Prentice-Hall.

Nisbett, R., & Ross, L. (1980). *Human inference: Strategies and shortcomings of social judgment.* Englewood Cliffs, NJ: Prentice-Hall.

Norman, D. A. (1988). *The psychology of everyday things.* New York: Basic Books.

Norman, D. A. (1993). *Things that make us smart: Defending human attributes in the age of the machine.* Reading, MA: Addison-Wesley.

Pennington, N., & Hastie, R. (1988). Explanation-based decision making: Effects of memory structure on judgment. *Journal of Experimental Psychology: Learning, Memory, and Cognition, 14,* 521–533.

Perkins, D. (1995). *Outsmarting IQ: The emerging science of learnable intelligence.* New York: Free Press.

Pervin, L. A. (Ed.). (1989). *Goal concepts in personality and social psychology.* Hillsdale, NJ: Lawrence Erlbaum Associates.

Putnam, H. (1981). *Reason, truth, and history.* Cambridge, England: Cambridge University Press.

Ranney, M. (in press). Explorations in explanatory coherence. In E. Bar-On, B. Eylon, & Z. Schertz (Eds.), *Designing intelligent learning environments: From cognitive analysis to computer implementation.* Norwood, NJ: Ablex.

Ranney, M. (1996). Individual-centered vs. model-centered approaches to consistency: A dimension for considering human rationality. *VIVEK, A Quarterly in Artificial Intelligence, 9*(2), 35–43.

Ranney, M., & Schank, P. (1995). Protocol modeling, bifurcation/bootstrapping, and *Convince Me*: Computer-based methods for studying beliefs and their revision. *Behavior Research Methods, Instruments and Computers, 27,* 239–243.

Ranney, M., Schank, P., Hoadley, C., & Neff, J. (1996). "I know one when I see one": How (much) do hypotheses differ from evidence? In R. Fidel, B. H. Kwasnik, C. Beghtol, & P. Smith (Eds.), *Advances in classification research* (Vol. 5) (ASIS Monograph Series; pp. 141–158). Medford, NJ: Learned Information.

Ranney, M., Schank, P., Mosmann, A., & Montoya, G. (1993). Dynamic explanatory coherence with competing beliefs: Locally coherent reasoning and a proposed treatment. In T.-W. Chan (Ed.), *Proceedings of the International Conference on Computers in Education: Applications of Intelligent Computer Technologies* (pp. 101–106). Artificial Intelligence in Education Society.

Ranney, M., Schank, P., & Ritter, C. (1992, January). *Studies of explanatory coherence using text, discourse, and verbal protocols.* Paper presented at the Third Annual Winter Text Conference, Jackson, WY.

Ranney, M., & Thagard, P. (1988). Explanatory coherence and belief revision in naive physics. In V. L. Patel & G. J. Groen (Eds.), *Proceedings of the Tenth Annual Conference of the Cognitive Science Society* (pp. 426–432). Hillsdale, NJ: Lawrence Erlbaum Associates.

Read, S. J., & Marcus-Newhall, A. (1993). Explanatory coherence in social explanations: A parallel distributed processing account. *Journal of Personality and Social Psychology, 65,* 429–447.

Read, S. J., & Miller, L. C. (1993). Rapist or "regular guy"?: Explanatory coherence in the construction of mental models of others. *Personality and Social Psychology Bulletin, 19,* 526–541.

Read, S. J., Vanman, E. J., & Miller, L. C. (in press). Connectionism, parallel constraint satisfaction processes, and Gestalt principles: (Re)Introducing cognitive dynamics to social psychology. *Review of Personality and Social Psychology.*

Ritter, C. (1991). *Thinking about ECHO.* Unpublished master's project, University of California, Berkeley.

Rumelhart, D., McClelland, J., & the PDP Research Group. (1986). *Parallel distributed processing: Explorations in the microstructure of cognition* (Vols. 1 & 2). Cambridge, MA: MIT Press.

Schank, P. (1995). *Computational tools for modeling and aiding reasoning: Assessing and applying the Theory of Explanatory Coherence.* Doctoral dissertation, University of California, Berkeley. (University Microfilms No. 9621352)

Schank, P., & Ranney, M. (1991). The psychological fidelity of ECHO: Modeling an experimental study of explanatory coherence. In J. K. Kruschke (Ed.), *Proceedings of the Thirteenth Annual Conference of the Cognitive Science Society* (pp. 892–897). Hillsdale, NJ: Lawrence Erlbaum Associates.

Schank, P., & Ranney, M. (1992). Assessing explanatory coherence: A new method for integrating verbal data with models of on-line belief revision. *Proceedings of the Fourteenth Annual Conference of the Cognitive Science Society* (pp. 599–604). Hillsdale, NJ: Lawrence Erlbaum Associates.

Schank, P., & Ranney, M. (1993). Can reasoning be taught? [Special issue]. *Educator, 7*(1), 16–21.

Schank, P., Ranney, M., & Hoadley, C. (1995). *Convince Me* [Computer program and manual]. In J. R. Jungck, N. Peterson, & J. N. Calley (Eds.), *The BioQUEST library.* College Park, MD: Academic Software Development Group, University of Maryland.

Shultz, T. R., & Lepper, M. R. (1992). A constraint satisfaction model of cognitive dissonance phenomena. In K. J. Hammond & D. Gentner (Eds.), *Proceedings of the Thirteenth Annual Conference of the Cognitive Science Society* (pp. 462–467). Hillsdale, NJ: Lawrence Erlbaum Associates.

Shultz, T. R., & Lepper, M. R. (1996). Cognitive dissonance reduction as constraint satisfaction. *Psychological Review, 103,* 219–240.

Scott, D., & Willits, F. K. (1994). Environmental attitudes and behavior: A Pennsylvania survey. *Environment and Behavior, 26,* 239–260.

Simon, H. (1955). A behavioral model of rational choice. *Quarterly Journal of Economics, 69,* 99–118.

Spellman, B. A., Ullman, J. B., & Holyoak, K. J. (1993). A coherence model of cognitive consistency: Dynamics of attitude change during the Persian Gulf War. *Journal of Social Issues, 49*(4), 147–165.

Taylor, J. (1985). Mona. On *That's why I'm here* [LP]. New York: Columbia Records.

Tetlock, P. E. (1985). Accountability: A social check on the fundamental attribution error. *Social Psychology Quarterly, 48,* 227–236.

Tetlock, P. E. (1992). The impact of accountability on judgment and choice: Toward a social contingency model. *Advances in Experimental Social Psychology, 25,* 331–376.

Thagard, P. (1989). Explanatory coherence. *Behavioral and Brain Sciences, 12,* 435–502.

Thagard, P. R. (1992). *Conceptual revolutions.* Princeton, NJ: Princeton University Press.

Thagard, P. R. (1996). *Mind: Introduction to cognitive science*. Cambridge, MA: MIT Press.

Thagard, P. (in press). Probabilistic networks and explanatory coherence. In P. O'Rorke & J. Josephson (Eds.), *Automated abduction: Inference to the best explanation*. Menlo Park, CA: AAAI Press.

Tversky, A., & Kahneman, D. (1974). Judgment under uncertainty: Heuristics and biases. *Science, 185*, 1124–1131.

Watterson, B. (1992). *Calvin and Hobbes* [cartoon]. Kansas City, MO: Andrews and McMeel, Universal Press Syndicate.

Wertheimer, M. (1982). *Productive thinking* (Phoenix ed.). Chicago: University of Chicago Press.

Wolf, G. (1996, February). [Interview with Steven Jobs]. Steve Jobs: The next insanely great thing. *Wired, 4*(2), pp. 102–107, 158, 160, 162–163.

SOCIAL INFLUENCE AND GROUP INTERACTION

TOWARD COMPUTATIONAL SOCIAL PSYCHOLOGY: CELLULAR AUTOMATA AND NEURAL NETWORK MODELS OF INTERPERSONAL DYNAMICS

Andrzej Nowak
Warsaw University

Robin R. Vallacher
Florida Atlantic University

The human brain is arguably the most complex structure in the universe. As Edelman (1992) noted, the cerebral cortex alone contains ten billion neurons, and the number of pairwise connections among them is approximately one million billion. The number of possible combinations of such connections, in turn, greatly exceeds the number of positively charged particles in the known universe. If one were to identify a candidate for greater complexity than the brain, it would have to be a structure composed of interacting brains—in effect, a social group. Like the brain, a social group is more than a mere collection of separate elements. To the contrary, what defines a group is the set of connections among the various elements (i.e., individuals) comprising the group. Just as the network of connections among neurons gives rise to identifiable brain states, the network of connections among members of a group give rise to identifiable group properties. The emergent nature of group properties has a long history in the social sciences, of course, dating back at least to Durkheim (1938).

Although the analogy between mind and society is a compelling one (see, e.g., Minsky, 1985), it has yet to be systematically explored with recourse to common tools. Neural network models have been successfully employed to expose the dynamic properties of neural and mental phenomena (e.g., McClelland & Rumelhart, 1986; Shultz & Lepper, 1995; Smith, in press), but the potential of this approach for uncovering the dynamic properties of social groups has yet to be realized. There is, of course, a vast difference between the respective elements in neural and social networks. Neurons, after all, are not people. The discoveries made in the physical sciences in the 1980s concerning dynamical and complex systems, however, proved that systems composed of entirely different elements may exhibit similar properties as long as the relationships among the elements are similar in a formal sense (Haken, 1982; Landau & Lifshitz, 1964; Weisbuch, 1992). In this light, it is encouraging that formal tools similar to neural networks have already been successfully applied to group-level processes. Bainbridge (1995), for example, applied neural networks to the emergence of religious beliefs in social groups.

The traditional approach to the description of social structure is the creation of social networks (e.g., Cartwright & Harary, 1956; Moreno, 1934). In this approach, interpersonal relations are depicted as connections among nodes in a graph (cf. Wasserman & Faust, 1994). Although this approach, like the neural network approach, is well suited to capture the structural properties of groups, it is not designed to reveal the dynamic nature of group processes. To be sure, it is possible to introduce rules governing changes in the states of nodes as a function of influence from connecting nodes. Such models, based on stochastic principles, lead to interesting predictions concerning the relation between network structure and network dynamics (e.g., Friedkin & Johnson, 1990). Because these models are based on assumptions and methods that predate the development of the complex systems approach, however, they do not incorporate insights from the natural sciences regarding the invariant properties underlying complex systems. More recently, cellular automata models, which were developed to model complex systems in the natural sciences, have become a tool of choice for modeling group-level properties and processes (e.g., Messick & Liebrand, 1995; Nowak, Szamrej, & Latane, 1990). Like neural networks, cellular automata are useful in revealing the dynamic as opposed to simply the static properties of the system in question. At the same time, though, cellular automata differ from neural networks in some potentially crucial respects.

Our aim in this chapter is to describe how complex social dynamics can be modeled and thereby understood in terms of an explicit neural network approach. We argue that the knowledge generated within this approach can provide important insights into the dynamics of social processes in general, and can specify how such dynamics depend on and give rise to the structure of social connections. We first describe cellular automata models of social processes, with an emphasis on social dilemmas, social influence, and social transitions. We then discuss the limitations of this approach and how these limitations are effectively handled within neural network models. We discuss insights provided by the neural network approach concerning social dynamics and we outline possible applications of this approach to various topics in group and societal dynamics. Finally, we argue that in social networks, in contrast to neural networks, there are processes operating to reduce the complexity of both structure and dynamics.

CELLULAR AUTOMATA MODELS

The relationship between micro and macro levels of description represents one of the most important and persistent issues in social psychology. This issue becomes particularly salient when one attempts to characterize the relationship between the individual and the group. On the one hand, an individual's behavior is heavily influenced by the social context in which he or she functions. On the other hand, each individual creates the social context for other individuals through his or her interactions with them. This mutual dependence is not easy to capture in traditional approaches to social psychology. In recent years, however, cellular automata models have been applied to this problem and have generated important insights into the nature of the feedback loop between the individual and the group.

The Nature of Cellular Automata

Cellular automata models (Ulam, 1952; von Neumann, 1966; Wolfram, 1986; see Gutowitz, 1991) represent prime examples of complex systems (cf. Casti, 1994). This class of models is widely used in physics and in various domains of biology, including neuroscience (Amit, 1989) and population dynamics (May, 1981). In each model, a finite set of elements is specified, each of which can adopt a finite number of discrete states. The elements are arranged in a specific spatial configuration that usually takes the form of a two-dimensional lattice or grid. Each element's location on this grid specifies the element's local neighborhood. Cellular automata are discrete dynamical systems in that the elements evolve in discrete units of time, such that the state of an element at $t+1$ depends on the states of the neighboring elements at time t. The exact form of this dependence is stated by so-called updating rules. The dynamics of cellular automata depend on the nature of the updating rule and on the format of the grid dictating the neighborhood structure.

Two classes of cellular automata models have been used to characterize social psychological phenomena. One class specifies that each individual's characteristics change as a result of updating rules. This approach is relevant for understanding the changes in attitudes, opinions, and so forth that occur as a result of social interaction. The other class specifies that individuals maintain stable characteristics but may change their physical location. Research based on this class of models revealed the emergence of spatial patterns on the basis of stable values, preferences, strengths, and the like. In an early application, Shelling (1969, 1971) developed an updating rule specifying that an individual who has more dissimilar than similar neighbors will move to a different random location. Simulations based on this simple rule demonstrated the emergence of spatial patterns reflecting social segregation.

Both classes of models are similar in that they reveal the emergence of regularities and patterns on a global level that were not directly programmed into individual elements. These regularities and patterns typically take the form of spatial patterns, such as the emergence of coherent minority opinion clusters from an initial random distribution of opinions. Regularities may also appear as temporal patterns, including such basic trajectories as evolution toward a stable equilibrium (fixed-point attractor), alternation between different states (periodicity), and apparent randomness (chaos).

Cellular Automata and Social Process

Models of cellular automata hold potential for characterizing the effects of different rules of interaction between individuals and the generation of societal level phenomena as a result of such rules. This linkage between micro rules and macro processes was investigated from several perspectives in recent years (cf. Hegselman, 1994, in press; Messick & Liebrand, 1995; Nowak et al., 1990). In these applications, each element corresponds to a single individual and the neighborhood structure is intended to capture the structure of interdependence among the individuals. Broadly defined, individuals are interdependent to the extent that they mutually affect one another's thoughts, feelings, and actions (cf. Thibaut & Kelley, 1959). Interdependence can take both indirect and direct forms.

Indirect interdependence exists when the actions of an individual have consequences for other people, whether or not these consequences are intended. This form of interdependence has most often been examined in the context of social dilemmas, in which an action intended to maximize one's personal gain has negative consequences for others (cf. Schulz, Alberts, & Mueller, 1994). In the tragedy of the commons (Hardin, 1968), for instance, a farmer may be motivated to overgraze an area of land shared with other farmers. In the short run, the farmer gains advantage over his neighbors, but in the long run, he as well as they suffer. Direct interdependence takes the form of social influence, in which one person directly influences the state or behavior of another person. Persuasion and modeling represent clear and well-documented examples of social influence. Both indirect and direct forms of interdependence have been examined in cellular automata models.

Social Interdependence and Social Dilemmas. Of all the long-standing issues in social psychology, none is more vexing than the puzzle of how altruistic behavior can emerge against the backdrop of self-interest (cf. Kelley & Thibaut, 1978). Recent applications of cellular automata models that simulate the short- and long-term effects of behavior in the Prisoner's Dilemma Game (PDG) are generating important insights into this puzzle. Axelrod (1984) pioneered this approach by demonstrating how cooperation can emerge in a group of individuals trying to maximize their respective self-interest. In his simulations, Axelrod found that cooperators survived by forming clusters with other cooperators with whom they could engage in mutual help without risking exploitation.

In an extension of this approach, Messick and Liebrand (1995) modeled the consequences of different strategies in the PDG. In their simulations, each interactant was located at a fixed position in a two-dimensional lattice and played a PDG with one of his or her nearest neighbors. On each trial, the interactant chose whether to cooperate or defect according to an updating rule. This rule, which could be looked upon as a social strategy, was assigned to all interactants in a given simulation. In the "tit-for-tat" strategy, each interactant's choice was simply an imitation of the choice made on the preceding trial by his or her neighbor. Two other updating rules were defined in terms of the respective outcomes experienced by the interactants on each trial. In the "win-cooperate, lose-defect" strategy, the interactant with the greater outcome cooperated, whereas the interactant with the smaller outcome defected. In the "win-stay, lose-shift" strategy, meanwhile, interactants who perceived themselves to be winning continued to behave in the same fashion on the next trial, whereas interactants who perceived themselves as losing changed their behavior on the next trial. It is important to note that these strategies were not derived from PDG rules per se, but reflect psychological considerations based on locally available information.

Simulations employing these updating rules reveal different results as a function of group size. In relatively small groups, equilibrium tends to be reached fairly quickly, with all the interactants converging on a particular choice. In relatively large groups, however, each strategy leads to continuous dynamics characterized by the coexistence of different behavioral choices. Eventually, though, each strategy leads to specific proportions of cooperating individuals. Interestingly, although these proportions tend to be maintained at the group level, the interactants commonly continue to change their choices.

A different approach to the issue of social interdependence was developed by Hegselman (1994, in press). Hegselman's research focused on the emergence of social support networks in a society. In his simulations, individuals lived on a two-dimensional grid containing some unoccupied sites and played a two-person "support game" with all of their immediate neighbors. Each individual in the neighborhood was characterized by some probability of needing help. On the one hand, a needy individual was clearly better off if he or she received help from a neighbor. On the other hand, providing help to a neighbor was clearly costly. With this trade-off in mind, each individual's preferred neighborhood was one in which he or she could obtain the degree of help needed while minimizing the help he or she provided. In accordance with some temporal rule, individuals were sometimes provided a migration option that enabled them to move to a more desirable location within a certain radius.

The results obtained by Hegselman reveal how support networks can evolve in a world of "rational egoists" who are differentially needy and but similarly motivated to choose partners in an opportunistic manner. Although social support inevitably develops, the emergent networks tend to be highly segregated. In particular, individuals who have a moderate probability of becoming needy tend to form relationships with one another, and also with individuals from somewhat higher and lower risk classes. Interestingly, individuals at the extremes of neediness—that is, those with very high or very low probabilities of needing help—tend to have the most difficulty in establishing support relations. If they do manage to form relationships, their partners tend to be from the same risk class.

Social Influence. The cellular automata model that has been analyzed most thoroughly from a dynamical systems point of view concerns the nature of social influence (e.g., Lewenstein, Nowak, & Latane, 1993; Nowak, Lewenstein, & Frejlak, 1995). In the initial formulation of this model (Nowak et al., 1990), the focus was on the emergence of public opinion in a society characterized by a diversity of attitudes. The model assumes that in the process of social interaction, individuals are motivated to sample the degree of social support for their position on a given topic. The model assumes further, in line with social impact theory (Latane, 1981), that each individual gives the greatest weight to the opinions of others who are spatially closest to him or her and who are the strongest (e.g., the most influential or persuasive). In the simulation, each individual compares the degree of support provided for each attitude position after each round of interaction and adopts the one with the strongest support in preparation for the next round of interaction.

Computer simulations of this model have repeatedly demonstrated the emergence of two basic processes (e.g., Nowak, Lewenstein, & Frejlak, 1995; Latane, Nowak, & Liu, 1994). First, there is a tendency for the initial minority position to decline in its proportion to some nonzero value representing a new stable equilibrium. This process is consistent with experimental research demonstrating group polarization (e.g., Moscovici & Zavalloni, 1969; Myers & Lamm, 1976). Second, attitudes that are initially randomly distrib-

FIG. 9.1. Initial distribution of opinions in the simulated group.

uted within the population tend to self-organize into a spatial pattern, such that the minority opinion becomes consolidated into coherent clusters. This process is similar in key respects to the emergence of group norms (cf. Festinger, Schachter, & Back, 1950). Figures 9.1 and 9.2 present representative results of computer simulations. The color of the bars corresponds to the opinions of the individuals, and the height of the bars represents individuals' relative strength.

These results, which were confirmed analytically (Lewenstein et al., 1993), indicate that polarization and clustering are order parameters of the underlying social influence processes. Four control factors, in turn, were identified as responsible for the emergence of these macroscopic properties; the magni-

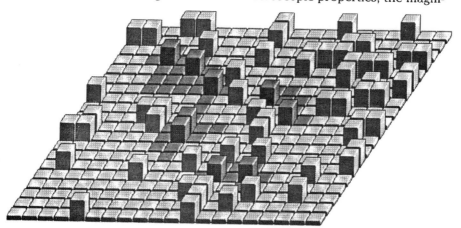

FIG. 9.2. Final equilibrium of opinions in the simulated group.

tude of individual differences, nonlinearity of attitude change (e.g., bipolar attitudes that change only when a threshold is reached), the degree of randomness in rules specifying attitude change, and the geometry of the social space (Latane & Nowak, in press; Lewenstein et al., 1993; Nowak et al., 1995).

The emergence of clustering means that most individuals eventually end up in a local majority surrounded by like-minded interactants. Because the greatest weight in opinion formation is given to nearby individuals, individuals in a minority cluster tend to have biased estimates of the relative popularity of opinions in the society as a whole. This means that individuals who hold a minority opinion are likely to maintain this opinion in the belief that it represents a majority position. It should be noted that these predictions, as well as the assumptions of the model, recently received support in experimental work (Latane & Nowak, in press; Latane, Liu, Nowak, Bonavento, & Zheng, 1995; L'Herrou, 1992).

A description of the model's effects at a macro level has recently been made possible with an analytical theory that characterizes changes in the model's order parameters (Lewenstein et al., 1993; Nowak et al., 1995). The derivation of analytical formulae is important for two reasons. This approach, first of all, provides a check on possible errors in the implementation of computer simulations. Second, it demonstrates that the same dynamics can be described at the micro level with cellular automata and at the macro level through a set of differential equations that can be solved analytically. In attempting to understand the relation between micro- and macrolevel phenomena, it is clearly helpful to have two descriptions representing different levels of analysis pointing to the same conclusions.

Social Change and Transitions. This general approach to the modeling of social process recently proved useful in generating insight into the dynamics of social change, including major societal transformations (Nowak, Lewenstein, & Szamrej, 1993). These models "work" when a source of bias is introduced that makes the minority opinion more attractive than the majority opinion. The simulations revealed that the occurrence of rapid social change is remarkably similar to the occurrence of phase transitions in physical phenomena. Metaphorically, changes enter as "bubbles of new within the sea of old," and social transitions occur as these bubbles expand and become connected to one another (see Fig. 9.1). This scenario stands in marked contrast to a scenario in which each individual gradually switches from an old set of attitudes to a new set of attitudes. Although the incremental scenario may effectively characterize changes in a stable society (e.g., a gradual shift from liberalism to conservatism or vice versa), it does not capture the nature of change during periods of rapid social transition.

These simulations also indicate, however, that the "bubbles of the old" stay entrenched in the "sea of the new." The strongest and best-supported individuals holding the old position, moreover, are the most likely to survive pressures associated with the new position. This means that the old position is likely to display a rebound effect when the bias toward the new disappears or is somehow reversed. This scenario provides an explanation for the return of leftist governments in Eastern Europe after their overwhelming defeat in the elections in the late 1980s. Empirical support for this perspective on social change is provided by two sources of data; the development of the private sector of the Polish economy and the emergence of voting preferences in the Polish parliamentary elections during the transition from socialism to private enterprise in the late 1980s and early 1990s (Nowak, Urbaniak, & Zienkowski, 1994).

Cellular Automata in Perspective

Cellular automata are useful in modeling a variety of social processes in which each individual's state is dependent on other individuals in his or her local neighborhood. Because updating rules can be designed to reflect virtually any form of local interdependence, a wide variety of social processes can be modeled and mapped over time. Social applications usually go beyond rigorous definitions of cellular automata by introducing characteristics of elements in addition to their state and location. This enables one to introduce updating rules with an almost unlimited range of characteristics, so as to capture variables believed to be important for social processes, such as individual differences in strength, resources, preferences, strategies, and so forth. It is possible, then, to use cellular automata to model any process, provided that it can be described in terms of local updating rules and elements with discrete states. Because such models have a well-defined spatial structure, they are ideally suited to the visualization of patterns produced by social interactions. Such patterns, which often have an appealing esthetic quality, are revealing of emergent group-level phenomena.

Although cellular automata are very flexible with respect to updating rules and individual characteristics, they are highly rigid with respect to the regularity of social structure. In classical square grid models, for example, each individual interacts with either four neighbors (in so-called von Neumann structures) or eight neighbors (in so-called Moore structures). In hexagonal models, meanwhile, each individual interacts with six neighbors. In yet another model, each individual is located along a single dimension, so that his or her interactions extend to either side. It is also possible to work with a three-dimensional model, in which each individual can interact with neighbors above and below as well as those on his or her four sides. Even more complex geometries can be envisioned (Lewenstein, Nowak, & Latane, 1993; Nowak, Latane, & Lewenstein, 1994; Nowak, Lewenstein, & Frejlak, 1996). The regularities inherent in these geometries may prove valuable in capturing the nature of certain social processes. A two-dimensional grid, for example, is well suited to represent the likely contacts among individuals in a town or village. Idealized structures of human contact may also prove useful in models of qualitative understanding, in which it is only important to define some local neighborhood, without worrying about the precise nature of the neighborhood.

At the same time, however, the inflexibility of such geometries makes them unrealistic as networks of social contacts. Even in models where individuals can change locations (e.g., Hegselman, 1994; Shelling, 1969), the constraints on social contact do not change. Such constraints are at odds with many well-established structures of contact among individuals. It is obvious, for example, that individuals widely separated in social space can strongly influence one another, a feature of social interaction not easily accommodated by cellular automata. It is also the case that individuals vary in the number of social contacts they have and in the strength of such contacts. Moreover, social contacts are generated on the basis of similarity in opinions and values. This means that there is bidirectional causality between the states of individuals and the connections between them. So, although friendship ties, for example, can promote opinion similarity, it is also the case that friendship ties are more likely to be formed between people who hold similar opinions. The second case may be modeled in cellular automata by movement to a new location, of course, but it is not possible to form only a single relationship in the new neighborhood. Rather, the individual has to adopt the whole structure of social ties inherent in the new location. In other words, the structure of social ties does not depend on individual choices but instead is dictated by the geometry of cellular automata.

There is another limitation of cellular automata apart from their inflexible geometry. In social reality, social ties vary not only with respect to their strength, but also with respect to their basic nature. Some ties are clearly positive, others are clearly negative. The adoption of a particular position by an individual thus will make some people more likely to adopt that position, but will make others less likely to do so. This basic feature of social reality cannot be modeled in cellular automata, because social ties are not a flexible property of individuals, but rather a fixed property of location in social space.

In summary, cellular automata are ideal for investigating individual differences and a wide variety of rules expressing mechanisms of individual change. This approach also has a clear advantage over other approaches in that it lends itself readily to visualization. The inflexibility of social ties in cellular automata, however, makes this class of models less appropriate for investigating the effects of realistic structures of social ties in general, and the dynamics of social ties in particular.

NEURAL NETWORK MODELS

Two features of social structure not easily captured by cellular automata seem particularly important. First, social connections can be negative and inhibitory as well as positive and excitatory. Thus, for example, a given individual may successfully influence someone else to embrace a particular opinion but tend to produce reactance (Brehm & Brehm, 1981) in someone else. Second, there is reason to believe that social structures are constrained in their evolution, in that certain patterns of connections are more likely to emerge and stabilize than are others. This idea is reflected, for example, in Heider's (1958) balance theory. In this model of social structure, knowing the sentiment relations between two people is useful in predicting the relations between each of them and a third person. Thus, if A and B like each other, there is a tendency for them to adopt a similar attitude (either like or dislike) toward a third person. If A and B have a negative relationship, on the other hand, Heiderian logic suggests that they will adopt different attitudes toward the third person. The extension of this principle to large groups of people suggests that some social structures will evolve toward only certain equilibria, with many possible structures never realized because of their psychological instability.

Both of these features can be modeled with attractor neural networks. Indeed, neural network models in general have become extremely popular in cognitive neuroscience precisely because of their ability to handle different types of connections (i.e., excitatory and inhibitory), and attractor neural networks in particular have received considerable attention because they reflect the tendency to evolve toward certain well-defined equilibrium (attractor) states (cf. Hopfield, 1982). Because we feel that the analogy between brains and groups provides a useful heuristic, it is tempting to consider how neural network models in neuroscience can be adapted to model the structure and dynamics of social groups. In this section, then, we discuss attractor neural networks as models of social networks.

The Basics of Attractor Neural Networks

Attractor neural network models are usually constructed in analogy with real neural nets. Neurons (or blocks of neurons in psychological applications) are modeled as relatively simple input–output elements (McCulloch & Pitts, 1943). Such elements, which we shall call "neurons" for simplicity, are connected with each other through so-called synaptic connections. Each connection can be represented as a number whose sign reflects the sign of the connection (positive or negative) and whose absolute value reflects strength or degree to which one neuron influences the other.

The most commonly investigated neural network models in psychology are so-called "feedforward networks." These networks are composed of layers of neurons, with adjacent layers connected by synapses. The flow of signals in feedforward networks is always unidirectional from input to output, such that the environment determines the states of neurons in the input layer, with the states of neurons in successive layers representing the results of computation. In attractor neural networks, there are no separate layers. The network instead is characterized by massive feedback loops between neurons. In a fully connected net, for example, each neuron is connected to all the other neurons. In the recognition process, the environment sets all of some neurons in specific states and then the network undergoes evolution, in which each neuron adjusts to the signal coming from other neurons. After some time, the network reaches some asymptotic state (i.e., attractor), in which the network's dynamics stabilize. Such attractors represent memories for the network. Quite often, for example, asymptotic states have the form of stable point attractors, in which no neurons change their state. In this case, the configuration of neurons in an asymptotic state represents the response of the network.

Attractor neural networks can be seen as programmable dynamical systems. The dynamics of the neurons depend on the connections among neurons and the states of the neurons. By the choice of appropriate connections, we can specify the asymptotic states (attractors) for a given network. The dynamics of the network then reflect the convergence from any state to the closest attractor. For some network architectures, the attractors may have forms different from stable points. Such attractors include periodic, chaotic, and purely random evolution.

Attractor Neural Networks as Social Networks

Although attractor neural networks were originally designed as models of brain function, their architecture may be interpreted as representing social groups and even societies. Such interpretation assumes that each neuron corresponds to a single individual and that the connections correspond to the relations among the individuals. This description is very similar to that employed in research on social networks (Wasserman & Faust, 1994). Attractor neural networks have the advantage, however, of enabling one to map the relationship between structure and dynamic properties. They also provide formal operators for dealing with graded connections and with negative as well as positive connections.

To analyze attractor neural networks as models of dynamic social networks, it is important to distinguish two fundamentally different types of dynamics. The first type occurs in neural networks during recognition and involves changes in states of neurons, with the connections among neurons remaining stable. Such dynamics correspond to the convergence of the state of the network to one of its attractors, and may be described as each neuron trying to adjust its state to the total input it receives from other neurons, from the environment, and from noise (i.e., random influences). The general rule is that if the sum of all inputs from other neurons exceeds a certain threshold, the neuron adopts an excited state. Otherwise, it adopts a low value corresponding to a nonexcited state. Interpreted in terms of social networks, the dynamics of neurons correspond to individuals' changing their opinions, moods, or attitudes, as a result of influence through existing social ties with other individuals.

The second type of dynamics occurs during learning and involves changes in the connections, with the neurons remaining stable. The dynamics of connections are defined in terms of a learning algorithm that guarantees that the desired configuration of neurons (corresponding to a memorized pattern) functions as an attractor. In the social interpretation, such dynamics correspond to the formation and dissolution of social relations based on the opinions, moods, and attitudes of the individuals. Because such changes converge on attractors, only certain configurations of opinions, and so forth are likely to be observed for a given social relationship. Later, we describe insights concerning both the dynamics of neurons and of connections that are relevant to understanding the dynamics of opinion change and the formation of social ties.

Dynamics of Opinion Change. In attractor neural networks, each individual is represented as a node (corresponding to a neuron) in the network. Although some continuous models of attractor neural networks have been proposed (e.g., Hopfield, 1984), we concentrate on the description of networks in which nodes are binary elements (i.e., nodes that adopt either +1 or a −1 value, corresponding to high and low states, respectively). Qualitative properties of dynamics in such networks are very similar to those in networks in which elements can adopt continuous values (see Hopfield, 1984). Because the attractor neural networks introduced by Hopfield (1982) are the easiest to understand, we describe them and develop their implications for the dynamics of opinion change.

In a Hopfield-type network, each node is connected to every other node. The strength or efficacy of the connections between neurons i and j is symmetrical and corresponds to the degree to which the state of neuron j influences the state of neuron i and vice versa. Such connections are represented by a real number, either positive or negative in value. Positive numbers represent excitatory connections, whereas negative numbers represent inhibitory connections. The influence of neuron j on neuron i is expressed as the product of j's state (+1 or −1) and the strength of the connection between i and j. It follows that if there is an excitatory connection between i and j, neuron j will influence neuron i to be in the same state, whereas if there is an inhibitory connection between i and j, neuron j will influence neuron i to be in the opposite state. At the same time, each node is trying to adjust its state in the next moment of time $(t + 1)$ to the total input it receives from other nodes, which may be expressed as a sum of all the inputs at the time t.

$$h_i(t) = \sum_{j \neq i} J_{ij} s_j(t) \qquad (1)$$

In this equation, $h_i(t)$ represents the total input neuron i receives from other nodes at time t, J_{ij} describes the connection (i.e., its sign and strength) from neuron j to neuron i, and $s_j(t)$ describes the state of neuron j at time t. If the sum is greater than some threshold (often set at 0), the node will adopt a high state at the next time moment; if lower than this threshold, the node will adopt a low state. For a threshold value equal to 0, the neuron updating rule may be written as:

$$s_i(t + 1) = \text{sgn}(h_i(t)) \qquad (2)$$

In this equation, the function "sgn" has a value +1 whenever $h_i(t)$ is positive and a value of -1 whenever $h_i(t)$ is negative. The dynamics may be realized in either a synchronous updating, in which the state of each neuron at one time is based on the states of all its connected neurons at the previous time (i.e., all the nodes are updated simultaneously), or in a Monte Carlo updating, in which one element at a time is randomly chosen and its states are updated based on the states of all other neurons (i.e., the nodes are updated sequentially). These two updating rules typically produce highly similar outcomes.

In a social interpretation, each node corresponds to a person and connections correspond to social relations. Positive connections represent relationships in which both persons influence one another to have similar moods, attitudes, and so forth. Negative connections represent reactance-like influence between both persons. Positive connections may often correspond to positively valenced relations (i.e., friendship, attraction, etc.) and negative connections often correspond to negatively valenced relations (i.e., dislike, resentment, etc.). Sometimes, however, the sign of a connection may correspond to strategic decisions concerning coalition formation rather than the affective quality of the relationship. For example, a person may have at best a neutral feeling toward someone else, but still adopt that person's position on a given topic because he or she wishes to have the backing of this person on another issue. This description follows Heiderian principles of relationship structure (Heider, 1958).

In reality, everyone is influenced by more than one other person. In balanced triads, for example, the distribution of opinions is stable, because all the pairwise relations support the distribution. If all the relationships are positive, everyone tends to have the same opinion. If one relationship is positive and two are negative, meanwhile, the persons connected by a positive relationship will share an opinion, whereas the third person will have a contrasting opinion. In unbalanced triads, on the other hand, no single configuration of opinions will satisfy existing relationships. If all three relationships are negative, for example, or if two are positive and one is negative, the opinion structure is necessarily strained and hence unstable. From the point of view of attractor networks, the actual configuration of opinions will depend on the relative strength of pairwise connections. Even an unbalanced triad may tend toward stability, then, if one of the connections is weaker than the others and can be effectively ignored.

In most real-world contexts, social relationships extend far beyond a triad. In large social systems, even relatively weak social ties can have significant impact on individuals when the effects of these ties are summed. Following the likely dynamics of opinions in larger unbalanced systems without the use of appropriate tools may thus be virtually impossible. Attractor networks provide a tool by which the dynamics of even very large and complex structures can be captured. If the connections among group members are primarily positive, the dynamics of opinions are relatively simple: After some time, everyone will converge on the same opinion. However, if there is a significant proportion of negative (inhibitory) connections (e.g., greater than 30%), the dynamics become much more complex. For a given set of existing connections, there may be several equilibria of opinions in the group. In the Hopfield model, for example, when connections are symmetrical, the number of potential uncorrelated equilibria is approximately $.14 \times n$, where n is the number of individuals. For asymmetrical networks (e.g., Gardner, 1988), the number of equilibria can approach $2 \times n$.

Some equilibria, however, are more stable than others. To understand the dynamics of social networks in the presence of several equilibria, we can use an energy metaphor. Given a set of connections, for every configuration of states of nodes we can assign a specific value of a so-called energy function. The energy of a given state (E) corresponds to

$$E = -\frac{1}{2}\sum_{j\neq i} J_{ij}s_i s_j \tag{3}$$

In this equation, J and s are used in the same way they were used in Equation 1. To compute the energy, one sums these terms over all the connected nodes. In the fully connected model, this corresponds to the summation of all possible pairs of nodes with the exception of the node with itself. To use a metaphorical description, one can imagine a landscape,

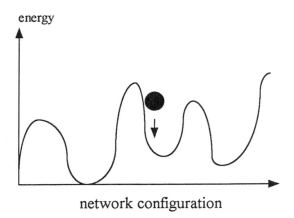

FIG. 9.3. Energy landscape.

where hills correspond to high energy and valleys correspond to low energy. We present a simplified depiction of such a landscape in Fig. 9.3.

In this figure, the x axis corresponds to configurations of states of nodes, such that neighboring points differ by the state of one node, and the y axis corresponds to the energy of each configuration. Each valley corresponds to a local minimum in the energy function (i.e., an equilibrium state), and the depth of each valley depicts the strength of the equilibrium. Dynamics of the network consist of the descent from any state to the closest equilibrium. In a metaphorical way, we can imagine a ball rolling on a hilly landscape. The ball will roll down a hill until it reaches a valley, at which point it comes to rest. We can check that the dynamics of attractor networks, in which each node adjusts its state to the total signal coming from other nodes, corresponds to the descent on the energy landscape.

The Role of Noise. If the influence of other nodes (e.g., the influence of other people in the social network) is the only source of dynamics, once a system achieves an equilibrium state, the dynamics cease. In reality, social influence rarely is the sole source of opinion change. Each individual's opinion depends on many other factors, such as the recall of idiosyncratic memories, communication from outside the group, mass media exposure, and so forth. The joint effect of all such factors may be represented as a random influence on each individual. In attractor neural networks, such random influences are commonly referred to as *noise*. The noise is added as a random number to the summed input of all the connections for each individual. If the addition of noise does not change the sign of the total influence acting on a node, its presence may be ignored. Sometimes, however, the noise will have an opposite sign to that of social influence, and if it is also of greater magnitude, an individual may adopt an opinion opposite to that suggested by the summed influence. The larger the magnitude of the noise, the more often this will happen.

In terms of network dynamics, if the value of noise relative to the value of social influence is very small, its influence is correspondingly subtle. Larger values of noise, on the other hand, tend to make weak equilibria unstable. This is because the introduction of randomness may cause the system to evolve in such a way that the energy function increases rather than decreases. With increases in noise, correspondingly stronger equilibria become unstable. Finally, for some value of noise, no equilibria will be stable so that the system evolves randomly. The introduction of noise can therefore qualitatively change the dynamics of processes in networks.

In the social interpretation, the greater proportion of outside and random influences on opinions, the weaker the role of equilibria produced by the structure of social relations within the group. In terms of the energy landscape metaphor, noise can be seen as shaking the landscape, with the ball leaving the relatively shallow valleys and settling in the deepest valleys. In neural network algorithms, in fact, the introduction of noise is often used in a so-called process of simulated annealing (Kilpatrick, Gelatt, & Vecchi, 1983) as a means of searching for the strongest energy minima. Understanding the role of noise in neural networks leads to a prediction concerning the role of randomness and outside influences on the structure of opinions, attitudes, and beliefs in a group. To the extent that social relations are relatively stable regardless of the opinion at issue, the same network structure applies when group members hold positions on multiple issues. The groups' position on each issue can be interpreted as a configuration of states of nodes. To examine how the relationship among different opinions evolve, we can portray the initial distribution of each opinion as a corresponding configuration of states of nodes and observe how these configurations change in the presence of noise. In a sense, we model the group as it discusses each issue in turn and note the resultant equilibrium for each issue.

In the absence of significant values of noise, even subtle equilibria should be visible, so that each starting configuration may end up in a separate equilibrium. For a given structure of social relations, then, there are many possible configurations of opinions. If the group members hold opinions on several issues, the opinions on each issue may reach equilibria that are independent of one another; in effect, the opinions are uncorrelated. With increases in noise and the concomitant destabilizing of weak equilibria, several opinions will necessarily come to share common and relatively strong equilibria. Eventually, all the opinions will tend to descend to the strongest equilibrium and thus become strongly correlated (either positively or negatively). This process is reminiscent of the emergence of ideology in a society. Thus, as Converse (1964) noted, issues that were previously uncorrelated develop correlation over periods of time. The process of emergent correlation among attitudes and opinions, in a similar fashion, may provide the basis for forming in-group identity (cf. Brewer & Kramer, 1985; Tajfel & Turner, 1986).

For even higher values of outside and random influences, each opinion begins to evolve independently of the internal group pressure. All the equilibria hence become unstable and the correlations among issues begin to dissipate. At extremely high values of randomness, the correlations vanish altogether. In terms of the energy landscape metaphor, as the landscape is shaken in a subtle manner, those balls that are resting in very shallow valleys roll into deeper ones. With progressively stronger shaking of the energy landscape, the balls gather in increasingly deeper valleys. At some point, however, even the deepest valleys cannot contain the jumping of the balls responding to energy. Hence, the balls begin to jump randomly and independently of one another. In the social interpretation, this is tantamount to the decoupling of attitudes and opinions, with each attitude and opinion becoming susceptible to different outside and random forces. This curvilinear relationship between noise and opinion correlation in a group is depicted schematically in Fig. 9.4.

The fact that the number of possible equilibria is limited means that if a large number of issues are discussed in a group, even unrelated issues are likely to become correlated as the issues achieve their respective local equilibria. It is also the case, however, that the number of possible equilibria changes as a linear function of group size (Hopfield, 1982; Hertz, Krogh, & Palmer, 1991). It is possible, therefore, for societies to hold uncorrelated positions on many issues, as long as interpersonal relationships (as opposed to, say, media influence) are the primary means of opinion change. In rela-

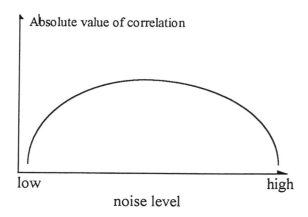

FIG. 9.4. Correlation among attitudes in a group as a function of noise.

tively small groups, however, it would be unlikely for even a small number of opinions to remain uncorrelated. It follows, then, that it is much easier for small groups to become cohesive than it is for large groups, a conclusion that is consistent with work on group dynamics (cf. Cartwright & Zander, 1968).

Dynamics of Social Relations

Thus far we have emphasized the dynamics of opinion change, assuming the stability of connections among group members. One of the most fascinating topics in the social sciences, however, is how the structure of social relations form and undergo change. Several rules relevant to this issue have been proposed in research on social networks. Stockman (1994), for example, proposed that individuals attempt to gain strategic influence in decision making by establishing connections (either direct or indirect) with decision makers. According to his friendship rule, individuals will establish connections with others who hold similar positions on issues.

Attractor networks allow one to describe the emergence of connections from a broader perspective that takes into account the overall group structure and dynamics. In neural networks, the structure of connections is established in the process of learning. In fact, all the memories of the network are coded in the connection strengths and signs among neurons. Several learning rules have been established for attractor neural networks (cf. Hertz et al., 1991). Two of these rules are representative of this approach; the Hebbian rule (Hebb, 1949) as implemented in a Hopfield model (Hopfield, 1982) and the perceptron as discussed by Gardner (1988).

The Hopfield Model. Hebb's rule specifies that if two neurons are in the same state simultaneously, the connection between them will become more positive, whereas if two neurons are in a different state at the same time, the connection between them will become more negative (inhibitory). Hopfield (1982) developed a learning algorithm based on Hebb's rule that establishes the representation of each of the learned patterns as a separate equilibrium. Each pattern corresponds to a set of opinions on different issues, and is represented as a specific configuration of states of neurons. The Hopfield learning algorithm is a direct instantiation of the Hebbian rule. The only difference is that the Hebbian rule states what happens as each pattern is learned and thus reflects the process of learning, whereas the Hopfield algorithm describes the connection strengths after all the patterns have been learned and thus reflects the result of learning.

Let us suppose that each pattern can be represented in a binary fashion as a string consisting of N elements, each of which has a +1 or −1 value. Assume further that there are k such patterns. Each element is represented

```
                    Element
              1   2   3   4   5
Pattern 1:   +1  -1  +1  +1  -1
Pattern 2:   -1  +1  -1  -1  -1
Pattern 3:   -1  +1  +1  +1  +1
```
FIG. 9.5. Example of pattern under learning rule.

by a node in the network. In Fig. 9.5, there are three patterns, each consisting of five elements.

The goal of the learning rule is to establish a structure for the network such that each of the above configurations would correspond to an equilibrium. In the Hopfield model, to establish the value of the connection between two nodes, one counts the number of patterns in which the two nodes have the same sign and subtract from this the number of patterns in which the two nodes have a different sign. In the above example, the connection between elements 1 and 2 would be −3, because they have a different sign in every pattern, whereas the connection between elements 4 and 5 would be +1, because they have signs in common for two patterns and signs that are different for one pattern.

The connection strength may be described more formally as

$$J_{ij} = \sum_{k=1}^{m} s_i^k s_j^k \qquad (4)$$

where J_{ij} describes the connection strength between elements i and j, and s_i^k describes the state of element i in the pattern k and s_j^k describes the state of element j in the pattern k, and m denotes the number of patterns to be learned. It follows from this formula that the connection between two elements is proportional to the correlation between their respective states. To allow for variation in the strength of different equilibria, one can introduce a weight for each pattern, such that more important patterns have higher weights. The formula then expands to the following (Lewenstein & Nowak, 1989):

$$J_{ij} = w^k \sum_{k=1}^{m} s_i^k s_j^k \qquad (5)$$

where w^k denotes the weight of the pattern k.

In the social interpretation, the above formula corresponds to the well-documented relationship between similarity and attraction (e.g., Byrne, Clore, & Smeaton, 1986; Newcomb, 1961). The greater the proportion of issues on which individuals share opinions, the more positive the relationship between the individuals, and hence the more positive the influence they have over one another. In effect, the opinions of every individual are anchored in the opinions of others with whom he or she has positive social relations. If the number of issues for which there is disagreement exceeds the number of issues for which there is agreement, a negative social relation develops. As differences in opinion are discovered, the positive ties will weaken and eventually negative ties will develop. The strength of negative ties is proportional to the number of dissimilarities minus the number of similarities. Influence in the context of such inhibitory connections is likely to be manifest as reactance (Brehm & Brehm, 1981), such that the recipient of influence adopts a position contrary to that advocated. In this model, then, individuals' opinions are anchored not only by positive social relations, but by negative relations as well.

As noted earlier, the Hopfield model can accommodate the fact that issues differ in importance for a group. In the final picture, then, it is the number of similarities, weighted by the importance of each, minus the number of dissimilarities, weighted by their respective importance, that determine the fate of a relationship. Those equilibria that correspond to more important issues will be stronger. It has been demonstrated that both strong and weak equilibria can coexist in neural networks (Nowak & Lewenstein, 1989). The introduction of stronger memories, however, tends to diminish the basins of attraction for the weaker memories. If the difference in weights becomes very pronounced, the weak equilibria may become unstable. This means that if a single issue becomes highly salient for the group, the structure of social relations may be shaped mostly by members' position on that issue, in effect dividing the group on that basis and preventing the attainment of equilibria with respect to different issues. The outcome of this would be a group split into "us" and "them," with the opinions on all issues homogeneous within each subgroup and different between subgroups. In this case, all the connections within each subgroup would be positive and the connections between subgroups would be negative.

To learn a set of stable patterns in the Hopfield model, it is necessary for these patterns to be uncorrelated. If the Hopfield algorithm is used to learn correlated (i.e., similar) patterns, the patterns become merged into a single equilibrium. In the energy landscape metaphor, this may be portrayed as an attempt to dig closely located holes in the sand. Instead of several separate small holes, one winds up with a single large hole. In the social interpretation, this implies that it would be very difficult to form a structure of relationships in which similar but distinct equilibria could be maintained. The tendency instead would be for similar distributions of opinions to merge, thereby increasing the strength of the correlations (either positive or negative) among opinions. This scenario may be observed in different social situations. In a political campaign, for example, somewhat related issues tend to become integrated in the public's mind.

The Hopfield model also proved useful in understanding the dynamics of coalition formation. In their landscape theory of aggregation, for example, Axelrod and Bennett (1993) analyzed how the elements in a system (where elements may be individuals, groups, or even nations) become organized into patterns in such a way that highly compatible elements are close together and less compatible elements are far apart. The rules by which this occurs are similar to those proposed by Hopfield. Their theory successfully predicted the formation of alliances during World War II and the alliances established in the creation of the UNIX standard in the 1980s.

The basic features of the Hopfield model are realistic from a social point of view in many situations. The requirement of symmetry in connections corresponds to the well-documented reciprocity of liking phenomenon (e.g., Dittes & Kelley, 1956). The scarcity of equilibria, meanwhile, corresponds to broad notions concerning the rather simple nature of social categorization (e.g., in-group vs. out-group differentiation). The assumptions of the Hopfield model may be limiting, however, with respect to other social situations. Social relations, after all, are not always perfectly symmetrical—not every romantic overture is reciprocated and opinion similarity is certainly not the only factor shaping relationships.

Perceptrons. A less restrictive model of social relationships can be derived from the perceptron learning algorithm (cf. Gardner, 1988). This algorithm describes a different approach to establishing connections among neurons that enables the storage of correlated patterns and also dramatically increases the memory capacity of the network. The primary difference from the Hopfield algorithm is that connections among elements are not symmetrical (i.e., the connection from neuron i to neuron j is not necessarily equal in strength to the connection from neuron j to neuron i). For this reason, the energy function, which is critical to understanding the dynamics of the Hopfield model, cannot be explicitly defined for networks within the perceptron approach. The analysis of the network thus requires the use of different formal tools than are used in the Hopfield model. In many important respects, though, Hopfield and perceptron networks are quite similar. Most importantly, in the recognition phase the updating rules in the perceptron model are identical to those in the Hopfield model, as previously discussed, and thus the dynamics in both models show similar convergence on attractors.

The perceptron algorithm takes the existing set of connections and states how to modify them gradually, such that the desired configurations of elements become attractors. In this algorithm, one starts from a particular set of connections, such as a random distribution. In the learning phase, all the neurons are set to correspond to a desired state for the network. Then a neuron is randomly chosen. If its state agrees in sign with the state dictated by the influence over existing connections of all other neurons, then nothing is changed and another neuron is randomly chosen. If, however, the influence of other neurons suggests a different state for the chosen neuron than the desired state, then all connections involving the chosen neuron are adjusted by a small constant, such that the conflict between the states of the neuron and the influences on it is minimized.

For example, if a given neuron is (and should be) in a +1 state, and the total influence of other neurons sums to a negative number, all the connections between this neuron and other neurons in the +1 state are changed by adding a positive constant value, and all the neurons in the negative state are changed in a negative direction. In the learning phase, then, the connections rather than the neurons change their state. Conversely, if a neuron is in a negative state and the influence of other neurons push it toward a positive state, the conflict is minimized by adjusting the connections involving positive elements in a negative direction, while adding a constant to the negative connections. This process of randomly choosing neurons and adjusting the connections so as to minimize "stress" is repeated until all the neurons coding a single pattern are stable, and repeated again for the next pattern, and so on. After the structure of connections accommodate the next pattern, it is likely that previously learned patterns become unstable. In successive iterations, then, one needs to return to previous patterns and relearn them. Such a process, in fact, may be very lengthy and requires hundreds or even thousands of iterations before all the patterns are successfully learned (i.e., established as equilibria of the system).

In the social interpretation, this model implies that social relations are changed in such a way that patterns of opinions in a group become stabilized. Each individual, therefore, attempts to establish those relationships that will stabilize his or her pattern of opinions and attitudes. We should note that connections are typically not symmetrical in this model, so that the number of possible equilibria approaches $2n$, where n is the number of nodes in the network, and thus is 14 times greater than in the Hopfield model. The perceptron algorithm captures the notion that people seek social support for their opinions and beliefs (e.g., Swann, 1990). Although the perceptron algorithm is clearly superior as a method for teaching neural networks, there are processes operating in social networks that tend toward simplification in a manner that is more compatible with the Hopfield model.

Repellor States. It is possible to generalize the class of attractor neural networks to so-called repellor states in network dynamics (Nowak, Lewenstein, & Tarkowski, 1994). In contrast to attractor neural networks, the dynamics in repellor networks are defined in terms of escape from the vicinity of repelling states. The dynamics of nodes is identical to those in attractor networks, but in the learning rules, the signs of the connections are reversed. In a reversal of the Hebbian rule, those nodes that adopt the same state for learned patterns will develop a negative connection and those nodes that adopt the opposite state for learned patterns will develop a positive connection. For this type of network, it is important that each element also influences itself, which has the effect of slowing down the dynamics. The issue of self-influence is discussed in detail in a later section.

In the social world, it is sometimes to easier to predict what cannot happen than it is to predict what will happen. It is difficult to predict the future spouse of young child, for example, but one can predict with practical certainty that it will not be his or her sibling. Negative prediction of this kind can be captured in terms of repellor neural networks. Unlikely configurations of opinions, for example, may be defined as repellors through the use of appropriate learning rules for establishing connections. If we can specify in advance that certain configurations of opinions cannot develop in a group, we can use this information to predict the structure of social relations in much the same way as that employed in attractor neural networks. Alternatively, if the structure of connections is already established, we may determine whether they are repellor states in the network. In general, repellor states in social networks are characterized by people with negative relations sharing the same opinions and people with positive relations holding different opinions. It is an open question, of course, whether real processes operate to generate specific configurations of opinions impossible to be obtained in a group. Nonetheless, even if such processes rarely occur in social groups, it is certainly possible to use the idea of repellor networks in a Machiavellian attempt to make undesirable configurations of opinions impossible in a group. Perhaps some instances of political intrigue play on this idea, in that negative feelings are generated between two people in order to prevent an alliance between them.

Bidirectional Causality in Social Relations

It follows from the description thus far that an existing structure of connections will generate changes in individuals' opinions, attitudes, and beliefs. At the same time, though, the opinions held by individuals will generate and change the nature of social relations. The first model of causality reflects the formation of attitudes through social influence processes, in which the relations among individuals are more stable than are the opinions of individuals. The second model of causality reflects the formation and change of social relations so as to maintain an existing structure of opinions and attitudes. Here the opinions of individuals are more stable than the relations among individuals and thus dictate the network of connections in a social group.

Taken together, these two perspectives capture the bidirectional nature of social processes. Such bidirectionality is consistent with research showing that attitude similarity promotes interpersonal attraction and friendship, and with research showing the complementary effect in which friendship and adversarial ties dictate the formation and change of attitudes. In a social group, then, those opinions that are strongly held by individuals and are not likely to change as a result of group influence provide a basis for the development of social relations. On the other hand, the distribution of opinions on new issues, especially those perceived to be of little importance, will be shaped by existing social ties. When a social group is being formed, initially held opinions will serve as the basis for establishing social relations. Opinions on issues that evolve later, however, are likely to display dynamics dictated by existing social connections. Those issues that are held strongly and are unlikely to change as a result of social influence processes, however, will tend to modify the existing structure of social relations. Such issues, for example, may be attitudes that are highly functional for individuals (e.g., opinions regarding taxation among people in vulnerable tax brackets).

Consider, for example, a person who enters a situation (e.g., a party) consisting of strangers. Because there are no existing social ties, the source of stability will be the person's existing opinions. Assuming he or she wishes to establish relations in this situation, he or she will seek out those who hold similar opinions. After social relations are formed in this way, however, the person's opinions on new issues will be formed on the basis of these relations. If, however, some positions are simply unacceptable for the person, the person may readjust his or her social relations, forming new alliances with those who hold similar opinions. In essence, then, both opinions and social relations can be the cause and effect in interpersonal processes. Attractor networks provide a rigorous formal model of capturing the dynamics of each process and for enabling prediction of one, given the other. It follows from these models that positive connections will develop among people with similar attitudes, whereas negative connections will develop among people with dissimilar attitudes. The tendency to form similar opinions on new issues, on the other hand, will be a function of the strength of the connections among the individuals.

The rules specified earlier may be used by individuals to develop social relations as a means of achieving other goals, such as gaining strategic influence. Thus, for example, an individual may try to forge a positive relation with someone else in order to influence that person's decision making. This may be done by displaying opinions similar to those of the other person on a number of issues that are not of strategic importance. Indeed, research on ingratiation and self-presentation demonstrated that displays of similarity are commonly used to gain advantage in social relations (cf. Jones, 1964; Schlenker, 1980). Another theoretically possible strategy, although no doubt unlikely, strategy is to build a negative relationship through displays of dissimilarity, and then basing influence on principles of reactance (Brehm & Brehm, 1981).

Attractor Networks in Perspective

Clearly, neurons are different from people and brains are different from societies. Although the formalisms developed to describe neural networks apply well to social computation, it is important to recognize that crucial differences may exist between social and neural networks. Some of these differences can be dealt with explicitly by modifying the assumptions and rules of neural network models so that they better reflect well-established principles of social psychology. Other differences, however, may reflect fundamental features of being human, such as consciousness, volition, goal orientation, as well as uniqueness and the potential for idiosyncrasy. In this section, we consider both the features that are open to realization in neural networks and those that pose serious problems for instantiation.

Individual Differences. It is clear that individual humans differ from one another in ways that individual neurons do not. Perhaps the most robust dimension of individual variation with respect to social relations concerns influence or potency vis-à-vis other people. Quite simply, some individuals have greater impact on their social contacts than do other individuals. We suggest that this aspect of personality, however, can be captured in attractor network models. The idea is simply that the connections coming from relatively influential people can be multiplied by a constant greater than 1, whereas connections coming from less influential people can be decreased by multiplying by a constant less than 1 (but greater than 0).

Although this possibility has yet to be implemented in attractor network models of interpersonal process, it is consistent with the SOREMO model of social relations developed by Kenny (1994). In an analysis of variance approach, Kenny decomposed the strength of sociometric choices into three components; the effect of actor, the effect of observer, and the interaction between actor and observer. By reversing this procedure, the actual connection between two elements can be established at such a value that they represent all three factors. We should note, however, that in the SOREMO model, the three factors are added rather than multiplied, as we suggest earlier.

Individuals also differ in their propensity to favor or adopt certain opinions. Opinion preferences bias the individual, such that he or she has a higher threshold for accepting contrary positions than does someone without the preference. It may be difficult, for example, for a rich person to have a favorable attitude toward high taxes, and it may require a correspondingly strong influence to change his or her position. This aspect of individual difference can be understood in terms of varying thresholds, a feature that is often incorporated into neural network models (cf. McClelland & Rumelhart, 1986). In particular, bias can be represented by adjusting the threshold of each neuron to values other than 0. If this threshold is high, the neuron will require stronger positive influence from other neurons to adopt a +1 state. If this threshold is below 0, meanwhile, a stronger negative influence will be required for the neuron to adopt a −1 state. We should note, however, that although the structure of connections for different issues may remain invariant, the threshold for each issue is likely to be different, because they may be salient with respect to different psychological and social characteristics. The differences in threshold may therefore lead to different equilibria for different opinions in a given social group.

Self-Influence. Most attractor neural networks assume that each neuron reacts to the influence from other neurons, but does not influence itself. In marked contrast, people are noted for their self-reflection (e.g., Vallacher, 1980), a capacity that implies the possibility of self-influence. Research on this point established that when people adopt a position on an issue and are made privately or publicly self-aware, they tend to embrace the position even more strongly and become correspondingly resistant to influence attempts (e.g., Wicklund & Frey, 1980). In attractor network models, self-influence can be represented as a connection from a node to itself, with the strength of this connection corresponding to the magnitude of self-influence. This form of influence has the effect of stabilizing the dynamics of the network. In terms of the energy landscape metaphor, it acts as friction to slow down the movement of the ball and enables movement cessation in areas that are not completely flat (Nowak et al., 1994). If self-influence becomes very strong, the dynamics of opinion change slow and may even cease altogether. Self-influence is, of course, apparent in everyday life and has been modeled in the context of cellular automata models of social influence (Nowak et al., 1990).

Reduction of Complexity. It is important to recognize that despite the basic similarity between formal descriptions of neural and social networks, the dynamics of the two types of networks differ. The basic goal of neural networks is to code a large number of complex memories and then retrieve them on the basis of minimal cues. Social networks have a very different goal. They provide for the coordination of individuals in social thought, emotion, and behavior. Although the architecture of neural networks should be optimized for complexity, the architecture of social networks should be optimized for social coordination. There are many goals for which cooperation is necessary. Scarce resources, however, induce competition. Social relations thus should form in such a way so as to enable cooperation among those with shared goals and competition with rivals. To accommodate social rules, standard learning algorithms of neural networks may need to be modified.

The equilibria of a neural network may have a very complex structure, and in fact learning algorithms are formulated in such a way as to accommodate a maximal number of memories. If the evolution of social ties simply mimicked such algorithms, the resultant social configuration might very well become incomprehensible for group members and the coordination of group action might be practically impossible. There is considerable evidence suggesting that social networks, unlike neural networks, evolve toward simplicity in both structure and dynamics. Although unbalanced triads in neural networks, for example, allow for multiple equilibria and thus a rich set of memories, Heiderian principles (Heider, 1958) state that unbalanced triads tend to evolve toward balance. Thus, a friend of our friend tends to become our friend, and an enemy of our friend tends to become our enemy, and an enemy of our enemy tends to be become our friend. Such processes aimed at minimizing frustration in a social network eventually lead to a situation of two groups with positive ties internally and negative ties externally (i.e., intergroup conflict).

This type of social structure may be further simplified by assuming that each group can be represented by a single node, with the members in each group having positive connections to the node representing their group. Negative relations between the two groups may be represented as a single, very strong negative connection between the two nodes representing the respective groups. To a certain extent, this description captures important features of the emergence of in-group identity (cf. Brewer & Kramer, 1985). In this formulation, the number of connections may be reduced from N^2, representing a situation where everyone is connected to everyone else, to $2 \times N$, representing a situation where everyone is just connected to their own group node. Such a simplified structure would provide a much more efficient mechanism for fast in-group coordination of thoughts, feelings, and actions.

Asymmetry in Social Networks. In attractor networks, there is symmetry between positive and negative connections, as well as between similarity and dissimilarity. In social reality, however, people tend to avoid both negative relations and displays of dissimilarity. Indeed, there is considerable evidence suggesting these forms of asymmetry. Kanouse and Hanson (1971), for instance, demonstrated positive–negative asymmetry with respect to evaluation, such that negative evaluations were displayed less frequently but were given greater weight in social relations. This type of asymmetry could be represented in attractor networks by assuming that whereas positive states are represented by +1, negative states are represented by a higher negative number (e.g., −2). The greater the asymmetry in the frequency of positive versus negative states, the greater the compensatory weighting of these states. In similar fashion, it is fair to say that in social groups, negative connections tend to be broken rather than maintained, so that the structure of connections is heavily biased in favor of positive relations. By virtue of their very infrequency, however, the few remaining negative relations are especially salient and thus their effective strength may be greatly increased. Such instances of positive–negative asymmetry can easily be coded into attractor networks, although this possibility has not been implemented to date.

Opinion Correlation in Social Networks. In developing the above considerations, we assumed that opinions on different issues are logically unrelated. This is rarely the case with social issues. The cognitive consistency theories (e.g., Festinger, 1957), for instance, share the assumption that individuals strive to establish and maintain consistency among their opinions concerning different issues. This well-documented tendency promotes correlations among the opinions in a group and makes different equilibria for similar opinions unlikely to exist. On the other hand, the similarity-attraction relationship, in combination with social influence processes, is likely to lead to the creation of small highly coherent groups. Those people whose opinions are similar are mutually attracted (i.e., the connections among them are positive and strong). Such connections generate similarity on other issues, which in turn strengthen the connections, and so on. Unless this process is disturbed by outside influences or by some internal mechanism (e.g., need for uniqueness), the self-reinforcing loop could plausibly lead to the fragmentation of society into small highly coherent groups that share opinions on all issues.

This process may be seen as establishing the basis for the emergence of social institutions, such as interest groups, fraternal organizations, clubs, political parties and lobbies, and religious cults. If subsets of individuals become very strongly connected, the individuals cannot evolve independently of other individuals in the group. When this happens, the group effectively loses many degrees of freedom and the group replaces the individual as the unit of analysis. This observation can be represented in neural networks by the simple assumption that each node reflects a group of like-minded people rather than an individual. In this very important sense, attractor network models hold potential for portraying how social fabric emerges from interacting individual cells.

SUMMARY AND CONCLUSIONS

One should not look at models of cellular automata and neural networks as replacements for social psychological theory and insight. Quite the contrary, the vast majority of rules governing the dynamics of social relations and opinions within social networks were developed within the framework of traditional social psychology. Thus, the similarity-attraction relationship, the tendency toward balanced structures, and the effects of social influence are all well-documented phenomena. Undoubtedly, the incorporation of yet other insights from social psychology would enhance the validity and utility of formal models such as those we describe in this chapter. It can be noted, too, that network models of social process are well known to social psychologists and predate the social applications of cellular automata and neural networks.

Cellular automata and attractor network models are formal tools developed in mathematics and physics to understand the dynamics of complex systems composed of many mutually interacting elements. As such, they allow for a precise description of both the structure and dynamics of phenomena that are not easily captured with traditional tools. At one level of description, for example, the Hopfield learning rule is simply a restatement of the similarity-attraction relationship. However, it goes beyond the verbal description of this relationship by enabling one to state precisely the evolution of the connections between two individuals holding particular positions on an issue. It also allows one to couch the dynamics of any given dyad in the context of other dyads in a larger social structure defined in terms of this relationship. Moreover, given the set of all connections in the social structure, the Hopfield rule allows for a precise description of all possible equilibria and their respective strengths. In addition, one can follow the change in each configuration of opinions in the social network and describe the resulting equilibrium. This potential for achieving precise description of complex social processes may set the stage for the emergence of computational social psychology.

In the natural sciences, an enormous amount of work has been devoted to formulating general laws concerning the dynamics of cellular automata and neural networks (cf. Amit, 1989, Hertz et al., 1991; McClelland & Rumelhart, 1986). The results of this work may be applied to social reality, once it is clear how these models can be instantiated in terms of social processes. We already know, for example, that if the connections in an attractor network are symmetrical, in the absence of noise, the network will always achieve a stable equilibrium. In a similar vein, we know that in the presence of small noise the network will tend to evolve toward stronger equilibria than it will without such noise. Paradoxically, then, the introduction of noise may increase rather than decrease order in the system. We also know how the number of possible equilibria is related to the number of elements, and so forth. Moreover, when modeling social networks, we can draw on rich technology concerning simulation and visualization.

It can be noted in this regard that many of the central theoretical issues concerning cellular automata and neural networks have already been resolved. Currently, then, we are witnessing a fascinating set of applications of these models to issues that spill well beyond the borders of the natural sciences. The knowledge concerning the basic properties of neural networks has generated designs of networks that carry out such tasks as risk assessment, face recognition, medical diagnosis, optical character recognition, statistical analysis, investment strategies, and expert systems. If we successfully map neural networks onto social networks, a rich set of practical applications are likely to be developed. It may be possible, first of all, to predict the course of social processes well into the future and with greater precision than is currently possible. Perhaps more fascinating, it may be possible to influence the course of social processes and thereby solve social problems, such as social polarization and fragmentation.

At the same time, it is important to keep in mind that people are not cells on a grid or neurons in a brain, and that social relations are not the same as neighborhood structures or synaptic connections. To be sure, there are important formal similarities between network models of brain and society, which we outline in this chapter, and many of the differences that exist are of little substantial consequence. Some differences, however, may prove to be crucial for understanding how people change their opinions, moods, and attitudes in a social context. First of all, people may use much more complex decision rules that are the result of factors other than whether social influence exceeds a certain threshold. We can note that although such rules are difficult, if not impossible in principle, to implement in attractor social network models, some relatively complex decision rules have been incorporated into cellular automata models (e.g., Hegselman, in press).

A second fundamental difference concerns the goal-oriented nature of human cognition and action (cf. Carver & Scheier, 1981; Miller, Galanter, & Pribram, 1960; Vallacher, Nowak, Markus, & Strauss, in press; Vallacher & Wegner, 1987). Individuals are not simply reactive, as implied in both cellular automata and neural network models, but rather are active and instrumental in their behavior. Specific models reflecting this feature of social as opposed to neuronal structure were developed by Stockman (1994). In these models, individuals are aware of the structure of social ties involving important decision makers and use this awareness to achieve influence over the decision-making process. In this process, an individual tries to establish either direct links with the decision makers or indirect links via intermediate people, whichever is more effective in light of the individual's resources. Social links may also be established for purely social reasons, such as romantic attraction or camaraderie. More generally, social relations are clearly instrumental in achieving a wide variety of goals (cf. Kelley & Thibaut, 1978).

The structure of goals may guide people's cognitions and actions in ways that are not easily represented in network models. Goal-oriented behavior in a social context may be better described by interacting autonomous agents in the artificial intelligence (AI) approach. The AI approach in general allows one to describe much more complex cognitive structures and processes than do the attractor network formalisms we have described. It should be noted, however, that it is possible to describe each individual as a neural network, and in such a description, very complex cognitive processes, perhaps even those pertaining to goals, may be captured if we assume that each individual corresponds to a whole network rather than to a single node.

Perhaps the most important characteristic of human psychology is the capacity for consciousness. Individuals are not only subject to influences, they are also conscious of the influence being exerted and can make an effort to resist it. Thus, social relations do not always evolve in accordance with similarity of opinions and other formal rules, but rather, may be reflected in consciousness and modified at will to match self-defined values and other prepotent conscious concerns. In a sense, consciousness and reflection create a barrier between individual decisions and factors influencing these decisions. Consciousness can therefore complicate to a high degree the rules of individual behavior and thereby undermine the rules of social dynamics. Simple effects of consciousness, like certain aspects of self-awareness described earlier, may be incorporated into both cellular automata and network models. It is conceivable, however, that other effects of consciousness cannot be captured by formal descriptions, even in principle.

Clearly, a great deal of work remains to be done before cellular automata and attractor network models achieve the status reserved for mature models of social reality. In view of its impressive track record in the natural sciences, though, we suspect that this approach—computational social psychology—will emerge as one of the dominant paradigms for understanding group and societal dynamics. In this role, it is likely to both provide integration to an admittedly fragmented field and generate new lines of theory and research in the years to come.

ACKNOWLEDGMENTS

Preparation of this manuscript was supported in part by Grant SBR 95-11657 from the National Science Foundation and Grant 1H01F07310 from the Polish Committee for Scientific Research. We thank Eugene Burnstein for his many helpful suggestions, especially those regarding the distinction between social and neural networks.

Correspondence concerning this chapter should be addressed to Andrzej Nowak, Department of Psychology, Warsaw University, Stawki 5/7, 00-183 Warsaw, Poland. Electronic mail may be addressed to ANOWAK@SAMBA. ISS.UW.EDU.PL.

REFERENCES

Amit, D. J. (1989). *Modeling brain function: The world of attractor neural networks.* Cambridge, England: Cambridge University Press.

Axelrod, R. (1984). *The evolution of cooperation.* New York: Basic Books.

Axelrod, R., & Bennett, D. S. (1993). A landscape theory of aggregation. *British Journal of Political Science, 23,* 211–233.

Bainbridge, W. S. (1995). Neural network models of religious belief. *Sociological Perspectives, 38,* 483–494.

Brehm, S. S., & Brehm, J. W. (1981). *Psychological reactance: A theory of freedom and control.* New York: Academic Press.

Brewer, M. B., & Kramer, R. M. (1985). The psychology in intergroup attitudes and behavior. *Annual Review of Psychology, 36,* 219–243.

Byrne, D., Clore, G. L., & Smeaton, G. (1986). The attraction hypothesis: Do similar attitudes affect anything? *Journal of Personality and Social Psychology, 51,* 1167–1170.

Cartwright, D., & Harary, F. (1956). Structural balance: A generalization of Heider's theory. *Psychological Review, 63,* 277–293.

Cartwright, D., & Zander, A. (Eds.). (1968). *Group dynamics: Research and theory* (3rd ed.). New York: Harper & Row.

Carver, C. S., & Scheier, M. F. (1981). *Attention and self-regulation: A control-theory approach to human behavior.* New York: Springer-Verlag.

Casti, J. L. (1994). *Complexification.* New York: HarperCollins.

Converse, P. (1964). The nature of belief systems in mass public. In D. E. Apter (Ed.), *Ideology and discontent* (pp. 206–261). New York: The Free Press.

Dittes, J. E., & Kelley, H. H. (1956). Effects of different conditions of acceptance upon conformity to group norms. *Journal of Abnormal and Social Psychology, 59,* 100–107.

Durkheim, E. (1938). *The rules of sociological method.* Chicago: University of Chicago Press.

Edelman, G. M. (1992). *Bright air, brilliant fire.* New York: Basic Books.

Festinger, L. (1957). *A theory of cognitive dissonance.* Evanston, IL: Row, Peterson.

Festinger, L., Schachter, S., & Back, K. (1950). *Social pressures in informal groups: A study of a housing community.* New York: Harper & Row.

Friedkin, N. E., & Johnson, E. C. (1990). Social influence and opinions. *Journal of Mathematical Sociology, 15,* 193–205.

Gardner, E. (1988). The space of interactions in neural network models. *Journal of Physics A, 21,* 257–270.

Glass, L., & Mackey, M. C. (1988). *From clocks to chaos: The rhythms of life.* Princeton, NJ: Princeton University Press.

Gutowitz, H. (1991). *Cellular automata: Theory and experiment.* Cambridge, MA: MIT Press.

Haken, H. (1978). *Synergetics.* Berlin: Springer.

Haken, H. (Ed.). (1982). *Order and chaos in physics, chemistry, and biology.* Berlin: Springer.

Hardin, G. (1968). The tragedy of the commons. *Science, 162,* 1243–1248.

Hebb, D. O. (1949). *The organization of behavior: A neurophysiological theory.* New York: Wiley.

Hegselman, R. (1994). Zur selbstorganisation von solidarnetzwerken unter ungleichen—ein simulationsmodell [On the self-organization of solidarity under inequality—A simulation model.] In K. Homann (Ed.), *Wirtschaftsethische Perspektiven I: Theorie, Ordnungsfragen, Internationale Institutuionen* (pp. 105–129). Berlin: Duncker & Humblot.

Hegselman, R. (in press). Modeling social dynamics with cellular automata. In W. B. G. Liebrand, A. Nowak, & R. Hegselman (Eds.), *Computer modeling of network dynamics.* New York: Elsevier.

Hegselman, R., & Nowak A. (1995). [The bargaining model of social interaction]. Unpublished raw data.

Heider, F. (1958). *The psychology of interpersonal relations.* New York: Wiley.

Hertz, J., Krogh, A., & Palmer, G. (1991). *Introduction to theory of neural computation*. Redwood City, CA: Addison-Wesley.

Hopfield, J. J. (1982). Neural networks and physical systems with emergent collective computational abilities. *Proceedings of the National Academy of Sciences, 79*, 2554–2558.

Hopfield, J. J. (1984). Neurons with graded response have collective computational properties like those of two-state neurons. *Proceedings of National Academy of Sciences USA, 81*, 3088–3092.

Jones, E. E. (1964). *Ingratiation*. New York: Appleton-Century-Crofts.

Kanouse, D. E., & Hanson, L. R. (1971). *Negativity in evaluations*. Morristown, NJ: General Learning Press.

Kelley, H. H., & Thibaut, J. W. (1978). *Interpersonal relations: A theory of interdependence*. New York: Wiley-Interscience.

Kenny, D. A. (1994). *Interpersonal perception: A social relations analysis*. New York: Guilford.

Kilpatrick, S., Gelatt, C. D., & Vecchi, M. P. (1983). Optimization by simulated annealing. *Science, 220*, 671–680.

Landau, L. D., & Lifshitz, E. M. (1964). *Statistical physics*. Oxford, England: Pergamon Press.

Latane, B. (1981). The psychology of social impact. *American Psychologist, 36*, 343–356.

Latane, B., Liu, J., Nowak, A., Bonavento, M., & Zheng, L. (1995). Distance matters: Physical space and social influence. *Personality and Social Psychology Bulletin, 21*, 795–805.

Latane, B., & Nowak, A. (in press). The causes of clustering in self-organizing social systems. *Journal of Communication*.

Latane, B., Nowak, A., & Liu, J. (1994). Measuring emergent social phenomena: Dynamism, polarization and clustering as order parameters of social systems. *Behavioral Science, 39*, 1–24.

Lewenstein, M., & Nowak, A. (1989). Fully connected neural networks with self-control of noise levels. *Physics Review Letter, 62*, 225–229.

Lewenstein, M., Nowak, A., & Latane, B. (1993). Statistical mechanics of social impact. *Physics Review A, 45*, 703–716.

L'Herrou, T. (1992). *Interacting in electronic space: Group dynamics resulting from individual change*. Unpublished master's thesis, Florida Atlantic University.

May, R. (Ed.). (1981). *Theoretical ecology: Principles and applications*. Oxford, England: Blackwell Scientific Publications.

McClelland, J. L., & Rumelhart, D. E. (1986). *Parallel distributed processing: Explorations in the microstructure of cognition* (Vol. 2). Cambridge, MA: MIT Press.

McCulloch, W. S., & Pitts, W. A. (1943). A logical calculus of the ideas imminent in neural nets. *Bulletin of Mathematical Biophysics, 5*, 115–124.

Messick, D. M., & Liebrand, V. B. G. (1995). Individual heuristics and the dynamics of cooperation in large groups. *Psychological Review, 102*, 131–145.

Miller, G., Galanter, E., & Pribram, K. (1960). *Plans and the structure of behavior*. New York: Holt, Rinehart & Winston.

Minsky, M. (1985). *The society of mind*. New York: Simon & Schuster.

Moreno, J. L. (1934). *Who shall survive?* [Monograph, No. 58]. Washington, DC: Nervous and Mental Diseases.

Moscovici, S., & Zavalloni, M. (1969). The group as a polarizer of attitudes. *Journal of Personality and Social Psychology, 12*, 125–135.

Myers, D., & Lamm, H. (1976). The group polarization phenomenon. *Psychological Bulletin, 83*, 602–627.

Newcomb, T. M. (1961). *The acquaintance process*. New York: Holt, Rinehart & Winston.

Nowak, A., Latane, B., & Lewenstein, M. (1994). Social dilemmas exist in space. In U. Schulz, W. Albers, & U. Mueller (Eds.), *Social dilemmas and cooperation* (pp. 114–131). Heidelberg: Springer-Verlag.

Nowak, A., & Lewenstein, M. (1994). Dynamical systems: A tool for social psychology? In R. R. Vallacher & A. Nowak (Eds.), *Dynamical systems in social psychology* (pp. 17–53). San Diego: Academic Press.

Nowak, A., Lewenstein, M., & Frejlak, P. (1996). Dynamics of public opinion and social change. In R. Hegselman & H. O. Peitgen (Eds.), *Modeling social dynamics: Order, chaos, and complexity* (pp. 54–78). Vienna: Helbin.

Nowak, A., Lewenstein, M., & Szamrej, J. (1993). Bable modelem przemian spolecznych [Social transitions occur through bubbles]. *Scientific American* (Polish version), *12*, 16–25.

Nowak, A., Lewenstein, M., & Tarkowski, W. (1994). Repellor neural networks. *Physical Review E, 48*, 1491–1498.

Nowak, A., Szamrej, J., & Latane, B. (1990). From private attitude to public opinion: A dynamic theory of social impact. *Psychological Review, 97*, 362–376.

Nowak, A., Urbaniak, J., & Zienkowski, L. (1994). Clustering processes in economic transition. *RECESS Research Bulletin, 3*, 43–61.

Schlenker, B. R. (1980). *Impression management: The self-concept, social identity, and interpersonal relations*. Belmont, CA: Brooks/Cole.

Schulz, U., Alberts, W., & Mueller, U. (Eds.). (1994). *Social dilemmas and cooperation*. Heidelberg: Springer.

Shelling, T. (1969). Models of segregation. *American Economic Review, 59*, 488–493.

Shelling, T. (1971). Dynamic models of segregation. *Journal of Mathematical Sociology, 1*, 143–186.

Shultz, T. R., & Lepper, M. R. (1995). Cognitive dissonance reduction as constraint satisfaction. *Psychological Review, 103*, 219–240.

Smith, E. R. (in press). Mental representation and memory. In D. Gilbert, S. T. Fiske, & G. Lindzey (Eds.), *Handbook of social psychology* (4th ed.). New York: McGraw-Hill.

Swann, W. B., Jr. (1990). To be adored or to be known? The interplay of self-enhancement and self-verification. In E. T. Higgins & R. M. Sorrentino (Eds.), *Handbook of motivation and cognition* (Vol. 2, pp. 408–448). New York: Guilford.

Tajfel, H., & Turner, J. C. (1986). The social identity theory of intergroup behavior. In S. Worchel & W. G. Austin (Eds.), *Psychology of intergroup relations* (2nd ed., pp. 33–47). Monterey, CA: Nelson-Hall.

Thibaut, J. W., & Kelley, H. H. (1959). *The social psychology of groups*. New York: Wiley.

Ulam, S. (1952). Random processes and transformations. *Proceedings of International Congress of Mathematics, 2*, 264–275.

Vallacher, R. R. (1980). An introduction to self theory. In D. M. Wegner & R. R. Vallacher (Eds.), *The self in social psychology* (pp. 3–30). New York: Oxford University Press.

Vallacher, R. R., Nowak, A., Markus, J., & Strauss, J. (in press). Dynamics in the coordination of mind and action. In M. Kofta, G. Weary, & G. Sedlek (Eds.), *Personality functioning and social cognition: An action control view*. New York: Plenum.

Vallacher, R. R., & Wegner, D. M. (1987). What do people think they're doing? Action identification and human behavior. *Psychological Review, 94*, 1–15.

von Neumann, J. (1966). *Theory of self-reproducing automata*. Champaign, IL: University of Illinois Press.

Wasserman, S., & Faust, K. (1994). *Social network analysis: Methods and applications*. New York: Cambridge University Press.

Weisbuch, G. (1992). *Complex systems dynamics*. Redwood City, CA: Addison-Wesley.

Wicklund, R. A., & Frey, D. (1980). Self-awareness theory: When the self makes a difference. In D. M. Wegner & R. R. Vallacher (Eds.), *The self in social psychology* (pp. 31–54). New York: Oxford University Press.

Wolfram, S. (Ed.). (1986). *Theory and applications of cellular automata*. Singapore: World Scientific.

10

ATTITUDE, BELIEFS, AND OTHER MINDS: SHARED REPRESENTATIONS IN SELF-ORGANIZING SYSTEMS

J. Richard Eiser
Mark J. A. Claessen
Jonathan J. Loose
University of Exeter

SOCIAL PSYCHOLOGY AND THE INDIVIDUAL

The trouble with most definitions, in psychology at any rate, is that they tend to invoke further concepts at least as ambiguous as the original. These in turn require definition, and so we can be led down a path of infinite regress. When Jones and Gerard (1967) defined the field of social psychology as involving "the scientific study of the behavior of individuals as a function of social stimuli" (p. 1), they were not unaware of these dangers. They anticipated the need for a justification of a scientific methodology, an emphasis on behavioral outcomes of various kinds, and a specification of what was meant by social stimuli. Jones and Gerard (1967, p. 1) defined these broadly as "stimuli that come from other people." The emphasis on individuals, however, seemed less in need of defense. Psychology as a whole shared this emphasis, and social psychology was part of this whole. What made social psychology "social" was that it studied how people can influence each other's cognitions and behavior through what they do. Yet, throughout this, the main unit of analysis remained the individual, both as an actor and as a perceiver of the world of other people.

No doubt, for much of the time, we take the individual as our unit of analysis merely for reasons of convenience rather than from explicit conviction. Even so, this approach carries a particular danger for social psychology. It leads too easily to the presumption that representations (including attitudes and beliefs) are a kind of private property. If we presume this,

313

it becomes hard to see how any such representations can be communicated or shared.

In this chapter, therefore, we deliberately depart from this convention. Instead of considering simply the question of how an individual social perceiver may interpret information from other people, we explore some of the products and processes of communication among individuals in interaction with one another. The starting point for this is the idea that the activity of any social group depends both on the information and challenges coming from outside and on the patterns of intercommunication and mutual influence among its members. It appears to us that such an idea can be translated fairly directly into the conceptual language of connectionism, with groups considered as networks and individuals—as a first approximation—as units within networks. Social relations and communication may then be defined in terms of the patterns of interconnectivity among the component units. Our purpose is to argue for the merit of attempting such a translation in general terms. We do not pretend at all to have identified the best form of network architecture or learning rule to produce convincing simulations of human social interaction, but hope to show something of what can be achieved with this approach, granted particular starting assumptions.

We first consider two concepts of fundamental importance to our argument, representation and self-organization, and then proceed to describe the findings of simulations of two rather different forms of social interaction. In the first of these, Heider's (1946) notion of cognitive balance is extended to the context of multiperson groups. As will be remembered, Heider predicted that individuals will seek to organize their attitudes and interpersonal relationships so that they agree with people they like (and like people with whom they agree), but will disagree with those they dislike (and dislike those with whom they disagree). Although this principle can be simply stated, it is unclear how, or how completely, it will be followed in larger groups where everyone is attempting to achieve balance with everyone else. The second set of simulations is not a test of any specific psychological theory, but instead considers some of the difficulties involved in individuals establishing, through communication with each other, a common linguistic code or label for specific objects. Finally, we draw some general conclusions regarding the merits of considering groups of individuals—no less than individuals within groups—as self-organizing systems, the activity of which reflects parallel constraint satisfaction and dynamic interaction among their members.

Representation

The term (mental) representation is used frequently, if loosely, to refer to people's interpretations and knowledge as distinct from the actual objects and events that are represented. This distinction allows for the obvious fact that our perceptions of physically present objects (or our memories of absent ones) can often be highly selective, and that other people's perceptions of the same objects can be selective in different ways from ours. As we move from consideration of physical object perception to social perception and attitude formation, this selectivity and relativity of viewpoint becomes not only even more self-evident, but theoretically central. People frequently disagree with one another in their views of attitudinal or social objects. Were this not so, there would be little, if anything, for theories of attitudes and social cognition to explain.

What is important, though, is not just that we can disagree, but that there is something we can disagree *about*. When we express an attitude, we are not just saying how we feel. We are making a reality claim that others may dispute. Disagreements matter precisely because they undermine a consensual definition of reality. Without consensus, it becomes difficult, as Kelley (1967) argued, to attribute objectivity to our impressions of objects and events. We can only talk about consensus or disagreement, however, if we have a means of identifying common objects of reference and of comparing different individuals' representations of these common objects. Interpersonal communication, and with it the attribution of reality to things, thus both requires and enables our representations to be *shared*. Interpersonal communication depends, obviously and crucially, upon our use of language. For this reason, it has frequently been assumed that representation itself is essentially a linguistic process (Fodor, 1975), depending on how we assign symbols to things, and how we combine such symbols into propositions. From a connectionist perspective, this assumption is unnecessary. If we are considering how information about the world can be encoded and stored within a cognitive system, we do not require any single component part or unit of the system to carry symbolic meaning in isolation from any other. It is sufficient that the different components or units can be organized or linked with one another in different ways, so that activation (that is, information) can pass from one unit or group of units to another. The distribution of activation across the different units of the network then constitutes the representation of any input pattern, whereas knowledge or memory is constituted by the weighted connections between the units. Because these connections or associative links are what determine, along with any input, the net activations of the separate units, they can be regarded as the cognitive structure through which the system encodes, stores, and accesses information about the world.

Although representation itself need not be symbolic, the achievement of shared representations through communication will almost certainly demand the use of some symbolic code. Applying a connectionist approach, communicative acts, such as expressing an attitude or simply assigning a name to an object, are forms of *output* (from the cognitive system of the communicator), which in turn constitute *input* for any recipients of the communication. We are thus dealing with a dynamic system, in which recipients associate others' expressive acts with their context and adjust their own expressive behavior accordingly. Representation and meaningful communication are thus properties of the system as a whole, rather than of any parts in isolation.

Self-Organization

The term self-organization highlights a very important assumption about how patterns can emerge from transformations of information within systems. There is no need for a grand design, unifying purpose, or "central executive" to hold things together. All that is required is that different units within the network each respond coherently to the information they receive, that is, to activation from other interconnected or nearby units. Coordination at the level of the system can thus be the cumulative effect of local adjustments by separate units to their immediate environment.

Examples of self-organization abound in nature. Indeed, many would argue that nature *is* self-organizing (Kauffman, 1993). Consider, for instance, the collective behavior of shoals of fish or flocks of birds. What can appear to an observer as coordination at the level of the group is in fact the outcome of fixed action patterns—essentially, behavioral algorithms—that govern the responses of each individual fish or bird, primarily to the movements and positions of its nearest neighbors. It is the repeated application of the same algorithm throughout the system that enables the shoal or flock to move as one. Local replication produces patterning at a higher level, rather than vice versa. Furthermore, the kinds of patterning produced by processes of self-organization become more complex as the system itself evolves. These same processes allow novel or creative responses to changed environments in the form of altered interactions between constituent parts of the system. The ubiquity of self-organization within all biological (and physical) systems testifies to its adaptive function. Cells, organisms, and ecosystems have evolved and coevolved to respond in such ways not so as to satisfy some drive to produce a higher order pattern, but because they simply would not have survived to this point if they had responded otherwise.

Intriguingly, one of the best examples of self-organization may be our own self, or self-concept. Hume (1740/1911) is possibly the best-known proponent of this viewpoint. He argued that we construct a sense of personal identity through applying principles of association to our successive "impressions." These principles are closely in keeping with more modern psychological principles of learning, whether in human beings, other animals, or connectionist networks. Specifically, he proposed that thoughts are associated with one another (to form concepts) on the basis of resemblance, contiguity in time and place, and "causation" (by which he simply meant if–then succession). Hence, according to Hume (1740/1911):

> we may observe that the true idea of the human mind, is to consider it as a system of different perceptions or different existences, which are linked together by the relation of cause and effect, and mutually produce, destroy, influence, and modify each other. Our impressions give rise to their corresponding ideas; and these ideas, in their turn, produce other impressions. One thought chases another, and draws after it a third, by which it is expelled in its turn. In this respect, I cannot compare the soul more properly to anything than to a republic or commonwealth, in which the several members are united by the reciprocal ties of government and subordination, and give rise to other persons who propagate the same republic in the incessant changes of its parts. (p. 247)

Using the societal metaphor of a republic accords closely with contemporary theoretical notions of systems and networks to describe mental processes. It implies also that it is reasonable to look for a common conceptual language or set of principles to account both for the intrapersonal cognitive activities of single individuals and the interpersonal interactions that define social groups. From the point of view of general principles that describe the activity of interactive systems, it can often be irrelevant whether we are talking about groups, single persons, or even single thoughts. What matters is how each constituent affects and is affected by the activity of other constituents within the network or system. Specifying how this works may seem a daunting task, but a few simple assumptions can allow us to at least make a start.

First, the system as a whole is dynamic, and we know that the repeated iteration of extremely simple transformations can lead dynamic systems to behave in extremely complex ways. Hence, the fact that we are trying to explain very complex phenomena, such as human thought and social behavior, should not deter us from seeking explanations in terms of simple underlying processes.

Second, if we conceive of a system as composed fundamentally of very simple constituent units, we should not expect these units to behave other than in very simple ways. The complexity comes from the interconnections between the units, and the massive number of permutations that these can conceivably involve. Hence, at the level of the unit, the processes must be simple if they are to be plausible.

Third, although we may be able to propose and test possible models to describe the activity of a system as a whole, we should not be unduly inhibited by the possibility that some other, untested, model might yield the same predictions. Principles of self-organization do not typically produce unique solutions, hence, biodiversity. For an illustration of this, consider the following example. Ask eight people to stand and form a circle, and they will do so quite easily. Yet there are 40,320 alternative solutions—that is permutations of positions—all of which would satisfy the same demand. Clearly, our eight people will not be concerned to find a unique solution, just one that works. Even so, granted particular initial conditions (e.g., where everyone was sitting or standing beforehand, who was most friendly with whom), we would expect some permutations to be more likely than others. We might, for instance, posit that everyone would try to move the shortest distance, and stand next to their best friends, both of which would be essentially "local" constraints. True, this is not quite a pure example, because it is implicit that the eight people (unlike flocks of birds) know what kind of shape it is that they are trying to form. But still, they do not have any *particular* circle in mind. Quite probably what will often happen is that everyone will start by trying to position themselves between two others, and only then will those at each end of the straggly line shuffle round to join up with each other. Even where people have a form of higher order knowledge (a concept of a circle) that can steer behavior in a "top-down" fashion, how this knowledge is put into practice can still depend on lower order or "bottom-up" processes of self-organization.

Connectionist methods and principles seem to us to be well suited to an exploration of such processes, both within and between individuals. From a connectionist perspective, individuals and social groups are both examples of systems. Systems, in their turn, can be characterized in terms of the connections among their component units. It is the presence of such connections that permits the transmission of information and hence coordination of activity at the level of the system as a whole. One feature that distinguishes connectionism from most other approaches is the assumption that such connections between component units are strengthened or weakened through learning so as to represent patterns and regularities in the information with which the system has to deal.

We attempt to illustrate the potential of this approach by describing two sets of simulations. The first considers attitude structure as a form of self-organization within a social system. Specifically, it simulates one theoretical account of how different individuals may come to evaluate an attitude object in ways that take account of their feelings of liking and disliking for each other. The second investigates how members of a social group may come to use symbols with a shared reference—specifically, how they may come to agree on how objects should be named. How we evaluate things and how we name them are only two relatively simple examples of representations that could come to be shared. Even so, the challenges they pose to a learning system are importantly different. Agreement at the attitudinal level can be achieved if, for instance, everyone rates a common object positively. This does not preclude these same people later giving the same positive rating to another object. Indeed, we know that this can happen very easily. However, naming requires a more distinctive association between a symbolic expression and its object of reference. We expect that the name assigned to an object will not merely be used in common by different interlocutors, but will distinguish that object from others to which different names have been assigned. As we shall see, this familiar aspect of language poses an additional challenge to the modeling of social and cognitive processes.

ATTINET: A SELF-ORGANIZING CONNECTIONIST SIMULATION OF COGNITIVE BALANCE

Introduction

We are claiming, then, that self-organization is a crucial feature of any complex system, and that there is therefore utility in taking social *systems* as our unit of analysis. This way, we may examine the impact of the system on the social cognitions of the individuals that constitute it. Further, by examining the social system using similar tools and techniques as are utilized in investigations of individual cognition, we support the notion that the society of mind and the societies of groups may be partially understood by virtue of the same underlying processes.

The first model to be explained conceptualizes Fritz Heider's cognitive balance theory (Heider, 1946) in terms of a highly recurrent connectionist network. Cognitive balance was chosen because it specifies a local rule, a rule by which each individual will seek to govern his or her attitudes and relations to others. A self-organizing system requires such a local rule, and hence cognitive balance theory would seem to be one very appropriate scheme for simulation. The development of such a model requires certain assumptions in Heider's work to be made explicit or criticized. Specifically, through an elaboration of the representation of an attitude, the notion of a negative relation is made explicit and the assumption that liking relationships must be reciprocal is questioned. Three experiments are performed with the model. The first demonstrates that the model is capable of restoring imbalanced structures to a balanced state, but notes that the model achieves this through modification of the relationships between individuals only, while leaving attitudes to impersonal objects largely unchanged. In order to try to explain why the model behaves in this way, the second experiment then asks whether balance may be restored to the model through attitude change alone. The question is answered in the negative for our model. Finally, a third experiment attempts to redress the balance between attitude and relationship change, and concludes that the relative rates of attitude and relationship change are critical for a solution to the problem of imbalance. On the basis of these experiments, we draw some conclusions about how balance may develop in n-person groups. Further, while noting the limitations of the model, we are able to see that a dynamical systems perspective can shed new light on well-established social psychological theories.

Cognitive Balance Theory

A cornerstone of much social psychological research over the last 50 years has been the notion of cognitive dissonance (Festinger, 1957) or cognitive imbalance (Heider, 1958). Common to all such theories is the notion that an undesirable state of conflict can arise within a cognitive system, such that the system seeks to reduce this conflict in some way. In the case of cognitive balance theory, the undesirable condition is termed an *imbalanced* state. Imbalance is understood in terms of a conflict within a triad of relations consisting of the attitude of an individual (P) to some object (X), P's perception of the attitude of a second individual (O) to X, and the relationship between P and O.

According to Heider, an imbalanced state exists when agreement regarding the evaluation of X is present alongside a negative liking between P and O, or when disagreement regarding the evaluation of X is conjoined with a positive liking relation between P and O. Others, especially Newcomb (1953), disagreed. They argued that an individual is disinterested in the attitudes of others whom he or she dislikes, and so there can only be a state of imbalance when the PO relation is positive. In terms of our model, the different assumptions amount to different algorithms for changing relationships and attitudes as a function of other relationships and attitudes. These differences are not investigated here.

Heiderian balance is easy to conceptualize in terms of a *triad*, with each of the entities P, O, and X occupying a vertex, and the connections representing the various relations between them. Heider included two kinds of relations in his theory-sentiment relations (such as liking) and unit relations that represent some kind of bond or link. Difficulties with the notion of a unit relation led to most work focusing exclusively on sentiment relations (Cartwright & Harary, 1956), and this trend is followed here.

Interest in theories of cognitive consistency peaked during the 1960s, but slowed greatly after that. Read and Miller (1994) argued that a key reason for this was the lack of a representational system powerful enough to investigate consistency in contexts broader than those of the simple structures provided by such as Heider. The preliminary model suggested here (along with others, for example, Read & Miller, 1994; Shultz & Lepper, 1996) demonstrates that the representational capacities of connectionist networks, and their potential for solving problems involving the satisfaction of multiple constraints, takes us beyond this impasse to a new consideration of imbalance or dissonance effects.

This new research into cognitive consistency must investigate how imbalance might develop and be conceptualized in a larger structure containing more individuals and more relations. We must ask what kinds of processes may be involved in achieving balance in a group consisting of both multiple individuals and multiple attitude objects. The present model seeks to do this, and thus not only begins to investigate the implications of balance theory, but extends it as well. This means that we are exploring areas where Heider's own predictions were not explicit. For instance, it is unclear whether it is plausible to expect total balance to be achieved in multiperson groups, or exactly what are the constraints that influence how much balance is attained. All that can be said is that Heider's theory should predict that multiperson groups, no less than dyads, will seek as much balance as is indeed attainable within the limits of any given set of constraints. Another significant question that was not addressed by Heider is that of which relations are likely to change in order to turn an imbalanced state into a balanced one. Again, it is unclear whether this is the kind of question that permits an absolute answer, as opposed to one contingent on specific conditions and assumptions about the kinds of interactions among different individuals making up a group. We cannot attempt to compare here the effects of all possible constraints on such interactions. However, with the important caveat that any findings are contingent on the specific constraints and assumptions built into the model we are using, this problem is one which the dynamical systems approach will turn out to answer very nicely. This approach can also help address the criticism that balance theory treats relations as reciprocal as a matter of course, although it is nevertheless clear that this may not be the case. Unrequited love represents imbalance for both parties!

Extending the Representational Model

One significant attempt was made to extend the concept of balance. Cartwright and Harary clearly outlined the inadequacies of Heider's original triadic structures, and applied more advanced graph-theoretical techniques in an attempt to provide a conception of balance extending to an arbitrary number of vertices and relations (Cartwright & Harary, 1956). The model presented here goes beyond their conceptualization in not only providing a representational system for *n*-person groups, but also a system in which balance is able to *develop*, in that each individual is motivated to seek balance in the context of a group of others motivated in the same way. Thus, we are able to look at the process by which balance may develop within a group, as well as the characterization of what balance may mean for a group.

Apart from claiming that Heider's theory should be able to encompass multiple vertices and relations, Cartwright and Harary criticized cognitive balance theory by claiming that the status of a negative relation is unclear in the model. More than that, however, the theory is limited in not being able to represent evaluations and liking relationships that vary as a matter of degree, assuming that a binary representation will suffice. It would be better to be able to place individuals somewhere on an agreement–disagreement dimension (cf. Osgood & Tannenbaum, 1955). This model maintains the notion that there is a binary element to attitudes, but places attitudes on a continuum from +1 (strong positive liking/evaluation) to 0 (no engagement or interest) to −1 (strong negative liking/evaluation). Like Thurstone, we do not consider attitudes to be this simple (Thurstone, 1928; see Eiser, 1994, for a complex alternative), nevertheless, again like Thurstone, the notion that attitudes can be measured on a dimension is seen as a step forward from a merely dichotomous representation. This extension to balance theory answers Cartwright and Harary's criticism, in that negative relations are now clearly defined.

Multiple Constraint Satisfaction in Balanced Structures

For the perceiver, the task of turning an imbalanced situation into a balanced situation is one of *constraint satisfaction*. Even in the simple case of a triad, in which the perceiver is considering his or her liking of the other person, the solution to the problem will depend on both the perceiver's attitude and that of the other person. In order for this traditional Heiderian triad to become balanced, the structure must be modified so that either only one or all three relations are positive. It is clear that even at this stage there are various ways of resolving the imbalance, and balance theory gives us no clue as to which of these relations is likely to be most susceptible to change. As the number of nodes increases, so the number of different balanced possibilities increases. Constraints will begin to conflict, because in attempting to resolve balance with one individual, there is the potential for a new state of imbalance to arise with many others. To take a simple example, at the time of this writing there is much contention about the role of the British monarchy. If Dick likes both Mark and Jon, but Jon and Mark disagree regarding whether or not the British monarchy should be disestablished, then it is clear that if Dick were to change his attitude toward the monarchy in order to be balanced with Jon, then this will cause imbalance with Mark, and vice versa. As groups increase in size, so the potential for this kind of situation explodes.

The constraints on the "multivertex" problem of balance are many, and are interactive. Each individual is involved in a process of multiple constraint satisfaction—he or she is involved in a balancing act in which the conflicting views of all the others in the social environment can determine a set of relationships that maximizes balance for the individual. At the same time, these relationships, thus determined, are capable of producing an attitudinal shift in the individual. When we realize that every individual in the group is involved in this interactive process of relationship and attitude change, the enormity of this interactive constraint-satisfaction problem becomes apparent. We have an example of a dynamical system.

ATTINET: A CONNECTIONIST MODEL OF COGNITIVE BALANCE

Multiple Constraint Satisfaction in Connectionist Networks

The most popular form of connectionist model, which tends to characterize what a connectionist network is, is a network in which the individual *units* are arranged into two or more layers, and are trained to associate an input to an output by some method of reverse error propagation that allows error to be corrected at the local (unit) level. Typically, there would be three layers of units, and some variant of back-propagation would be used (Rumelhart & McClelland, 1986). These networks are trained to associate a set of arbitrary patterns presented on the input with a corresponding set of patterns presented at the output. The same set of connection weights must be adjusted by a process of gradient descent such that they satisfy each of the input–output mappings. Over time, the weights evolve to a point at which they satisfy the multiple constraints inherent in the different mappings. Later, we describe a model built from these feedforward networks. However, the basic principle of multiple constraint satisfaction, which as we have already seen is analogous to the problem of n-person balance, is exemplified even more clearly by a recurrent architecture.

Attinet is a completely recurrent network, in which the output of every unit is connected to the input of every other unit. The implication of this is that the network cannot be seen in terms of layers, but must be viewed as a thoroughly interactive system. There are no separate input and output units as in the feedforward case. In a recurrent network, the input is provided to each unit, and the network is then allowed to settle down to a stable state at which the new output can be read off from the same units. The recurrent nature of the network causes its behavior to seem more opaque, and it is therefore useful to remember that just as in the feedforward case, the network is attempting to satisfy the multiple constraints inherent in the inputs; it is just that the recurrent net is satisfying constraints in *parallel*. Allowing such intense interaction makes it practically impossible to discover in advance whether constraining the network on the basis of balance theory will cause it to settle to a stable state, or what kinds of rules would be required to make it do so.

From Nodes to Units—Attinet's Representational Scheme

There is clearly an analogy between Heider's conception of a social structure, and the structure of a connectionist network like Attinet. Individuals changing both their patterns of interaction and their evaluations of shared attitude objects are analogous to units or subnetworks modifying their connections with one another, and their activations over time.

Attinet assumes that individuals may be represented as connectionist units (hereafter, units). Figure 10.1 illustrates the structure of a typical unit of the network. It can be seen that fundamental to each unit is its activation level and its weighted connections to other units. Each time that input is received from other units, the *activation function* produces a new activation as a function of both the input to the unit, and the unit's previous activation. This activation then constitutes the output to further units in the network.

Figure 10.1 also shows the network's representational scheme. Attitudes toward impersonal attitude objects are to be thought of as activations, and interpersonal liking relationships as connection weights. Immediately we find that we have the potential for a model that represents evaluations and liking relationships on a continuum. Activation does not have to be binary, and in this case, activation may range between ± 1, thus the activation of a single unit is able to represent both positive and negative evaluations of varying degree, as well as a midregion (0) representing no involvement. Similarly, connections can be weighted in the range ± 1, and can thus represent the range from strong dislike, through indifference, to strong liking.

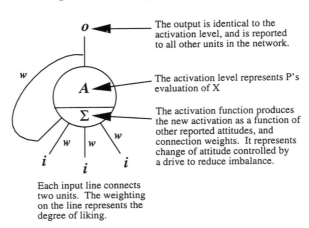

The output is identical to the activation level, and is reported to all other units in the network.

The activation level represents P's evaluation of X

The activation function produces the new activation as a function of other reported attitudes, and connection weights. It represents change of attitude controlled by a drive to reduce imbalance.

Each input line connects two units. The weighting on the line represents the degree of liking.

FIG. 10.1. A single unit within the Attinet model.

Note that a network constructed of these units will not assume reciprocity of relationships. Because every unit has its own input connection from every other unit, the weighting of the link between any unit a and any other unit b is independent of the link between unit b and unit a.

Hence, we have a representational scheme for a social structure. The next problem is how balance might be measured in such a structure. The simplest method for characterizing balance, and the method used here, is to break down the network into a set of traditional Heiderian triads, each involving two units and a connection between them. Each network triad can be considered balanced so long as either one or all of the values are positive. The percentage of all triads that are balanced represents a global balance measure for the entire network.

Modeling a "Pressure Toward Balance"

Pressure on Evaluations. Having set up the social structure, some local rules must be devised that allow each "individual" to adjust its evaluations in order to attempt to place itself in a balanced environment. It turns out that a standard connectionist activation function will do just that.

Typically, a unit's activation function will first produce the dot product of the input—the sum of individual inputs multiplied by their corresponding connection weights. Because both weights and inputs may be positive or negative, the dot product, when applied to the activation (evaluation of impersonal object) represents a pressure toward balance. If the dot product is positive, then the pressure is to generate a balanced structure in which the individual's attitude is also positive. Conversely, if the dot product is negative, then the pressure is to produce balance with a negative attitude.

For example, let us assume that unit P has a positive activation (i.e., P approves of X), and has a negative weighting on the connection that provides input from unit O (i.e., P dislikes O). Let us further assume that the output of unit O (its activation) is positive (i.e., O approves of X). In this case, we have a representation in which P dislikes O (because the connection weight is negative), but nevertheless agrees in the evaluation of the impersonal object (because the activations of P and O share the same sign). This should cause P to be under pressure to disagree with O, if balance is to be restored (without changing the status of the liking relationship). This is in fact what happens, because the product of a positive input and a negative weight is itself negative—and would therefore lower the value of the activation of P if the two were summed. The amount by which P's activation is lowered will be proportional to the strength of O's attitude, and the strength of the relationship between them.

The dot product of all the inputs, then, represents a group average pressure toward balance over all the relationships in which the individual is involved. This is combined with the previous activation of X by feeding X's activation back to the input via an autoweight (see Fig. 10.1) that does not change it (i.e., it has a value of 1). The activation function described can be expressed mathematically thus:

$$A_t = \left(\sum_{i=1}^{n} \frac{w_i x_i}{n} \right) + A_{t-1}. \tag{1}$$

In fact, the activation function also includes the standard sigmoid squashing function (see chapter 2, Rumelhart & McClelland, 1986), and is therefore actually:

$$A_t = \frac{1}{1 + e^{-\left(\sum_{i=1}^{N} \frac{w_i x_i}{n} \right) + A_{t-1}}}. \tag{2}$$

In this way, pressure toward balance has been modeled to change evaluations of impersonal attitude objects as a function of interpersonal liking. Of course, interpersonal liking should also be free to vary under the constraint of balance, and at this point, we must ask how to characterize agreement and disagreement.

Pressure on Liking Relationships. If we are to modify a relationship on the basis of the level of agreement or disagreement between two individuals, then we must quantify what agreement and disagreement mean to our model. Clearly the level of disagreement is going to be a function of the attitudes of the two people involved. One possibility that we initially investigated was to multiply the two attitudes together, and consider a negative result to be disagreement, and a positive result to be agreement. However, this was found to produce some artifacts not present with an additive rule.[1] The

---

[1]The appeal of a multiplicative rule was that the function used for modifying relationships would be identical to that which modifies the attitudes. In the case of attitudes, the pressure toward balance from any individual would be the product of that individual's attitude and the relationship between the two. In the case of relationships, the pressure toward balance exerted by an individual on another would be the product of the attitudes of the two individuals. Thus, the learning rule and activation function would operate identically on different relations within a Heiderian triad. The chief problem with this measure is that a multiplicative rule gives a different value of disagreement for two individuals who are totally agreed, but not highly polarized as compared with two individuals who are totally agreed but highly polarized. This makes it difficult to justify the computed value as a measure of disagreement at all. A second problem is that the use of a multiplicative rule tends to pull the connection weights to zero. This happens because the product of any two numbers i where $0 < i < 1$ will be smaller than either of the original values.

Hebbian learning rule states that connections are to be strengthened when two units are simultaneously active. For our purposes, we modify this principle slightly, strengthening a connection when two units are *similarly activated*. This means the reduction of connection weights when the activations of the two units are discrepant, and the increasing of weights when the activations are more similar. We are therefore interested in the difference between the two activations as opposed to their product. The implemented rule uses this principle to compute either a measure of agreement or a measure of disagreement between two units.

If a particular relationship is to be made more negative, then this should be done as a function of the level of disagreement between the two individuals, whereas if a relationship is to be made more positive, this should be a function of agreement. Thus, we need two additive rules. If we consider the two individuals to disagree (to whatever extent), then we decrease the strength of their relationship by an amount proportional to their disagreement (which is taken to be the difference between the two attitudes). If we consider the two individuals to agree, then we increase the strength of their relationship by an amount proportional to their agreement. All that is needed then is some definition of agreement. We have taken agreement to be the complement of disagreement. If two individuals have attitudes of, say +0.4 and −0.3, then we have a disagreement of 0.7. This is 35% of the maximum possible disagreement (which is $1 - (-1) = 2$). Thus, if the two individuals are 35% disagreed, we would say they are also 65% agreed.

The final thing that the learning rule must do is to decide what constitutes agreement, and what constitutes disagreement. There are two options here. Either we can take the zero point on the scale as not being significant, and consider two individuals to disagree when the differences between their attitudes are greater than a specific value, or we can take the zero point to be the arbiter, considering only attitudes on opposite sides of zero to be in disagreement. We use the latter strategy here, leaving the comparison between the two as a question for future work.

Thus, we can now state our learning rule mathematically as:

If $A_i.A_j \geq 0$ (i.e., there is agreement between the two units) then:

$$\delta \propto 1 - \left| \frac{A_i - A_j}{2} \right|. \tag{3}$$

If $A_i.A_j < 0$ (i.e., there is disagreement between the two units) then:

$$\delta \propto - \left| \frac{-A_i - A_j}{2} \right|. \tag{4}$$

Simulations

In order for changes in evaluation and liking relationship to occur simultaneously, an epoch of the simulation consisted of all units updating their activations and weights simultaneously. Hence, every activation and every weight was updated once per epoch. The relative significance of weight change and activation change was controlled by a pair of constants, β, which is identical to the traditional *learning rate* in a connectionist network, and α, which was a similar multiplier applied to the input to each unit, and so scaling the overall impact.

RESULTS

Three experiments are reported, each providing an insight both into Attinet and balance theory. The networks used each consisted of 10 units. Initial investigations with group size demonstrated no major effect of scaling between 5 and 50 units, and hence these results are generalizable over that range. Each experiment began with all connection weights and activation levels being set randomly within the ± 1 limit. The reported results represent generalizations on the basis of multiple simulations from differently seeded random starting points.

Basic Algorithm

Initially, the development of balance was simulated with α and β set to the same value (.50). With all activations and weights initially randomly distributed, typical results are shown in Fig. 10.2. A number of points are significant. First, the level of balance in the network rose quickly from its initial value of around 50% of all triads, to the 100% mark. In the example shown, complete balance was found after only five epochs of training. It is interesting, although not necessarily surprising, that the percentage of relationships that were reciprocated increased quickly and tracked the development of balance.

The most significant feature of the initial simulations comes from the observation that balance was achieved by virtue of changing relationships as opposed to evaluations. Careful consideration of the network reveals that this occurred because each individual had 10 degrees of freedom available with which to solve the balance problem. Nine of these degrees of freedom were connection weights, and only one was an activation. Hence, the majority of the change was likely to occur in the connection weights, as it did.

This observation led to the speculation that perhaps the activation function is irrelevant, and that, given enough individuals in the group (i.e., enough degrees of freedom in the connection weights), the learning rule

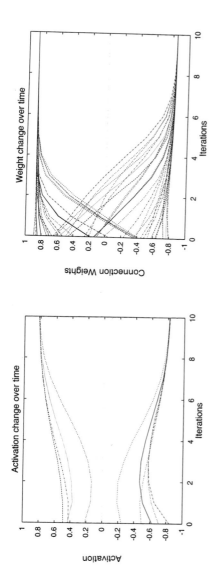

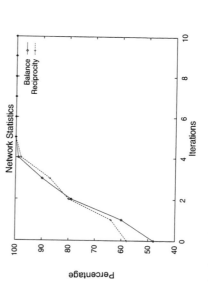

FIG. 10.2. Results for a 10-unit network demonstrating a fast resolution of imbalance.

would be able to produce balance on its own. Subsequent simulations in which activations were held constant throughout demonstrated that this was in fact the case. Throughout, the learning rule was able to find an entirely balanced solution from the initial random configuration.

Activation Modification Only

In order to investigate further the utility of the activation function, a number of simulations were run in which the relationships were held constant, and only evaluations were allowed to vary (see Fig. 10.3). As predicted, the activation function was not able to bring the networks to 100% balance. However, it was not known prior to simulation whether the activations would settle to a steady state, or whether they would oscillate perpetually. Interestingly, the network did settle to a steady state. As can be seen from the example simulation in Fig. 10.3, the network took longer to settle, and settled with only 58% of triads balanced. This might suggest that the network is falling into a local minimum during its futile search for a solution to the imbalance problem. Without more degrees of freedom, the network might be expected either to do this or to oscillate continually (although we found no evidence for the latter behavior with this model). An alternative possible interpretation is that the network in fact found a global minimum—albeit one of less than total balance—that is the best solution that can be achieved granted the specific constraints and starting conditions under which the simulation was run. The point, however, is that there is nothing in Heider's theory to suggest that groups, of whatever size, should be satisfied with anything less than total balance. Thus in theory, if not in real life, groups would be predicted to continue to engage in cognitive work (reappraising attitudes and/or relationships) so long as *any* imbalance persists. Whether such extra cognitive work actually succeeds in further reduction of imbalance must clearly depend on the general constraints on the model, and the configuration of the network at the time.

Slow Learning ($\beta \ll \alpha$)

The final set of simulations reported attempted to redress the distribution of power across the activation function and learning rule by reducing β to be orders of magnitude smaller than α. Both activations and weights were able to change, but the change to the weights was insignificant compared to the change in activations for each epoch of the network. Power was redistributed by reducing the ease with which the connection weights changed. This was achieved by limiting the influence of the learning rule.

A typical set of results is shown in Fig. 10.4. Significantly, the network took a large number of epochs to stabilize (around 150), and stabilized without achieving a complete solution to the imbalance problem.

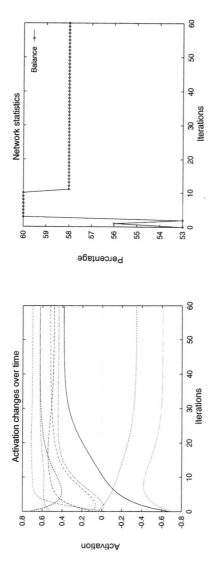

FIG. 10.3. Results for a 10-unit network attempting to resolve imbalance without recourse to relationship change.

331

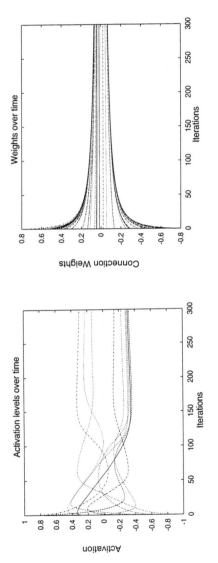

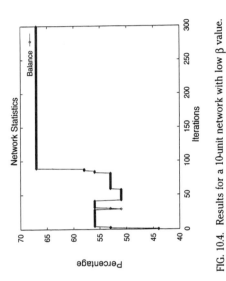

FIG. 10.4. Results for a 10-unit network with low β value.

332

It seems that the learning rule was unable to respond quickly enough to the activation function for the two parts of the algorithm to work together, and hence, there was an imbalance within the individual units. In other words, while revising his or her attitude in the direction of balance with a given set of interpersonal relationships, the individual also starts to modify the relationships in an attempt to achieve balance with the prior attitude. However, by the time such relationship changes are under way, a new attitude position will have already been adopted. The changes in the relationships will therefore no longer be appropriate for achieving balance with the new attitude. When it comes to finding balance, the learning rule and activation function can sometimes be said to be working against each other.

Discussion

The model utilized a dynamical systems approach, taking the system rather than the individual as the unit of analysis, and demonstrating that balance can develop in a system as a function of individual elements seeking balance for themselves, each responding to their own unique environment.

The initial simulations demonstrate that the network can become totally balanced under the right conditions and that the simplest solution to the balance problem does imply total reciprocity of relationships, as Heider originally assumed.

More significantly, the model suggests the possible constraints on the development of balance. What determines whether or not a social system will become balanced is both the number of parameters that an individual can change (i.e., attitudes or liking relations) and how easily or rapidly these can be changed. Granted the specific assumptions incorporated in our model, it is clear that Heider's theory, when extended to more individuals than the two he began with, is typically going to imply that attitudes influence liking, and not the other way around. The reason for this asymmetry is that changing PX to produce balance in triad PO_1X may simultaneously produce imbalance in another triad PO_2X, whereas changing PO_1 leaves the PO_2X triad unaffected. Furthermore, the model demonstrates that much of the influence that attitudes and relationships exert on each other is wasted if the two are not free to change at roughly the same rate. This may offer an insight into why imbalance persists somewhere within almost every social group, presumably despite all the best efforts of the individuals concerned.

In sum, then, the constraints on the development of balance are as follows:

1. Individuals should have enough degrees of freedom available to them to be able to solve the problem. Where the degrees of freedom lie will determine how balance will develop.

2. If both attitude and liking relations are allowed to vary, attitude change and relationship change must keep in step with one another. If they do not, the two processes are likely to work against each other to some extent and it is less likely that balance will be achieved.

These constraints carry a number of further implications. First, processes of attitude change to impersonal attitude objects and processes of relationship change may confound or interact with one another, with the form of organization achieved by the system depending to a great extent on their respective rates of change. This suggests that we are looking at a dynamical system in which changes may be nonlinear and where Heiderian balance is only one of a number of possible attractors, or relatively stable forms of organization, onto which the system may converge.

Second, we have only just begun to touch on the potential complexities inherent in an extension of balance theory to multiperson groups, even with respect to the simplified case where only a single attitude object is considered. It is worth reiterating what our network does and does not do. The classic POX triad is expanded into one of $PO_1O_2 \ldots O_nX$. The system is interactive to the extent that each individual serves both as a P for some calculations and as an O for others. However, from the perspective of any given P, the relationships between O_1, O_2, and so forth are not considered directly. The impact of these other interpersonal relationships on triads involving P is one step removed, in that P has to try and achieve balance (separately) with O_1 and O_2 (so any change to the PX relation in the triad PO_1X is constrained by what is happening in PO_2X); also, the O_1X and O_2X relations are influenced by the O_1O_2 relationships, as a consequence of what is happening in the triads in which O_1 and O_2 respectively take the place of P. This, however, glosses over the distinction, which Heider would have insisted upon, between the O_1O_2 relationship as perceived by O_1 and O_2 themselves, and the same relationship as perceived by P. To take account of the latter kind of perceived relationship directly would require a different kind of network architecture. The same conclusion would probably apply to any attempt to model multiperson POQ structures (Heider's notation for triads in which a third person is substituted for an impersonal attitude object).

Third, because our results reflect the different degrees of freedom associated with attitude and interpersonal relations, the question arises whether such a model could be extended to encompass more than a single object of evaluation. In fact, the point could be made more strongly that balance theory is of limited applicability *unless* it can also deal with multiple attitude objects. If we are to deal with multiple attitudes, however, we must begin to ask questions about how individuals represent and develop their own knowledge structures, for we cannot consider different attitude objects independently. Rather little would be gained by simply running, say, five parallel simulations (even with the same prior random settings of interper-

sonal relations, i.e., connection weights) using five notionally different attitude objects, unless, at the very least, the changes in connection weights
within one network were allowed to affect those in the others.

Even if this were accomplished, however, we would still be left without
a representation of any patterning between the attitude objects themselves
(i.e., any covariation between individuals' evaluations of these different
objects). If we were to attempt to take such patterning into account, we
would need an architecture in which individuals are represented, not by
single units, but by separate subnetworks or groups of units, capable of
learning pattern discriminations. Also we would need a conceptual definition
of attitudinal agreement or disagreement, applicable to sets of related attitude objects. This could then be used as a criterion for judging the extent
of balance or imbalance within any such complex structure, and hence as
the basis of an error or discrepancy measure to be incorporated in whatever
learning algorithm was best suited to producing a convergence of the system
onto a balanced solution.

Before tackling such issues of higher order complexity, a simpler assumption needs to be examined. If individuals are to influence each other as a
function of their respective attitudes and the extent to which they like or
dislike each other, such attitudes and feelings need somehow to be communicated. It may be attractive to think of different individuals within a group
as constituting a network, and of communication among them as the spreading of activation through a network of associative links. But what is implied
by thinking of communication in this way? Surely the first requirement is
that such activation is informative, that is, that it actually represents something. In other words, we need to assume that the different members of the
social network are all responding to (broadly) the same environmental
context, that is, that they are talking about the same thing.

Communication thus requires a shared language or symbolic code, representative of a shared reality. If we know we share a common language
with another person, we know we can communicate our thoughts with each
other adequately enough. However, it is far from obvious how different
individuals could acquire a shared language or symbolic code if they did
not have one provided for them. The next question we address, therefore,
is whether a network of individuals can organize itself so as to develop a
shared code that links symbols to objects.

MODELING COMMUNICATIVE PROCESSES USING
CONNECTIONIST CELLULAR AUTOMATA

> It disperses the fog to study the phenomena of language in primitive kinds of
> applications in which one can command a clear view of the aim and functioning
> of the words.
>
> —Ludwig Wittgenstein (1958, p. 4e)

Introduction

People's models of the world are in part shaped by their social environment. Although no two people's models will be the same, we can communicate effectively through the use of language. Language consists of words, and some words refer to objects. Wittgenstein's (1958) language games focus our attention on how words acquire their meaning, or more fundamentally, on how names become associated with (classes of) objects. In these games, a pupil is taught the names of objects by a teacher, who points out the objects while naming them. This process is called *ostensive teaching* (see also Harnad, 1996). Although this picture of language learning is grossly oversimplified, as Wittgenstein was quick to point out, in the simulations described here we see just how far we can get with such a simple notion of learning through ostension.

Typically, in connectionist simulations of the learning of object-name pairings (categorization), the category name associated with each object is a given (see, for instance, Kruschke, 1992, and Shanks, 1991). Although it is undoubtedly the case that we learn to name many objects in this way, as a general description of language learning, this picture is too constrained: Words are not always given, but sometimes have to be agreed on. For instance, in a number of languages, there has been a battle between the word "computer" and the alternative word in the particular language ("Rechner" in German, "rekenmachine" in Dutch, "ordinateur" in French). Whereas simulations up to now have tended to totally constrain the relation between an object and its name, the goal of the present simulation is to look at the case where this relation is totally unconstrained. The focus is not on how a pupil is taught the naming of objects by a teacher, but on the development of shared names in a group of people who as yet have no shared vocabulary. Rather than an asymmetrical relationship between a teacher and a pupil, there is the requirement that a larger group of people reach a consensus on how to name the objects in their environment. As we see later, this distinction between *constrained* and *unconstrained* name-object relations leads to some surprising results in the simulations, with some important theoretical consequences.

The sort of simulation described here requires two ingredients; learning agents and an environment in which these agents are placed and that contains the objects that have to be named. This can be achieved by placing connectionist networks (the agents) in a cellular automaton (the environment), which renders what we have coined a connectionist cellular automaton.

Connectionist Cellular Automata (CCA)

A standard cellular automaton (CA) is a two-dimensional lattice of cells, in which the behavior of a cell is determined locally, that is, by its immediately neighboring cells. Each cell has a finite set of possible states, and there are some global transition rules that determine what state each cell will take on in the next generation, based on the cell's current state and the states of its eight neighboring cells. Although the transition rules are global, the information that determines a cell's transition is strictly local. Once the new states of all the cells in the lattice have been determined, all the cells change their states simultaneously, and the cellular automaton is said to have proceeded to the next generation.

A simple example should make this easier to understand. We can think of the two-dimensional lattice as a checkers board, where each square is either occupied or unoccupied. The board corresponds to what we called the lattice, and a square stands for a cell. Starting from an initial distribution of the pieces, we apply some simple rules to determine what should happen to each of the squares: Should an empty square be left empty, and should an occupied square still be occupied next time? To determine this, each square "looks" at its eight neighboring squares, and counts the number of occupied squares. The *transition rule* (which determines what should happen to this square next) could be that if the number of occupied squares that neighbor this particular square is exactly three, the square will either stay occupied, or become occupied. The trick is that we do this for all the squares *at the same time*, so that each of the squares on the board "decides" what state it is going to be in next. Only then do we change all the squares that need changing. Once we have done this, the "game" has progressed to the next generation, and we start the process all over again. If we do this very fast, we see a film of moving patterns of pieces over the checkers board. Although these patterns display some regularities, which we can come to recognize, these regularities are hard to describe in precise words. For instance, we would see that areas with many occupied squares are almost empty a few generations later.

In nonstochastic cellular automata, the transitions are *deterministic*: The only thing that has to be set is the starting configuration, but from there on, the behavior of the automaton is predetermined. This is not the same as saying that the behavior of the CA is *predictable*: To say this means that one is able to predict if, for instance, the CA will eventually settle into a steady state. With cellular automata, this is not possible: The shortest way to "predict" generation $n + x$ from generation n is to go through all x intermediate steps—there is no faster way in which information can travel.

Although cellular automata can be described by very simple rules, the behavior they display is very complex. Conway's game of life (Berlekamp, Conway, & Guy, 1982) allows the specification of self-replicating systems, with just two states for the cells, and three simple transition rules. As far as social psychology is concerned, Nowak and May (1992) modeled a population of individuals playing the prisoner's dilemma game. They found that under certain conditions, it was possible for minority groups of cooperators to survive among a majority of competitors by sticking together. Ohnishi (1991) used cellular automata to model people's attitudes toward nuclear energy. He used actual opinions in Japan to set model constants, as well as cells that acted as opinion leaders, from which positive and negative attitudes were spread among the wider population of cells.

As a cell in a cellular automaton can stand for anything, and as the state of a cell is determined locally, a natural extension of this class of models is to let each cell be a connectionist network, so that cells become capable of learning. In connectionist cellular automata (CCA), the neural network that occupies a cell receives input from all (or a subset) of its neighbors, and computes an output that is received as input by its neighboring cells in the next generation of the automaton. A learning cell can thus "decide" on the name it gives to an object, compare that name to the names associated with this object in its neighbors, and decide whether it should adjust the name *it* gives to the object. The input to the network thus corresponds to (a description of) an object, and its output to the name it associates with that object.

Cellular automata are topographically organized, and they are therefore ideally suited to model communicative processes: They allow for communicative messages to slowly spread through a population of cells—as every cell only communicates with its direct neighbors in the lattice, messages can only travel the distance of one cell in every direction in a single generation. The CCA that is introduced here is called ObjectWorld.

ObjectWorld

Because of the computational complexity of a combination of connectionist networks and cellular automata, the lattice size should not be too large. The cellular automaton could just be a rectangular lattice of fixed size, in which case the cells on the edge of the lattice have fewer neighbors. Alternatively, one can warp the rectangular grid around its two edges, ending up with a torus, so that every cell has the same number of neighbors.

The sort of connectionist cellular automata that are investigated here model communicative processes. In each generation of the simulation, every network "talks" to all, or some, of its neighbors. This means that a given network trains its neighbors on the name that it produces when presented with a certain object. As a network is also trained *by* its neighbors, and as in a cellular automaton, all cell states have to be updated simultaneously, the weights of the networks can only be updated at the end of a generation, after all the individual networks have "talked" to all of their neighbors. This means we have to use *batch updating of weights* (Rumelhart, McClelland, & the PDP Research Group, 1986).

Each learning agent in the CCA is a simple three-layer backpropagation-error network (Rumelhart, McClelland, & the PDP Research Group, 1986), or backprop network for short. The input layer encodes the objects the network comes across as n-digit binary patterns. For an input layer of size n, it is therefore possible to encode 2^n different objects. The hidden layer is of variable size, with smaller sizes allowing for more generalization, whereas larger sizes make the learning of specific knowledge easier. The output layer represents a phonetic encoding of a two-syllable word associated with the object represented over the input, where each syllable has the form *consonant–vowel–consonant*. Consonants are binarily encoded in three digits (three output units), allowing for the use of eight consonants; F, K, L, N, P, R, S, T. Vowels are binarily encoded in two digits (two output units); A, E, I, O. The total output string is therefore 16 digits, or 16 output units, long (an example would be "KAPLOT"). As the output of a back-propagation network is continuously valued, the output is made binomial with a cut-off point of .50. All the networks are identical and initialized with random values before the simulation is run. The same seed is used when comparing networks, so that the results from different runs are directly comparable. We choose the size of the pool out of which we draw the objects that have to be named, and the number of objects that we present to the neural networks (all networks work on the same set of objects), as well as the number of units in the hidden layer.

For the initial simulations, cellular automata of size 10×10 are used (so that there are 100 individual networks), where the lattice is warped around both edges, so that the whole is shaped like a torus (something like a doughnut). A torus has the property, just like a globe, that moving up, you end up at the bottom of the lattice, and moving left, you eventually end up at the right. The difference with a globe is that one can more easily map a torus in two dimensions, which renders a rectangle—the original lattice.

Earlier we said that a cellular automaton is defined by the states of its cells and the global transition rules, which determine what states the cells will take on next, for any given situation. In the case of ObjectWorld, the state of a cell corresponds to the activation and weight matrices of the neural network that occupies the cell. The state of a network determines what name it will come up with when presented with the objects in its environment.

The transition rules should represent the amount of influence one network has on another: If a certain network is highly influential, it has a large coercive impact on its surrounding networks, which will then be more likely to change the names they give to the objects in the environment. With neural networks, this influence can be moderated using the learning rate λ: If a network has a higher learning rate, it is more susceptible to changing its weight matrix, and therefore the names it gives to the objects. The transition rules that are used will therefore work directly on the learning rates. As each network teaches its neighbors (i.e., provides them with the network's names for the objects), the amount of influence that a network has on a neighbor can be modeled by varying the learning rate. This learning rate in effect determines how much the neighbor will be inclined to change the neighbor's names for the objects (through the adjustment of its weight matrix). Remember that every network talks to its neighbors, and that the weights are only updated at the end of the epoch, according to the batch updating of weights mentioned previously, so that a network training one of its neighbors does not directly lead to a change in that neighbor's names, but only after all the networks have talked to all of their neighbors.

The transition rules model communicative constraints in two ways; through the *pattern of connectivity* between cells, and through the adjustment of learning rates based on *Euclidean distances* (disagreement) between networks.

Pattern of Connectivity.   A *fully connected* cellular automaton corresponds to a world where everyone is free to "talk" to all their neighbors. Under full connectivity, there are no constraints on communication, and therefore the learning rate is not adjusted. Although the assumption of full connectivity might be true for small groups of people, once we look at things at a societal or even cross-societal level, this is no longer a valid assumption to make. A *partly connected* cellular automaton can be used to model geographical or sociopolitical constraints. These constraints take the form of barriers, across which it is impossible, or at least more difficult, to communicate. This can be modeled by multiplying the learning rate between two networks on different sides of a barrier by some constant b, where $0 \leq b < 1$.

Euclidean Distances.   We can compute a measure of similarity between two networks by computing the Euclidean distances between each of their output vectors and summing these. In geometry, Euclidean distances represent the shortest distance between two points in space. Here, we use them as a measure of disagreement. The higher the summed Euclidean distance, the more dissimilar two networks are in the names they give to the objects. (The Euclidean distance between two vectors can be calculated by first taking the sum of the squared differences between all the elements of the two vectors, and then taking the square root of this sum. For instance, the Euclidean distance between the vectors $[\mathbf{0,0,0}]$ and $[\mathbf{1,0,1}]$ is $\sqrt{1^2 + 0^2 + 1^2} = \sqrt{2}$.) We can now try several functions that map this summed Euclidean distance to a value for the learning rate. (The learning rate is adjusted for every generation of the CCA, based on the new Euclidean distances between the cells after communication.) As a consequence, the degree to which two neighboring networks disagree on the names of the objects determines the amount of coercive influence they have on each other. As these functions directly work on the learning rate (λ), they are called *Lambda functions*. By using different Lambda functions, we can represent different theoretical notions about whether we are more inclined to communicate with like-minded or differently minded people (see also Fig. 10.5):

1. *Constant function:* The learning rate does not change as a function of Euclidean distance; everyone has an equal coercive impact on everyone else.

2. *Sigmoid function:* The learning rate increases as a function of Euclidean distance; there is a preference for communicating with differently minded individuals; neighboring networks that disagree on the names of objects have more coercive influence on each other.

3. *Inverse Sigmoid function:* The learning rate decreases as a function of Euclidean distance; we prefer to communicate with those individuals that are similar to ourselves; neighboring networks that agree on the names of objects have more coercive influence on each other.

4. *Gaussian function:* The learning rate is highest for those individuals that are neither very dissimilar nor very similar; neighboring networks that moderately (dis)agree have more coercive influence on each other.

5. *Inverse Gaussian function:* The learning rate is highest for those individuals that are either very similar or very dissimilar; neighboring networks that either disagree or agree have more coercive influence on each other.

This set of functions exhausts the major possibilities. These different functions are compared in order to see whether the results from simulations based on them correspond to what we would expect, and under what conditions consensus is reached. Clearly, consensus is a necessary precondition for the development of language, so it is important to know, at the group level, what factors contribute to reaching a consensus, and how fast agreement on the names of objects is reached. For instance, we might be inclined to think that when two neighbors who disagree on the names of the objects in their environment have a high coercive influence on each other, this will lead to a quick resolution of conflict, and that therefore we would see the community of individuals (the CCA) quickly settle into an agreed upon set of names for the objects. Because of the complexity of the pattern of interactions (everyone is communicating with all of their neighbors), this might not actually be what is happening at the level of *the system as a whole*.

The Simulations

Smurfing Behavior. The first thing that becomes apparent when one tries to run any of the CCAs outlined earlier is that, if there are two or more objects that have to be named, the networks collectively display what we have termed

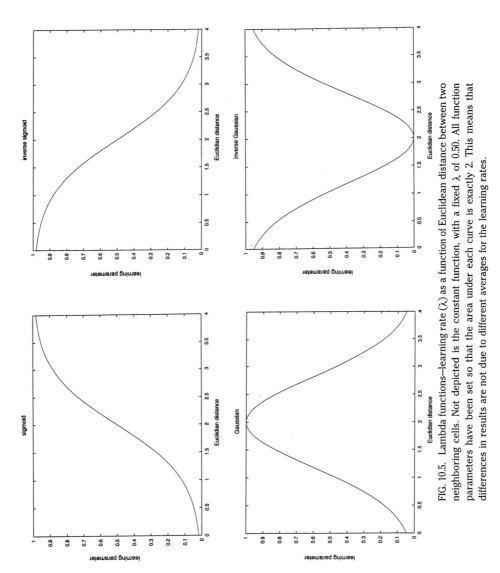

FIG. 10.5. Lambda functions—learning rate (λ) as a function of Euclidean distance between two neighboring cells. Not depicted is the constant function, with a fixed λ of 0.50. All function parameters have been set so that the area under each curve is exactly 2. This means that differences in results are not due to different averages for the learning rates.

smurfing behavior. Soon after the simulation starts, all objects become associated with the same name. The reasons for this are discussed later. For now this means that we have to limit the simulations to just one object. As the computational complexity of learning just one object-name mapping was not very great, the size of the hidden layer was set to 3 units, and the size of the input layer to 6 units (limiting the pool from which the one random object could be drawn to 64 or 2^6 objects). As there is only one object, and therefore one output vector, it no longer makes sense to talk about the *summed* Euclidean distance between two networks, and the term *Euclidean distance* will be used. (This explains why in Fig. 10.5 the Euclidean distance ran from 0 to 4, as the maximum Euclidean distance equalled the square root of the number of output units, when the output of a unit ran from 0 to 1.)

Simulations With Fully Connected CCAs

For the first set of simulations, fully connected CCAs were used, as described earlier. All the simulations were run until the Euclidean distance averaged over all possible pairs of neighbors dropped below 0.10 (at which point the CCA would almost have converged to a single name), *or* until 10,000 generations had passed.

From Fig. 10.6, it is apparent that the five Lambda functions lead to very different behavior. (Although the simulations were run for a maximum of 10,000 generations, all of them either converged to the 0.10 average Euclidean distance criterion within 1,000 generations, or reached a stable condition up to generation 10,000 with higher average Euclidean distance.) The constant and the inverse sigmoid functions quickly converged, which meant that all networks had the same name for the object. The Gaussian function took longer to converge, but did eventually. The sigmoid function did not converge to a single name, but settled to a state where about two thirds of the networks produced the name "TOSNOF," with the remainder settling on "TOTNOF."

Finally, the inverse Gaussian function settled to a state with many different names, some of which resembled each other. Figure 10.7 (left pane) shows how these names were distributed. Figure 10.7 (right pane) is a plot of the Euclidean distances of all the networks, averaged over all their neighbors: Each point in the figure is the average distance between the network at that position in the automaton and its surrounding networks. In Fig. 10.7 (left pane), we can see that there is a "ledge" of networks at the back of the map that converged on the most common name, which corresponds to the near-zero Euclidean distances at the same position in Fig. 10.7 (right pane). Another interesting phenomenon (see Fig. 10.7, right pane) is that networks that converged on the same name were often organized in diagonal bands. This behavior flowed forth from the asymmetrical connectivity patterns

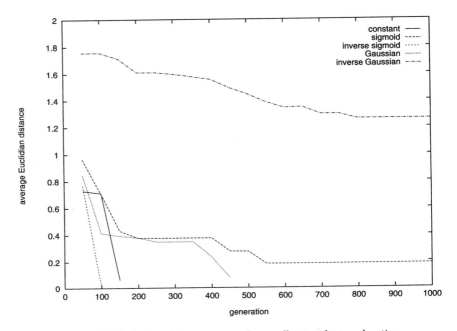

FIG. 10.6. The Euclidean distance averaged over all networks as a function of the number of generations.

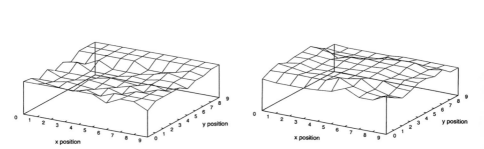

FIG. 10.7. Words and Euclidean distances for the converged solution with the inverse Gaussian function. Left pane—most frequent words in the converged solution (greater z-value is more frequent). Right pane—average Euclidean distance with neighbors for all networks in the CA lattice.

between networks that were organized in a lattice. In general, the functions that converged slowly were those in which networks were inclined to communicate with differently minded neighbors (the sigmoid and inverse Gaussian functions, see Fig. 10.5).

Simulations With Connectivity Constraints

Further simulations were carried out with larger lattice sizes (20 × 20), and with additional connectivity constraints (previously discussed). To keep things simple, a single L-shaped barrier was put up, with sides of 10 cells long (see Fig. 10.8). Across this barrier, no direct communication was possible. Of course, indirect communication via intermediate cells was possible, but the reason for this manipulation was to see what the effect was of the partial isolation of the population of cells in the shadows of the barrier.

Figure 10.9 shows the average Euclidean distances for every 50th generation of the simulations for the five Lambda functions (up to generation 5,000 at which point all simulations either converged to the 0.10 average Euclidean distance criterion, or settled up to generation 10,000 to a stable condition with higher average Euclidean distance). The behavior of the simulations under the five Lambda rules is comparable to the simulations run under full connectivity (Fig. 10.6; bear in mind that Fig. 10.9 shows 5,000 generations as opposed to just 1,000 for Fig. 10.6). As not all networks were connected to all of their neighbors, for most Lambda functions, it took longer to converge than in the condition without constraints on the pattern of connectivity. The most noteworthy differences were that the simulation using the sigmoid Lambda function did now converge to within the specified criterion (average Euclidean distance smaller than 0.10), and that the simulation using the inverse Gaussian function converged to a higher Euclidean

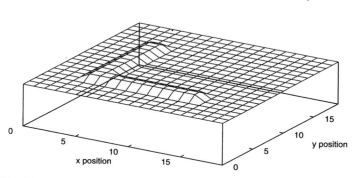

FIG. 10.8. Connectivity constraints: All cells with connectivity constraints are raised above the plane.

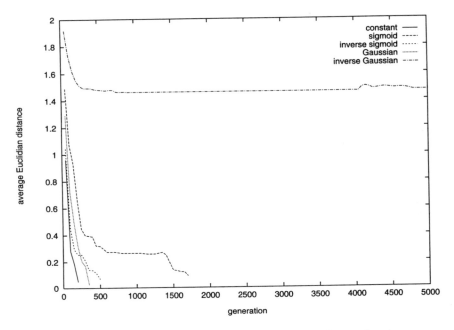

FIG. 10.9. The Euclidean distance averaged over all networks as a function of the number of generations.

distance (1.47 compared to 1.26). Another interesting aspect of the simulation using the inverse Gaussian was that there was no change for about 3,000 generations (roughly between 1,000 and 4,000), after which the average Euclidean distance rose again, to finally settle to a constant level until the end of the simulation at generation 10,000.

Figure 10.10 again shows the distribution of the names and the Euclidean distances for the converged inverse Gaussian simulation. If we compare this figure with the position of the barrier as depicted in Fig. 10.8, we can see that the shape of the barrier is apparent in both the distribution of the names and the Euclidean distances. This is most clear in the case of the names with the vertical part of the L-shaped barrier. As in the simulations without connectivity constraints, networks that converged to the same name were often organized in diagonal bands: The two longest bands start at the horizontal part of the L-shaped barrier. From Fig. 10.10 (left pane) we can further see that a large group of networks with infrequent names (the flat, trapezoid-shaped area extending from the middle to the back of the map) were shielded from the influence of networks with more frequent names by the barrier.

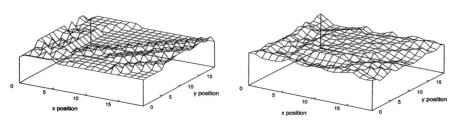

FIG. 10.10. Words and Euclidean distances for the converged solution with the inverse Gaussian function (constrained connectivity). Left pane—most frequent words in the converged solution (greater z-value is more frequent). Right pane—average Euclidean distance with neighbors for all networks in the CA lattice.

DISCUSSION

Discussion of Results

The results from the simulations show that we can model different communicative constraints (both interpersonal and global) using a cellular automaton with learning cells (CCA). As a reminder, the interpersonal constraints are modeled by varying the learning parameters of the networks as a function of the Euclidean distance between pairs of networks: In other words, the coercive influence of two neighbors on each other is a function of their (dis)agreement on the names of objects. The global constraints take the form of barriers thrown up across the automaton, which prevent networks on different sides of the barriers from communicating with each other. As mentioned earlier, the reason for introducing these constraints was to see what the impact of these constraints on communication was on how a consensus was reached (or not) at the level of the system as a whole, which might not correspond to our ideas at the outset.

Indeed, a somewhat counterintuitive result is that a consensus within a group is reached faster if individuals mainly communicate with similar, rather than dissimilar, neighbors. If we consider that communication is reciprocal, this becomes understandable: The net balance of two individuals who disagree communicating with each other is normally that they reach a stand-off, whereas two individuals that already mostly agree might more easily reach a consensus. However, if both of these are combined (as in the inverse Gaussian function) a global consensus is never reached, and minority groups are able to withstand the coercive influence from surrounding groups. This is because this function allows individuals in the center of a group to strengthen group cohesiveness by reinforcing the current name, keeping those at the border of the group from joining other groups, whereas communication between individuals belonging to different groups suffers from the stand-off effect described earlier.

Using global connectivity constraints (barriers), which model geographical or sociopolitical borders, minority groups can fight off influence from neighboring groups (longer), because they are shielded from that influence in one or two directions. In the present simulations, only absolute barriers were used—no direct communication across the barrier was possible—but it would be interesting to look at the effect of permeable barriers. Another extension would be to appoint some networks as opinion leaders, who have a greater effect on their neighbors (as in Ohnishi, 1991).

An Explanation of the Smurfing Behavior

Earlier we mentioned that a CCA based on backprop networks was unable to learn more than one object-name pair without resorting to calling all objects by the same name. To understand this behavior, we have to look at the task that the CCA *as a whole* is set to perform, and then it will follow why *individual* networks show smurfing behavior. First, the naming of objects is a few-to-many problem, which means that in natural language, there are many more (possible) signifiers than signifieds. This is so because the connection between objects and the words in a lexicon is largely arbitrary: Nothing would change if all of a sudden everyone started calling "tables" "hables."

Second, backpropagation-of-error is a gradient descent learning rule. If we have a network with n weighted connections, we can create an $n + 1$ dimensional space, where the first n dimensions represent the weight matrix, and the $n + 1th$ dimension represents the error associated with this weight matrix. What the backprop rule does is start at a given point of this *error space* and find the steepest way down into the bottom of the error valley, which signifies minimal total error.

It does not matter greatly if during the course of training a network we change the error surface a little, as long as this change is small compared to the rate of descent with which the backprop rule moves down the error surface. In a CCA however, there is no absolute training set representing the desired outputs given certain inputs. What the networks in a CCA have to do is arrive at a shared representation of the problem domain, which is done as much by moving the problem domain itself as by adjusting the weight matrices of the individual networks. If we try to store even just three objects in each network, then, under the condition that all three objects have unique names attached to them, there are $(2^{16})^3$ possible solutions if there is total convergence within the CCA (we arrive at this number because the output is a 16-digit binary vector, and we need to produce three distinct names). However, under the condition that all three objects have the same name, there are "only" 2^{16} possible solutions. This means that giving every object the same name is a much easier solution (by several orders of magnitude) than attaching a unique label to every object.

Conclusions

There are three ways in which the smurfing problem might be solved. First, we could use some learning rule other than backpropagation-of-error. The necessity to use a supervised learning rule—we are dealing with communication, so there has to be feedback—means that there is no connectionist learning rule (at least that we know of) that will overcome this problem while still allowing for groups of networks in a CCA to converge on the same names. Remember that most simulations have used object-name pairings that were set out in advance by the experimenter. This was called the *constrained* approach to learning object-name pairs. Under the constrained approach, smurfing does not occur, because the learning targets (the names of the objects) are fixed, and the network is able to gradually learn the correct mappings between objects and names. But in the *unconstrained* condition, there is no fixed, "correct" mapping between objects and names. The only sense in which a mapping is correct is when it is shared by a large group of networks in the automaton, but because this leaves the networks (as a group) free to determine exactly *which* mapping this one agreed-upon mapping should be, this situation is far less constrained. As these simulations show, this lack of constraints means that by far the easiest way to settle into an agreed set of names (within a group of individuals) is the trivial solution of giving all the objects in the environment the same name. As this is clearly not what is happening in the real world, a "bare-bones" supervised-learning rule is not powerful enough to enforce that different objects have different names. In a nutshell, backprop smurfs.

Second, we might adjust our model by using a specific connectionist *architecture* that imposes some constraints on the task (Murre's CALM, 1992, is one example of such a model).

Third, we might use a learning rule that reduces a measure of error through some process other than gradient descent, because gradient descent allows the networks in the automaton to gradually converge the different names they have for the objects at the outset to a single name. Genetic algorithms are an instance of this class of learning rules. These relatively simple algorithms work on binary strings (much the same as we have been using here as output vectors) and the fittest strings are allowed to reproduce and recombine. It can be mathematically shown (Goldberg, 1988) that genetic algorithms actually asses the fitness of many substrings (or parts of the solution) in parallel, so that this method is very powerful despite its apparent simplicity. This corresponds to a sampling of the error surface at different points, with successive generations of strings gradually increasing in fitness. Which strings are the fittest is determined by a fitness criterion. We used error (disagreement), not fitness, but this is inconsequential, as our error was based on dissimilarity of vectors, so a fitness criterion would simply be based on the similarity of vectors (or strings). A drawback of standard genetic algorithms is that they are limited to searching a problem space. More complex models based on genetic algorithms, called classifier systems (Goldberg, 1988) overcome this limitation. Further simulations will investigate whether a CCA employing genetic algorithms (a GCA) would actually avoid the smurf trap.

Although limited to one object-name pair, the present simulations allowed us to study the impact of different communicative constraints (the Lambda functions and the connectivity constraints; interpersonal and global) on the speed and manner in which (local) consensus is reached on the names of objects. This was done by organizing learning networks in a cellular automaton. This model, which we termed CCA, poses some challenges to the way that neural networks are ordinarily trained: Not only do the individual networks have to adapt their responses to the vicissitudes of the environment, but they have to reach a consensus on how to represent things as a group as well.

The value of doing these sorts of simulations is not just that they give us insight into how humans perform a certain (social) task. An equally important aspect is that they isolate factors that any adequate theory of the behavior under investigation should incorporate. If we had not looked at the case of totally *unconstrained* communication (no object-name pairs are fixed in advance), we would not have realized that *constrained* connectionist models of categorization can only work (i.e., not smurf) because they oversimplify things by imposing excessively stringent constraints. Obviously, the present simulations commit a sin in the opposite direction, in that they use a model that is too unconstrained. Arguably, it is better to start without constraints, and then introduce more constraints as we go along, because in this way, we get a clearer view on all the possible factors that influence our behavior.

OVERALL CONCLUSIONS

The application of connectionist approaches to the field of social psychology is an exciting development, but one that is still extremely new. Only a small sample of topics has yet been studied from this perspective and only a small range of network modeling techniques has yet been exploited. We believe that the potential for such approaches is far greater than might be supposed even from the considerable amount that has so far been achieved. The focus of much research so far has been on the individual perceiver or social actor. This has exploited the very close fit between many of the theoretical questions addressed by mainstream cognitive science and cognitive psychology and those studied within the field of social cognition. As Smith (1996) argued, one of the major insights that connectionism can provide is that social cognition does not need to rely exclusively or even typically on the use of symbolic rules and forms of reasoning, as many theories imply.

Still, with reference to the individual social perceiver, the question of *representation* emerges as a key issue. According to a connectionist approach, concepts and memories are not to be thought of as "things" lurking in some storage bin or filing cabinet, waiting to be found, but as patterns of *activity* that are reconstructed, and not merely retrieved, on the presentation of appropriate cues. This argument can be applied just as directly to more social objects, such as other people or either side of a political debate, as to more physical stimuli. The complaint that social objects can be vastly more complex than physical ones is already a familiar one in the field of social judgment (Eiser, 1990; Eiser & Stroebe, 1972). In principle, such complexity is no barrier to the applicability of theories that take the multidimensionality of incoming information as their starting point (although it is acknowledged that modeling is more difficult when the inputs are less precisely specified). The idea that representations are not fixed in memory extends also to our definitions of social groups and categories. These are neither static, nor unproblematically given by the wider social structure, but are continually reconstructed by individuals as a function of previous and current experience (Eiser, 1996; Turner, Oakes, Haslam, & McGarty, 1994).

In all of this, however, the focus remains on the individual perceiver. The "objects" being perceived have become more complex and social, but the perceiver—the cognitive system being described—is still the single person. In the explorations described in this chapter, we seem, with hindsight, to have crossed a border without noticing that we had done so. The very fact that we slipped across so easily makes us question whether this border is more than an arbitrary convention. Compared with the predominant emphasis on the modeling of intrapersonal processes, the notion that interpersonal processes too may be explicable in terms of parallel-constraint satisfaction has remained relatively unexplored (but see Hutchins, 1991; Nowak, Szamrej, & Latané, 1990). Yet, we would not be content with a situation in which studies of intrapersonal and interpersonal processes were regarded merely as complementary to each other. The theme of our work here was that the intrapersonal and interpersonal are interconnected with each other, and that these interconnections deserve special study in and of themselves.

We have taken intrapersonal phenomena, that is, attitudes and the association of names with objects, and attempted to simulate, albeit in a highly simplified way, some of the interpersonal processes by which they are shaped. These topics of attitudes and communication are very much within the traditional territory of social psychology.

However, the issues raised are very much of relevance to individual cognitive processes too. If the mind can indeed be thought of as a network, then the question of how different parts of that network achieve forms of coordination with each other is just as relevant if the network corresponds to intrapersonal as interpersonal structures. Remember Hume's metaphor of the mind as a republic. If shared representations among different members of our "republic" are necessary for those individuals to constitute a group, then why should such sharing be any less essential for different units to constitute a mind?

What of the border guards we initially evaded but may now need to pacify? The most probable charge against us is that we ignored the importance of different levels of description of (social) psychological phenomena. Undoubtedly, there are many things to be said about people at the level of the person that cannot be said about, for instance, brains, neurons, or artificial neural network simulations of hypothesized cognitive processes. In the same way, there are things to be said about groups at the level of the group that are not merely "reducible" to the *noninteractive* activities of separate individuals. By the same token, there are properties we may attribute to individuals but not to groups. The idea that members of a group may share a "single" mind or consciousness is a loose and potentially dangerous metaphor. We accept all of this, although we would warn against uncritical acceptance of *all* descriptive distinctions. For instance, concepts such as attitude, meaning, and the self have very often been described as though they are fixed entities, thereby ignoring their underlying dynamic complexity.

Nonetheless, our main response is simply that we are not suggesting that there should or could be unity at the level of *description*, but rather that some unity might be established at the level of *explanation*. Indeed, the evident need for different levels of description is quite compatible with the notion that a vast number of complex and very different forms of organization can potentially emerge from interactions between a more limited number of very simple processes. To adopt a connectionist or other soft-computational approach to the study of such processes may potentially lead us to explanatory principles that generalize across different levels of description.

This hope coincides with what Seidenberg (1993) called "explanatory connectionism"—the interpretation of connectionism as the basis for a general explanatory theory of psychological phenomena. Like any general theory, its principles are formulated at quite an abstract level. This, however, can sometimes lead to the suspicion that it is a theory that, by claiming to explain everything in general, explains nothing in particular. One response to this is that many very specific empirical predictions can be both confirmed and generated through the use of specific kinds of neural networks. A less orthodox response is provided by the findings presented in our chapter. Different kinds of networks have different kinds of limitations. Finding out what kinds of phenomena are *difficult* to simulate with specific kinds of networks and algorithms forces us to refine our ways of conceptualizing these phenomena and the processes that underlie them. We are not dealing with unfalsifiable generalities, but with precise applications of general principles. Sometimes these applications can generate predictions of effects likely to be observed under novel conditions. Just as valuably, though, they can sometimes illustrate how incomplete our understanding still is of many familiar aspects of human thought and behavior.

REFERENCES

Berlekamp, E., Conway, J. H., & Guy, R. K. (1982). *Winning ways for your mathematical plays* (Vol. 2). New York: Academic Press.

Cartwright, D., & Harary, F. (1956). Structural balance: A generalization of Heider's theory. *Psychological Review, 63,* 277–293.

Eiser, J. R. (1990). *Social judgment.* Pacific Grove, CA: Brooks/Cole.

Eiser, J. R. (1994). *Attitudes, chaos and the connectionist Mind.* Oxford: Basil Blackwell.

Eiser, J. R. (1996). Accentuation revisited. In P. Robinson (Ed.), *Social groups and identities: Developing the legacy of Henri Tajfel* (pp. 121–142). Oxford: Butterworth-Heinemann.

Eiser, J. R., & Stroebe, W. (1972). *Categorization and social judgement.* London: Academic Press.

Festinger, L. (1957). *A theory of cognitive dissonance.* Evanston, IL: Row, Peterson.

Fodor, J. A. (1975). *The language of thought.* New York: Cromwell.

Goldberg, D. E. (1988). *Genetic algorithms in search, optimization, and machine learning.* Reading, MA: Addison Wesley.

Harnad, S. (1996). The origin of words: A psychophysical hypothesis. In B. Velichkovsky & D. Rumbaugh (Eds.), *Communicating meaning: Evolution and development of language* (pp. 27–44). Mahwah, NJ: Lawrence Erlbaum Associates.

Hebb, D. O. (1949). *The organisation of behavior: A neuropsychological approach.* New York: Wiley.

Heider, F. (1946). Attitudes and cognitive organisation. *Journal of Psychology, 21,* 107–112.

Heider, F. (1958). *The psychology of interpersonal relations.* New York: Wiley.

Hume, D. (1911). *A treatise of human nature.* London: Dent. (Original work published 1740).

Hutchins, E. (1991). The social organization of distributed cognition. In L. B. Resnick, J. M. Levine, & S. D. Teasley (Eds.), *Perspectives on socially shared cognition* (pp. 283–307). Washington, DC: APA.

Jones, E. E., & Gerard, H. B. (1967). *Foundations of social psychology.* New York: Wiley.

Kauffman, S. A. (1993). *The origins of order: Self-organization and selection in evolution.* Oxford: Oxford University Press.

Kelley, H. H. (1967). Attribution theory in social psychology. In D. Levine (Ed.), *Nebraska Symposium on Motivation* (Vol. 15, pp. 192–238). Lincoln: University of Nebraska Press.

Kruschke, J. K. (1992). ALCOVE: An exemplar-based connectionist model of category learning. *Psychological Review, 99,* 22–44.

Murre, J. M. J. (1992). *Categorization and learning in modular neural networks.* Hillsdale, NJ: Lawrence Erlbaum Associates.

Newcomb, T. M. (1953). An approach to the study of communicative acts. *Psychological Review, 60,* 393–404.

Nowak, A., Szamrej, J., & Latané, B. (1990). From private attitude to public opinion: A dynamic theory of social impact. *Psychological Review, 97,* 362–376.

Nowak, M. A., & May, R. M. (1992). Evolutionary games and spatial chaos. *Nature, 359,* 826–829.

Ohnishi, T. (1991). A cellular automaton model for the change of public attitude regarding nuclear energy. *Progress in Nuclear Energy, 26,* 163–205.

Osgood, C. E., & Tannenbaum, P. H. (1955). The principle of congruity in the prediction of attitude change. *Psychological Review, 62,* 42–55.

Parisi, D., Cecconi, F., & Nolfi, S. (1990). Econets: Neural networks that learn in an environment. *Network, 1,* 149–168.

Read, S. J., & Miller, L. C. (1994). Dissonance and balance in belief systems: The promise of parallel constraint satisfaction processes and connectionist modeling approaches. In R. C. Schank & E. Langer (Eds.), *Beliefs, reasoning, and decision making: Psychologic in honor of Bob Abelson* (pp. 209–235). Hillsdale, NJ: Lawrence Erlbaum Associates.

Rumelhart, D. E., McClelland, J. L., & the PDP Research Group (1986). *Parallel distributed processing: Explorations in the microstructure of cognition* (Vol. 1). Cambridge, MA: MIT Press.

Seidenberg, M. S. (1993). Connectionist models and psychological theory. *Psychological Science, 4,* 228–235.

Shanks, D. R. (1991). Categorization by a connectionist network. *Journal of Experimental Psychology: Learning, Memory, and Cognition, 17,* 433–443.

Shultz, T. R., & Lepper, M. R. (1996). Cognitive dissonance as constraint satisfaction. *Psychological Review, 103,* 219–240.

Smith, E. R. (1996). What do connectionism and social psychology offer each other? *Journal of Personality and Social Psychology, 70,* 893–912.

Thurstone, L. L. (1928). Attitudes can be measured. *American Journal of Sociology, 33,* 529–554.

Turner, J. C., Oakes, P. J., Haslam, S. A., & McGarty, C. (1994). Self and collective: Cognition and social context. *Personality and Social Psychology Bulletin, 20,* 454–463.

Wittgenstein, L. (1958). *Philosophical investigations.* Oxford: Basil Blackwell.

AUTHOR INDEX

SUBJECT INDEX

A

Abortion, 259
Acceptability, 12
Accessibility, 114, 123-127, 182, 183
ACME, 20
Action, 29, 51, 54
Adaptive network model, 143
Adaptive readiness, 35
Adaptive response, 184
Additive similarity model, 96, 97
Adversarial problem solving, 13
Affect, 20, 36, 181-187, 190, 194, 198,
    see also mood and emotion
    affective mediating units, 182-186
    affective modules, 135, 136
ALCOVE, 85
Alternative explanation, 57, 61
Altruistic behavior, 280
Ambiguity, 28, 30
Ambivalence, 215, 216
Analogy, 4, 13-22, 40, 73, 184
    coherence, 5, 13, 16, 17, 18
    mapping, 14, 15, 241
    retrieval, 241
Animal conditioning, 143, 154
Arousal, 217, 228, 229
Aspect extraction, 102
Associative learning, 154
Associative model, 143, 149
Associative processes, 21
Associative thinking, 153
Attention, 40, 99, 162, 255
Attitude, 211, 212, 223, 224, 230, 240,
    265, 279, 282, 289, 290, 294, 300,
    301, 307, 313, 314, 315, 318, 320,
    321, 322, 324, 326, 327, 330, 333,
    334, 335

change, 184, 213, 231, 232, 233,
    241, 284, 319, 334
similarity, 301
Attraction, 296, 298
Attractor system, 41-46, 287-292,
    295, 299, 300-308, 334
Attribution, 13, 19, 41, 64, 144, 153,
    164
Augmenting, 41, 56, 57, 62, 144,
    153-157, 163
Autoassociator, 46, 114-116
Automatic process, 10, 11, 19-21,
    40, 113, 181
Automatic trait inference, 20
Autonomous agents, 308
Availability, 21
Avoidant coping strategies, 203
Awareness, 10, 20

B

Backpropagation, 44, 162, 163, 165,
    166, 323, 338, 339, 348, 349
Balance theory, 64, 211, 241, 250,
    287, 290, 304, 306, 314, 319-325,
    328-335
Basin of attraction, 43, 44, 297
Batch updating of weights, 338
Belief, 182-187, 211, 217, 250-259,
    265, 313
Belief disconfirmation, 213
Belief revision, 13, 241, 255
Believability, 260
Behavioral identification, 58
BIAS (Brunswikian Indiction
    Algorithm for Social Cognition), 99
Bias terms, 151, 166, 303
Blocking, 153, 156

DATE DUE

Connectionist models of
social reasoning and social